CYBERMEDIA
GO TO
WAR

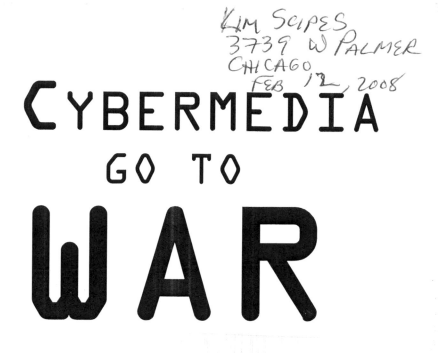

D0675194

Other Books of Interest from
MARQUETTE BOOKS

Stephen D. Cooper, *Watching the Watchdog: Bloggers as the Fifth Estate* (2006). ISBN: 0-922993-46-7 (cloth); 0-922993-47-5 (paperback)

Jami Fullerton and Alice Kendrick, *Advertising's War on Terrorism: The Story of the Shared Values Initiative* (2006). ISBN: 0-922993-43-2 (cloth); 0-922993-44-0 (paperback)

Mitchell Land and Bill W. Hornaday, *Contemporary Media Ethics: A Practical Guide for Students, Scholars and Professionals* (2006). ISBN: 0-922993-41-6 (cloth); 0-922993-42-4 (paperback)

Joey Reagan, *Applied Research Methods for Mass Communicators* (2006). ISBN: 0-922993-45-9

David Demers, *Dictionary of Mass Communication: A Guide for Students, Scholars and Professionals* (2005). ISBN: 0-922993-35-1 (cloth); 0-922993-25-4 (paperback)

John C. Merrill, Ralph D. Berenger and Charles J. Merrill, *Media Musings: Interviews with Great Thinkers* (2004). ISBN: 0-922993-15-7

Ralph D. Berenger (ed.), *Global Media Go to War: Role of Entertainment and News During the 2003 Iraq War* (2004). ISBN: 0-922993-10-6

Melvin L. DeFleur and Margaret H. DeFleur, *Learning to Hate Americans: How U.S. Media Shape Negative Attitudes Among Teenagers in Twelve Countries* (2003). ISBN: 0-922993-05-X

CYBERMEDIA GO TO WAR

Role of Converging Media During and After the 2003 Iraq War

Foreword by
Everette E. Dennis

Edited by
RALPH D. BERENGER

MARQUETTE BOOKS
SPOKANE, WASHINGTON

Library of Congress Cataloging-in-Publication Data

Cybermedia go to war : role of converging media during and after the 2003
Iraq war / edited by Ralph D. Berenger ; foreword by Everette E.
Dennis.
  p. cm.
Includes bibliographical references and index.
ISBN-13: 978-0-922993-48-2 (hardcover : alk. paper)
ISBN-10: 0-922993-48-3 (hardcover : alk. paper)
ISBN-13: 978-0-922993-49-9 (pbk. : alk. paper)
ISBN-10: 0-922993-49-1 (pbk. : alk. paper)
1. Iraq War, 2003---Mass media and the war. 2. Iraq War,
2003---Press coverage. I. Berenger, Ralph D., 1945-
P96.I73C93 2006
070.4'4995670443--dc22

                                          2006031083

Marquette Books LLC
3107 East 62nd Avenue
Spokane, Washington 99223
509-443-7057 (voice) / 509-448-2191 (fax)
books@marquettebooks.com / www.MarquetteBooks.com

DEDICATION

This book is dedicated to two cyberspace heroes: TIM BERNERS-LEE, who created the World Wide Web and the Internet domain system, which should have made him richer than Bill Gates, but who settled instead to content himself as a lowly academic basking in the knowledge that he changed the world by insisting that the Web remain free for all users; and MARC ANDREESON, who created Mosiac, the first effective and user-friendly Internet browser. Without them there would be no on-ramps to the Internet Superhighway and a lot more toll booths. Obviously this book would never have happened without them.

Contents

About the Authors

Amy Mowafi Ahmed (BSc. University of Bath) is a Master of Arts candidate in Journalism and Mass Communications at the American University in Cairo. She has published several academic journal articles and a book chapter. She is senior editor at *Enigma Magazine*, a Middle East-based lifestyle publication and writes for several publications in the United Kingdom.

Lama Al-Hammouri (M.A., American University in Cairo) has presented papers at several academic conferences. Trained as a desk reporter by the Associated Press TV News (APTN), Cairo, she worked as a staff journalist for several newspapers in Jordan. She is currently working as a media trainer, anchor (Saudi Radio) and a freelance writer in Saudi Arabia.

Ibrahim Al-Marashi (Ph.D., Oxford) lectures at the Department of International Relations at Koç University in Istanbul, Turkey, and is a Fellow at University of Pennsylvania, Annenberg School for Communiation, Program for Global Communication Studies, where he is working on a project for the media in post-war Iraq. He received a master's in Arab Studies at Georgetown University and a Ph.D. at the University of Oxford, Centre for Middle Eastern Studies. He is a specialist on Iraq's intelligence agencies and Iraqi public diplomacy during the 1990-1991 occupation of Kuwait. Al-Marashi is author of the *Middle East Review of International Affairs* article, "Iraq's Security and Intelligence Network: A Guide and Analysis," which was plagiarized by the British government in February 2003 as part of its case for going to war in Iraq.

Emmanuel C. Alozie (Ph.D., University of Southern Mississippi) is university professor of media communications at Governors State University, University Park, Illinois. His research interests are in development communication, international/cultural journalism, advertising and public relations. A former assistant editor with *Democratic Communiqué*, Alozie is author of *Cultural Reflections and the*

Role of Advertising in the Socio-economic and National Development of Nigeria (2005, Edwin Mellen Press), and co-edited *Toward the Common Good: Perspectives in International Public Relations* (Allyn and Bacon, 2004). He has published several refereed articles.

Muhammad I. Ayish (Ph.D., University of Minnesota) is dean for the College of Communication at the University of Sharjah. He had worked at Yarmouk University in Jordan and in UAE University and Ajman University of Science and Technology in the United Arab Emirates. His research interests include Arab world broadcasting, media convergence, political communication and culture-based communication perspectives. He has published scores of journal articles or book chapters in Arabic and English.

Tal Azran (Ph.D., University of Melbourne) is a lecturer at the Interdisciplinary Center in Herzliya and the Hebrew University in Jerusalem. His main field of research is the reception of Al-Jazeera in Western countries and its ability to mediate cultural differences. His interest in mediating cultural differences stems from his direct interaction with students of Palestinian descent during his postgraduate studies and lecturing in New York and Australia. He holds an master's from New York University.

Eric Bain (B.A., University of Wisconsin-Madison) is a project manager/consultant at Hiebing, a marketing and advertising agency in Madison, Wis. His papers, which have focused on international political news coverage, have been presented at the Association for Education in Journalism and Mass Communication and the International Communication Association. He is a founding member of Analyzing Media Perspective (AMP), which studied news coverage of the war in Iraq.

Ralph D. Berenger (D.A., Idaho State University) is a professor of journalism and mass communication at the American University in Cairo, Egypt, where he teaches courses in international communication, ethics, media management and communication theory. He has published scores of scholarly articles, book chapters and book reviews and has more than 30 years of professional experience as a newspaper and magazine reporter, editor, publisher and international consultant. His edited or coauthored books include *Global Media Go the War: Role of News and Entertainment During the 2003 Iraq War,* and *Media Musings: Interviews with Great Thinkers* (both Marquette Books, 2004).

Timothy J. Boudreau (Ph.D., Southern Illinois University) is an assistant professor in the Central Michigan University Journalism Department. He has published several scholarly articles dealing with political coverage and newspaper management. Prior to entering academe, he had a 10-year career as a reporter, editor and copy editor in several southern and Midwestern U.S. newspapers.

Lisa Brooten (Ph.D., Ohio University) is an assistant professor at Southern Illinois University Carbondale, College of Mass Communication and Media Arts, and a member of the Advisory Board for the college's Global Media Research Center. Brooten's research interests include militarization and media, gender, human rights, community and indigenous media, social movements and globalization. Her research on the Independent Media Center examines its strengths and weaknesses as a technological tool for the global linking of locally based alternative media groups. Her current work includes the attempt to theorize the similarities found in the work of alternative or opposition media groups in vastly different media environments (e.g., the United States, Burma and Thailand).

Elaine Cardenas (M.B.A., George Mason University) is a doctoral student in the Cultural Studies program at George Mason University. She teaches in the Communication Department at the university and is also an executive at The Gallup Organization and CEO of Redwood, Inc., a government consulting firm that specializes in knowledge-transfer. She is co-editor of *The Hummer: Myths and Consumer Culture* to be published December 2006 by Rowman and Littlefield and was managing editor of Dorling Kindersley's *The Book of Rule* (2004). Previously, she was an executive at several Washington, D.C.-based social policy think tanks and public opinion research firms.

Shaun P. Cannon (B.A. [Hons], Deakin University) is the executive officer of the Melbourne Catholic Commission for Justice, Development and Peace, where he researches human rights injustices, develops policy recommendations and advocates for their effective introduction in social and economic disciplines. He has been a university lecturer of labor history and served as a trade union organizer. In 2006, he edited *Work, Ethics and Values: Labouring Ideals in the Century Ahead*, a collection of essays on Australian industrial relations reform. He is currently completing his Ph.D. studies on the reconfiguration of community.

Everette E. Dennis (Ph.D., University of Minnesota) is Felix E. Larkin Distinguished Professor at the Fordham Graduate School of Business in New York City, where he is also director of the Center for Communication. He is author and coauthor of various books about the media, including several on international and global topics, notably a monograph on the Persian Gulf War of 1991. He was founding executive director of the Media Studies Center at Columbia University, a senior vice president of the Gannett/Freedom Forum Foundation and founding president of the American Academy in Berlin. He is a member of the Council on Foreign Relations and concurrently with his Fordham appointment is executive director of the International Longevity Center, a population-aging think tank.

Daniela V. Dimitrova (Ph.D., University of Florida) is assistant professor at Iowa State University, where she teaches multimedia production and communication technology courses. Her research interests focus on new media technologies and political communication. Dr. Dimitrova's research has been published in *Journalism Studies, Telecommunications Policy,* and *Gazette: The International Journal for Communication Studies.* She received her Masters of Arts from the University of Oregon.

Andrea Falkenhagen (B.A., University of Wisconsin-Madison) is a reporter for the *Casper Star-Tribune* in Wyoming. She reports on education, child welfare issues and Wyoming's emerging Latino population.

Carlos Fontes (Ph.D., University of Massachusetts) is associate professor of communication and director of the Center for Community Media and Global Studies at Worcester State College, Mass., where he teaches courses in alternative media, visual literacy, communication theory and video production. His research focuses on alternative media, globalization, and media, technology and society. He is also a media activist who has worked in community video with women's and youth groups. He volunteers with Western Mass Indymedia and is a founding organizer of Worcester Indymedia. He has given many presentations about alternative media in the United States, Portugal and Brazil and has published "Alternative Video: Community, Culture and Counter-Hegemony" in J. Miranda and J. Silveira, J. (eds.), *As ciencias da comunicação na viragem do século* (Lisboa: Vega, 2002).

Tao Lam Fung is an undergraduate student majoring in journalism and international studies at the University of Wisconsin in Madison. Sponsored by the Committee on Institutional Cooperation, the academic consortium of 12 major teaching and research universities in the Midwest, she participated in the Pathways Scholars Program (2003) in which she did a research on comparison of media coverage of SARS in Toronto and Hong Kong. She is working on her senior honors thesis about influence of embedded journalism in media coverage during the 2003 Iraq War.

Injy Galal (M.A., American University in Cairo) has more than seven years of professional experience in marketing and public information, as well as in freelance journalism. She taught media writing at the Modern Science and Arts University in Cairo. She is currently an adjunct professor at the American University in Cairo, where she teaches media ethics. She also is the managing editor of an English-language publication, published in Egypt and in Europe. Ms. Galal has published research on public diplomacy and Internet communications in *Global Media Journal*, *Transnational Broadcasting Studies* journal, and the Arabic *Global Media Journal*.

Naglaa Hassanein (M.A., American University in Cairo) earned a master's degree from the American University in Cairo.

Dina Hussein (M.A., American University in Cairo) is a Ph.D. candidate at the University of Alexandria, Egypt. She taught media writing and editing at The American University in Cairo and at the Modern Science and Arts University in Cairo. She has presented papers at several academic conferences. Her research interests include mass communication education, political communications, and the impact of new communication technologies on Egypt. Her studies have focused on Egyptian mass communication education; research productivity of Egyptian journalism and mass communication educators; the Internet and war; Islamic Web sites; and Arab identity in Web sites.

Thomas J. Johnson (Ph.D., University of Washington) is the Marshall and Sharleen Formby Regents Professor at Texas Tech University. His fields of interest are public opinion and political communication research, particularly the role of the media in presidential elections. More recently, he has concentrated on how people use the Internet and what effect online media have on them.

Barbara K. Kaye (Ph.D., Florida State University) is associate professor in the School of Journalism and Electronic Media at the University of Tennessee-Knoxville. Her research interests include media effects and consumer uses of new communication technologies especially the Internet. Her work has been published in many academic journals. Additionally, she is lead author of *The World Wide Web: A Mass Communication Perspective* (McGraw Hill/Mayfield, 1999, 2001), *Just a Click Away: Advertising on the Internet* (Allyn & Bacon, 2001), and is coauthor of *Electronic Media: See It Then, See It Now, See It Later* (Allyn & Bacon, 2004).

David D. Perlmutter (Ph.D., University of Minnesota) is a professor and associate dean for graduate studies & research at the University of Kansas' William Allen White School of Journalism & Mass Communications. A documentary photographer, his books on war, media and politics include: *Photojournalism and Foreign Policy* (Greenwood, 1998), *Visions of War* (St. Martin's, 1999), *Policing the Media* (Sage, 2000) and *Blogwars* (Forthcoming, Oxford University Press). He writes about the use of blogs in politics, journalism and government at http://policybyblog.squarespace.com/.

Jon R. Pike (M.S, Southern Illinois University-Edwardsville) is a Ph.D. student in communication at North Dakota State University, where he teaches an introductory class in mass communication and advanced undergraduate classes in media writing. At Southern Illinois University-Edwardsville, he wrote a master's thesis on Indymedia and taught courses in audio and video production. He spends his spare time helping out with a student radio station and writing for small circulation publications.

Stephen Quinn (Ph.D., University of Wollongong, Australia) is an associate professor of journalism at Deakin University in Australia. From 2001-2003, he ran the center for media training and research at Zayed University in the United Arab Emirates. He is the author of *Convergent Journalism: An Introduction* (Boston: Focal), *Convergent Journalism: The Fundamentals of Multimedia Reporting* (New York: Peter Lang, 2005), and *Conversations on Convergence* (New York: Peter Lang, 2006). He is the sole academic on the advisory counsel of the Newsplex (www.newsplex.org).

Shafiqur Rahman (M.A., University of Louisiana, Monroe) is a Ph.D. candidate in the College of Mass Communication and Media Arts,

Southern Illinois University, Carbondale. His research interest includes globalization of media, representation of Islam and South Asian Muslims, the Internet and international communication, and diaspora and diasporic media. His research was published in academic journals, including the *Gazette*. He presented his research in various conferences, including the International Communication Association.

Jyotika Ramaprasad is associate professor in the School of Journalism, College of Mass Communication and Media Arts, Southern Illinois University, Carbondale. Her teaching and research interests are largely international and have spanned Asia and Africa. She has published in *Journal of Advertising, Journal of Advertising Research, Journalism Quarterly, Newspaper Research Journal, Gazette,* and *Mass Communication & Society*. Ramaprasad has also produced a TV documentary on the Asian Indians of Carbondale, has worked as a consultant for a social marketing project in Vietnam, and has received journalism-training grants from the U.S. Department of State for work in South Asia and Tanzania.

Chelsea Ross is an undergraduate student in journalism and mass communication and sociology at the University of Wisconsin in Madison.

Carol B. Schwalbe (M.A., George Washington University) is an assistant professor at the Walter Cronkite School of Journalism and Mass Communication at Arizona State University, where she teaches magazine writing and online journalism. Before moving west in 2002, she enjoyed a long career at the National Geographic Society as a senior text editor for *National Geographic* magazine, senior articles editor for *National Geographic Traveler,* senior producer for nationalgeographic.com, and editor-writer in the book division. She lives in Tucson with her husband, two cats, 13 snakes and four Gila monsters.

Atsushi Tajima (Ph.D., University of Wisconsin-Madison) is a lecturer in the Communication Department at the University of Wisconsin-Whitewater. His research interests and recent publications concern news coverage and media representation in an international context. He is a founder and supervisor of Analyzing Media Perspective (AMP), a research circle that has produced several conference papers and publications related to the 2003 Iraq War.

Lamya Tawfik (M.A., American University in Cairo) is a mass communication lecturer at the Misr International University in Cairo. She is also a freelance journalist and a doctoral student at Ain Shams University in Cairo. Her research interests include children's media education, and she has presented papers at international academic conferences on the subject.

Kaye D. Trammell (Ph.D., University of Florida) is on the faculty of the Grady College of Journalism and Mass Communication at University Georgia. Her research interests revolve around the intersection of computer-mediated communication and political communication. She is a former Navy journalist and currently serves as a public affairs officer in the U.S. Naval Reserve. She is an accredited public relations practitioner (APR).

Melissa A. Wall (Ph.D., University of Washington) is an associate professor at California State University–Northridge, where she studies international communication, social movements and alternative media, including blogs. A former journalist, she has trained Ethiopian journalists in Addis Ababa, volunteered at a homeless newspaper in Seattle and works with an independent radio collective that broadcasts on the Pacifica station in Los Angeles.

David Weinstock (MMPh.D., Michigan State) is an assistant professor of journalism in Grand Value State University's School of Communication. In addition, he is a freelance journalist who writes about computer technology and the environment. Prior to his university career, he had a 10-year career as a magazine editor, reporter and photographer. He won a number of national writing and photography awards.

Andrew Paul Williams (Ph.D., University of Florida) is an assistant professor in the Department of Communication at Virginia Tech University. His primary research interests are political communication and media studies. The theoretical perspectives of framing and agenda setting guide much of his scholarship. Williams is interested in political public relations and marketing and how political figures, issues, and events are portrayed in candidate-controlled media and traditional and alternative mass media content. Methodologically, his preferred approaches are content analysis and experimental research design.

FOREWORD

EVERETTE E. DENNIS

Nothing inspires critical analysis of media — whether traditional or alternative — than war. The 2003 Iraq War, which continued as an insurgency three years later, is no exception. Like other wars that came before, it is the "Big Story" — one that commands attention in the nations involved and elsewhere. And always for the communicator and the audience, there is concern about the pursuit of truth, which ancient commentator Aeschlus called "the first casualty" of any war. Communicating the essence of war also employs the technology of the day, whether that is the telegraph and the photograph in the Crimean War, radio in both World Wars, television in Vietnam and digital media in the two Gulf Wars.

There is much controversy about the origins and rationale for the war in Iraq, officially called Operation Iraqi Freedom by the coalition forces, made up mainly of U.S. and British troops. There is, however, less mystery about the role of media in covering this war from the embedded reporters (mostly representing major news organizations) to various alternative and insurgent voices that have less official access. Both use modern digital technologies to tell their stories. Lessons from the Persian Gulf War of 1991 are abundant. That was the first "real time" war, which included what several colleagues and I in a study called "the Charge of the E-Mail Brigade," because various new technologies were employed to cover the news and engage opinion and advocacy. That was before the Internet and World Wide Web were fully accessible to most citizens even in information societies, let alone the developing world.

One lesson from the first Gulf War, evident then and now, is the reality that government control and the inevitable desire to censor has suffered a lethal blow. New technologies simply won't allow it since Internet users can make end-runs around old barriers that ranged from military-sanctioned messages from the war zone to the jamming of radio signals. The first Gulf War benefited from early e-mail messaging, digital transmission of still photographs, fax machines, satellite phones, laptop computers and satellite uplinks. How quaint those tools seem today in a more seamless digital world with easy access to the Internet and the dynamism of interactivity at the core. In this new world of converging media, full-motion video is easily transmitted while high-speed Internet and broadband service offer instantaneous connections.

Once "war correspondence," another seemingly antiquarian term these days, was limited to accredited correspondents, like those embedded with U.S. and British forces in Iraq, but the convergence of all media in global networks opens the possibility that formerly "enemy" communicators get access to information and can transmit it almost anywhere they wish, something unprecedented in the history of wartime coverage and communication. No longer can censors block "correspondence," including that delivered by active bloggers. Suddenly borders are porous and addressable messages can reach almost anyone, anywhere.

The conditions suggested in communicating on and about the Iraq War bring together three of my favorite topics: global and international communication in the context of war; alternative media; and media technologies. I have explored these topics in various studies and research projects over the years, beginning with work on the New Journalism and alternative media during the Vietnam era. This was a time when war critics mostly had to operate on fugitive platforms (alternative, underground, and military underground newspapers) within the United States, where they were pariahs to establishment media, let alone government sources. Even before that I was interested in the role of technological change in media, working on convergence issues nearly two decades before the Internet would triumph and take terms like cybernetics and cyberspace from technical reports to popular parlance. And finally, war coverage from the long forgotten "digestible bite" in Granada, through the Persian Gulf and beyond, provides compelling terrain for understanding media government relations.

That and more is what media scholar Ralph D. Berenger and his colleagues have done in *Cybermedia Go to War: Converging Media During and After the 2003 Iraq War*, which is a vital companion to Dr. Berenger's earlier volume, *Global Media Go to War: Role of News and Entertainment During the 2003 Iraq War*. In *Cybermedia Go to War*, Dr. Berenger and some 33 media scholars, many of them young and promising new contributors to our literature, explore the nature and impact of Web-based digital communication on media content and its distribution while also probing deeper to see what impact these new transitional forms have on news and entertainment itself. This means considering media functions — information, entertainment and opinion — and how they fare in the world of cyberspace. Whether the interactive environments blur and merge in new configurations or are actually transformative in some other fashion is a matter of debate.

Behind several of the essays and studies presented here is a nagging question about whether cybermedia are independent (or alternative) media that are part of a larger professional media system or more akin to pamphleteering and propaganda, a subset of marketing and promotion. As the authors posit, they are both, which means that sorting out and distinguishing information is more difficult than it was when media were more singular and perhaps more predictable.

What editor Berenger and his colleagues offer here causes us to think more deeply about the impact and influence of cybermedia — what they are, their known extensions and connecting links as well as the role they play in informing ordinary citizens and policymakers alike. The authors explore important questions about the extent to which cybermedia are genuine agents of change as well as agents of control — or both. Of course, this is virgin territory and few, if any, other studies offer this kind of thoughtful, speculative analysis.

Based at the American University in Cairo, Dr. Berenger has enlisted a cadre of cooperating researchers, many of them also located in the Middle East, who offer a perspective not often found among media scholars whose international and regional experience is more limited. That's one of the great benefits of these studies that cohere nicely with unifying themes and critical integration. The result might have been confusion and complexity, given the range of material and admittedly ephemeral examples, but instead what we have are media studies in real time, a visual portrait of contemporary communication at the dawn of a new era.

Cybermedia are much more mature today than they were when early e-mail brigades set their course in the 1991 Gulf War, but this work offers a foundation for understanding cyber communication while charting its changes — and ultimately its consequences — for us all. Happily, Dr. Berenger and his coauthors have produced a well-written and accessible volume whose value will be self-evident to any reader.

CYBERMEDIA GO TO WAR

Ralph D. Berenger

M uch of what the world learned about the 2003 war in Iraq was learned from nontraditional news sources, often before the mainstream media reported the stories. The Internet, while in a neophytic stage of development during the 1991 Iraq War, was widely available to the average computer user a dozen years later and played a large role in how people gained, internalized and, in some cases, shared that information with others. E-mails have replaced handwritten notes and letters as the interpersonal communication of choice. Digital photographs and messages can be sent around the world with the speed of a single key stroke. Online diaries and logs — called Weblogs — allow professional journalists and amateur writers alike to communicate with huge mass audiences, sometimes numbered in the millions, with links to other blogs and computer sites. It was, as suggested by Rodney Weideman of IT Net and others, America's first global Internet war.

The computer and Internet made communications instantaneous while obliterating the concept of a news cycle. That infinite realm known as cyberspace also contained its share of rascals and scoundrels. Internet users had to develop a skeptical as well as a discerning eye about information coming out of or about the 2003 Iraq War. Even visuals, digital still photographs and video, could be altered and manipulated with the help of photo- and video-editing programs. Hoaxes abounded. Fact-checking sites like www.snopes.com were busy tracking down e-mail hoaxes and misinformation passed from one inbox to another.

Supporting the notion that nothing is private in cyberspace, photographs intended for archival or personal use were intercepted from online photo albums, which happened to a Seattle-based contractor whose j-pegs of flag-draped coffins in a cargo-hold provoked immediate outrage by U.S. government officials, and her removal from Iraq. Digital photos posted online by guards at Abu Ghraib prison and downloaded by newspapers and Web sites around the world sparked an immediate outcry by already-angry Arabs around the globe. Those pictures fueled a media frenzy in the United States. A Google search in 2005 found that the prison abuse was mentioned at 5.4 million of the 188 million sites that discussed the war. E-mail messages from military-sponsored cybercafes and soldier Weblogs also provided grist for the mainstream media.

Meanwhile, a cyberwar of sorts broke out on the Internet, with the English Al-Jazeera Web site being hacked shortly after its launch in March 2003 with a picture of an American flag superimposed over a map of the United States. As Naila Hamdy and Radwa Mobarak pointed out in *Global Media Go to War*, thousands of chat rooms with millions of hits a day debated the merits of the war and its outcome. Converging to the newest medium, traditional news sites reported an increase of between 30% and 150% during the last two weeks of March 2003, when shooting broke out. The BBC Web site recorded 150 million visits alone. CNN Online posted similar numbers. Responding to the demand of up-to-the-minute news of the war, BBC broadcast around the clock on its Web site to a global audience.

Even after George Bush's presidential "mission accomplished" pronouncement May 1, 2003, the rationale for going to war in the first place continued to be debated in chatrooms, listservs and e-mail exchanges. Did Saddam Hussein really threaten regional peace? Did Iraq possess weapons of mass destruction (WMD) or did American and British governments lie to their peoples to get their support for the war? Can democracy be imposed? Did Iraq provide aid and comfort to terrorist organizations? Are the Iraqi people worse off under the American occupation than they were under Saddam? Is any country in the Middle East capable of civil, democratic societies given their histories and cultures? Was the war all about America's thirst for cheap oil? Or was it about the political ambitions of George W. Bush to win a second term, and his desire to finish the job his father started in 1991 by removing Saddam Hussein from power? Or were there grander issues? Was Iraq invaded because Israel felt threatened by the growing economic and military capabilities of neighboring Arab states, sworn enemies of the Jewish state? Were Afghanistan and then Iraq the first two dominos to fall in the Near East? Who was next: Syria or Iran? Since the two invaded countries were Muslim, was this an abject example of Samuel Huntington's clash of civilizations and a gloomy portend of things to come?

The Internet is no respecter of national borders, of time, or, for that matter, of unquestioned patriotism or nationalism. Charges can be quickly matched by counter charges, simple assertions can be stripped away by clicking on the next link. Cyberspace is both a vast reservoir of useful information and a babbling brook of streaming consciousness. All is there for the world to see and ponder; to ignore and absorb; to mobilize or remain silent. In short, the new media offered users an unparalleled array of choices to become either passive or active consumers of information — and for traditional news consumers this blizzard of conflicting digital images, facts, sources, and access to information from all sides of the conflict was as unsettling as it was satisfying. The cyberspace war's information blitzkrieg might have caused at least one casualty: understanding. In this case, Neil Postman might have gotten it right when he warned that too much information could be as debilitating on an individual's comprehension of events and knowledge-building as not enough information.

Of course, consumers of information are selective in what they seek out. Psychologically, individuals are more apt to choose information that strengthen and support their preconceptions, biases, ideologies and core beliefs. Rarely does selected information alter individual schema. Information that challenges a person's belief system can result in what Leon Festinger called "cognitive dissonance." Very few humans are like F. Scott Fitzgerald's Daisy in *The Great Gatsby*. Individuals are simply incapable of holding contradictory viewpoints of equal weight and importance, and they will reject, rationalize and repress cognitive stimuli that cause psychological discomfort. Selective perception and cognitive dissonance are two possible explicates of what happened to audiences in the 2003 Iraq War.

Those who strongly favored the war, either out of revenge for 9/11 or fear that Iraq posed a threat to world peace, were supportive to the end, although they tended to rationalize the reasons of going to war in the first place. War opponents sought out information that supported their opposition, especially in the Arab World, where a generation of media consumers has been "cultivated" by its media systems, controlled by authoritarian regimes, to accept certain precepts as "true" and contrary viewpoints as "false" because they came from lands that allegedly are ignorant of Middle East cultures and have media systems that allegedly portray Arabs and the dominant religion, Islam, unfavorably (as was the case of the 2005 Danish political cartoon controversy that was believed to depict the Prophet Muhammed, a cultural taboo). The digitalized cartoons, by the way, were widely distributed by Islamic activists over the Internet, thus expanding globally the reach of these drawings and eliciting violent protests in places that are densely populated by Muslims around the world. So access to vast repositories of information over the Internet does not necessarily change hearts and minds because, again, individuals "choose" message frames that reinforce what they already believe.

Scholarship has affirmed the concept that opinion formation is enhanced if the receiver of a message knows, trusts and identifies with the sender. The stronger the affinity and identification, the stronger impact messages have on recipients' opinion formation. Given that e-mail messages and forwarded Web links are often sent to individuals in a sender's address book, the impact of those messages on opinion formation cannot be disregarded. Again, individual schema are generally reinforced because the receiver knows, trusts and identifies with the sender of the message. As is often the case, the receiver of a message forwards it to friends and relatives in his or her address book with a predictable impact on the second set of receivers thus contributing to a multiple flow of the message content. The challenge for subsequent media scholars will be to continue their research into this dynamic of media effects, deriving significance and understanding from those studies.

CHARACTERISTICS OF "NEW MEDIA"

The characteristics of the "new media" — usually defined as anything digital that communicates to known and unknown audiences in actual (synchronic) or delayed (asynchronic) time — fall into several broad categories.

> *Convergent.* Nearly all new media use or have the capabilities of using a variety of different media that converge or synthesize into a new type of communication media. Of course, it can be argued that there is no such thing as "new media." When telegraph messages sped the process of communicating from far-away places in the 19th century, it could have been regarded as a new media. The same could be said of commercial radio when it emerged early in the 20th century, and television as it became the dominant medium in the last half of that century. The adaptation of the Internet for information, combining words, pictures, sound and video, and allowing for interactivity, is only the latest to fall under the rubric of a new media, while predecessors join the category of traditional or legacy media. Logically, there is no such thing as a new media, some skeptical scholars assert, only "preconvergent media." During the 2003 Iraq War and its aftermath, Web sites carried text messages, audiovisual material, some of it created specifically for those Web sites, and links to similar sites with multimedia formats. A recent development has

been downloadable multimedia material to iPods and hand-held telecommunications devices such as inepensive mobile phones.

Ubiquitous. Preconvergent media are everywhere in cyberspace and accessed by mobile telephony as well as computer users. Clearly, the exponential growth of cyberspace and its asynchronous/synchronous nature makes information and analysis available to more people than ever before. Individuals can connect to the wide information reservoir at home, in the office, at their university, or at the proliferating cyber cafés that pop up even in remote locations. Wireless technologies, available during the 2003 Iraq War, allowed millions of users to access information on the Internet from a park bench or a parked car, or simply while walking down the sidewalk. Advances in computer science have led to more user-friendly programs that anyone, young or old, can use. Governments and non-governmental organizations, concerned about the digital divide, are globally stepping up efforts to make computers and Internet connections accessible not only to the elites in those countries, which is the case now, but the average person as well. In some regions, like the Middle East, which lags everywhere else in the world except Sub-Sahara Africa, growth will have to be exponential to catch up. But Internet access during 2003-2005 doubled in the Middle East.

Agenda-setting. Many stories covered in cyberspace set the agenda for mainstream media, and monitoring Web sites and blogs is an essential weapon in the arsenal of all reporters. Search engines such as Google, Ask, Netscape and Yahoo! are used in newsrooms to fact-check stories and collect story background. Stories carried on Weblogs and Web sites often set the tone for "water cooler" discussions as well as listservs that target specific interest groups, as well as mainstream media reporters. This agenda-setting function of the new media was evident during the 2003 Iraq War, as Internet discussants often quoted Weblogs with the same authority as they would cite newspaper and television reportage or academic studies. Bloggers such as Salam Pax were often quoted in newspaper and magazine reports, giving them the same attention as governmental sources of the war. Such a rich diversity calls into question the "social control" function of media and their ability to set national and international agendas.

Credibility. The adage of "seeing is believing" is a chief characteristic of the preconvergent media. Puzzling to some scholars is how

Weblogs have acquired instant credibility with a vast number of users because they often mix analysis with interpretation of news stories, and the bloggers' credentials — which are highly valued in academia as evidence of credibility — are often lacking. They are credible because *they* are there, in cyberspace for the world to see; without mediation from journalism professionals, and without pressures advertisers and clients, elites, routine newsroom practices and customs. Unlike Gertrude Stein's derision of Oakland as "there's no *there* there," virtual space does not need *place, time* or even some acknowledged *controlling authority* like a government to have a presence. Anyone with a computer, modem and a perspective can find a home in virtual space and attain instant credibility. The legacy media also have a presence on the Internet. Hardly a newspaper or magazine is absent from the Internet, and those blogger sites that link or quote these sites add to bloggers' credibility.

Interactivity. The new media are interactive, and perhaps this characteristic is what sets them apart from their predecessors. This interactive characteristic allows anyone to express his or her views, often without mediation or editing, on topics raised by Internet sites or Weblogs.

Transferability. The cut and paste function of the digital realm allows large blocks of information to be transmitted as well as linked. Material contained on Web sites can be cut and pasted into e-mails and sent to other users who might have missed the initial posting. Since individuals seem to be greatly influenced by opinion leaders they perceive to share their worldviews, interests and similar societal, political or sociological orientations, these transferred messages are generally given a high degree of credence by recipients. The multi-step flow of information's impact on opinion formation has never been as evident as it is in the digital age.

PURPOSE OF THIS BOOK

In *Global Media Go to War* (Marquette Books, 2004), scholars and working journalists contributed 34 essays and studies about media behavior during the 2003 Iraq War in the first compendium of its type to be published. Although several chapters centered on uses of alternative media in a specific section called "The War in Cyberspace," the intent of that book was to paint in broad strokes about the role and behaviors of mostly traditional news and entertainment media in helping global audiences come to grips with the run-up, prosecution and aftermath of the war.

It was clear toward the end of that project, however, that a companion volume was needed to complete the picture of war coverage, but this time from a nontraditional media's focal point. Hence was planted the seed for *Cybermedia Go to War: Role of Converging Media During and After the 2003 Iraq War*. Readers seeking a fuller picture of how the media behaved during the war will find themselves referring, as I did, to *Global Media Go to War* to provide cross-media context and historical timelines to better understand many of the studies presented in this volume even though this work stands on its own as well.

This book attempts to answer questions raised by preconvergent or new media's behavior. What impact, if any, did cyberspace have on the creation and distribution of news during wartime? Did it rob traditional media of their iron-vise grip on news and information? Could the Internet hold government — and the mainstream media — more accountable for getting the facts and interpretation of those facts? Could it help mobilize opposition to or support for a war? Was it an agent of control or change or both?

The answers to these questions were inconclusive, fragmentary and situational, this book expectedly found. Yet, it moves the ball closer to the goal of full and complete understanding of the role of the new media in war coverage in the digital era.

Following the benchmarks set by *Global Media Go to War*, the authors were asked to write chapters that resulted in a book that was cross-disciplinary in nature; cross-cultural; cross-generational and which focused on the behavior of the digital media. Senior and junior scholars present perspectives from both sides of the conflict from a variety of cultural orientations and nationalities. Surprising cogency emerged from this eclectic mix, which should add to the book's readability. Speaking of which, readability was high on the list of desirables contained in the call for chapters. Like *Global Media Go to War*, I wanted a book that could be read and understood by undergraduates, professional journalists and the general reading public, devoid of much of the academic language that often sacrifices clarity for exactness that unfortunately results in obfuscation. Credit deservedly belongs to the authors, most inculcated with academese in their everyday lives, who admirably accomplished this goal.

How This Book is Organized

This book of 23 chapters is divided into five parts containing studies and essays by 33 authors or coauthors for readers who have a special interest in various aspects of the converging new media, or for researchers seeking studies on alternative media uses during times of conflict.

The book was designed with classroom use in mind. At the end of each chapter are five discussion questions that can be used by instructors to stimulate students to develop a deeper understanding of the issues and theories raised by the authors. Like its predecessor, this book would be suited for courses in international conflict studies, international communication studies, undergraduate and graduate seminars on uses of new and alternative media, and courses in public diplomacy, itself a converged discipline emerging from international relations and diplomacy, and mass communication. The nonacademic reader, however, should find the discussion questions provocative and illuminating as well as they try to assimilate the ideas contained in the chapters.

Writing the foreword to this book is media scholar Ev Dennis, creating a reunion of sorts between professor and student. Dr. Dennis was my thesis advisor at the University of Minnesota some 30 years ago. He has had a profound influence on media studies worldwide and an even greater impact on my thinking about how media facilitate or hinder audience's understanding of information they disseminate.

Part I — The 2003 Iraq War in an Era of Convergent Media

The first seven chapters address the issue of how converging media behaved during the war. Stephen Quinn brings the reader immediately into the realm of media technologies and war, recounting how communication technologies have always helped war correspondents do their job, from the Crimea War of the mid-19th century to the first war of the 21st century. The multimedia reporter, he says, arrived in full flower in the 2003 Iraq War. The availability of inexpensive hardware, he hints, raises an intriguing possibility that amateur journalists might one day rival their paid brethren in collecting news and disseminating news.

While most of the book deals with the digital media, the second chapter by Atushi Tajima, et al., puts the pre-Iraq War into perspective by studying the front pages of 523 newspapers around the world, all of them with their own Web sites that now reach global audiences. A recent study, reported in *Editor & Publisher Online*, says that because of online newspapers and gateway sites, like drudgereport.com and others on the Internet, more people around the world than ever are reading stories generated by newspapers, even as print edition circulations are shrinking. How these newspapers "framed" the Iraq War debate was the focus of this chapter.

Shafiqur Rahman and Jyotika Ramasprasad build on Tajima, et al., by comparing the venerable *New York Times* coverage of the war with its online edition and *Yahoo! News* to see if there were differences in coverage between a local newspaper designed for local and national readers, and the Internet versions designed for a global audience.

Daniela V. Dimitrova concentrates on the BBC News' online coverage of the war and how the news organization found itself making news during the Dr. David Kelley incident, all dutifully reported on its Web site. The BBC obviously recognized its importance to satisfy global audience needs of news, often at the expense of Britain's international political interests.

Chapters 5-7 focus on the Middle East, and how the region coped with the war over the Internet despite the fact that fewer than 10 million residents of that region had access to the Web during the war. That figure that has been climbing steadily, however, as regional governments are making access to the Information Superhighway one of their national development goals.

Tal Azran reports in Chapter 5 his study of english.aljazeera.net and how the West perceived this instrument of information counter flow that reported news of the war through an Arab filter.

In Chapter 6, three Middle Eastern junior scholars — Injy Galal, Amy Ahmed and Lama al-Hammouri provide an Arab perspective of CNN and Al-Jazeera's coverage of the war to determine how either media outlet framed the conflict for their respective audiences.

Following up on Al-Jazeera's impact on Arab audiences, senior scholar Muhammad Ayish takes a closer look at the aljazeera.net Web site and probes how the site shaded the news for an Arab audience, sometimes at the loss of what Westerners would consider objective news coverage.

Part II — The Convergent Media's Power to Mobilize

Chapters in this part deal specifically with the ability of the converging media to mobilize large numbers of like-minded individuals around a specific issue. The huge, international antiwar rally Feb. 15, 2003, was an abject example. Never before had so many people — variously estimated up to 50 million people worldwide — been moved to congregate in world capitals to protest an impending war.

The first two chapters in this part deal with Independent Media Centers. Carlos Fontes, in Chapter 8, draws broad strokes around the use of alternative media from his vantage point inside the WestMass IMC, while Lisa Brooten looks at the inner workings of the St. Louis IMC in Chapter 9. Both chapters allude to the mobilization ability of computer-based activist organizations.

In Chapter 10, Jon Pike studies how small social movements, like moveon.org, can become important, sustained political forces with the potential of influencing national affairs and possibly international policy, while in Chapter 11, Shaun Peter Cannon reports on his study of how a couple of volunteer workers with a computer and modem, who called themselves the Victoria Peace Network, mobilized tens of thousands of antiwar protesters by e-mail. Mobilization over the converging media also took place in the Middle East, as Ibrahim Al-Marashi in Chapter 12 found. He writes about the cyber-insurgency and Iraqi resistance movements.

Part III — How People Used New Media During the War

While Part II centers on the mobilization aspect of the alternative media, this part focuses on the various uses of media by individuals and groups during the war. The first chapter explores how e-mails, developed less than a decade earlier as a communication device with worldwide reach, were used during the 2003 war. In Chapter 13, Emmanuel Alozie investigates e-mail as an instrument of war propaganda and finds that the U.S. government's destabilization strategy had only marginal success.

In Chapter 14, Egyptians Dina Hussein and Naglaa Hassanien report on a uses and gratifications study of Internet use by elite Arabs during the war, while in Chapter 15 Lamya Tawfik looks at young Arabs' home pages to see if they created an identifiable Arab identity and found that the Iraq War was not the main thing that interested them. Across the oceans, Elaine Cardenas found essentially the same thing in Chapter 16 among predominantly American users of online diaries.

Part IV — Blogging During War: A New Journalistic Form or Trivial Self Expression?

Weblogs entered public consciousness — and lexicon — during the 2003 Iraq War and in many cases rivaled traditional news reports in credibility and readability for Internet users.

Blogging, technically available since the 1990s, increased in popularity after 9/11 and reached public acceptance during and after the 2003 Iraq War. Of the 865 blogs in 2005 concerned with the Iraq War, 600 of them were started during the war and insurgency in 2003 and 2004, according to the Blogosphere Ecosystem at truthlaidbear.com. Millions of people followed the writings of a Baghdad blogger, Salam Pax, during the war as well as dozens of amateur and professional journalists, who shared their impressions of the conflict, their media organization's response to it, and their political perspectives by writing Weblogs, some of them interactive and most of them linked to traditional media Web sites for background information. At first, mainstream media eschewed this rival, forbidding their reporters to post blogs online, but as Weblogs grew in popularity, some traditional media encouraged their reporters to post links to their individual blogs on the news organization's Web sites.

In Chapter 17, Melissa A. Wall ponders the question of whether blogs are a new genre of war reporting, and if so what changes in media strategies would result. In the next chapter, Kaye D. Trammell examines celebrity Weblogs and how well known personalities treated this conflict. In Chapter 19, scholars Thomas J. Johnson and Barbara K. Kaye ask the salient question of whether blogs are siphoning off audiences from traditional media sources.

Part V — Effects of Convergent Media

This final segment looks at the effect on users of the alternative media and attempts to connect the dots of the previous chapters by examining how digital media might impact individuals and society.

David D. Perlmutter (Chapter 20) ponders "The Big Picture" in his examination of the Fallujah incident and documents how the photojournalistic event faded from youthful consciousness over time. Similarly, Carol B. Schwalbe investigates mainstream U.S. news Web sites in Chapter 21 to show how the faces of war we do not see can be as important as those we do see.

Andrew Paul Williams in Chapter 22 reinforces Marshall McLuhan's dictum that the media are the message, not merely the messengers, in what he calls "Net narcissism." Finally, in Chapter 23, David Weinstock and Tim Boudreau continue their study from the previous volume of the effect of online Iraq War news on young audiences, and find leading TV Web sites had as much appeal for young audiences as spinach and liver.

A FINAL THOUGHT

This introduction asserted earlier that all new media are more accurately described as preconvengent media, which begs the question: preconvergent with what?

The correct answer is: who knows? Did anyone predict at the birth of the telephone in the 19th century that one day call-in radio stations would widely use it — often distributing their programs globally via satellite and the Internet? Or when radio was in its infancy, did anyone imagine how television would one day bring war into the living room? Or when television was first broadcast in England in the late 1930s, did anyone suspect that viewers in 1996 would hear and see choral groups on five continents singing in unison in real time Beethoven's *Ode to Joy* at the Sydney Olympics, or would be witnessing in 1991 the eerie night-vision live broadcasts via satellite of the bombing of Baghdad? And at the height of the Golden Age of TV in the 1960s did anyone imagine that those programs would have global appeal decades after they were originally broadcast? Or when home computers became available in the 1980s, who could have predicted the impact of the Internet on shaping opinions and attitudes of a global audience? Yet all of these media have converged into common usage today. So it is logical to assume that the Internet one day will also converge into something new and different. After all, we've only had a few decades of experimentation with this "new media."

If we have learned anything from two centuries of technological development in mass communication it is this: No one can foresee either the effects of new media on mass audiences or what the final — if that is a correct word to use — form media and the content they carry will take. At best we can only study what is in front of us, and speculate on what will be.

ACKNOWLEDGMENTS

While dozens of people have been involved in various aspects of this book, led by the authors who contributed to it, a special thanks goes to David Demers at Marquette Books, who has put up with my chronic tardiness in meeting deadlines and who constantly and consistently cajoled, critiqued and counseled me on the direction of this book; Hussein Y. Amin, chairman of my university's journalism and mass communication department, who has been most understanding for my requests for easier teaching schedules and relief from committee work so

I could work on this compendium while at the same time tutoring me on Middle East media; Naila Hamdy, a valued colleague, who teaches and writes about communication technology and who has reshaped my thinking about the subject; Mona Badran, my research and teaching assistant, who has helped organize my class load, which freed my time from routine academic tasks and who helped edit some of the chapters; my long-suffering wife, Carol, who similarly relieved me of household tasks and gently prodded me to stay on schedules, while applying her formidable intellect and talent in helping copyedit and proofread this book; and finally my undergraduate and graduate students in international communication who are constantly updating my knowledge of youthful Arab culture and technological communication innovations they seem to readily adopt.

PART I

THE 2003 IRAQ WAR IN AN ERA OF CONVERGENT MEDIA

CHAPTER ONE

WAR REPORTING AND THE TECHNOLOGIES OF CONVERGENCE

STEPHEN QUINN

W ar may be horrid and brutish, but journalism usually benefits from coverage of conflict. Technologies developed for war coverage tend to improve newsgathering processes in general, accelerating the speed at which news is delivered and boosting the quality of coverage. Baron Paul Julius von Reuter gave the news agency that bears his name a head start on its rivals when, from about the middle of the 19th century, he introduced pigeons to speed correspondents' reports from the fronts of various wars. Journalists were still using pigeons to avoid traffic as recently as the Tokyo Olympics in 1964.

Photographs helped document the American Civil War (its introduction was during the Crimea War six years earlier, along with the concept of the foreign correspondent), along with the telegraph, which linked battlefields with major newsrooms in the United States. Fear of disrupted telegraph lines during the American Civil War taught journalists to send the essence of the story early, leading to the development of the inverted-pyramid structure and summary lead. Interestingly, this was probably the first war in which Americans saw live fighting. Audiences at the first battle of Bull Run on July 21, 1861, watched the conflict from the comfort of their picnic blankets until the horror of what they were witnessing set in and they fled back to Washington. It took another 142 years before American audiences were able to watch live fighting, this time in the comfort of their homes and offices via satellite from Iraq.

During the wars in Afghanistan and Iraq, small digital video cameras, satellite phones and laptop computers proved a boon for broadcast and print journalists alike. These technologies allowed them to feed stories and images quickly back to their newsrooms, and freed news teams from being tethered to a large satellite uplink. Those computers and satellite phones were the descendants of technology developed during World War II and the Cold War, respectively.

Computers were developed to accelerate the calculations needed to provide accurate ballistics charts for artillery. And U.S. military spending on space boomed after the Soviet Union put the first Sputnik satellite into orbit in 1956. A major newsgathering innovation, the videophone, came of age during the wars in Afghanistan and Iraq, especially in areas where electricity was scarce, weather conditions appalling, and transport and telephone connections unreliable. BBC correspondent Ben Brown told of how he rode a horse for two hours to reach the front in Afghanistan because the roads were so poor. Dick Tauber, CNN's vice president for satellites and circuits, said sand was the worst enemy his staff encountered in Iraq. "The sand is so fine, it's insidious," he said at the time.

News organizations have employed what they learned during war to improve newsgathering during peace. During the 2004 U.S. presidential primaries, cable news network MSNBC embedded a young reporter with each of the Democrat candidates. MSNBC gave each reporter technology tested on the Iraqi battlefields: A small video camera, a tripod, and a powerful laptop for editing footage. The reporters were one-person operations, sending their reports to MSNBC over any available high-speed Internet connection. Often this was from the nearest Starbucks coffee shop. Reporters set up their cameras before interviewing and filming the candidate. Each edited his or her footage on a laptop, wrote articles for the Web, and reported live. Mark Lukasiewicz, executive producer of NBC's "Campaign Embed," said viewers responded to the concept based on their knowledge of embedded reporters in Iraq. "The part of it we're applying to the campaigns is having reporters with the campaigns, with their stories, all the time, living and breathing it." *Wall Street Journal* reporter Michael Phillips said the network "saved a bundle," because the one-person reporting teams did not need camera or sound crews or expensive satellite hook-ups. The candidates got "straight coverage with minimal spin" and many junior reporters had the chance to prove themselves (Phillips, 2003).

This chapter argues that the vast improvements in newsgathering technologies at the start of the 21st century are finding fruition in the arrival of a single, multimedia journalist, and the evolution of a new form of journalism around the world known as convergence, or multiplatform publishing.

What is convergence? It is a form of journalism where newsrooms (often from rival companies) work together to deliver news in a variety of formats. They aim to reach a range of audiences with interactive content on a 24/7 basis. In some cases, one editorial staff produces multiple types of journalism for multiple platforms. The nature of convergence varies from country to country and from culture to culture, both within countries and within companies. But it is happening. In 2001, Earl Wilkinson, executive director of the International Newspaper Marketing Association, noted that most major publishers worldwide had "accepted the multimedia, brand-oriented future for newspapers." That year the Innovation International media consulting group estimated that perhaps 100 companies worldwide had embraced the concept. Four years later Ifra, the media research company, estimated that 560 publishers around the world had a "declared and major emphasis" on gathering and delivering news in a variety of platforms and anticipated the number would rise.

The multimedia journalist is also an increasing trend around the Western world. As of early 2005, they tended to be in the minority in most newsrooms, but that will change as candidates graduate from journalism programs. At the pioneering News Center in Tampa, Florida, six of the just over 400 editorial staff at the *Tampa Tribune*, WFLA-TV and tbo.com are true multimedia reporters. Prestigious internships there go to students who are aware of the potential of multimedia reporting. The single journalist who can write, shoot, edit, and package multimedia content will become increasingly valuable, especially in situations where it is not possible to get a group of journalists into an area such as wars or isolated regions, or in small markets. With time, these reporters will attract a premium in terms of salary and recognition.

Photojournalists tend to be early adopters and represent examples of what is possible. In Austria, for example, photojournalists at the *Vorarlberger Nachrichten* in Schwarzach have carried camera-enabled cell phones as well as standard digital cameras since 2002. On arrival at a news event, they were all expected to take photographs with the cell phone and immediately send images to the newspaper's Web site before using their other cameras. Jochen Hofer, editor-in-chief of Vorarlberger Online, said the policy started in July 2002 after a photographer found he could not send images taken with his digital camera via the local phone lines because the files were too large and the connection poor. "That's why we tried our MMS [multimedia messaging system] mobiles. We knew we had to win time," Hofer said. Photojournalists sent MMS images to online editors via the cell phone and then telephoned the newsroom to dictate two or three sentences about what happened. Hofer said his photojournalists used MMS for most news events such as accidents, fires, and avalanches, plus sporting events. "The photographers get a new mobile every year, so the quality of the pictures sent by MMS is improving steadily" (quoted in Northrup, 2004, p. 18).

SMALLER TECHNOLOGY AND FASTER NEWS

The war in Iraq that started in March 2003 was a watershed in terms of journalists' use of technology. The biggest changes involved a major reduction in the size and weight of the equipment, and considerable improvements in the speed of delivery.

During the Gulf war of 1991, the available satellite newsgathering technology weighed more than a ton, was packed into perhaps a dozen boxes, and took a team two hours to unpack. Jump forward just over a decade to the invasion of Iraq and journalists' satellite newsgathering gear weighed about 45 kilograms — about 100 pounds — and two people could set it up in less than half an hour. Everything could fit into two suitcases rather than a dozen. The units combined MPEG-2 encoders, miniature antennae and a multiplexer. The last is a device that combines several inputs into one signal so it can be transported via a single transmission channel. The system employed lower-power amplifiers and smaller dishes than previous packages. The mobile, very small aperture terminal (MVSAT) fold-up antenna — a mere 1.2 meters (48 inches) in diameter — could handle voice, video and data at the same time at speeds of up to 3.8 megabits a second. Alternatively, a solo multimedia or backpack journalist with a camera, laptop, digital camera, satellite phone and accessories often carried less than 40 kilos — about 90 pounds — even when their kit included a chemical suit, gas mask and other safety gear. Many correspondents typically connected their digital video camcorders to Macintosh G4 laptops. They used Apple's Final Cut Pro to edit video, and then transmitted their packages via satellite phones.

HISTORY, TECHNOLOGY AND WAR

It's useful here to briefly consider the lessons of history. New technologies have always had an impact on newsgathering. Media historian Anthony Smith noted that the telegraph had a "substantial" impact on the English provincial press from the middle of the 19th century, because it allowed them to "hold their own against metropolitan newspapers" (Smith, 1978, p. 209). In the early part of the 20th century, the telephone changed the structure of American journalism, producing "legmen" who collected news and phoned it in, and "re-write men" in the office who tailored the news to fit the personality of the newspaper. The telephone switchboard later transformed the nature of reporting in the 1920s and 1930s (Smith, 1979, p. 150), just as the computer changed newsgathering from about the 1980s through the development of computer-assisted reporting.

Dr. Mark Deuze, a visiting professor at Indiana University journalism school, noted that war and technological developments had always complemented each other. "Their respective impact on the acceleration of certain trends and technology-related developments in journalism is important," he said.

This situation had important cultural implications. It was reflected in the style of involved reporting in World War II of people like Ernie Pyle, which in turn could be related to the New Journalism movement in the United States decades later, Deuze said. In the first Iraq War in 1991, the U.S. networks' use of satellite broadcasting technologies triggered the popularity of 24/7 live television. The invasion of Iraq propelled Webloggers — both professional and amateur — to center stage (Deuze, 2005).

Nigel Dacre, the editor of London's Independent Television News, noted that a new technology seemed to emerge in every recent war or conflict. Videophones had "really come into their own during the Afghanistan campaign," he said. CNN reporter Nic Robertson was one of the first reporters to experiment with the videophone. He broadcast video of a hijacking in Kandahar, Afghanistan, in 1999. The BBC first used one in the spring of 2000, when correspondent James Reynolds reported from Santiago, Chile, on the lead-up to the arrest of General Augusto Pinochet. John Simpson used a videophone in Afghanistan on the night the United States started its bombing campaign. Sky News correspondent Geoff Meade also sent pictures from near Kabul that same night. In January 2001, Nic Robertson reported from the scene of the Bhuj earthquake in India in a fraction of the time it would have taken with conventional equipment. And on April 12 that year, CNN showed live the U.S. Air Force lifting its people from Hainan Island, off the Chinese mainland, after a collision with a Chinese F-8 fighter had forced their plane to land 11 days earlier. Videophones also played an important role in CNN's coverage of the attacks on the World Trade Center and the Pentagon on September 11, 2001. Reporters also used them to interview rescue workers and survivors from the scene at Ground Zero.

The big difference with new technology in the early 21st century compared with a generation earlier was speed, ITN's Nigel Dacre said. During the Vietnam conflict, for example, it would have taken at least 24 hours to get the Hainan Island footage to air. With the videophone, it was almost instantaneous. The nature of the conflict in Afghanistan and Iraq made reporting difficult and expensive, Dacre said, but even more so without the new technologies. Afghanistan was the first main story that ITN had covered using videophones. John Beeston, news director for CNN Online in Hong Kong, said the development of small and inexpensive digital equipment such as cameras had enormous implications for the way in which journalists worked.

> A traditional camera crew in its four-wheel drive with many boxes of gear is pretty obvious. People know they are a television crew. When a camera is pointed at people, it changes the dynamics of the situation. People behave differently. A single video-journalist is less intimidating. Film crews are all about deadlines. A single video-journalist can produce material for a variety of formats: television, real audio or video on the Web, [even] stills. It changes the dynamics of the reporting process and it changes the deadline from the next news bulletin to any time (Beeston, 2001).

THE PRIMACY OF IMAGES

It is a truism that television needs graphic pictures. Otherwise it becomes radio with wallpaper pictures.

Until the invasion of Iraq, news desks would tolerate poor quality or grainy images from videophones if they showed live or important news. Grainy images gave a mood of reality. Newspapers similarly published poor-quality photographs if the image had sufficient news value (such as the explosion of the Challenger shuttle in January 1986). All that changed with the war in Iraq. Ian Ritchie, chief executive officer of Associated Press Television News (APTN), said his broadcast clients expected to see quality images immediately the fighting began in Iraq. "With this one you need to be live or very close to live ... our biggest investment before the conflict was in insuring live coverage." APTN set up 40 operational cameras in Iraq and neighboring countries in the months prior to the fighting. Many of the cameras on the road had a "store and forward" capability. This meant that images could be transferred from camera to laptop, and from there to a satellite telephone or to a satellite news gathering facility. "We were the first with live pictures out of Um Qasr in the beginning of the war and we were the first with live pictures from Baghdad airport [after it was captured]," Ritchie said (Schleifer, 2003).

Former BBC correspondent David Cass, who presented news for the English-language news programs of Al-Arabiya in Dubai, said image quality was one of the key issues during the Iraq War:

VIDEOPHONES JOIN THE FRAY

After CNN used a videophone on Hainan island in April 2001, manufacturer 7E Communications said they had difficulty filling orders from broadcasters around the world. In November 2001, the company won the prestigious *Wall Street Journal* Business Innovation Award for the phone.

"We are selling them as fast as we can make them to news organizations around the world," said company spokesman Peter Beardow at the time.

A UK company, 7E Communications is based near Heathrow airport. Their technology enables journalists to file reports that would have been impossible with traditional satellite equipment.

The 7E phone employs the H.263 compression algorithm and can either use one channel of ISDN to operate at 64 kilobits a second or by combining both ISDN channels can send at 128 kilobits a second. It also has built-in audio mixing capabilities.

A videophone can send images at up to 20 frames a second. These phones are based on video-conferencing technology and cost $8,000-10,000. A videophone is about the size of a laptop, weighs about 10 kilos (22 pounds), and a single person can operate it. Phone line costs are about a tenth of the cost of traditional satellite transmission.

Though battery operated, they can also be used with other power sources.

CNN reporter Nic Robertson is said to have once powered one using his car battery via its cigarette lighter.

In this environment, quality is the single most important factor. In just the same way as the news organizations want to upgrade their signals sent by correspondents in the field, from the jumpy, grainy sat-phone quality that came to prominence in Afghanistan, to full-on broadcast quality, so the viewer sitting at home needs at least the quality in light entertainment, sports, and movies to which he has become accustomed.

Cass noted that a Russian TV network, RTVI, had pioneered sending quality images between New York and Moscow using Internet protocol television (IPTV). Path 1 Network Technologies, a San Diego, California, company, developed the software. This technology saves money by removing satellite costs, which Cass said were "crippling" the big news organizations. RTVI was able to send four to six megabits of live video from New York to Moscow. Image quality was excellent despite the poor Russian telecoms infrastructure. The potential return on capital investment of this technology was almost immediate, Cass said.

Most news organizations managed to produce excellent images from the heat of battle in Iraq. The late NBC correspondent David Bloom broadcast from on top of a tank recovery vehicle with the Third Infantry, while technician Craig White controlled the camera from inside the vehicle. White sent full bandwidth video and audio via microwaves to a satellite-equipped truck two miles behind the advancing military. From that vehicle, full bandwidth video was sent to the network. Stacy Brady, vice president of field operations for NBC News, described the pictures as "fabulous" (quoted in Johnston, 2003).

THE POWER OF THE LAPTOP

In November 2003, BBC journalists became the first in the world to employ innovative software to broadcast video news live via laptop computers. Laptop newsgathering (LNG) requires a digital video camera, a laptop, and some proprietary software called Quicklink. Loaded onto Panasonic Toughbook laptops and used in conjunction with Avid editing software, the software compressed broadcast quality video into a file that could be transmitted as an e-mail attachment. The compression algorithm enabled one minute of quality television to be transmitted in somewhere between 90 seconds and two minutes. This was a vast improvement on the grainy images of the videophone. It took a videophone about 20 minutes to transit a one-minute report and the quality was not as good. The software needs a high-speed Internet connection such as an ISDN line or wireless connection, using IPTV.

Peter Mayne, executive editor of BBC newsgathering, said the BBC had provided Quicklink to all its reporters around the world. "The system was used extensively during the Iraq War by our news teams who were in the most forward positions. Being in the thick of the action [they] needed to travel with the smallest and lightest equipment possible." Mayne said the BBC could easily update the software to its correspondents. It was scalable depending on the available Internet connection, and could operate from about 64 kilobits a second through to one megabit a second. "The greater the bandwidth, the better the picture quality," Mayne said. Ken Herron, director of Quicklink, said several other broadcasters were experimenting with the software. Videophone connections could only transmit live video at a maximum speed of 128 kilobits a second, Herron said, while Quicklink software allowed feeds of up to one megabit a second depending on the speed of the connection (Quicklink press release 2004).

Editorial managers are always balancing the key equations of time versus money and flexibility versus cost. Delivery over the Internet, if available, is cheap but limited in terms of flexibility because it is fixed in place. Satellite phones allow for greater mobility, but the costs are much higher than an Internet connection because bandwidth is limited and the cost-per-minute charges are higher. Combined with laptop computer newsgathering (LNG), satellite phones give journalists considerable independence. BBC's Peter Mayne said correspondents had tested LNG in West Africa before the Iraq invasion and were satisfied the system was rugged enough to cope with battlefield situations. "LNG software integrates well with our editing platform on one laptop [which is] a distinct advantage for teams that need to travel light," Mayne said. The U.S. television network, ABC News, also used LNG in the Gulf.

Conventional satellite hardware costs much more than LNG hardware. Satellite uplink technology costs at least $100,000. These transponders typically send real time video at about three megabits a second. Satellite phones are cheaper. A videophone costs about $8,000 for a single delivery channel of 64 kilobits a second, or $10,000 for two kilobit-a-second channels. Any video transmitted live by videophone will be of poor resolution because of the low frame rate compared with broadcast-quality video. A LNG laptop with Quicklink software costs about $4,000. Michael Murrie, professor of broadcast journalism at Pepperdine University in California, said that for the price of one satellite newsgathering (SNG) unit, a news organization could deploy several reporters each with a laptop, digital camcorder, and satellite phone. A SNG unit would usually need at least a technician and a reporter, Murrie said.

> With less bulky equipment, the laptop news gatherers are more mobile. These crews can go to more remote locations. Transmission costs may be higher, but they can operate more efficiently as one-person crews saving personnel costs (Murrie, 2003).

CONSEQUENCES FOR NEWSGATHERING

Because of the availability of relatively cheap digital equipment, the BBC has been experimenting with the concept of the single reporter able to shoot, write, edit, and package an entire news story for domestic news programs. This person is known as a video-journalist, or VJ.

The VJ was the brainchild of Michael Rosenblum, a former CBS news producer turned media consultant. Rosenblum developed this idea at NY1 in Manhattan and convinced the BBC that it could boost newsgathering efficiency by using the latest digital technology. Rosenblum said the scheme was an attempt to "build television along the lines of a newspaper" operation. "We want to take them [journalists] out of the newsroom and put them in the field where they can gather news," he said. Rosenblum said his process would cut the cost of production by 20-70 percent and the BBC contracted him to train about 600 BBC staff. Groups of journalists and other staff such as cameramen and production assistants volunteered to attend three-week training courses.

The process became known as personal digital production (PDP), and the BBC established a training center in Newcastle in the north of England. Paul Myles, the PDP center coordinator, said all VJs used a firewire cable to transfer footage from a camera to a laptop or desktop computer. A firewire cable links a camera and computer, and transfers data rapidly from one to the other. Trainees at the Newcastle center learned nonlinear editing during their three-week course. Myles said most video editing was done with Avid DV Express 3.5.4 when trainees returned to their newsrooms, but they had to learn about other software because a handful of newsrooms used Final Cut Pro and Liquid Edition. Video journalists were initially given a Sony PD150 digital video camera. After 2004, course attendees received a later model, the PD170.

> It's a lightweight camera that has two channels of audio. We make several alterations to the basic camera. We have replaced the onboard Sony domestic microphone with a Seinhesser 416 microphone. It's a sensitive and directional microphone that helps us acquire excellent actuality. (Myles, 2004)

Myles's team also added a wide-angle lens and lens hood.

> This allows us to get closer to the subjects we are filming, providing the benefits of a steadier shot, better depth of field, clearer audio and greater intimacy with character. (Myles, 2004)

Myles said video-journalists mainly contributed to the BBC regional evening news programs, but they also contributed to current affairs, political, Welsh language, and children's programs.

The range of stories and techniques are almost as numerous as the trainees themselves. Many find the access and the ability to tell stories through real people's eyes the big attraction. For the others, multiple deployments are a big draw offering the ability to show several dimensions of a story simultaneously (Myles, 2004)

Myles said the flexibility offered by the nonlinear editing systems helped producers create "very individual styles." Video journalists were not intended to replace television news crews, but to supplement traditional ways of working and to offer more "up-close-and-personal" stories.

It is inevitable that the use of "self operating" staff will reduce the use of traditional crews but this wasn't the reason for doing it. The big attraction was that this way of working would give greater access, more freedom and creativity to the video-journalist, and a more honest and interesting final product (Myles, 2004).

Newspapers are also embracing the concept of the single multimedia reporter. Regina McCombs is a multimedia reporter and producer for startribune.com, the online division of the *Star Tribune* in Minneapolis, Minn. She spent 13 years as a television photographer and producer at the award-winning KARE-TV in Minneapolis before joining the newspaper. McCombs said multimedia gave journalists the chance to produce stories in whatever form was most understandable and enjoyable for audiences.

We say this story would be best served with a graphic and a short video, or this would be great with text and audio, or whatever. (McCombs, 2004)

Each year Ifra, the international association for media publishing, publishes the NewsGear, a suite of tools designed for the multimedia journalist. It was a project of the Advanced Journalist Technology Project, an initiative of Ifra's Center for Advanced News Operations. Kerry Northrup, the center's executive director, said Ifra had been studying the technological needs of media organizations since 1998, when it assembled the first NewsGear. Northrup said several of Ifra's members asked for recommendations on the best equipment that would let their reporters become more mobile. Northrup's team began evaluating hundreds of technologies for their usefulness in a networked, converged newsroom. They brought together the best laptop, digital camera, digital camcorder and mobile networking device.

"After a while," Northrup said, "it dawned on us that we were essentially creating a backpack toolkit for journalists." It was vital that all the pieces worked together "without having to make a reporter carry around a ton of cords and power bricks." His team had focused on getting all components into a manageable size that a correspondent could work with in a car or take on an aircraft (quoted in Lasica, 2002).

Chris Cramer, former president of CNN International, predicted that the future of television journalism would involve multi-skilling, smaller bureaus, lightweight editing equipment and small cameras, videophones, and satellite telephones. "We have a new array of firepower at our disposal," he told the NewsXchange conference in Budapest in November 2003. "Covering the world shouldn't just be for the big boys and girls to handle," he said. "All of us need to change the way we think. Change the way we practice our craft. And we need to keep changing all the time." He cited the example of CNN correspondent Nic Robertson's exclusive when he acquired Osama Bin laden's personal video collection in August 2002. Robertson's success came about because he was multi-skilled, Cramer said.

> If Nic couldn't shoot, edit, engineer, and report he couldn't possibly have picked up and smuggled that remarkable piece of TV journalism out of Afghanistan. And he is just one example of the new breed of broadcaster (Cramer, 2004).

The availability of sophisticated equipment such as the satellite phone and LNG has the potential to produce changes in management policies. With major breaking news, it must be tempting to fly a big name reporter to a country, rather than having people on the ground all the time who know the region and its history. The latter are always going to be more expensive. Nadia Bilbasey, Africa correspondent for the Middle East Broadcasting Center, objects to the concept of flying international correspondents to hot spots, which critics have called, "parachute journalism."

> You have to have specific knowledge about the region you're covering. American networks have maybe two people to cover the entire continent of Africa. And when something happens they fly in someone who doesn't know the area and has to rely on the entourage of people around them and simply appear in front of the camera. (Hachten, 1999, p.132)

Khalid Kazziha, senior producer for East/Central and West Africa for Associated Press Television, believes the real threat facing news agencies and media organizations comes from local stringers armed with digital cameras and laptop computers and the ability, as technology advances, to send images over the Internet.

> It will revolutionize the way people watch the news. Perhaps it will mean the news will come faster, and maybe it'll be told in a better way because it'll be coming from someone at the location. Our region is really big. If our stringer in Congo or Rwanda has the ability to send pictures, we're not going to be traveling anymore. So I'm then the stranger, I don't have to be there to tell their story anymore. More and more, people in each location can tell their own stories. (TBS, 2001)

Murrie agreed. He suggested that over time, because digital newsgathering equipment was relatively cheap and common, an increasing number of freelance materials from more diverse locations could appear on news programs. "If cell phone operators begin contributing video, the news gathering process will open dramatically." Technicians at the BBC have conducted experiments using Nokia digital cellular phones to deliver video from the field. A typical phone can store about two minutes of audio and video. At 15 frames per second (the highest resolution) it takes about 40 minutes to transfer two minutes of video. Murrie does not believe that low-cost digital video from journalists armed with laptops and cell phones will replace heavyweight satellite newsgathering equipment for live coverage "in the near future." Satellites would still be needed for high quality images and for producing complex news programs on location—the kind of images that people had become accustomed to seeing.

> Laptops and even cell phones are just additional tools that can be used to gather more diverse stories, more quickly from a broader range of sites. (Murrie, 2004)

Against this milieu, it may be significant that in March 2005 the BBC announced it would cut 3,230 jobs in an attempt to trim $664 million from the budget. This included 420 journalists. The job losses involved redundancies and plans for more extensive use of freelance rather than full-time positions

Inexpensive tools that can be purchased off the shelf increase the potential for flexibility, an attractive option during wars. In the first weeks of the war in Iraq, harsh conditions such as sand storms ruined many journalists' equipment. "Iraq is tech hell," CNN's Kevin Sites wrote in his Weblog a few days before the war started (quoted in Johnston, 2003). David Schleifer, a senior executive with Avid, maker of video-editing software, said journalists on the Inside Edition program found one of their laptops had failed.

> They literally had sand stuck in one of the cards and couldn't make it work. They went to a local computer store in Kuwait and picked up a firewire card, and they were [soon] up and running. (quoted in Johnston, 2003)

Developments in technology make the military nervous. Theoretically, censorship is no longer possible if television reporters can carry their means of transmission with them. During World War II, military censors reviewed reporters' dispatches before those reports were released. And during the 1991 Gulf War, the 1,400 reporters based in Saudi Arabia got much of their news at daily briefings that the military ran. That conflict was widely seen as the place where reporters had the least opportunity to see first-hand what was going on. It prompted legendary CBS News anchor Walter Cronkite to comment in a PBS documentary:

> We have no independent film of the Persian Gulf War, none. Correspondents should be with the troops, everywhere where the troops are. But our film crews were not permitted to go out on the front. They should have been. Then their tape should've been sent back to censorship; if it couldn't be released immediately, at least it would be held for eventual release and history. We don't have that history now. That history is lost to us. (Pollak & Ives, 2003)

Imagine what an independent reporter armed with a videophone, laptop and satellite phone could do in future conflicts? We may be seeing only the start of a newsgathering revolution.

REFERENCES

Beeston, J. (2001, June 12). Interviewed in Hong Kong.
Cramer, C. (2004, Spring/Summer). NewsXchange 2003 looks at war coverage? *Transnational Broadcasting Studies* 12. Retrieved March 24, 2005, from http://www.tbsjournal.com.
Deuze, M. (2005, March 24). E-mail interview.

Johnston, C. (2003). TV goes to war. Retrieved March 24, 2005, from http://www.tvtechnology.com

Hachten, W.A. (1999). *The world news prism: Changing medias of international communication.* Ames, IA: Iowa Sate University Press.

Lasica, J. (2002, December 10). Gear for the multimedia newsroom. *Online Journalism Review.* Retrieved March 23, 2005, from http://www.ojr.org/ojr/lasica/1039552387.php

McCombs, R. (2004, December 3). Interviewed by telephone.

Murrie, M. (2003 December). New products. *Communicator.*

Murrie, M. (2004, Spring/Summer). Technical review. *Transnational Broadcasting Studies* 12, Retrieved March 24, 2005, from http://www.tbsjournal.com.

Northrup, K. (2004 April 12). Newsplex models mobile publishing in *The Seybold Report*, pp. 16-18.

Phillips, M. (2003 December 29). Embedded reporters tell campaign tales: Iraq war concept of 'living' with the story lands MSNBC's Schein a road trip with Dean, *The Wall Street Journal*, p. 15.

Pollak, A., & Ives, S. (Producers); Ferrari, M. (Writer); Ives, S. (Director). (2003 November 12). Reporting America at war, Episode 2. Washington: WETA. Transcript retrieved April 3, 2005, from http://www.pbs.org/weta/reportingamericaatwar/about/ep02_transcript.html

Quicklink press release, accessed March 24, 2005, at http://www.Quicklink.tv.

Schleifer, S.A. (2003 Summer/Spring). Interview with Ian Ritchie, CEO of Associated Press Television News. *Transnational Broadcasting Studies* 10. Retrieved March 24, 2005 from http://www.tbsjournal.com.

Smith, A. (1978). *The Politics of information: Problems of policy in modern media.* London: Macmillan.

Smith, A. (1979). *The newspaper: An international history.* London: Thames and Hudson.

TBS. (2001 Spring/Summer). Growth of new technology. *Transnational Broadcasting Studies* 6. Retrieved March 24, 2005, from http://www.tbsjournal.com.

Discussion Questions

1. New technologies have always changed the way reporters have filed stories from the field. The telegraph, for example, resulted in development of the inverted pyramid and summary news lead (the classic Five Ws and H — "who," "what," "where," "when," "how" and sometimes "why"). Now reporters must be aware of the images as well as narratives they show to tell the story. In what ways has this affected the types of stories they cover?

2. Convergence might have more to do with altering a journalist's concept of how he or she will fashion their news reports. In what ways do journalists have to ensure the accuracy of their field reporting since they are also reporting in "real time?"

3. While this chapter deals with technology driving war news reporting, what

other considerations should media decision makers make regarded the preparedness of their field reporters. Should their multi-tasking, multimedia skills give them preference over experience and knowledge of local cultures they cover?

4. Why do these new technologies make military planners uneasy as they develop ways of satisfying the often-divergent needs for military operational secrecy and journalists' needs to report fully and fairly from areas in conflict?

5. Knowing that technological advances will continue at a breath-taking rate in the future as digital convergence becomes the norm, how should journalism curricula adapt to these new ways of covering war and other societal upheavals?

CHAPTER TWO

HOW INTERNATIONAL NEWSPAPERS FRAMED THE PRE-IRAQ WAR DEBATE

ATSUSHI TAJIMA, ERIC BAIN, TAO LAM FUNG, ANDREA FALKENHAGEN AND CHELSEA ROSS

On March 22, 2003, *The New York Times* examined claims that the news media failed to challenge the Bush administration aggressively enough as it made its case for war. The article said reporters did not adequately scrutinize the alleged link between Iraq and Al-Qaeda. *The Times* cited a Knight Ridder poll taken in early January 2003 that showed half of the Americans polled believed at least some of the 9/11 hijackers were Iraqis. None was (Rutenburg & Toner, 2003, March 22, p. D10). One might argue that American media had been framed to speak for their own government, neglecting to include diverse perspectives from other governments, positions and organizations.

As the lone superpower after the Cold War, the United States is the most powerful nation in international politics in various ways. In addition to its diplomatic presence, it possesses the largest military force that can rapidly deploy anywhere in the world. The extensive "attempt to affect what happens beyond its border" (Chanley, 1999, p.23) is what makes U.S. foreign policy powerful and influential. This influence has become crucial in the post-9/11 world, including the overthrow of the Taliban regime in Afghanistan and the Ba'ath regime in Iraq.

According to *The Times'* article,

> experts say the news media's role was particularly important this time because Congress offered such a muted challenge until the final weeks of the buildup to war ... the burden fell more heavily on the news media to examine and analyze the administration's rationale for war. (Rutenburg & Toner, 2003, p. D10)

Due to the extensive role the media have in influencing public opinion, especially in foreign policy, and the enormous global importance of the conflict with Iraq, careful comparative analysis of such media coverage is crucial to clarify what is or what is not covered as well as how the coverage constructed. With this understanding, does the public have access to the kind of information needed to make informed opinions? Are hidden biases in the news causing misperceptions of the world situation? Do the news media "frame" issues in certain ways, and how?

To explore these questions, this study employs the theoretical framework of "framing." We first briefly review the concept and its effects, and later provide two empirical analyses to demonstrate how different frames are constructed. Finally, we discuss the implications of our findings on media practice and public opinion.

Framing refers to the journalistic practice of highlighting certain aspects of an issue and excluding others. More broadly, Nelson, et al. (1997) define framing as "the process by which a communication source, such as a news organization, defines and constructs a political issue or public controversy" (p. 567). For example, certain social moods were created through "framed" media discourse of Iraqi President Saddam Hussein during the run-up to the 2003 Iraqi War. Conners (1998) noted that "describing Iraqi president Saddam Hussein as evil, menacing, or mad, could rally support for U.S. involvement and sway public opinion in the direction of the U.S. government's position" (p. 96). Conners then argued that such framing could create a "psychological need" that could result in a "variety of beneficial outcomes on people, including stress reduction, emotional release, and reduction of inner conflict by projecting negative qualities onto an external source" (p. 97).

To negatively portray, frame and ultimately delegitimize Hussein, some linguistic elements were employed in media coverage. Hussein was often equated with Adolf Hitler during the previous Gulf war (Iyengar & Simon, 1993, pp. 381-382; Seaver, 1998, p 81). The "Hitler analogy" labeled Hussein as a powerful and dangerous dictator. The term "Hitler," though a mere proper noun, functions as a "value word" (Nelson, Clawson & Oxley, 1997; Brewer, 2002). Dorman and Livingston (1993) found that between Iraq's invasion of Kuwait (Aug. 2, 1990) and just before the war began (Jan. 15, 1991), *The Washington Post* and *The New York Times* published a total of 228 articles that used the Hussein-Hitler analogy. A *Times* editorial read, "President Bush may or may not be right that Saddam Hussein is worse than Hitler" (Digiacomo, 1990, p. Section 4, 16).

Even simpler, one might keenly recall that news stories often addressed Mr. Hussein without official title but only by his first name,

"Saddam," while the same stories constantly addressed other political leaders like "President George W. Bush," "Mr. Bush," and "Prime Minister Tony Blair." This is a very unusual media practice since Hussein was still the legitimate head of a state. It is absolutely unthinkable to address President Bush as "George" in the press. Simple linguistics, such as the omission of an official title and the use of a first name, powerfully delegitimize Hussein as a political leader but, simultaneously, stress him as "a dictatorial human agency."

Apart from linguistic elements, sources being quoted have been acknowledged as an important element of framing. Coverage of foreign-policy issue especially tends to rely on governmental sources, which can control information. Page and Shapiro (1989) note that "on foreign policy matters government officials often control access to information and can conceal or misrepresent the truth with little immediate danger of being challenged. ... With regard to domestic policy, sources of information are usually more diverse" (pp. 310, 313). Particularly, warfare and national security are areas where journalist's sources can be limited to governmental, often top-down, sources. How they are presented and quoted to frame news stories provides for important analytical consideration.

METHODS: TWO ANALYSES

This study consists of two analyses. The first is a quantitative coding of frames over a three-month period. The second is an in-depth textual analysis.

For the first coding analysis, we featured 14 different papers from 10 different nations around the world and coded a total of 523 articles from Oct. 10, 2002, through Jan.15, 2003 (see Table 2.1). Our period of analysis was intended to coincide with the international debate following U.S. President Bush's threat of taking unilateral military action against Iraq in September 2002. This study limited coding to the front pages, including jumps. Regardless of different journalistic cultures around the world, all news organizations typically place the most important articles on the front page, which is a feasible way to compare different papers of different national origins.

In our coding scheme, frames were determined to be biased as "supporting war," "opposing war," "balanced (both 'supporting' and 'opposing' views were quantitatively and qualitatively equally politically weighted information). This categorization seems relatively simple.

TABLE 2.1
NEWSPAPER SAMPLE AND FRAMING DISTRIBUTION

Name of Newspaper Analyzed 10/10/02 to 1/15/03	Country	Support war	Oppose war	Balanced coverage	Other	Total
Asahi Shinbun	Japan	0	15	2	22	39
Financial Times	United Kingdom	18 .	3	5	0	26
Frankfurter All Gemeine Zeitung	Germany	0	6	2	4	12
Guardian	United Kingdom	30	13	22	2	67
La Nacion	Argentine	7	3	6	7	23
Le Monde	France	0	11	1	5	17
Los Angeles Times	United States	17	2	15	19	53
New York Times	United States	26	19	9	23	77
Peninsula News	Quarter	19	50	9	5	83
Straits Times	Singapore	1	4	2	12	19

However, the most fundamental debate throughout the period we analyzed was essentially trichotomous: whether the international society should terminate the UN inspections and go to war (supporting war), whether it should allow more time for the inspections instead of going to war (opposing war), or other (included for coverage that did not present either side and showing both sides). Our primary interest follows this important trichotomy. Taking into consideration the numerous studies conducted through and on framing, certain guidelines and methods were agreed upon before determining the type and value of the frames for the articles coded. With this taken into account, a uniform procedure was employed to determine the frames for all articles, as 15 coders undertook this task. Given the idea that sources being quoted are one of the fundamental factors to constitute frame (e.g., Entman, 1991), we also coded a total of

3,045 sources (See Tables 4.2 and 4.4).

Assuming there are many models for frames, types of frames can be distinguished as either issue-specific news frames or generic news frames. "Issue-specific frames pertain to specific topics or news events, whereas generic frames are broadly applicable to a range of different news topics, some even over time, and potentially, in different cultural contexts" (de Vreese, et al., 2001). As this study focused on the particular topic of the conflict and eventual war with Iraq, the research was restricted to coverage containing issue-specific frames.

For the in-depth textual analysis, we featured a single event: Chief UN Weapons Inspector Hans Blix's Jan. 27, 2003, presentation to the UN Security Council — a crucial event and turning point of the disarmament discussion. Examining world media coverage of this event provided for fruitful scrutiny since it was an action of no particular country and independent of nationalistic forces. As an impartial public figure, Blix presumably was immune from the biases national newspapers often display towards particular friends or enemies. The frames constructed by each national newspaper should provide insight into how Blix and his claims were framed by the media. For example, it is reasonable to expect that each paper representing a nation reflected the stance, reactions and opinions of its own government. By seeing Blix as a non-national figure, analysis of such discursive interaction should provide us with richer insights about specific frames.

For this textual analysis, we chose articles, dated Jan. 27 and 28, 2003, from nine newspapers in four countries: the United States, United Kingdom, France and Germany. Not only were they the most crucial nations leading the Iraq debate, but they have shown a bipolar contrast in their political stances: the United States and the U.K. were proponents of war, while France and Germany opposed it.

FINDINGS: DISTRIBUTION OF FRAMES

Table 2.2 presents overall numerical findings of how the 523 front-page articles were framed.

If we dichotomize from the U.S./U.K., the two leading nations in support of war, and other regions, we see that newspapers from the former show more support for war, while the newspapers from the latter more frequently opposed war. A chi-square test clearly indicates that the difference between the two groups supporting and the nations opposing war is statistically significant. ($p < .000001$, $df = 2$).

TABLE 2.2
DOMINANT FRAMES

		Dominant Frame				Total
		Supporting War	Opposing War	Balanced	Other	
U.S.	(n)	66	30	46	49	191
	%	34.55	15.71	24.08	25.61	100
U.K.	(n)	48	16	27	2	93
	%	51.61	17.20	29.03	2.15	100
U.S./U.K. Total	(n)	112	46	73	51	284
	%	39.43	16.20	25.70	17.96	100
Non-U.S./U.K. Combined	(n)	30	110	34	65	239
	%	12.55	46.03	14.22	27.19	100
French/German*	(n)	0	23	11	12	46)
	(%	0.0	50.0	23.91	26.09	100)
All Regions Total	(n)	144	156	107	116	523
	%	27.35	29.82	20.49	22.17	100

* French/German papers are included in "Non-U.S./U.K.."

Since the literature has suggested that news sources and the ways they are quoted contribute to framing, we also coded types of quoted news sources and the frequencies of sources being quoted. The simplified summary is shown in Table 2.3.

Needless to say, each paper presented its own nation's governmental sources frequently. The U.S. papers featured 45% of their quotations from U.S. governmental sources, while the U.K. papers devoted less than half as many (20%) of their quotations to U.K. official sources.

A few additional quantitative figures were noteworthy. Papers from "other regions," devoted about 15% of their quotations to Iraqi governmental sources. It is important to note that this analysis did not feature any Iraqi papers. This phenomenon cannot be attributed to the notion of "quoting one's own governmental sources," as discussed through the U.S. and U.K. cases. This is a relatively high frequency.

TABLE 2.3
SOURCES (CATEGORICAL) QUOTED
BY NATIONALITY OF NEWSPAPER

Source category	U.S. Papers		U.K. papers		France/ Germany Papers		Non-U.S./ U.K. Papers	
	n	%	n	%	n	%	n	%
U.S. government	746	44.80	69	17.69	43	28.29	208	25.09
U.S. non-government	139	8.35	26	6.67	4	2.63	59	7.12
Iraqi government	128	7.69	41	10.51	8	5.26	124	14.96
Iraqi Non-government	83	4.98	18	4.62	2	1.32	28	3.38
U.K. government	35	2.10	78	20.00	8	5.26	29	3.50
German/French government	35	2.10	9	2.31	32	21.05	35	4.22
Russia/Chinese government	22	1.32	8	2.05	5	3.29	28	3.38
Other governments	106	6.37	42	10.77	9	5.92	116	13.99
United Nations	193	11.59	34	8.72	23	15.13	92	11.10
Other sources total	178	10.69	65	16.67	18	11.84	110	13.27
Total	1665	100	390	100	152	100	829	100

Incidentally, they featured "other governmental sources," which included their own governmental sources, only 14% of the time. The high proportion of "opposing war" frames among those papers may be attributed to their focus on Iraqi sources when compared with U.S. and U.K. papers.

Furthermore, newspapers from all regions relied on U.S. sources on the Iraq issue, although their degrees varied. For example, German and French papers featured U.S. governmental sources 28% of the time, while they featured their "own governmental sources" 21% of the time, which theoretically should have distinctively opposing viewpoints from U.S. and U.K. sources. Interestingly, while the pro-war papers quoted each other's government sources, they hardly featured their opponents: France and Germany. The U.S. papers showed that 47% of their quotations were from the U.S. and the U.K. governments, while only 2.1% of their quotations were from the two most vocal opponents of war.

A possible explanation for this discrepancy could be that the war debate was primarily led by the United States and, to a lesser degree, the United Kingdom. The idea of going to war became an "official international agenda" when Bush announced that possibility at the UN. Since then, high-level U.S. government sources continuously broached the idea of attacking Iraq. At the same time, the governmental officials of "opposing-war" nations were not actively vocal because they favored retaining UN weapons inspectors. Symbolically, this disproportionate feature of U.S. officials implicitly illustrates the "unilateral" nature of the U.S. policy. In the following textual-analysis section, we attempted to demonstrate how a heavy reliance on certain governmental officials could create certain frames.

TEXTUAL ANALYSIS

Through a textual analysis, the constructions of frames were dissected to investigate the techniques employed in developing the form and style of particular frames. Fundamentally, frames were determined by various factors that all contribute to the construction of frames: headlines, quoted sources, legitimization or illegitimization of sources, placement and structure of information, and the use of value words. For this particular event, Blix's UN speech, all of the nine articles were framed "supporting-war" except for a "balanced" *Washington Post* article, a "balanced" *Le Monde* (French newspaper) article, and one "opposing-war" *Sueddentsche Zeitung* (German newspaper) article.

Intended to grab a reader's attention, consideration was initially placed on headlines, because they are boldly printed abstracts that succinctly summarize and represent an editor's view of the story. Headlines introduce and summarize the main content of an article, thus contributing to the overall framing. The headline for the *Financial Times'* lead story read, "Blix attacks Baghdad over lack of co-operation." Adjacent to the headline is a quote box that read: "Iraq appears not to have come to a genuine acceptance, not even today, of the disarmament that was demanded of it." The same quote also appeared in the second paragraph of the article. Consequently, this article was framed "supporting-war." The reporters consciously chose to stress Blix's statement that Iraq had not accepted disarmament and articulate that to mounting U.S. and U.K. impatience. As a case in point, the two upper headlines suggested that Iraqi noncompliance only accelerated any use of force. This framed the article in a way that implied any evidence of Iraqi hostility towards cooperation was a threat to peaceful inspections.

However, not all headlines elaborately contribute to frames. Many are much more direct. In Britain's *Guardian,* the headline stated, "Another step towards war." Despite the fact that this "step" actually involved giving UN inspectors more time, this rather presumptuous headline resonated throughout the rest of the article so as to construct a "supporting-war" frame. On the other hand, the headline in Munich's *Sueddeutsche Zeitung* stated, "Schroeder: War only after a second UN-Resolution." This succinct summation of the German response to Blix's presentation similarly added to an "opposing-war" frame, which was prevalent throughout the remainder of the article.

Beyond headlines, how sources are quoted in the main text of each article largely influence how frames are determined. A journalist's treatment of quoted sources can often tip the scale, throwing off the balance of an article, thus creating a frame. Though the ideal of objective journalism supposedly presents the views of diverse quoted sources, affording equal and impartial priority to all angles of the debate, it is not always realized. Nevertheless, a "balanced" frame exists within this context.

As certain figures push specific agendas, who is being quoted can lead to particular frames. For example, heavy reliance on hawkish U.S. official sources contributed to "supporting-war" frames. Additionally, beyond who is being quoted, it is important to consider how sources are quoted. Blix was directly quoted in every article covering his presentation. However, as every article framed "supporting-war" used his quotes speaking of Iraq's failure to cooperate, Munich's *Sueddeutsche Zeitung* framed its article "opposing-war" by quoting Blix as calling for more time for inspections.

Furthermore, the amount of space allotted to each quote, the location of each quote, and how each quote is prioritized and interrelated with other quotes all contribute to frames. In the *Washington Post,* a "balanced" frame was constructed. Suggesting inspections had failed, the *Washington Post* reported, "'It is not enough to open doors,' [Blix] said, adding that the level of cooperation by Baghdad required by UN resolutions continued to be often 'withheld or given grudgingly.'" This was immediately followed by, "In a more positive overall assessment, Mohamed El-Baradei ... said the IAEA [International Atomic Energy Agency] should be able 'within the next few months to provide credible assurance that Iraq has no nuclear weapons programs,'" negating the previous "supporting-war" argument by Blix and lending to a "balanced" frame.

However, quotes can also be weighted to contribute to a particular frame. In *The New York Times*, immediately following Blix's main quote on Iraq's noncompliance of disarmament, the reporter choose to mention that U.S. Secretary of State Colin Powell believed "time is running out," reinforcing Blix's report as a trigger for military action, which contributed to a "supporting-war" frame. The *Los Angeles Times'* article, "Damning Portrait of Arms Programs" is framed "supporting-war" for its failure to equally present arguments opposing war. The article contained only one quote by El-Baradei that supported more inspections, as opposed to four quotes from inspectors, as well as seven Blix quotes that spoke of Iraq as a threat. Whereas Blix's "supporting-war" opinions were backed up with facts from his report, IAEA Director General Mohamed El-Baradei's "opposing-war" quote was not backed up with any facts thereafter, but left dangling at the end of the article.

The location of quotes within an article can also affect the frame. *The New York Times* constructed a "supporting-war" frame because of the prioritization of certain quotes. Although many quotes from representatives of UN veto-wielding nations are given, they are relegated to the end of the article. The reporter instead chooses to highlight quotes supporting military action in the beginning, while placing the "peace-seeking" quotes toward the end.

In addition to quoted sources, the construction of frames can be influenced by how journalists treat the organization of information and sources. For example, the "balanced" frame constructed in the *Washington Post* article is achieved by pitting Blix's statements against nations, such as France, Russia and South Africa, which all supported more time for inspections. In contrast, *The Guardian* constructed a "supporting-war" frame. Here the reporters mentioned Blix had "acknowledged that Baghdad had granted access to weapons inspectors." However, this is instantly followed by "But he said:" — then trailed by his primary quote. Later, in the fifth and sixth paragraphs, the reporter mentioned that France, China, Russia and El-Baradei were all calling for the "inspectors to be given more time." Following this quote, the reporter reinforces a "supporting-war" frame by mentioning Blix's references to Iraq's possession of chemical and illegal weapons.

Legitimization and delegitimization are both techniques of organizing information to construct particular frames. It is possible that a slight "supporting-war" frame exists in The *Los Angeles Times'* article, "Iraq Seems Unwilling to Give Up Weapons, UN Inspector Says," because it relied so heavily on "official" sources. Little space is given to balance the article with "opposing-war" arguments. The "supporting-war" frame of the article is strengthened as the reporters delegitimized the single "opposing-war" voice—an Iraqi official quoted with vague rhetoric, speaking of "warmongers."

As another example, the "supporting-war" frame of the *Guardian's* article left audiences conscious of the debate within British parliament. The reporters chose to counter the Liberal Democrats' argument of supporting indefinite time for inspections with the Tories' complaint that ministers "have not argued the case they could do" to persuade voters. The Liberal Democrat's argument was essentially dismissed as repetitive by the Tories' fresh critique of waning public support in Britain for military action, ultimately sealing a "supporting-war" frame for the article.

Newspaper reporters also use various linguistic expressions to frame their news stories. Brewer (2002) argues that "frames use 'value words' to link a particular position on an issue...to an abstract value" (p. 303). By attaching "value words" to a particular issue, readers are most likely to adopt such perspective as their own (Brewer, 2002). However, blatantly strong or harsh "value words" are not always overtly present in many frames. Rather, reporters simultaneously rationally present "vague" words or phrases lending to a particular frame by either justifying one angle or delegitimizing the opposing angle.

The use of "value words" was taken into consideration in coding, and numerous cases illustrate their powerful role. Proponents of regime change, national security and Iraqi liberation frame the issue with the language of support for war, or "supporting war," arguing the use of "force" is the best means to ensure such. Opponents of war, or those who are "opposing war," frame the same issue with the language of peace, providing humanitarian justifications and legitimizing increased time for UN inspections. Presenting an equally dichotomous debate, "balanced" frames serve as a detached intermediary lacking any unilateral agenda.

For example, in *The Financial Times'* "supporting-war" article, the reporters chose to play on an already fearful audience by mentioning specific examples of Blix's inspections turning up "mustard gas" and illegal "long-range missile projects." Similarly, *The New York Times* reported that Blix had found "indications that Iraq had created weapons using the nerve agent VX, which he described as 'one of the most toxic ever developed.'" In turn, these specific references only garnered support for war by painting Iraq's guilt as a threat to world peace.

Summary and Discussion

This analysis revealed that more than half of each newspaper's coverage of the conflict with Iraq was framed as either "supporting war" or "opposing war." Specifically, papers from the United States and U.K. were more frequently framed as "supporting war," while papers from other nations were more often framed as "opposing war." The sources quoted in each article are pertinent in determining the frame. The U.S. and U.K. papers relied heavily on their own official sources and local reporting, although the action and conflict took place in Iraq.

Our analysis also coded the location of reporting and found that the majority of articles from U.S. and U.K. papers were reported from within the United States or U.K. (62% of the U.S. articles were reported from the United States; 53% of the U.K. articles were reported from U.K.). The textual analysis illustrated how the effects of various elements of framing, such as the role of the headlines, value words, journalists' selection of salience, and the complex roles of sources being quoted, all function to construct frames.

The data revealed that the Anglo-American newspapers provided more balanced coverage. The U.S./U.K. papers had a total of 26.62% balanced coverage compared with the 14.22% balanced coverage papers from other regions displayed. This could be due to the Anglo-American journalistic tradition that expects newspapers to provide all sides of a story for fair and balanced reporting. However, if we examine the entire framing distribution, over 50% of U.S./U.K. articles were determined as "unbalanced" (i.e., "supporting" [40%] or "opposing" [10%]). In sum, while they provide more balanced coverage, they do not provide balanced frames.

French and German papers are apparently biased as well — 50% of the coded articles contained an anti-war frame. But unlike their U.S. counterparts, these papers do not make much attempt to appear unbiased. They have an agenda, and European readers recognize that fact. Chalaby (1996) credits part of this disparity to the political histories of the different countries and the journalistic traditions that historically developed as a result of them.

In the United Kingdom. and the United States, political struggles were generally confined to parliamentary or congressional bipartism.

Journalists could claim to be "neutral" simply by proclaiming to be "impartial" by giving an equal amount of attention to each political party. This bimodal view of the political struggle evolved to a high professional value of reporting news and information rather than only political opinion. In France, journalists faced a more complex political landscape as the space of political positions was much wider and the field of political possibilities was more open (p. 319).

However, while U.S. reporters and editors might strive to provide objective accounts of news and factual information, it is unrealistic to believe that they do not have their own opinions or agendas that subtly affect the framing of their work. There are inevitably biases in all reporting — they are perhaps more hidden (e.g., structural linkages between newspapers and the centers of power), if not insidiously covert, than the biases published in papers from other regions with different journalistic traditions.

Similarly, sources quoted in the non-U.S./U.K. papers appeared to be more diverse and well-rounded, although almost a quarter were still coming from U.S. governmental sources. However, we have to remember that it is framing that ultimately conveys the actual weight and meaning of any number of sources and quotes.

It is also imperative to analyze how the sources are presented and interact with each other in the article. For example, not only significantly more U.S. sources were quoted than Iraqi sources, but U.S. sources were also presented differently than Iraqi sources. Iraqi sources were rarely quoted as dominant sources. In some instances, Iraqi sources were quoted as counter-offensive to the U.S. sources (mostly to U.S. policy-making officials). However, the Iraqi sources were typically limited to statements by the country's very limited high-ranking officials, specifically Foreign Minister Naji Sabri and Iraqi Ambassador to the UN Mohammed Douri, who were readily available in New York. The number of their quotes as well as the space devoted to them, is relatively small—typically one or two lines. For example, while a *New York Times* article quotes nine American sources describing Iraq's "maliciousness" in interrupting the weapon inspection, only one Iraqi source is quoted for two lines. And they were only quoted as saying, "We don't have weapons of mass destruction." There were no other details. This does not provide any new information or insight to the readers.

Another key example lies in the discussion of Hans Blix's report on weapon inspections. In a *Los Angeles Times* article, Blix was quoted giving many "damning" facts of Iraqi weapons violations, and several former weapons inspectors praised Blix's strong words. However, the viewpoints supporting further inspections were framed quite differently. Iraqi foreign Minister Naji Sabri was quoted as saying:

> We have done everything possible to let this country and this region avoid the danger of war by the warmongers in Washington and their ally British Prime Minister Tony Blair. They are fond of exporting destruction and death to other parts of the world.

No rational or clearly articulated quotes from any Iraqi or another nations' source in the region was quoted.

We argue that quoting Iraqi sources, however sparingly, might superficially function as journalists' cross-check practice of "fair and balanced" reporting. The opposing Iraqi sources do not actually provide any substantial information, statements, or opinions. Seemingly, they were quoted to merely fulfill the "both sides" requirement for journalists in the most basic way. Such news stories did not actually present a diverse array of information on which readers could base an opinion. If journalists seriously desired to achieve real "fair and balanced" coverage, they had to treat Iraqi sources the same as the U.S. and UN sources, both quantitatively and qualitatively.

Often reporters superficially present "both sides," then delegitimate one side with a discrediting analysis or negating quote. For example, in the same *Los Angeles Times* article, Blix was quoted as saying that Iraq has cooperated "rather well" in providing access to inspection sites. However, within the context of the article, "Iraq has cooperated rather well" is preceded with "although" and directly followed by information stating authorities have blocked flights of U-2 surveillance planes and seem to have intimidated scientists into refusing private interviews. Suggesting incomplete Iraqi compliance, the manner in which this information is constructed delegitimizes Blix's initial statement recognizing Iraqi cooperation.

Through the delegitimization of such quotes, this framing technique provides a "sentiment" of a non-cooperation by Iraq. The sentence would have had a completely different tone and meaning if it read, "while authorities have blocked some flights and intimidated some scientists to refuse interviews, Blix said that overall Iraq has cooperated, 'rather well.'" This would change the frame to be much more positive. Instead the reporter chose to pick a positive-sounding quote and sandwich it between two negative word choices.

This research has also led us to speculate on the relationship between the number of sources quoted and the overall balance and objectivity of the article. It is generally believed that more quotes means less inference and elaboration from the reporter, which could possibly increase the objectivity of the overall article. However, our analysis has found some occasions where presenting more sources and "both sides" does not necessarily show diverse perspectives and "unframe" an article.

Thus, we argue that superficial Anglo-American journalistic norms and practices possess a danger to deceive audiences. By recognizing the presentation of two sides to a story, audiences may assume they are "reading unbiased media text." They may then believe to be well-informed without bias. This essentially produces less-critical audiences. To further analyze this, as other researchers have suggested, using the current data as an independent variable to explore "audience framing," could further an understanding about the effects of framing in a larger context.

REFERENCES

Brewer, P. R. (2002). Framing, value words, and citizens' explanations of their issue opinions. *Political Communication, 19*(3), 303-316.

Chalaby, J. K. (1996). Journalism as an Anglo-American invention: A comparison of the development of French and Anglo-American journalism, 1830s-1920s. *European Journal of Communication, 11*(3), 303-326.

Chanley, V. A. (1999). U.S. public views of international involvement from 1964 to 1993: Time series analyses of general and militant internationalism. *Journal of Conflict Resolution, 43*(1), 23-44.

Conners J. L. (1998). Hussein as enemy — The Persian Gulf War in political cartoons. *Harvard International Journal of Press-Politics, 3*(3), 96-114.

De Vreese, C., Peter, J., & Semetko, H. A. (2001). Framing politics at the launch of the euro: A cross-national comparative study of frames in the news. *Political Communication, 18*(2), 107-122.

Digiacomo, M. (1990, November 18). Negotiating an Iraqi withdrawal beats war: Chamberlain lives. *The New York Times*, p. D16.

Dorman, W. A., & Livingston, S. (1993). News and historical content: The establishing phase of the Persian Gulf policy debate. In Lance B. W., & Paletz D. L. (Eds.), *Taken by storm* (pp. 63-81). Chicago: The University of Chicago Press.

Enteman, R. M. (1991). Framing U.S. coverage of international news: Contrasts in narratives of the KAL and Iran air incidents." *Journal of Communication, 41*(4), 6-27.

Iyengar, S., & Simon, A. (1993). News coverage of the Gulf crisis and public opinion: A study of agenda-setting, priming, and framing. *Communication Research, 20*(3), 365-383.

Nelson, T. E., Clawson, R. A., & Oxley, Z. M. (1997). Media framing of a civil liberties conflict and its effect on tolerance. *American Political Science Review, 91*(3), 567—583.

Page, B. I., & Shapiro, R. Y. (1989). Educating and manipulating the public. In Margolis, Michael M., & Gary M. A. (Eds.), *Manipulating public opinion* (pp. 294-320). Pacific Grove, California: Brooks/Cole Publishing Company.

Rutenburg, J., & Toner, R. (2003, Mar. 22). A nation at war: The news media; critics of Iraq war say lack of scrutiny helped administration to press its case. *The New York Times*, p. D10.

Seaver, B. M. (1998). The public dimension of foreign policy. *Press/Politics, 3*(1), 65-91.

ARTICLES USED FOR IN-DEPTH TEXTUAL ANALYSIS

Borger, J., White, M., & MacAskill, E. (2003, January 28). Another step towards war. *The Guardian,* p. A1

DeYoung, K., & Lynch, C. (2003, January 28). Report faults Iraq on arms hunt; Blix: Access is given, but not cooperation. *The Washington Post,* p. A1.

Drogin, B. (2003, January 28). Showdown with Iraq; damning portrait of arms programs. *Los Angeles Times,* p. A1.

Farley, M. (2003, January 28). Showdown with Iraq; Iraq seems unwilling to give up weapons, UN inspector says. *Los Angeles Times,* p. A1.

Fried, N. (2003, January 29). Schroeder: War only after a second UN-Resolution. *Sueddeutsche Zeitung,* p. A1.

No 'genuine acceptance' of disarmament, Blix says. (2003, January 27). *The Washington Post,* p. A14.

Patrick Jarreau (2003, January 29). War in Iraq: George Bush Gives Himself Time to Convince. *Le Monde,* p. A2.

Preston, J. (2003, January 28). Threats and responses: Report to council; UN inspector says Iraq falls short on cooperation. *The New York Times,* p. A1

Turner, M., & Khalaf, R. (2003, January 28). Blix attacks Baghdad over lack of cooperation. *Financial Times* (U.S. edition), p. A1.

DISCUSSION QUESTIONS

1. Content analysis of major newspapers is one way to establish news frames. Are these frames conscious attempts at manipulating reader receptions or unconscious results of writer/editor biases?

2. One of the findings in this study shows that American newspapers generally supported the war in Iraq while European newspapers were against the incursion for a variety of reasons. Why do you think is the main reason for the bifurcation of these editorial positions?

3. The main source for news around the world tended to be U.S. government sources, but Anglo-American newspapers tried to give more balanced coverage than their European counterparts. What, if anything, does this say about biased news coverage, and its impact on public opinion?

4. How do journalists use language to legitimize or delegitimize war supporters and opposition? Give examples of both.

5. Both the governments of France and Germany opposed the 2003 Iraq War.

Who can be said to set the agenda for national policy in those countries on the war issue? The newspapers, the politicians, or the public?

CHAPTER THREE

A COMPARATIVE ANALYSIS OF COVERAGE OF THE IRAQ WAR IN *THE NEW YORK TIMES*, ITS ONLINE VERSION, AND *YAHOO! NEWS*

SHAFIQUR RAHMAN AND JYOTIKA RAMAPRASAD

The Internet is a unique medium given its interactivity, its largely free access, its unlimited space and its global audience. Does this uniqueness shape its content in ways that make it different from the content of print newspapers? This study makes an effort to answer the question by comparing content on the Iraq War in three media: *The New York Times* print version, *New York Times* online and *Yahoo News*.

The 2003 Iraq War triggered worldwide attention and interest for various reasons. The modern technologies of communication, including the Internet, were used extensively to disseminate war-related news to a global audience. If the 1991 Iraq War is remembered as a "real time" war presented by CNN, then the 2003 Iraq War will be associated with an increased presence of online and digital media. Online media, with their round-the-clock breaking news and riveting audio-visual battlefield reporting, became a major player in this war's reporting.

The 2003 Iraq War generated widespread anti-Americanism throughout the world, largely because the United States and its allies waged a preemptive war without United Nations approval. A substantial portion of this anti-American sentiment was vented on the Internet. In fact, new Web sites were created with the sole purpose of attacking the war. Most of these sites were created and maintained not so much by individuals as by different organizations including those representing religious extremists. Web sites of different media organizations, such as *Al-Jazeera*, also became popular for presenting non-American perspectives on the Iraq War.

Because the Internet is a global medium, developers of media Web sites are aware that different news perspectives, particularly on international news and issues, need to be presented for the site to appeal to an international audience. In fact, online media have the potential to reach the smallest niche. Their content can be customized according to the specific needs and orientation of small segments of the audience. In an interview with the *Online Journalism Review*, Emily Bell, editor-in-chief of *Guardian Unlimited*, the online version of the British newspaper *Guardian*, said that, since September 11, 2001, they have been doing journalism from a "slightly more liberal" perspective (hAnluain, 2003). She also said that the *Guardian Unlimited* was publishing more stories from foreign correspondents simply because space was not a problem and there were readers of these stories somewhere in the world. Online media thus have the potential to be different in content from traditional newspapers because of their diversified audience and their unlimited space.

FACTORS INFLUENCING MEDIA CONTENT

No media content is created arbitrarily. Rather, the content of every medium — print, electronic, or online — is the result of a process that includes many factors, such as journalists' traits and roles, audience likes and dislikes, advertiser pressure, media organization policies and procedures, and the ideological values of the country. Thus, media content is not necessarily an accurate reflection of reality.

Numerous studies have investigated whether journalists' background, education, personal values and beliefs, political attitudes, religious orientations and ideological biases influence the content of news (Hess, 1981; Goodrick, 1991; Shuster, 1988; Gans, 1979). Results of these studies are inconclusive. Consequently, researchers maintain that journalists' personality variables are minor factors in shaping news content, and it is organization-level influences such as media routines that are critical (Weaver & Wilhot, 1991). In fact, according to Gans (1985), media routines and organizational constraints may negate the effects of journalists' personal attitudes, values and beliefs on news content.

Media routines are the patterned, routinized, repeated practices and forms that media workers use to do their job (Shoemaker and Reese, 1996). Media routines provide journalists with a structured way of looking at events and issues.

The concept of media routines may be illustrated by gate-keeping theory. Gate keeping refers to a process by which journalists select certain stories from a wide variety of probable stories and present these stories in the media using the treatment (placement, angle, etc.) they think appropriate. Because of the gate-keeping role of journalists, certain stories receive front-page treatment, some are buried on inside pages, and some are left out. As gatekeepers, journalists also determine the length of the stories and decide whether the stories will be accompanied by photographs. Gatekeepers make these journalistic decisions regarding the content of media largely on the basis of the organization's routine practices, which constitute the immediate environment in which these decisions are made (Hallin, 1992; Bantz, McCorkle, & Badde, 1981).

To cope with the challenges of newsgathering, media organizations have developed practices that give journalists clearly defined and specialized roles and expectations. For example, media organizations set up news bureaus and beats. The beat obliges the reporter to write something even when nothing of significance is happening (Fishman, 1980). Or, media organizations classify news into *hard news* and *soft news* (Tuchman, 1973). This distinction is less a function of the nature of the content than how the event is scheduled. Hard news is most often based on scheduled events such as political conventions and court trials or events that suddenly happen. The hard news/soft news distinction facilitates media organizations in covering events. For example, it is acceptable that media report hard news immediately with whatever information they have. For soft news or feature stories, media are expected to provide detailed information. Also, these stories are featured mainly when space is available, as hard news takes priority.

Media routines are intimately related to what is popularly known as news values. Examples of news values include timeliness or immediacy, conflict, significance, proximity and human interest. News that focuses on conflict or is about a country that is geographically or culturally close is more likely to be covered. The use of news values to determine what is covered is fairly predictable.

Another routine practice is journalists' dependence on news sources, more often institutional or official sources. Sources can influence media content by withholding or giving false information, providing the context within which all other information is evaluated, and providing easy access, thereby keeping journalists from seeking sources of alternative information (Shoemaker & Reese, 1996). Shoemaker and Reese also suggest that interest groups capable of retaliating economically can force journalists into self-censorship.

Extra organizational factors also shape the content of news, in particular, audiences and advertisers. In the Western tradition, news media sell their audiences to advertisers who consider them as potential consumers of their products. Therefore, the ideal target audience for these advertisers is one that is wealthy enough to buy products (Bagdikian, 1983). Media organizations and professionals therefore tailor their content to attract the "right" audience. Studies have found that newspapers cultivate high-income readers by intentionally structuring content for them, marketing selectively and concentrating circulation drives in the "right" neighborhood (Fink, 1989). Media organizations in fact make systematic efforts to know their audience (e.g., demographic profile). The circulation and advertising sales departments, which have this information, generally provide journalists with a picture of the audience for which they are writing (Smith, 1977). Content of media is then shaped according to the needs and orientation of this audience.

Although the editorial and business departments of media organizations remain separate in the traditional sense, with increasing pressure for corporate profit in the media industry, this wall is disappearing. Journalists are more susceptible to pressure from their business-department colleagues when advertising support is scarce (Shoemaker & Reese, 1996).

Finally, ideology also influences media content. From an ideological perspective, the previously discussed factors (influence of media sources, advertisers, ownership, etc.) are not individual and separate shapers of media content. Rather, the content of media is the result of a systemic and coherent act on the part of capitalist, advertiser-supported media systems to maintain the supremacy of their political and economic system.

Ideology and power are central concerns in Marxist and critical media theory. A central premise of these theories is that media generally tend to propagate the dominant ideology by having their content conform to these ideologies. Researchers who hold the view that ideology influences media content consider media as a means of social control. These researchers (Hall, 1982) believe that the media's ability to define reality gives them their ideological power.

ONLINE NEWS MEDIA

Today, news publishers and newsreaders show an increasing interest in online news. In 1993, there were just 20 online newspapers. By 1996, the number jumped to 1,300 (Lasica, 1997). By April 2000, there were 5,400 online news publications (Gunter, 2003).

Besides newspapers, other online sources for news are also available. The broadcasting industry has a strong presence online. By April 2000, 1,895 Web sites of radio stations and 1,305 Web sites of television stations were recorded (*Editor & Publisher* online, mediainfo.com as quoted in Gutner, 2002). People also get news from portal sites. Portal sites are those sites through which people start their online sessions. Portal sites are the gateways of online traffic.

Various surveys reported that the September 11, 2001, terrorist attacks in the United States as well as the 2003 Iraq War substantially increased online news readership. A Pew Internet and American Life survey (2003) found that more than half of wired Americans went online to get news and commentary about the Iraq War, at least twice the number of people who usually turn to the Internet for news. The survey also reported that although the Internet was the main source of news for only 17% of wired Americans, more than three quarters (77%) of them used the Internet for information on the war in Iraq.

Research on online news media has mainly focused on overall patterns of online media or comparisons between traditional and online news media in terms of use, recall/retention, and differences in knowledge gain. Only a few scholars have examined differences between newspapers and their online versions.

Analyzing the content of 80 online newspapers and surveying their editors, Peng, Tham, and Xiaoming (1999) found that online newspapers were published primarily for reaching more readers, generating income and promoting print newspapers. The authors also found that, because of the availability of worldwide readers, more national and metropolitan dailies than local dailies had online versions. Also, 43% of the respondents, editors of online newspapers, believed that their online versions differed from their print versions.

In a similar study, involving the content analysis of 422 Web sites associated with local newspapers, radio stations and television stations, Lin and Jeffers (2001) found that each medium had a relatively distinct content emphasis, while each attempted to utilize its Web sites to maximize institutional goals.

In a comparison of print and online versions of six Colorado newspapers, Singer (2001) concluded that gatekeepers of online newspapers failed to utilize the potential of the online medium as they put fewer stories online and concentrated on local issues. However, data for that study was gathered in 1998, when online newspapers were in their earlier days.

Analyzing the content of the *New York Times*, *Chicago Tribune* and

Portland Oregonian, Burnhurst (2002) found that online newspaper stories differed very little from those printed in the originating newspapers. He found that online versions reproduced the content of print versions in a way that related similarly to the readers. The author concluded that publishers used the online versions of their newspapers as low-cost placeholders to keep the audience that guards their U.S. market position and to put up a barrier to the entry of geographical competitors and ideological alternatives in the U.S. news arena.

In sum, only a few studies have concentrated on the comparative content of online and print media. To the best of the authors' knowledge, no previous studies have incorporated portal news sites in their comparison of print and online newspapers. Previous studies have also not focused on a specific issue, such as the Iraq War, which has a relatively strong universal news appeal. And results on comparative news content of print and online versions of a newspaper are mixed.

This study uses the Iraq War as its topic and includes portal sites in a comparison of print and online media. While the unique characteristics of online — space and global audience — suggest that content will differ between online and print, it is also possible that, for an online version of a newspaper (as compared with a portal site), the differences may not be large. Still, this study expected to find differences between online and print.

HYPOTHESES

People all over the world are potential users of Internet news. Although it is difficult to have a comprehensive picture of the readers of online news globally, it can be argued that these readers will be educated, middle to upper class and active information seekers.

A study of media consumption in the United States (Pew Research Center 2000) indicated that Internet users were generally young and comprised information-hungry groups. More than half (54%) of the users went online to get more information about a story they first saw or heard about from a more traditional news medium. Research among readers of Arab electronic newspapers found that the most popularly mentioned reason for using the Internet was to obtain news (Alshehri, 2000).

Still, only the well-to-do in many countries of the world have access to the Internet. Further, because several countries directly or indirectly control news through traditional media, online news is a critical source of information in such countries. The Internet appears to have a diverse, information-hungry, somewhat affluent global audience, for some of whom the Internet may be the only reliable and accessible news source. These audience characteristics are likely to influence the content of online news.

On any major news event/issue, such as the Iraq War, worldwide audiences might seek alternative points of view. People with different ethnic, cultural and political backgrounds might search for news on this issue from their perspectives. People's use of the Internet for news soared after Iraq was invaded. The Pew survey (2003) found that 66% of Internet users cited Internet's ability to provide news from a variety of sources as their primary reason for using the Net to find information on the Iraq War. The same study reported that 63% of the respondents chose the Internet because it could provide up-to-the-minute news on the Iraq War, while 52% said that they used the Internet to hear points of views different from those in traditional media.

Online news media have the technological capability to meet the varied needs of this diverse global audience. Unlimited Internet space might encourage online news editors to publish more stories and various perspectives.

The Iraq War created widespread anti-American sentiment throughout the world. World media questioned the U.S. government's perspective on the Saddam Hussein regime. The U.S. government framed the conflict as a war to liberate the Iraqi people. The general premise of the U.S. and U.K governments was that Iraq posed a regional if not global threat because it had weapons of mass destruction and that a military rather than diplomatic solution was the proper road to take to remove the threat. They believed that a "liberated" Iraq would make the world a safer place.

Once the war began, the U.S. government repeatedly reinforced its view that Iraq would be a better place after the war with a different government. Many countries did not subscribe to this view. As a result, news in these countries might focus on topics different from those promoted by the U.S. government such as rebuilding Iraq, diplomatic activities, war protests, other countries' involvement, UN activities, growing insurgency and lack of security. Because of their global audience, online media may also provide such perspectives. To do this, they may rely on non-U.S. news agencies/outlets, news datelined from non-U.S. locations, non-U.S. sources, and non-U.S. people (people in the news).

For a global audience, online media might provide non-U.S. government perspectives on the Iraq War, compared with U.S. print media, which was more likely to adopt a U.S. government perspective. Studies have found that U.S government policy influences U.S. media content. Studying the coverage of *The New York Times* and *The Washington Post* between 1950 and 1984, Chang (1989) found that the more the U.S. government favored the U.S.-China relations, the more the newspapers presented better relations between the two countries. Studies have also found that news coverage of world events involving U.S. military operations in U.S. media favor the broad perspective of the incumbent administration (Kellner, 1993; Hallin & Gitlin, 1993: Pedelty, 1995; Reese & Buckalew, 1995).

Based on differences between print and online media, the following hypotheses are proposed:

H1: Compared to the *New York Times* print version, the *New York Times* online version and *Yahoo News* will have a larger percent of stories on the Iraq War.

H2: The *New York Times* online version and *Yahoo News* will have a larger percent of stories on topics other than immediate military operations in the Iraq War, while the *New York Times* print version will have a larger percent of stories on military operations in the Iraq War.

H3: The *New York Times* online version and *Yahoo News* will have a larger percent of stories on the Iraq War circulated by non-U.S. news agencies and media outlets, while the *New York Times* print version will have a larger percent of stories circulated by U.S. news agencies and media outlets.

H4: The *New York Times* online version and *Yahoo News* will have a larger percent of stories on the Iraq War originating from non-U.S. locations, while the *New York Times* print version will have a larger percent of stories originating from U.S. locations.

H5: The *New York Times* online version and *Yahoo News* will have a larger percent of non-U.S. sources in stories on the Iraq War, while the *New York Times* print version will have a larger percent of U.S. sources in stories on the Iraq War.

H6: The *New York Times* online version and *Yahoo News* will have a larger percent of non-U.S. people in stories on the Iraq War, while the *New York Times* print version will have a larger percent of U.S. people in stories on the Iraq War.

H7: The *New York Times* online version and *Yahoo News* will have a larger percent of stories that provide a non-U.S. government perspective on the Iraq War, while the *New York Times* print version will have a larger percent of stories that present a U.S. government perspective on the Iraq War.

METHOD

The method of the study was content analysis. *The New York Times* and its online version as well as *Yahoo News* were selected for the study. *The New York Times* was selected because it is the most prestigious U.S. national newspaper and more likely to present news for a global audience than other newspapers. *Yahoo News* was selected because it was ranked as the most accessed portal news site in the world.

The selection of only two online news outlets for the study can be justified on the grounds that although there are thousands of Web sites, people tend to visit a few popular sites. Using a database created from a survey of 33,000 people, Webster and Lin (2002) found that Internet audiences are concentrated in a relatively few sites. A similar pattern was found for the audience of newspaper sites. In a survey in Austin, Texas, Chy and Lasorsa (1999) found that online newsreaders mainly visit Web sites of large national and metropolitan newspapers.

A nonprobability sample of one week (November 5-11, 2003) was taken for the study. All the stories on the Iraq War from the selected publications were downloaded and printed. Online content is ephemeral and changing and represents a document model that coexists between recorded and unrecorded documents (Koehler, 1999). Because of the ever-changing nature of Web content, stories from the online version of *New York Times* and *Yahoo News* were downloaded and printed at the same time for each sample. Altogether, 355 stories were included in the sample.

Variables and Operational Definitions

Each story was coded for name (categories = *New York Times* print, *New York Times* online and *Yahoo News*), topic, news provider (i.e., agency/outlet), origin of news (i.e., dateline), news source, people in the news, and perspective (categories = U.S. government or not) on the Iraq War. Not all stories had all of these variables in them. For example, not all of the stories had a perspective on the war. All variables were coded only once for each story with the exception of source, which was multiple coded.

A preliminary look at the stories on the Iraq War revealed that news stories focused on the following topics: U.S./British Army action; terrorists' attacks; rebuilding Iraq; UN activities; war plan/Pentagon activities/war strategy; diplomatic activities regarding Iraq; internal politics in Iraq; debate on U.S. involvement in Iraq; Iraqi oil/resources; U.S. casualties; Iraq casualties; consequences of the Iraq War for the Middle East; Saddam Hussein; life in Baghdad; war protests; inspections for arms/weapons of mass destruction; other countries' involvement in Iraq; world reaction on Iraq War; censorship complaints, and other topics. These were used in the study as starter topic categories but the list was kept open-ended by including the category "Other." The list under "Other" was then divided into categories if the number of mentions of a particular category warranted it. The first few paragraphs of the story were used to determine topic. At the end of the coding, topic categories emerged (see Table 3.1).

Determination of news provider (i.e., which news agency or media outlet provided the news) was made by looking at the beginning of each story. Origin of the story was determined by looking at the dateline of the story. Usually newspapers do not use a dateline in reporting news originating from the city in which the newspaper is published. Therefore, undated items, in both the print and online versions of the *New York Times,* were attributed to New York.

Almost every piece of information in a news story is attributed to a certain individual or group. These individuals or groups were coded as the source of news. Usually news sources are clearly defined, but in some cases news sources are implied. Implied news sources were determined by reading the whole story carefully. If a source could not be determined, it was coded as unclear and this category was not used in later analysis.

People in the news were defined as a group or individual who actively say or do something. People also included individuals or groups who were covered in the media for their importance. Inanimate objects such as a government, council, etc., were not considered people.

Perspective was defined as point of view of the U.S. government (included the U.K. government point of view because of the similarity between the two) versus a non-U.S. government point of view. At the end of the coding, for several variables conceptually similar categories were collapsed into one because many cells had small frequencies making statistical tests difficult. Particularly for topic, while the study began with several topics, these were ultimately collapsed into four.

One of the authors of the paper did the coding. A second coder recoded 35 stories (10%) after the first coder completed coding. The inter-

TABLE 3.1
IDENTIFICATION OF TOPICS
AND OPERATIONAL DEFINITIONS

Topic	Operational Definition
Attack on U.S. troops/establishments	Any attack inflicted on U.S. troops or establishments with or without casualty or injury.
Attack on Coalition troops/establishments	Any attack inflicted on Coalition troops or establishments with or without casualty or injury.
U.S. military operations	Any U.S. military operation or action including arresting people, searching sites, etc.
Coalition military operations	Any Coalition military operation or action including arresting people, searching sites, etc.
Conditions in Iraq	Any description by any party that relates to the situation in Iraq
Iraq policy/strategy	Any statements or actions that reflect policy or strategic aspects of the Iraq War, such as strategic speeches, strategic troop deployment, and strategic visits. For example, when military officials said that the army would be tough in dealing with "terrorists," it was coded as policy/strategy.
Rebuilding of Iraq	Any activities with a reference to rebuilding Iraq. For example, building Iraqi security forces.
Iraq economy	Any reference to the economy or oil of Iraq. If both rebuilding and economy were present as topics, the dominant theme was coded. The dominant theme was determined by looking at the headline and by reading the full story.
War protest	Any type of protest on the war against Iraq, ceremonial or non-ceremonial.
Iraq internal politics	Any internal debate on the sharing of power between different groups in Iraq.
Other countries' involvement	Activities or statements concerning other countries' involvement in Iraq's affairs.
Military family/support	Any activity that covers the non-combat aspects of the military, support for the troops.
Anti-U.S. sentiment/actions	Any activities/statements denouncing U.S. presence and policy in Iraq, Anti-U.S. rhetoric related or unrelated to Iraq.

coder reliability scores were: Name: 100%, topic: 86%, news provider: 97%, news origin: 100%, news source: 97%, people: 91%, and perspective: 89%. The variables in the study, their operational definitions and their categories are presented in Table 3.2.

FINDINGS

Findings of the study are presented in Table 3.3. *Yahoo News* published the largest percent of stories (60%, N=355) in the selected week on the Iraq War, followed by *New York Times* online (31%), and *New York Times* print (9%) ($p<.05$). Thus, H1, which stated that compared to *New York Times* print, *New York Times* online and *Yahoo News* would publish a larger percent of stories on the Iraq War, was supported.

H2 posited that *New York Times* online and *Yahoo News* would have a larger percentage of stories from non-U.S. media outlets, while *New York Times* print would have a larger percent of stories from U.S. media outlets. The chi-square test was significant ($p<.05$), but an examination of the table reveals that percentages were not all in the expected direction. Therefore, H2 was not supported. Still, the table shows that *Yahoo News* published the largest percent of news stories (55%) provided by non-U.S. news outlets, while *New York Times* print published the largest percent of news from U.S. media outlets. This interaction possibly resulted in the significant chi-square and, thus, supports at least two of the three directional expectations. However, even though *New York Times* online, compared to its print version, also published more news provided by non-U.S. media outlets (20% compared to only 6% by print *New York Times*), it did not use non-U.S. media outlets more than it used U.S. outlets, which is what had been hypothesized.

None of the other hypotheses were supported. Thus, *New York Times* online and *Yahoo News* did not differ from *New York Times* print for the following five variables: topics discussed, origin of news, sources used, people portrayed, and perspective presented. A descriptive analysis is provided below for the sample stories, but without statistical significance these may not be generalized to the population of stories.

A pattern was present for topic, origin, source, people and perspective, whereby differences were evident between print and online in most cases. For origin this difference was in the expected direction; more stories datelined in non-U.S. locations were published in *New York Times* online and *Yahoo News* (54% in both), while more news stories datelined in the United States were published in *New York Times* print (63%). For

TABLE 3.2
IDENTIFIED VARIABLES, OPERATIONAL
DEFINITIONS AND CATEGORIES

Variables	Operational Definition	Categories
Topic	The main subject matter of the story	War; conditions in Iraq; rebuilding of Iraq; Iraq economy/oil; effect on the region; war protest; Iraq internal politics; U.S. involvement; other countries' involvement; U.S. casualties; Iraq casualties; Coalition casualties
News provider	The staff reporter, news agency, newspaper, other media outlets that provide news	U. S.: Staff reporter; U.S. media; U.S. news agency; press releases Non-U.S.: Staff reporter; U.K. media; Arab media; Western (but non-U.S.) news agency; non western news agency; press releases; other
Origin/ dateline	The originating place of the news, the dateline	U. S.: U.S. Non-U.S.: U.K; UN; Iraq, Arab countries, other countries
News source	Individual, group of office to which information in the news is attributed	U. S.: U.S. leaders/officials; U.S.groups; journalist-witnesses/eye witnesses Non-U.S.: U.K. leaders/officials; Iraqi leaders/officials; Arab leaders/officials; UN officials; Turkish officials/leaders; other countries' leaders/officials; Iraqi people; Arab people/groups; journalist-witnesses/eye witnesses; Iraqi insurgents; other
People in the news	Individual or group that actively says something or performs a job or are mentioned in the media for their importance.	U. S.: U.S. leaders/officials Non-U.S.: U.K. leaders/officials; UN officials; other countries' leaders/officials
Perspective	The point of view of various countries/ groups/parties/in dividuals	U. S.: U.S. government; U.K. government Non-U.S.: U.S. opposition; U.K. opposition; Iraqi leaders; Iraqi people/groups; UN, Arab countries, European countries, other countries; international panels; U.S. polls; media; other

perspective, all three used a non-U.S. government perspective, but the online media did this much more than did the print media.

For source and people in the news, all three news media mostly used U.S. sources and U.S. people, but the print media did this to a larger degree than did the online media. For topic, too, a similar pattern was evident. All three media focused mostly on military affairs (a U.S. topic mostly), but the online media did this to a smaller extent. In reverse, all three focused less on two of the other three topics — rebuilding Iraq and the post-war condition in Iraq (a non-U.S. topic mostly), but the online media had a considerably larger percentage of news using these foci and the print media had a very minor focus on these.

Thus, in the sample at least, it appeared that *New York Times* print was more likely to report from a U.S. outlook than were *New York Times* online and *Yahoo News*.

DISCUSSION

The objective of the study was to examine news content on the 2003 Iraq War to discern whether print and online media differed in terms of topic, news provider, origin, source, people, and perspective. The study found mixed results — online and print media were different in a few aspects, but similar in most others.

Findings show that online media published significantly more stories on the Iraq War. As we know, unlike print media, space is unlimited in online media, enabling online media to contain large amounts of information on any topic. News is updated instantly in online media. As the process of updating goes on, "old" stories neither disappear nor are they merged with the latest story versions. In addition, online publications put almost identical stories side by side — the only difference is that two different news agencies supplied these stories. As a result, at any given time, online media usually contain more stories than print newspapers.

As hypothesized, *New York Times* depended on U.S. media outlets to a large extent. This paper is primarily targeted to U.S. readers. *Yahoo News*, on the other hand, used non-U.S. media outlets. This site is primarily targeted to a global audience. *New York Times* online fell somewhere in between. It depended largely on U.S. outlets, but not to the extent the print *New York Times* did. It is possibly balancing the interests of its U.S. and foreign readers. Also, because it belongs to the same company, The New York Times Company, it would be practical for it to

TABLE 3.3
FREQUENCY OF COVERAGE BY MEDIA OUTLET

	Media Outlet		
	NY Times Print N(%)	*NY Times* Online N(%)	*Yahoo News* N(%)
No. of stories (N = 355)	32 (9)	111 (31)	212 (60)*
Topic (N = 355)			
Military Affairs (N = 125)	14 (47)	41 (38)	70 (36)
Rebuilding Iraq (N = 58)	2 (7)	20 (19)	36 (18)
Iraq policy/strategy (N = 94)	13 (43)	27 (25)	54 (27)
Post-war condition in Iraq (N = 58)	1 (3)	19 (18)	38 (19)
News Provider (N = 355)			
U.S.Media Outlets (N = 214)	30 (94)	89 (80)	95 (45)*
Non-U.S Media Outlets (N = 141)	2 (6)	22 (20)	117 (55)
Origin (N = 339)			
U.S.(N = 162)	20 (63)	50 (46)	92 (46)
Non-U.S Media (N = 177)	12 (37)	59 (54)	106 (54)
Source (N = 333)			
U.S.(N = 192)	24 (75)	59 (57)	109 (55)
Non-U.S (N = 141)	8 (25)	44 (43)	89 (45)
Main people (N = 182)			
U.S.(N = 121)	16 (76)	32 (63)	73 (66)
Non-U.S (N = 61)	5 (24)	19 (37)	37 (34)
Perspective (N = 161)			
U.S.Government (N = 41)	4 (33)	10 (22)	27 (26)
Non-U.S.Government (N = 120)	8 (67)	35 (78)	77 (74)
* p<.05			

use some of the same stories and resources that its print counterpart has.

While *New York Times* used stories datelined in the United States and depended mostly on U.S. sources a majority of the times, it had 37% of its stories datelined in places other than the United States and had a quarter of its stories utilize non-U.S sources. This is probably a reflection of the fact that the *New York Times* has the resources to employ reporters in non-U.S. locations and makes use of them to some degree.

Fifty-five percent of the stories on Iraq War published on *Yahoo News* came from non-U.S. outlets, including non-U.S. news agencies and newspapers; 54% came from non-U.S. locations; and 45% used non-U.S. sources. *Yahoo News*, as an aggregator of online media, republishes the work of about 100 news outlets (Palser, 2002). The Iraq War, being a controversial global event, initiated reactions throughout the world. *Yahoo News*, taking full advantage of technology, gathered news from various outlets, locations and sources, and presented it to its global audience.

All three vehicles — both versions of the *New York Times* and *Yahoo News* — published more news using a non-U.S. government perspective. *New York Times* online published the largest percent of stories (78%) using this perspective. As mentioned earlier, the war in Iraq was a controversial one from the beginning, both in the United States and elsewhere in the world. By November 2003, when this study was conducted, many of the American people and media had become disenchanted with the war. The possibility of finding weapons of mass destruction on which the war was based was fading away rapidly. Opposition political parties and other groups had also become increasingly vocal against the war. All these possibly explain the anti-U.S. and anti-U.K government content in both versions of the *New York Times*. This explanation is possibly true for the high percentage of such news in *Yahoo News*, too, but *Yahoo News's* need to cater to a global audience might be an additional reason.

For main character, the opposite was true; all three depended on U.S. people. For topic, all three focused mainly on military topics and then on Iraq policy/strategy, which was a somewhat mixed category using both U.S. and non-U.S. focus. This use of U.S. people and focus on military topics and strategy possibly resulted from the fact that it was, after all, a U.S.-led war. This and event-oriented nature of most news as well as a system that positions reporters in institutions of the establishment (whether it is a beat or the embedding of reporters) are, therefore, likely explanations.

While the study's hypotheses were not completely supported, there is some indication in the sample that online news does differ from print news. This difference likely arises from the needs of a global audience. To some extent, this wider audience also impacts the online version of print newspapers. Earlier studies had found that the online version of *The New York Times* and other major newspapers reproduced the content of the original publications (Burnhurst, 2002), but this appears to be changing. *New York Times* online, while not quite like *Yahoo News* in its orientation, was still somewhat different from its own print parent. It did not imitate the print version.

At the same time, a global audience is only one of the factors that influences news content. The resources of the media, new technology and the possibilities it offers, the routines of news such as dependence on establishment sources, beats, and news values, and government/patriotic pressures are all additional factors that interact in ways which are not always predictable.

LIMITATIONS, CONTRIBUTIONS AND FUTURE STUDY

The one-week convenience sample is a weakness of the study. Its non-random nature and its small time frame provide only a small and sliced picture of the reporting of the Iraq War. While the number of stories coded was not small and Kerlinger and Lee (2000) suggest that many statistical tests are robust enough to handle the nonrandom nature of many samples, this is still a limitation, particularly because this study did not use statistics other than chi-square.

At the same time, this study makes a few contributions. Its descriptive analysis of the sample findings provides some insight into how the Iraq War was covered across three different media. The study is also one of few comparing print and online versions of one newspaper and a portal site. The study's variables were developed to be conceptually and theoretically relevant and had sufficient detail so that their coding was highly reliable. Particularly for topic and perspective, considerable pilot reading of the content on non-sample data was done to reflect the subject matter the media may cover if they adopted a U.S. government orientation.

Future studies may conduct personal interviews with print and online journalists and editors to determine what factors influence which content in online media. Given that these media do not suffer the limitations of print in terms of space, the gatekeeping process may be different for such media. Researcher observation might also be useful in rounding out findings of empirical studies.

REFERENCES

Alshehri, F.A. (2000). *Electronic newspapers on the Internet: A study of the production and consumption of Arab dailies in the World Wide Web.* Unpublished Doctoral dissertation, department of journalism studies, University of Sheffield, England.

Bagdikian, B. (1983). *The media monopoly,* Boston: Beacon Press.

Bantz, C. R., McCorkle, S., & Badde, R. C. (1981). The news factory. In G.C. Wilhoit & H. D. Bock (Eds.), *Mass Communication Review Yearbook,* Vol. 2. Beverly Hills, CA: Sage, pp. 336-390.

Barnhurst, K.G. (2002). News geography & monopoly: The form of reports on U.S. newspaper Internet sites, *Journalism Studies, 3*(4), 477-490.

Chang, T.K. (1989). The impact of presidential statements on press editorials regarding U.S-China policy, 1950-1984. *Communication Research, 16,* 486-509.

Chy, H.I., & Lasorsa, D. (1999), Access, use and preferences for online newspapers, *Newspaper Research Journal, 20*(4), 2-14.

Fink, C.C. (1989, March). How newspapers should handle upscale/downscale conundrum, *Presstime,* pp. 40-41.

Fishman, M. (1980). *Manufacturing the news,* Austin, Texas: University of Texas Press.

Goodrick, E.T. (1991). Editorial writers' approaches to selected women's issues. *Newspaper Research Journal, 12*(3), 20-31.

Gunter, B. (2003). *News and the Net,* Mahwah, NJ: Lawrence Erlbaum Associates.

Gans, H. (1979). *Deciding what's news.* New York: Random House.

Gans, H. (1985, November-December). Are U.S. journalists dangerously liberal? *Columbia Journalism Review, 24*(6): 29-33.

Hall, S. (1982). The rediscovery of "ideology": Return of the "repressed" in media studies. In M.Gurevitch, T. Bennett, J. Curran & J. Woollacott (Eds). *Culture, sociology and media,* (pp.56-90). New York: Routledge.

Hallin, D. L. (1992. The passing of the "high modernism" of American journalism, *Journal of Communication,* 42 14-25.

Hallin D., & Gitlin, T. (1993). Agon and ritual: The Gulf War as popular culture and as television drama. *Political Communication,* 10, 411-424.

hAnluain, D.Ó. (2003 Sept. 11). The Guardian of the web, *Online Journalism Review.* Available at www.ojr.org.

Hess, S. (1981). *The Washington reporters,* Washington D.C.: Brookings Institute.

Kellner, D. (1993). The crisis in the gulf and the lack of critical media discourse. In B.S. Greenberg & W. Gantz (Eds.) *Desert storm and the mass media.* Cresskill, NJ: Hampton Press, Inc., pp. 37-47.

Kerlinger, F. N., & Lee, H. B. (2000). *Foundations of behavioral research* (4th Ed.). New York: Harcourt College Publishers.

Koehler, W. (1999). An analysis of Web page and Web site constancy and permanence, *Journal of the American Society for Information Science, 50*(2), 162-180.

Lasica, J.D. (1997, June). Time to freshen up online newspapers, *American Journalism Review Newslink.* Available at http://www.newslink.org/ajrlasica697.html.

Lin, C.A., & Jeffres L. W. (2001). Comparing distinctions and similarities across Web sites of newspapers, radio stations, and television stations. *Journalism and Mass Communication Quarterly,* 78(3). 555-573.

Palser, B. (2002). Is it journalism? Yahoo attracts a large audience but does not original reporting, *American Journalism Review, 24*(5), 62-63.

Pedelty, M. (1995). *War stories: The culture of foreign correspondents*, New York and London: Routledge.

Peng, F.Y., Tham, N.I., & Xiaoming, H. (1999). Trends in online newspapers: a look at the U.S. web. *Newspaper Research Journal, 20*(2), 52-64

Pew Research Center (2000, January). The Internet news audience goes ordinary. Retrieved May 30, 2005, from at http://www. people-press.org/reports/display.php3?ReportID=72

Pew Internet and American Life (2003). The Internet and Iraq war: How online Americans have used the Internet to learn war news, understand events, and promote their views. Retrieved June 1, 2005, from http://www.pewinternet.org/report-display.asp7r=87.

Reese, S.D., & Buckalew, B. (1995). The militarism of local television: The routine framing of the Persian Gulf War, *Critical studies in Mass Communication. 12*(1), 40-59.

Smith, A. (1977). Technology and control: The interactive dimensions of journalism. In J. Curran, M. Gurevitch, & J. Woolacott (Eds.) *Mass Communication and Society.* Beverly Hills, CA: Sage, pp. 174-194.

Singer, J.B. (2001). The Metro Wide Web: Changes in newspapers gate-keeping roles online, *Journalism and Mass Communication Quarterly,* 78(1). 65-80

Shuster, S. (1988 May/June). Foreign competition hits the news, *Columbia Journalism Review,* pp. 43-45.

Shoemaker, P.J., & Reese S.D. (1996). *Mediating the message: Theories of influence on mass media content,* New York: Longman.

Tuchman, G. (1973). Making news by doing work: Routinizing the unexpected, *American Journal of Sociology, 79,* 110-131.

Webster J.G., & Lin, S. (2002). The Internet use: Web use as mass behavior, *Journal of Broadcasting and Electronic Media,* 46(1), 1-12.

Weaver, D.H., & Wilhoit, G.C. (1991). *The American journalist: A portrait of U.S. news people and their work,* (2nd Ed.). Bloomington: Indiana University Press.

DISCUSSION QUESTIONS

1. The authors make a point of routinized news coverage by beat reporters. In what ways did war correspondents practice routinization of news during the 2003 Iraq War, and how did the new, digital media contribute to or detract from such traditional approaches toward war news coverage?

2. What examples can you give of the "social control function" of media as practiced during the 2003 Iraq War?

3. In what ways did global audiences impact the way online newspapers covered the war, and how did this differ from Yahoo.com?

4. The authors argue that the 2003 Iraq War contributed to anti-American sentiment around the world. What, if anything, does this tell us about the global news reach of online newspapers and news sites?

5. International communication scholars maintain there is an imbalance of news flow from developed countries with media centers to developing

countries without them. What do you think is the prospect of a more even "playing field" of international media flows because of the Internet?

CHAPTER FOUR

ANALYSIS OF BBC NEWS ONLINE COVERAGE OF THE IRAQ WAR

DANIELA V. DIMITROVA

T he BBC and its coverage of the 2003 Iraq War have received much criticism as well as much praise around the world. Some observers have attacked the news coverage of the BBC, claiming it was clearly biased in support of the war, serving as a propaganda tool for the British government. Others have credited the BBC for its in-depth reporting from the war zone, juxtaposing it to the blatantly patriotic U.S. news coverage. This chapter examines the news coverage the BBC provided on its Web site during the 2003 Iraq War and analyzes the themes and Web-specific features used to enhance war reporting.

THE BBC AND THE IRAQ WAR

The BBC, a respected news source worldwide, was established as a radio station in 1922 when it began medium-wave services from London (Wikipedia, 2004). The BBC was founded as the British Broadcasting Corporation and remains a publicly funded broadcaster.

BBC provided the first television broadcasts of entertainment programming to a limited number of homes in 1936, long before the Americans, but suspended them in 1939 at the outbreak of World War II, fearing the transmissions would act as a homing device for enemy bombers. The first regular television news broadcasts were transmitted in 1954. The BBC began to air broadcasts overseas shortly after that (Wikipedia, 2004). The online service is among the many branches of the BBC, founded in 1997 by Mike Smartt, a BBC television reporter. The BBC news Web site was established in November 1997 and began with only a staff of 30 (BBC, 2004). It has grown substantially since then. Today it has an estimated global user base of around 30 million, according to its director of new media and technology Ashley Highfield (Kiss, 2004).

Immediately after the start of the 2003 Iraq War, the BBC news audience increased substantially. Traffic statistics show that the online BBC audience skyrocketed with a 103% increase during the first week of the war (Nielsen NetRatings, 2003). The BBC News World Edition Web site recorded 400 million page views for the first two weeks of the war (BBC Press Office, 2003). The online traffic of the site increased not only at home, but also abroad — by 41% in United States and 10% in Canada (BBC Press Office, 2003). In sum, BBC News World Edition Web site became a major news source visited by audiences all over the world immediately after the war broke out.

Covering the Iraq War and the build-up to the war presented some challenges for BBC reporters and executives, which, among other things, included the resignations of the BBC managing director, its board chairman and a defense reporter. On May 29, 2003, reporter Andrew Gilligan said in an interview on the Today Programme of BBC Radio 4 that the British government probably knew some of the claims that Iraq possessed weapons of mass destruction (WMDs) were wrong or questionable and published them in a 2002 dossier anyway. The government fired back with a rebuttal and accused the BBC of anti-war reporting. In a subsequent investigation by Lord Hutton (named the Hutton Inquiry), the conduct of BBC was investigated along with some other issues, the central of which was the apparent suicide of Iraq weapons expert Dr. David Kelley. The conclusions of the Hutton Report were that Gilligan's allegations on the BBC Today were "unfounded" (Hutton Report, 2004). The report also concluded that BBC management failed to investigate complaints that the Gilligan broadcast was inaccurate and, further, that BBC executives failed to make proper investigations if Gilligan's report was actually supported by his sources (Hutton Report, 2004).

In sum, the Hutton Inquiry found that Andrew Gilligan's accusation that the British government was "sexing up" reports on WMDs in Iraq before the war began was unfounded (Hutton Report, 2004). Two days after the Hutton Report was released, the BBC Director General (managing director) resigned on January 30, 2004 (Wikipedia, 2004). In addition to managing director Greg Dyke, the chairman Gavyn Davies as well as Andrew Gilligan also resigned from the BBC. The Hutton Report criticized the standards of journalism at the BBC, specifically the editorial system that allowed Gilligan's report to go to air and the internal system through which complaints were investigated. The incident did not seem to substantially harm BBC's global reputation.

Contrary to some expectations, the BBC online coverage was not supportive of the war and sometimes seemed anti-coalition in nature. The justification of the war was questioned and the news reporting frequently showed the dark side of war, focusing the reporters' camera on the lives of everyday Iraqis, children in the street, wounded in hospitals, and civilian casualties of war. That is evident from the themes present on the BBC News Web site; in particular, through the violence of war reporting. Similarly, the human-interest frame, which was also common, brought to the fore personal stories of Iraqi families.

Another tool worth analyzing is the use of Web-specific features to augment the reporting about the Iraq War. Online visitors from around the world could not only read about the events in Iraq, they could see the pictures of the victims, hear interviews with the main actors, watch videos of military briefings, and learn about the perspective of the journalists covering the war through their Web diaries.

The rest of this chapter shows in more detail what kinds of themes were discussed and what other online features were employed to present the online audience with a comprehensive picture of the war. The first half of the chapter examines the themes in the online war coverage while the second half focuses on the use of online features. The chapter is based on content analysis of the BBC Web site. It focuses on the BBC News World Edition available online at *http://news.bbc.co.uk*, which provides continuous coverage of news events. The BBC News home page was downloaded and saved during the official period of the war, March 19, 2003 to May 1, 2003. The analysis of the online news reporting on the recent Iraq War suggests that despite some skepticism, there is hope for thorough and balanced reporting of war. The chapter leads to the conclusion that other news media can emulate BBC's comprehensive reporting, which offered multiple perspectives on its Web site and used online features skillfully to augment traditional news coverage.

THEMES IN BBC ONLINE WAR COVERAGE

Media frame events for the public, focusing on some aspects of the event while ignoring other aspects. Just like a video camera pointed at a specific scene of interest, journalists can capture only a limited amount of reality in their reporting. Where they focus the camera, what they zoom in on, becomes of concern to the general public, which relies on media coverage to form their interpretations of the event. In a democratic society, we trust news media to tell us what is happening in the world and why.

When news media cover controversial events, however, their role as an objective observer and government watchdog is put to the test. Journalists who cover war and international conflict often find it difficult to remain neutral and may offer diverse, disparate coverage of the same event. In fact, previous research has shown that Coalition and non-Coalitions countries provided different framing of the 2003 Iraq War in their national media (Dimitrova, Kaid, & Williams, 2004). Because of such differences in coverage, it is not uncommon for people who live in different countries to see the event through different angles as a result of reading reports that focus on different themes and actors, cite different sources, and vary in tone of news coverage.

Scholars have labeled this different construction of the same event in the media text *framing* (e.g., D'Angelo, 2002; Entman, 2004). While different paradigms exist in framing research, all agree that framing is important to study and may influence audience cognitions, attitudes, and beliefs (D'Angelo, 2002). According to D'Angelo (2002, p. 873), "news frames are themes within news stories that are carried by various kinds of framing devices. The content of the frame amalgamates textual items (words and images) with the contextual treatment that they receive from framing devices." Frames are important because they have been found to shape public opinion in general as well as individual cognition (D'Angelo, 2002; Entman, 2004). The process of framing is complex and results from multiple external factors around the journalist who writes the media text. These factors include the surrounding culture and ideology and journalistic values and practices. The government administration, other elite, the news media as well as the public at large all contribute to the development of news frames (Entman, 2004). Internal influences such as individual journalists' attitudes and schemas also impact news framing. These influences, however, are beyond the scope of this chapter.

The BBC News World Edition Web site represents a prominent and respected news source worldwide available to global audiences via the Internet (Wikipedia, 2004). As shown above, it became a popular online news destination during the 2003 Iraq War. That makes it even more interesting to see how it framed the war, a controversial international event, which received limited support outside of the Coalition of the Willing. Even within the Coalition countries, the public was split and sometimes the majority opposed government decisions to send troops to Iraq. We begin the examination of the online war framing by first looking at the main actors in the online BBC coverage.

The Actors

The online news reporting on BBC was, of course, focused on its domestic political leaders, such as Tony Blair, and the British position on the war. The official position of the U.S. government and its political and military leaders also were covered closely. At the same time, the BBC journalists did not ignore the views from the rest of the world.

Articles on the Web site often focused on the Middle East, Russia, and other European countries. Foreign political leaders such as Jacques Chirac and Vladimir Putin were often cited. Among the countries mentioned in the BBC war coverage were Australia, France, Jordan, Kuwait, Malaysia, Somalia, South Korea, Syria and Turkey. The positions and views of the Arab world were often discussed, both in text and in pictures. The perspectives of international organizations such as the European Union and United Nations were also mentioned.

The Sources

Staff reporters wrote all articles published on the home page of the online BBC edition. The main sources cited within the articles were government officials and military personnel. Some criticized the fact that official sources were quoted most frequently. As Entman (2004) notes, however, top administration officials are regular sources for the news media. Thus, they contribute to framing of events in certain ways. According to Entman's cascading activation model, that is one way in which the current administration and other national elite influence how the news media frame events.

Reasons for War

The BBC's online journalists rarely discussed the reasons for war. It seems that the causes for the military action as well as responsibility for the war and its consequences became "nonissues" in this case. One of the few reasons for war mentioned on the BBC News Web site was that "America does not tolerate dictators." This was one of the rare occasions in which the righteousness of military action was implied.

Tone of Reporting

Understanding that objectivity is difficult to achieve in a war situation, when access to sources is most challenging and journalists have to protect their own lives, we attempted to measure the tone of the online reporting. Overall, BBC journalists stayed objective, avoiding explicitly stating either support or opposition to the war. The online news coverage rarely contained positive or negative moral terms. The content analysis showed that explicit support or direct condemnation of the war was absent.

Frames

Despite the fact that BBC journalists refrained from voicing biased opinions about the war and their own attitudes about the conflict, they certainly presented various war frames. War reporting, as expected, incorporated discussions of military action and strategy, military advances and losses. This type of framing exemplifies the *military conflict frame,* where the journalist focuses on military strategy and action on the field.

Another common frame on the BBC news home page was the *violence of war frame*, which zoomed in on the violence of the conflict, presenting human casualties of war as well as destruction of cities, roads and other infrastructure. The BBC online coverage portrayed a comprehensive picture of the destruction caused by the war. Pictures and text showed the negative consequences that resulted from war violence, touching everyday Iraqis and soldiers.

A third common frame was the *human interest frame*. BBC reporters who brought to the attention of the online reader the personal stories of those involved in the war — the Coalition soldiers, the Iraqis, and the journalists themselves — used it skillfully. Even though the human-interest angle often ignores the broader context of the war and provides only isolated snapshots of reality, it allows readers to empathize with the actors as they see deeply personal stories and reactions of everyday people faced with the harsh realities of war.

Another interesting frame was the *anti-war protest frame*. The BBC home page often included stories about anti-war marches not only in the U.K. but also abroad. The March 23, 2003, home page, for example, included a story (with a photo) about demonstrations against the war in Asia titled "Thousands March for Peace." The home page contained as many as three stories about anti-war protest in some cases.

Another noteworthy war frame was the *prognostic frame*. This frame is exemplified by discussion about the future consequences of the war, both for Iraq and other countries or regions. Such analysis was common in the BBC online coverage even during the time of war when official military actions were not declared over. The prognostic frame provides the audience with a more comprehensive picture of the war, portraying the short-term and long-term effects it may have on people, countries, and international relations in general. BBC journalists offered a comprehensive look at the possible consequences of the Iraq War.

WEB-SPECIFIC FEATURES USED TO AUGMENT ONLINE REPORTING

The BBC News World Edition Web site was applauded as an "exemplary news site" immediately after the war began. According to the Poynter Institute, the BBC had planned its online coverage well in advance and, as the war broke out, offered a large amount of war content that combined text, photos, video and audio in an impressive way (Poynter Institute, 2003). Below, we discuss how various online features contributed to rich, comprehensive online coverage of the war.

Hyperlinks

The BBC News Web site offered multiple sections about the war, starting with its home page and letting the user browse further for more in-depth information. While most links took the online reader within the BBC's own Web site, the sheer number of links about the war was impressive. During the official war period, March 19-May 1, 2003, the number of war-related links ranged from 24 to 30 and often exceeded 26 per day. Some links took the user to a special section with in-depth coverage dedicated to the war — "War in Iraq: In Depth" — while others linked to multimedia, video, or audio features, photo galleries, or audience opinion polls. Each of those Web elements is briefly analyzed below. The number and position of the links were consistent from day to day, which allowed easy and quick browsing throughout the BBC site.

Web Diaries

One of the most innovative reporting tools on the BBC Web site was a section titled "War Diaries." This section was prominently featured on the BBC News home page. It included journalists' diaries, which represented a creative way of reporting.

The BBC online editors chose to enrich war reporting by allowing their team of journalists to share brief chronological reports in a log format. Entries were provided in reverse chronological order. These "mini-blogs" allowed the online reader to experience the war from a first-person perspective, seeing through the eyes of the journalist and realizing that what was actually going on in the battle field was often unclear, leading to questions, conjectures, and mixed expectations. The Weblog of the team of BBC correspondents stationed in the Gulf region was perhaps the most notable feature of the Web site, because it combined traditional reporting with an innovative blogging perspective. It also allowed reporters from various locations to share their impressions: for example, online visitors to the BBC site could read the entries from journalists in Northern Kuwait, Qatar, Baghdad, and Amman simultaneously. According to the Poynter Institute, this feature was "really excellent" and should be emulated by other news sites (Poynter Institute, 2003).

Photos

Another, more traditional, feature of the online reporting was the use of visuals. The BBC News Web site incorporated a large number of photos, ranging from four to seven only on the home page. Sometimes, a picture is worth a thousand words. Therefore, it is worth examining the content of the BBC photographs.

Instead of merely focusing on military action and victory for the Coalition of the Willing, the BBC News Web site always included thumbnail pictures of ordinary Iraqis. The faces of Iraqi children orphaned by the war were often pictured on the site. BBC photographers also showed the reality of war in pictures from local hospitals, schools, and mosques. The site often featured slide shows of still photos from the war region. The BBC News home page presents a good example of how photography on the Web can be utilized to supplement traditional media coverage.

Multimedia

Another noteworthy feature of the BBC News Web site was the use of multimedia and interactive elements to enhance their online coverage. The site employed *audio and video-related material* regularly, creating links to interviews and video coverage of war progress in Iraq. The site featured as many as three video segments.

Examples of typical links include live broadcasts of Coalition war briefings, latest war coverage, and live videos from the streets of Baghdad. Audio links to interviews with American military or political leaders were also frequently provided. These audio and video features presented the online audience with a more complete picture of the war. Of course, adding substantial video and audio material will be a challenge for smaller media organizations.

The BBC News Web site also allowed online readers to express their opinions about the war via online polls and surveys. The site often offered a section called "Have Your Say," in which users could post their comments about current developments in Iraq. That was a unique feature of the site. In addition to engaging the online user, it also allowed BBC editors to gather audience feedback and thus better tailor their online content.

Among the online features used by the BBC News Web site was the ability to sign up for e-mail alerts. That was another way to personalize the BBC online content to individual interests and preferences.

Other Online Features

The BBC News World Edition home page offered an excellent example of a well-designed and well-structured Web site. The daily hierarchy of news was clearly outlined. Multiple sections about the war were provided to the online user, combing text, pictures and multimedia elements in innovative ways. The site always included a summary section titled "Iraq Latest: At-a-glance," which presented the latest news from Iraq in reverse chronological order. This section of the site can be used for chronological purposes as well as a pointer to the latest developments in the war.

Another way in which the BBC site appealed to diverse audiences was by allowing customization of the site in different languages—for example, the site content is available in Arabic, Russian, and Spanish. The BBC online content also attempted to offer multiple perspectives originating from different geographic areas such as the Middle East and Asia. News stories did not focus only on U.S. and British perspectives on the war.

CONCLUSION

This chapter analyzed the online content of the BBC news coverage of the 2003 Iraq War. We found that, overall, the Web coverage was substantial, balanced, and presented international perspectives on the ongoing Iraq War. The online reporting was also inclusive of multiple war frames. The four major frames that emerged from the content analysis were military conflict, violence of war, human interest, and anti-war protest. These four frames dominated the BBC News online content. As most national news media, the BBC relied mostly on official sources — government representatives and military personnel. At the same time, the online coverage attempted to incorporate views from around the world.

The BBC Web site also used online reporting elements in innovative ways. The most interesting elements, which contributed to a richer picture of the war, were the reporters' Web diaries and the use of multimedia. The large amount of hyperlinks and photographs was also impressive. These online features can and should be incorporated by other news sites whenever possible in order to augment their own online reporting.

The analysis of the BBC war coverage was limited to the BBC News World Edition home page. It was also limited to news coverage published online during the official war period. Extending the analysis to the whole Web site and examining a longer time period may enrich this analysis. Comparisons with other countries' news media as well as other types of media are also recommended.

REFERENCES

BBC Press Office. (2003, April 11). More people turn to the BBC for news of war in Iraq. Retrieved Dec. 26, 2004, from http://www.bbc.co.uk/pressoffice/pressreleases/stories/2003/04_april/11/iraq_audiences.shtml

BBC. (2004, Dec. 9). BBC website founder picks up OBE. Retrieved Dec. 30, 2004, from http://news.bbc.co.uk/1/hi/uk/4082733.stm

D'Angelo, P. (2002). News framing as a multiparadigmatic research program: A response to Entman. *Journal of Communication, 52*, 870-888.

Dimitrova, D. V, Kaid, L. L., and Williams, A. P. (2004). The first hours of the war: Online news coverage of Operation "Iraqi Freedom." In R. D. Berenger (Ed.) *Global Media Go to War* (pp. 255-264). Spokane, WA: Marquette Books.

Entman, R. (2004) *Projections of power*. Chicago: University of Chicago Press.

Nielsen NetRatings. (2003, March 27). Round-the-clock news coverage of the war in Iraq draws surfers online. Retrieved Dec. 26, 2004, from http://www.nielsen-netratings.com/pr/pr_030327.pdf

Kiss, J. (2004, Sept. 2). Global BBC site could be pay per play. Retrieved December 30, 2004, from http://www.journalism.co.uk/news/story1037.shtml.

Lord Hutton. (2004). Hutton Report. Retrieved Dec. 30, 2004, from http://www.the-hutton-inquiry.org.uk/content/report/huttonreport.pdf

Poynter Institute. (2003, March 20). A special war edition of e-media tidbits. Retrieved December 26, 2004, from http://poynteronline.org/column.asp?id=31&aid=25856

Wikipedia. (2004). BBC. Retrieved Dec. 30, 2004, from http://en.wikipedia.org/wiki/BBC

DISCUSSION QUESTIONS

1. To what extent do you think the BBC's coverage of the events leading up to the 2003 Iraq War enhanced or tarnished its image as a premier news

organization, particularly in the wake of Andrew Gilligan's reports and the controversial suicide of Dr. David Kelley, who was "outed" by the news organization as its news source on Iraq's WMD program?

2. Why do you think the BBC's Web site differed in its news coverage of the war from the coverage offered by CNN and Fox News Web sites? In what ways was the coverage different?

3. Increasingly news consumers are turning away from the traditional mediums and getting their news from Web sites like the BBC, especially for fast-developing news stories. How are Web sites, like the BBC's, adjusting to this new-found popularity?

4. News organizations' Web sites feature a variety of converged multimedia devices like video and audio to augment the printed words. What new challenges do these communication techniques pose for new journalists and journalism trainers?

5. Web pages change frequently, often several times a day — or more often if breaking news requires. What are the limitations and problems these Web pages face in forming an historical record for Internet users to research? How are Web sites meeting these challenges?

CHAPTER FIVE

FROM OSAMA BIN-LADEN'S MOUTHPIECE TO THE DARLING OF THE ALTERNATIVE MEDIA WEB SITES: REPRESENTATION OF ENGLISH·ALJAZEERA·NET IN THE WEST

TAL AZRAN

Al-Jazeera launched an English-language version of its Arabic Web site Sept. 1, 2002, a few months prior to the start of the 2003 Iraq War (*http://english.aljazeera.net*, hereafter referred to as english.aljazeera.net).

According to its mission statement, the Web site was designed "to fill a niche for English speakers who want to get the other side of the story, the Arab perspective" by breaking the traditional "language barrier" (Dube, 2003) that exists between Western audiences and the Arab television network. The launch of this English language news service represents an unprecedented attempt by a foreign network to directly target a Western audience with broadcasts from "behind enemy lines," with the potential to influence public opinion through reports that frequently contradict the mainstream news media.

The degree to which Western audiences accept english.aljazeera.net will determine the success or failure of this ambitious project. Success will likely encourage other non-Western news channels to follow Al-Jazeera's footsteps in reaching out to an English-speaking audience. The development of such a trend would have major implications for the traditional global news media, as well as break the hegemony of Western news organizations as the sole providers of information for Western viewers, readers and (more recently) Internet users during wartime.

This chapter provides a survey of how english.aljazeera.net has been received by Western news and current affairs Web sites and Internet users. Specifically, it examines the Western-based news Web sites and blogs that *re-present* reports from english.aljazeera.net and the *representation* of english.aljazeera.net as a news source. Deacon, Pickering, Golding, and Murdock (1999, p. 397) note that representations are "built around conceptions of other groups; they inevitably have 'us' and 'them' implications, and in this way they function as vehicles of ideological transmission."

METHOD

This study utilizes two research techniques: content analysis and virtual ethnography. Content analysis identifies and classifies the type of Web sites that systematically re-present reports from english.aljazeera.net. Virtual ethnography (Hine, 2000), which perceives Internet users as a specialized audience that not only consumes but also "culturally produces" content, can highlight the representation of english.aljazeera.net among this audience.

This report explores the re-presentation and representation of three randomly selected reports from english.aljazeera.net's coverage of the U.S. occupation of Iraq and Afghanistan from October 1, 2003 to November 30, 2003. The first piece, "The Picture Which Shames U.S. Army" (October 17, 2003) by Yvonne Ridley, depicts U.S. soldiers searching young Afghan children for explosives in the village of Zermit. The photograph — taken secretly — was given to Al-Jazeera by the Islamic Observation Centre. In response to the article, U.S. Army Major Peter Mitchell stated it was conceivable that the children could have carried explosives, and U.S. troops had to respond to any potential threat accordingly. The second article, "Shocking Images Shame U.S. Forces" (November 10, 2003) by Yvonne Ridley and Lawrence Smallman, showed U.S. soldiers tying up Iraqi women and children in their homes. The third article, "U.S. Continues to Humiliate Iraqis" (November 23, 2003) by Lawrence Smallman, depicted U.S. soldiers searching young Iraqi girls for explosives. The piece quoted an Iraqi father who "promised" that if U.S. soldiers intended to "humiliate" his daughter in such a way he would rather die "and take a few soldiers with him."

These news reports appeared on 118 English Web sites, with 102 originating in Western countries or operated by Westerners. Eighty-eight of the Web sites were based in the United States, six in the United Kindgdom, six in Canada and two in Ireland. The results were retrieved through searches on *Google* and *Alta Vista* in order to maximize the number of results and avoid exclusions stemming from the individual search algorithms.

The primary limitation of this study is the inability to confirm the identities of the Internet users and Web site content designers that re-presented the english.aljazeera.net reports (gender, ethnicity, age etc.). Many of the respondents did not reply to requests for interviews or refused to be identified. As such, this report relies on previous studies that have identified the active users of blogs and alternative Web sites as generally "upscale males" with a high level of education and income (Rainie, Fox & Fallows, 2003).

THE RE-PRESENTATION OF ENGLISH · ALJAZEERA · NET REPORTS

Of the 102 Web sites that re-presented reports from english.aljazeera.net, the majority (55) could be characterized as alternative media. The rest were as follows: unaffiliated (19), blogs (11), unclassified (11), hate groups (4), and mainstream (2). Given the substantial number of alternative media organizations that reported on various elements of the War in Iraq and Afghanistan, this result is not surprising.

This number would have been much larger if the study included the blogs that frequently re-presented the english.aljazeera.net reports. However, this study distinguishes between blogs and alternative news Web sites in order to examine the differences in representation between these distinct formats. A single user usually operates a blog, while alternative news Web sites are often semi-professional operations (see *Indymedia* below). Moreover, many blogs follow mainstream media; thus, they cannot be classified as "alternative" in content or perspective.

The ratio between the alternative media and mainstream media (55:2) that referred to the english.aljazeera.net reports is the most surprising result of the study, especially considering the online 'buzz' that Al-Jazeera's exclusive images created (as shown below), the fact that some of the stories were followed-up in Western forums, and the availability of the reports and images (in English) to Western news outlets.

As Table 5.1 shows, an overwhelming number of the surveyed Web sites openly declared a political orientation (66 of the 102 Web sites examined). This contradicts the findings of a comprehensive study (Michalsky & Preston, 2002) of audience reception in the aftermath of the terrorist attacks on September 11, 2001, which noted the emergence and

Type/orientation (N=102)	Liberal	Conservative	Other (Unclassified/ Unaffiliated)
Alternative	47	5	3
Blogs	6	3	2
Politically Unaffiliated	4	7	8
Hate groups	1	3	---
Unclassified	---	---	11
Mainstream	---	1	1
Total	58	19	25

growth of "skeptic" and nonaffiliated audiences. The study found that the proliferation of transnational news channels and alternative news sources generated a heightened awareness of a diversity of perspectives on political events among those able to access such sources. One practical result was the fostering of an attitude of skepticism towards the content and perspective of the mainstream media. These "skeptic zappers" characteristically skip between television channels in order to compare and contrast different news bulletins (e.g., CNN vs. BBC vs. Al-Jazeera), and supplement their consumption of traditional TV news with a highly selective but extensive use of the Internet. The study noted that general distrust of available TV and print media news sources "was the single biggest reason given for the vastly increased use of Internet sources following September 11" (Michalsky & Preston, 2000, p. 37).

In contrast, the present study found that most re-presentations of english.aljazeera.net content occurred within the context of political affiliation.

Next, the table shows that the ratio of re-presentation between liberal-oriented and conservative-oriented Web sites was more than 3 to 1 (58:19). This result is also not surprising given that the english.aljazeera.net content implicated U.S. soldiers in questionable activities and was presented from the "Arab perspective." It may also be relevant that the alternative, liberal-oriented media specifically aims to publish reports (and use sources) that contradict the mainstream U.S. media, which naturally makes Al-Jazeera an invaluable source for news.

Finally, the relatively small number of "hate" Web sites is a surprising result. This might be because such Web sites focused on Al-Jazeera's perceived "anti-American bias" rather than the re-presentations of its reports. In fact, it can be argued that by re-presenting the reports, hate Web sites acknowledged the de facto importance of Al-Jazeera.

WHAT DID WESTERN INTERNET USERS PRODUCE FROM THE ENGLISH·ALJAZEERA·NET REPORTS?

This section focuses on the representation of the three previously mentioned reports among Internet users. Overall, representations were favorable toward Al-Jazeera on alternative Web sites, mixed on blogs and unaffiliated Web sites, and generally hostile for hate Web sites and Web sites affiliated with the mainstream media. Given the overwhelming number of re-presentations on alternative Web sites, the analysis revealed a slight tendency to embrace english.aljazeera.net as a credible news source.

How are alternative media Web sites — the main groups that used the english.aljazeera.net reports — different to the mainstream media Web sites? First, while the mainstream media seeks to maximize profits or sell advertisers access to a specific audience, the alternative media are often non-profit or free and, thus, can target a broad and nonelite audience. Second, it has been argued powerful social institutions (particularly corporations) control mainstream media that seek to reinforce elite hegemony and hierarchical social relationships (Chomsky, 1997). In contrast, alternative media are structured to "subvert society's defining hierarchical social relationships, and sees itself as part of a project to establish new ways of organizing media and social activity" (Albert, 2003).

Western-based alternative media organizations originated from the recognition that the mainstream media are restricted or controlled by a concentrated number of agents or corporations that hold a similar socio-political ideology. Many alternative news sites certainly have their own agendas, which some clearly declare in their mission statements. For example, the Centre for Research on Globalization (CRG) presents itself as "an independent research and media group of progressive writers, scholars and activists committed to curbing the tide of "globalisation" and "disarming" the New World Order" (http://www.globalresearch.ca/about). Thus, while Al-Jazeera was constantly framed in mainstream media as a "mouthpiece" for Osama bin-Laden, a significant number of liberal-oriented alternative Web sites embraced the Arabic network as a credible news source. A typical example is the following posting from a respondent on Indymedia Vancouver:

> [T}hank god we have al-jazeera and other news media that present an alternative view to the U.S. propaganda machine. Have you not already learned how many lies the U.S. administration and main stream media have fabricated to justify this illegal and atrocious war? Your attempt to justify treating women and children as such only reveals your true racist agenda (Indymedia Vancouver, Nov. 10, 2003, http://vancouver.indymedia.org/ news/2003/11/81153.php).

Similarly, on Indymedia Portland, the respondent "Zach" argued that the Fox News slogan of "fair and balanced" actually fit Al-Jazeera better:

> [L]ast night I listened to the founder and owner of the Aljazeera network speak. He spoke about the shit they get from the United States for showing certain things, but he said he also gets the same shit from every country in the Middle East for reporting 'not so nice things' about them too. Now that's "Fair & Balanced" (Indymedia Portland, Nov. 10, 2003; http://portland.indymedia.org en/2003/11/274602.shtml).

Bloggers often indicated mixed feelings about using Al-Jazeera as a news source. One respondent posted the following message on the Whiskey Bar blog:

> I hesitated to put this link here, because after all it is Al-Jazeera and it could somehow be a fake (although I have found, to my surprise, that one of the best places to get fairly unbiased news lately is their site). Anyway, since TGS and Dongi mentioned the dire possibility, here it goes: *Shocking images shame U.S. forces*. I really don't know what to make of it. You may judge for yourselves (Whiskey Bar blog, Nov. 15, 2003, http://billmon.org/archives/000883.html).

Like many alternative news Web sites, bloggers often noted that english.aljazeera.net reports were not "picked up" by the mainstream U.S. media:

> [N]o wonder the world is hating us. the arab [sic] world is seeing these pictures. and the american [sic] media will never show them (Blog for

America, Nov. 12, 2003, http://www.blogforamerica.com/archives/002241.html).

However, some bloggers concurred with the mainstream perception of Al-Jazeera that is frequently associated with Fox News:

I'm sure this actually does cause international outrage — but consider the source, Americans. This is coming from Al-Jazeera, aka the Bin Laden Network. My guess is the story that goes with these pictures is not the one told in the article (Riz's blog, Nov. 10, 2003, http://www.rizzn.com/2003/11/osint-shocking-images-shame-us-forces.php).

Web sites with no political affiliation were the source of the most heated debates regarding the nature and credibility of english.aljazeera.net, particularly because such forums invite users with less defined or rigid views. On Govteen.com, a non-profit U.S.-based corporation that aims "to provide interactive and engaging educational opportunities for teenagers by teenagers" logged more than 50 posting after its re-presentation of the english.aljazeera.net report on the restraining of Iraqi women and children. This is interesting because the participants are American teenagers whose opinions regarding the war could be significantly shaped by the content of these forums. "Weejoby," the first user to post a message about the article, wrote:

Why did i have to go to aljazeera to find out about this? Can anyone find it on CNN for me? (Govteen.com, Nov. 12, 2003, http://forums.govteen.com/showthread.php?t= 52516&page=1)

Other users supported this perspective. "Cicero17" wrote:

You think they would show this on CNN? Of course they wouldn't; our media is VER[R]Y [sic] biased (Govteen.com, Dec. 4, 2003, http://forums.govteen.com/showthread.php?t= 52516&page=1)

It should be noted that some unaffiliated forums took a distinctly oppositional stance towards Al-Jazeera. On Rantburg.com, a discussion board "dedicated to a civil, well-reasoned discourse," the editors of the Web site deformed the original english.aljazeera.net article by adding "entertaining" side-notes. For example, in response to the photograph of the U.S. soldier frisking the Afghani child, one side-note read: "Get his name! I want him court martialed!" In addition, next to the text recounting the U.S. army's response to the photograph, the side-note reads: "At least the major had the good grace not to burst out laughing in their faces" (Rantburg, Nov. 24, 2003, http://rantburg.com/default.asp?D=10/24/2003&C=Fifth%20Column). This spirit of mockery was clearly present in many of the following 21 'talk-back' postings.

Skeptical perspectives were also republished on some of the unaffiliated forums. On Cruel.com, which offers a "cruel site of the day," "Forum Maniacs" wrote:

> Not the most unbiased of sources I must say so. The pics look genuine, but could have been doctored. There could have been any number of reasons that it occurred, if it has at all. All in all, im gonna take this with a hefty pinch of salt (Cruel.com, Nov. 11, 2003, http://www.cruel.com/discuss/viewTopic.php/60405)

In response, "Please do not feed the troll" wrote:

> Nothing fake about it. Nothing fake about the 500,000 children who died during the boycott. Like CNN is objective, an U.S. propaganda machine (Cruel.com, Nov. 12, 2003, http://www.cruel.com/discuss/viewTopic.php/60405)

The fourth and smallest group (2) was Web sites affiliated with the mainstream media. A reference that was made to the english.aljazeera.net report on the frisking of the Afghani children from Opinionjournal.com — which is the Web site of *The Wall Street Journal's* editorial page — characterizes Al-Jazeera as an unworthy voice. James Taranto called the report a "fascinatingly weird, and rather funny, example of Islamist propaganda." Tarano then purported to "expose" the source for the article as unreliable. He claimed that the spokesman for the Islamic Observation Centre (responsible for releasing the photograph to Al-Jazeera) was "known as the mouthpiece of Al-Qaeda in Britain," and that he had sought asylum in Britain after fleeing Egypt, where he had been convicted and sentenced to death for a bomb attack that killed a 12-year-old girl. Tarano also stated that the author, Yvonne Ridley, was a Muslim convert who made "the extraordinary claim that Western intelligence agencies tried to get her killed to bolster public support for the air strikes on Afghanistan" (Tarano, Opinion Journal, Oct. 23, 2003, http://www.opinionjournal.com/best/?id=110004208).

Hate Web sites comprise the fifth category of Web sites that republished english.aljazeera.net reports. These groups rely on the Internet to present and propagate their hate-based perspective to a worldwide audience of like-minded individuals. How are hate Web sites differentiated from extremist alternative news Web sites? A U.S. Senate Judiciary Committee review of hate Web sites in the late 1990s defined hate messages as messages that "can be interpreted as threatening to some groups [and] may demonstrate a degree of criminal intent" (Currie, 2002). In this study, some of the hate groups that discussed the english.aljazeera.net reports included anti-gay Web sites. The following posting from Thundermonkey (noisyprimate.com, a Web site that identifies itself as a forum for extreme right-wing groups) typifies the perspective towards Al-Jazeera on these sites:

> Listen up you hypocritical motherfuckers. If you savages didn't use any and all methods of employing civilians to wage your jihad maybe our soldiers wouldn't have good reason to frisk 4 year old children. In the mean time while you goat r****s continue to pull stunts like this one don't complain when our troops get a little jumpy doing the dirty work of rebuilding your country, sans fascism. Aljazeera.Net - The all whiney maggots, all the time, channel (Thundermonkey, Oct. 17, 2003, www.noisyprimate.com/ archives/ 000188.html).

This analysis has demonstrated that the more liberal and "alternative" the Web site (alternative news media and blogs), the more they are willing to use english.aljazeera.net reports and the more likely they are to accept Al-Jazeera as a credible news source. In contrast, Web sites related to the mainstream media and hate groups rarely use english.aljazeera.net reports and regard Al-Jazeera as a "mouthpiece" for Osama bin Laden.

IMPLICATIONS OF THE STUDY

This study has found that english.aljazeera.net has become a major source of news for specific types of Western-based Web sites, primarily alternative news Web sites, blogs, and a number of other politically unaffiliated Web sites. Many of the Western Web sites that republished the reports were popular news-hubs for Internet users, and thus have dramatically increased Al-Jazeera's exposure. For example, dailykos.com reportedly attracts about 8 million unique visits a month and won the Forbes "best blog" award; this means that the english.aljazeera.net reports reached a substantial Western audience.

Equally important, the study reveals that while many users took the english.aljazeera.net reports "with a hefty pinch of salt," the general tendency was to accept Al-Jazeera as a credible news source. Moreover, most of the Web sites that republished the reports were loyal to the original published version. This is significant since one study of the representation of Al-Jazeera content in the mainstream media during the War in Iraq found that "Western [mainstream] news outlets use[d] Al-Jazeera as a convenient source of information in the Middle East, but rarely convey its take on any of the stories they use," as well as generally "overlook the Qatari channel's value as a source for news" (Cassara & Lengel, 2003, p. 230).

In addition, while the mainstream media often filtered out Al-Jazeera's original news angle, an identifiable *"transculturation"* process is occurring in the online media. Transculturation occurs when "cultural flows ... interact with other cultural forms, influence each other, and produce new forms" (Lull, 2000, p. 153). Examples of transculturation include the interaction of Rap music with Asian cultures or the influence of Latin music and dance on the work of mainstream Western artists such as Madonna (see Fouz-Hernández & Jarman-Yvens, 2004). By definition, the ongoing process of transculturation contributes to cross-cultural heterogenization and to the establishment of a balance of cultural flows. When the flow originates from the periphery to the core — i.e., from Al-Jazeera to U.S./West — "counter-flow" is established (Sinclair et al., 1995). This counter-flow is a reverse of the traditional one-way information flow from the core to the periphery, which is also known as "media imperialism" (Boyd-Barrett, 1998).

Moreover, the study shows the tendency among Western Internet users to turn to Al-Jazeera's English Web site in order to complete the picture depicted to them by their own mainstream media in order to "put together" a larger picture. Thus, the Internet, I would argue, is taking on an important role in "contextualizing" all media stories that disrupts conventional media "framing" through the wide variety of "voices" and opinions available online. Furthermore, this suggests that, in creating the wider narrative or world picture, the Internet is more important than any other information technology for some people; accordingly, television becomes simply a receptacle of images which are understood through the Internet rather than through the media which channels them.

Finally, the republication of english.aljazeera.net reports break — to some extent — traditional Western conceptions of the East (see Said, 1978). In this respect, a new bond is being formed between english.aljazeera.net and alternative Web sites (and, to a lesser extent, with blogs and unaffiliated Web sites), who are searching for credible alternative news sources due to dissatisfaction with the mainstream media. These Web sites and their audiences have embraced english.aljazeera.net, blurring the borders and traditional divisions between "us" (the West) and "them" (the Other). In fact, some Western Internet users who operate or frequently rely on alternative Web sites have come to view CNN and Fox as "unreliable" (a term which is traditionally affiliated with the "Orient"). For such users, english.aljazeera.net is seen as an ally that shares the goal of fighting the corruption of the mainstream media and, thus, becomes part of the new "coalition of the alternatives."

REFERENCES

Albert, M. (2003 October). What makes alternative media alternative? Toward a federation of alternative media activists and supporters — FAMAS', *Z Magazine*. Retrieved May 29, 2005 from http://www.zmag.org/zmag/articles/albertoct97.htm.

Boyd-Barrett, O. (1977). Media imperialism: Toward an international framework for the analysis of media systems. In J. Curran, M. Gurevitch, & J. Woolacott (Eds.), *Mass communication and society*. London: Arnold

Cassara, C., & Lengel L. (2003). Move over CNN: Al-Jazeera's view of the world takes on the west. In R.D. Berenger, (Ed.) *Global Media Go To War: Role of News and Entertainment Media During the 2003 Iraq war*. Spokane, WA: Marquette Books, pp. 229-34.

Chomsky, N. (1997 June). What makes mainstream media mainstream? From a talk at Z Media Institute. Retrieved May 30, 2005, from www.zmag.org/chomsky/articles/z9710-mainstream-media.html

Currie, D.W. (2002 July). Hatred on the Web: It's not over 'til it's over. *NetNacs.com*. Retrieved May 29, 2005, from http://www.netnacs.com/news/archive/nn-0207.htm

Deacon, D., Pickering, M., Golding, P., & Murdock, G. (1999). *Researching communications*. New York, NY: Oxford University Press, p. 397.

Dube, J. (2003 Sept. 4). Al-Jazeera launches English site. *Pointer Online*. Retrieved May 30, 2005, from http://www.poynteronline.org/dg.lts/id.32/aid.46709/column.htm

Fouz-Hernández, S. & Jarman-Iven, F. (2004) *Madonna's drowned worlds: New approaches to her cultural transformations, 1983—2003*. Aldershot and Burlington VT: Ashgate.

Hine, C. (2000). *Virtual eEthnography*. London, UK and Thousand Oaks, California: Sage.

Lull, J. (2000). *Media, communication, culture : A global approach*. Cambridge: Polity Press.

Michalsky, M., & Preston, A. (2002 Sept. 9). After September 11: TV news and transnational audiences, presented at an international symposium held at the Stanhope Center for Communications Policy research, London England. Retrieved May 30, 2005, from http://www.afterseptember11.tv.

Rainie, L., Fox, S., & Fallows, D. (2003). *The Internet and the Iraqi War: How online Americans have used the Internet to learn war news, understand events, and promote their views.* Washington: Pointer Institute. Retrieved May 30, 2005, from http://www.pewinternet.org/reports

Said, E. (1978). *Orientalism.* New York : Pantheon Books.

Discussion Questions

1. As the title suggests, Al-Jazeera's English Web site exposed the philosophical divide between mainstream media, which on sum, supported the U.S. government's war in Iraq, and alternative media that was opposed not only to the war but in many cases America's mainstream values and beliefs. To what extent did this divide contribute to global anti-Americanism?

2. Why did alternative media, such as Indymedia, find Al-Jazeera more credible than mainstream U.S. newspaper Web sites?

3. What assumptions can you make about the agenda-setting function of media and their perceived reliability by users? Which Web site or sites set the anti-war agenda in this instance, and how effective were they?

4. What about "transculturalization" dialectic? Could Al-Jazeera's English site contribute to a synthesis and create, according to the theory, of a "third culture" with elements of both the West and the Middle East lines of thought? If so, could this result in a "Big Media Effect?"

5. The author calls news Web surfers "skeptic zappers," which means they search various news Web sites for different versions of the same story. Does this constitute an important diversion from traditional news source users? And if so, what is the likely contribution of such a multiple search on schema development within each user?

CHAPTER SIX

OPERATION IRAQI FREEDOM OR INVASION OF IRAQ: ARAB INTERPRETATION OF CNN AND AL-JAZEERA COVERAGE OF THE 2003 IRAQ WAR

INJY GALAL, AMY AHMED AND LAMA AL-HAMMOURI

Before the 2003 invasion of Iraq, it had been argued that if a new Gulf war were to break out in the region, it would be a vastly different media affair than its predecessors. Alternative media, some of it transnational, exploded in the years between the 1991 Desert Storm and the 2003 Operation Iraqi Freedom, including a spate of new Arab-language satellite channels such as Al-Jazeera, the Qatari-based Arab satellite news channel, and their Web sites.

As a result, Arab viewers in 2003 no longer depended on American lenses and words to understand battles fought in their own backyard. At same time, these same viewers still had access to CNN's broadcasts, on which they had been totally dependent during the 1991 war. The international press devoted reams of analysis about the differences in content, framing and agendas of each of these channels.

An article in *Newsweek* summarized the differences when it noted that

> in this war the mighty but merciful allies target bombs carefully and tend to the enemies' wounded. In that war the allies blow up women and babies. In this war, Iraq is postponing certain defeat by cheating, killing civilians and unsuspecting human shields. In that war, a weak nation is steadfastly defending itself using the only effective means available. This war on American television is alternately "the war on Iraq" or "Operation Iraqi Freedom." That war, broadcast by the media of the Arab and Muslim world, is "the invasion" (Alter, 2003, April 7, p. 49).

While concentrating on the differences of two satellite broadcasting giants — both considered as alternative media to the mainstream broadcasters in the countries in which they are viewed — this chapter attempts to understand how Arab audiences interpreted the CNN and Al-Jazeera coverage of the 2003 Gulf War.

INTERPRETATION OF LITERATURE AND SCHEMATIC FRAMEWORKS

There are many theories on how interpretation and perception of media texts work. It has been argued that there are no purely objective "findings" that settle the matter (Chandler, 1995). This study is based on the assumption that meaning is actively created through a dynamic process of interpretation, rather than by passive assimilation. In other words, the meaning exists not in the text but in the reading (Chandler, 1995; Hall, et al., 1980; Hanes, 2000; Hart, 1991).

Interpretation varies so greatly because everyone has varying degrees of interest and prior knowledge of the news (ViAfaf, 2002). The strategy used to make sense of the news is to link the text's information to prior information or schema that we possess. Schemas are the deeply ingrained psychological frameworks that mediate perception, comprehension, interpretation and memory (Chandler 1995). Readers draw upon different repertories of schemata, partly as a result of their cultural background, experience, knowledge and social roles. This highlights the fact that meaning-making is a conceptually driven process that starts with expectations and cultural cues, which are always present (the schema). Berenger (2002) refers to this schema as components of "core opinion frames."

Graber (1988) noted that when watching news there are three main information-processing strategies or types of "schematic thinking" (p.250). First, "relatedness searches" seek out the most relevant schema. This often leads to wrong perceptions if relevant prior knowledge is absent (p.158). Second is "segmentation," which enables the viewer to divide information and integrate it into several schema to find the most relevant (p.160). And last is "checking," which searches and finds the most appropriate schema, and "comes into force when people think out loud testing several possibilities" (p.164).

Most content is written with certain intended meanings or "preferred readings" (Chandler, 1995). Television programming can be subject to three different types of interpretations or readings (Hall, et al., 1980).

First, the dominant "hegemonic," which embraces the intended meaning; second, the "negotiated" reading, which accepts the preferred reading but does not totally embrace it; and third, the "oppositional" reading, which radically opposes the preferred reading. Factors that affect the type of reading include the reader's point of view, the degree of reader involvement, perceived credibility and even gender (Chandler 1995).

In the seminal Liebes & Katz study (1993), schematic frameworks combined with other intervening factors (as discussed above), causing the audience to interpret the text through certain frames or themes. Such frames may be cultural, ideological, political, historical or any other. Berenger (2002) distinguishes between this schematic framework and an individual's ability to selectively perceive information in a peripheral opinion frame of "the world around him within his mental and emotional grasp" (p. 60). This interaction of selective perception and schema can result in widely varied understanding of media messages.

As Hanes (2000) noted, the message has different meanings because the reader decodes it according to his/her world-view and horizons. Hence there is an interaction between the text's construction and the reader's worldview. The reader can only approach the text with his/her own understanding, which is grounded in history. For example, Chandler (1995) describes early experiments by Sir Fredric Bartlett (1932) that showed "how readers employed schemata to interpret stories from an unfamiliar culture in a manner, which made more sense to them." Chandler also points to Richard Anderson (in Singer & Ruddell, 1985, pp. 347-50) as another proponent of framing theory. Anderson conducted cross-cultural experiments in derived meaning from letters about an Indian-American Indian and an American wedding, reflecting the cultural biases affecting meaning by the reader.

METHODS

Two discussion groups were formed. Participants were chosen via a nonprobability convenience sample, which consisted of Egyptian men and women aged 18 to 57. They all belonged to the elite class, had higher education degrees, and came from different walks of life. They were engineers, bankers, teachers or housewives, among other occupations.

A background questionnaire on participants' opinions of CNN and Al-Jazeera, was distributed prior to the discussion group. Participants were then shown a 20-minute recording of either CNN or Al-Jazeera's footage for April 9, 2003, midnight (Cairo time), the day coalition forces entered

Baghdad and toppled Saddam Hussein's statue. Each session lasted about two hours and was led in Arabic by a trained facilitator. The tape was paused several times for discussion, initiated by the facilitator's questions on the participants' opinions and perceptions of what they saw.

Findings

After transcribing the discussion tapes, we validated them against the background questionnaires. The opinions expressed by participants seemed to genuinely voice their interpretations of what they saw. The discussion transcripts were reviewed. Cultural, political, media, and historical frames were identified.

Interpretive Media Frame

One important interpretive frame was the media frame. It was manifest when one member of the focus group viewing Al-Jazeera's coverage said, "The footage gave the impression that this is the Iraqi population, whereas the truth is that these are the few people looting government properties."

Ironically, the voice-over did describe that scene as an "operation in which only a few Iraqi juveniles participated alongside American soldiers." The claim that Iraqis pulled down the statue was made on channels other than Al-Jazeera. Apparently, even though they had all stated they watched Al-Jazeera, the participants were all affected by what they saw and heard on other channels. This might mean that the audience expects what they watch and hear through one medium to be echoed on all others. This is in line with Chandler's (1995) description of conceptual schema, patterns of cognitions already constructed and ready for use and reuse. In this case, a schema was constructed in their minds into which was poured all they received through any medium. They seemed to do so regardless of the content.

An explanation for this might rest in the historical background or schema present in their minds about Egyptian media. During the Nasserite era (The socialist period of the 1950s and 1960s), all media was state-owned and repeated the same government-influenced messages. Even those who did not live during this era had internalized that experience through collective consciousness.

Another sub-frame was evident in their mode of interpretive reading of both channels. While CNN was immediately dismissed as being biased and uncredible, critical thinking was deployed before describing Al-Jazeera as being somewhat credible. Hence, CNN was noncritical oppositional reading, while Al-Jazeera was critical negotiated reading.

Such judgment was obviously based more on where the channel was located rather than what content the channel carried. In CNN's case this was obvious. A participant said the channel possessively referred to American troops as "our" and "we." One of the CNN group participants said "CNN creates a story and expects us to believe it." As for Al-Jazeera, the connection is less direct. As one Al-Jazeera focus group participant said,

> I was confused with the coverage of Al-Jazeera during this war. It was trying to portray itself as an objective channel that is extremely against the United States, but at the same time broadcasting the daily report from the military base in Qatar. America is invading Iraq from American bases in Qatar. This is hilarious.

Once again, the historical schema was being called upon, when all media was state-owned and, thus, reported whatever the government permitted. Egyptian viewers, listeners and readers had only two types of media: government mouthpiece or enemy propaganda. The idea of independent media still has not taken root in their minds.

The idea of propaganda impelled the audience to dismiss much of what politicians said or did. For example, participants in the CNN group described the war as "purely a media war; the two counterparts are [Al-Sahhaf, the Iraqi information minister, and the U.S. spokesman]." Also, a scene showing Saddam touring the streets of Baghdad was dismissed as propaganda. "Any dictator should create this image and propaganda around him," one of them said.

Pulling down Saddam's statue and covering its face first with an American flag then with an old Iraqi flag was also dismissed as a propaganda stunt. A participant in the Al-Jazeera group called it "an American movie," while another from the CNN group described it as a "stunt." They seemed immunized to "propaganda." As one Al-Jazeera participant put it, "It shows the silliness of the Americans. They thought that toppling the statue would symbolize the freedom of Iraq." A participant from the CNN focus group said, "CNN showed the toppling of the statue followed by Rumsfeld's comments about liberation and freedom in Iraq. The channels tried to symbolize in the mind of viewers the end of a dictatorship era and the beginning of freedom."

The idea of government control of local media has converged into the superpowers' control of global media. The audience seemed convinced the U.S. controlled or at least intimidated even Arab channels. As a participant in Al-Jazeera group said,

> I think that the shift happened after the death of their correspondent, Tareq Ayoub. All the media channels changed their coverage and softened their anger against the United States

A participant in the same group said,

> I noticed that none of the reporters covered how the museum and other sites had been robbed. This is history. I can't believe that no one thought of shooting what is happening there. Media people were asked to be blind.

A CNN participant said, "I noticed a huge shift in the Arab media coverage of the war after April 9." Another in the same group said, "I believe that there has been an order from senior officials for these channels to soften the tone they adopt against the United States."

Credibility is a fragile quality that risks being lost upon the slightest mistake. Ironically, if the audience feels a channel has a particular point of view, even if it shares their own, they discredit it immediately. For example: "I noticed that the Al-Jazeera channel had a standpoint against the U.S. and its anchors were really pleased when they hear any statements against the U.S.," said a participant in Al-Jazeera group, who also described the channel as not credible. If the same channel gives conflicting statements, it is discredited. For example, "When the station office in Baghdad was under siege, the CEO of the Qatari station came out and announced that Qatar is supporting the United States and that the people who are surrounding the office are Iraqis not Americans. This was only announced on Reuters and on Al-Jazeera Web site."

The audience was in shock, confusion and uncertainty. They could not accept nor believe that the war had ended so quickly and that the United States had taken over Iraq with minor military opposition. As a CNN group participant put it: "We do not know who are these people and where did they come from." An Al-Jazeera focus group member said, "I felt weird when I saw people ... saluting what happened but at the same time I saw people protesting against invaders. These are two contradictions in the mentality of the same people." A CNN group participant said,

> The media are trying to convince us that Saddam sold the country to Americans. CNN is saying he escaped to North Baghdad. Other media say that he is in Russia or Cuba. It is all guessing. Nothing is definite.

And at the end the media are asserting that he [sold out] his country.

The interpretive media frame illustrates the fact that media in general are not credible in Egypt. Members from both groups explicitly indicated:

"The media in the Arab world is not credible."
"We lost trust in the media during this war. Everybody relies on their own frame of reference and interpretation of the events."
"It might be a fake story. Nobody knows the truth."

This mistrust is so common that Egyptians often reflexively dismiss something as untrue by saying: "That is newspaper talk." Many scholars trace this mistrust of media to the 1967 War with Israel, when the Egyptian press repeatedly reported false victories of the Egyptian army against Israel. The reality was Egypt suffered a humiliating defeat which traumatized the Egyptian public's collective consciousness for nearly two generations.

Interpretive Historical Frame

Egypt had suffered to varying degrees British occupation until 1952. For decades Egyptians struggled against the occupation. This embedded collective memory was often triggered while watching news coverage of the war; sometimes unintentionally, at others intentionally.

According to Stuart Hall (1980), a text or script may be implanted with statements, assumptions and attitudes that trigger certain memories, cognitive associations or address certain schema in respondents. This was often evident in the case of Al-Jazeera channel. For instance, its use of the Arabic word "anew" to refer to foreign presence on Iraqi land was aimed at instigating memories of occupation. Its description of the statue's fall scene — "Even after its fall, its feet remain embedded in Iraqi concrete planted in the heart of Baghdad" — appears to draw upon memories of resistance.

The presence of such historical schema in the participants' minds was obvious from their statements. In fact nothing can explain this frame better than the explicit statement from one of them: "We, as Egyptians, suffered from the occupation for a very long period, and we know for a fact that Americans will not leave Iraq." Another participant said,

I hate Saddam and I hate dictatorship in all its forms, but I don't call in the Americans to take hold of my land. At the end Saddam and his sons will be dead but nobody knows when will the Americans leave.

In light of the Egyptian experience, there is an expectation that any kind of foreign occupation must be met with popular resistance. Since the Iraqi position appeared to contradict this schema, selective perception was employed. In other words, the audience seemed to make excuses for the Iraqi people. For example Al-Jazeera participants said, "It is the shock. People are scared, unbalanced. The natural reaction will appear after a while," and "We can not consider these escaped burglars as the whole Iraqi population." A CNN group participant said, "It is really weird to see the troops just marching into Baghdad without any kind of resistance."

Interpretive Cultural Frame

Egyptians and Iraqis share a common Arab cultural identity, even though a sizable portion of Iraq is populated by non-Arabs. People identify and sympathize with those they feel are similar to them. The audience from the CNN focus group openly admitted: "We, as Arabs, felt sympathy towards Iraqis, and we would love to believe them." Again the issue of Arab identity came up in Al-Jazeera focus group: "If I were not an Arab, I would view the Arab as barbaric."

Another important cultural sub-frame is the Egyptian perception of America and Americans. The audience viewed the United States as an arrogant nation: "All Americans feel the superiority. The rest of the world is less than them." However, some sympathy with the American people was present, as many felt they were conned and misled by their government's leaders. The following was collectively expressed by participants: "I believe that Americans are not dumb. They are just ready to believe the message. Americans are people who have been always in a calm atmosphere. They don't understand the war," and "If this war started two years ago, no American would support it. But they kept on repeating the same message for more than two years and people started to believe in their intentions to eradicate terrorism."

Interpretive Ideological Frame

Conspiracy theory is an important part of the Arab political culture. It came up repeatedly in the audience perceptions. It seems that when the audience is unaware of the complete truth, the truth seems to conflict with existing schema or is just difficult to understand or believe, it is either rejected, repressed, denied or rationalized as a conspiracy by powerful forces.

For instance, CNN group participants commented on Ahmed Chalaby's criticism of the United States, saying, "It is kind of bluffing. Chalaby had to show some disagreement with the Americans to portray himself as a loyal Iraqi citizen who cares for his nation and tries to show sympathy towards his people." A participant from Al-Jazeera focus group described the channel as "a fake channel, part of the American game: deceiving Arabs and creating hatred amongst them."

Gender Interpretive Frame

Gender may play a role in text interpretation. According to Chandler 1995, men and women may understand the texts differently. This was evident in the focus groups, as when participants were asked what they viewed as the biggest loss. Women replied that it was the wounded, maimed and killed children as well as the allegedly looted Baghdad museum artifacts. Men replied that it was the toppling of the statue as well as the economic losses. The comments suggested that women are more concerned about humanitarian and cultural losses, while men are more concerned about materialistic and symbolic losses.

CONCLUSION

The Egyptian audience might have perceived news coverage of the 2003 Iraq War quite differently than might have been intended. Over a generation this audience has built perceptive schema through which they interpret what they see. Years of state-controlled media during the Nasserite socialist era have compelled Egyptians to view all media sources as one and the same. Moreover, Egyptians do not trust independent media outlets because they view all media as either a government mouthpiece or an instrument of propaganda. All this combined to create in their minds an inherent doubt in media credibility. The biggest blow to news media credibility might have come from the 1967 war in which Egyptian media repeatedly lied about the progress of the war. The result today is mistrust of media in general and severe doubt in its credibility. This might partly explain why Al-Jazeera was viewed as only partially credible, primarily because it addresses viewers in their own language.

Decades of foreign occupation and an inherent belief in conspiracy theory have Egyptian audiences suspicious of foreigners and foreign media. This (among other things) might help explain their tendency to media. This (among other things) might help explain their tendency to regard CNN as completely lacking credibility. In other words, it might help shed light on the reason why they interpret CNN as oppositional reading, despite the fact that its content did not differ drastically from that of Al-Jazeera.

However, there is light at the end of the tunnel. In the discussions, Al-Manar South Lebanese Satellite channel was repeatedly referred to as credible. It seems that this channel is being perceived as a preferred reading.

References

Alter, J. (2003, April 7) The other air battle. *Newsweek,* pp.48-49.

Berenger, R.D. (2002) Frame theory and political behavior by candidates, national media and voters in the 2000 primary election. Dissertation Abstractions International. 63(02), 397A. (AAT No. 3042255).

Chandler, D. (1995). The active reader (Selected Lecture Notes UWA) [online] Retrieved January 3, 2004, from http://www.aber.ac.uk/media/Modules/MC10220/active.html

Graber, D. (1988) *Processing the news: how people tame the information tide.* (2nd Ed.) New York: Longman.

Hall, S., Hobson D., Lowe A., & Willis, P. (Eds). (1980). *Culture, media, language.* London: Methuen

Hanes, P. (2000). *The advantages and limitations of a focus on audience in media studies.* Cambridge: MIT Press

Hart, A. (1991). *Understanding the media: A practical guide.* London: Routledge

Liebes T., & Katz. E. (1993). *The export of meaning: Cross-cultural readings.* Dallas. Polity Press.

Singer, H., & Rudell, B. (Eds.) (1985). *Theoretical models and processes of reading* (3rd Ed.) Newark, NJ: International Reading

ViAfaf M. (2002) Interpreting TV news, [online]. Retrieved August 3, 2003, from http://www.aber.ac.uk/media/Sections/interp02.html

Discussion Questions

1. How did media images from the 2003 Iraq War contribute to the formation of individual schema of Arab viewers?
2. Why do attempts at propagandizing a population succeed or fail? What factors contribute to the success or failure of such propaganda efforts?
3. Why do you suppose Al-Manar, a station operated by Hezbollah from South Lebanon and decidedly anti-American, was regarded as most credible by the focus group in this study? What inferences can be drawn

4. Other studies have shown that Al-Jazeera, the Qatar-based satellite channel, is regarded as a local station by Arabs despite reaching 50 million viewers worldwide, the most watched international channel. Do audiences develop a "place or origination bias?" Explain.
5. If women do, in fact, interpret information differently than men, what is the long-term effect of their interpretations, given their gender roles as primary conveyors of culture to their children?

CHAPTER SEVEN

HEROES & VILLAINS IN THE LAND OF THE TWO RIVERS: HOW ALJAZEERA·NET TOLD THE STORY OF THE ANGLO-AMERICAN INVASION OF IRAQ

MUHAMMAD I. AYISH

During the past decade, the Arab World has witnessed sweeping media changes marked by the introduction of satellite television and the World Wide Web. One writer has noted that global political, economic and technological transformations have changed the face of Arab communications, offering individuals and groups unprecedented opportunities for expression outside established official channels (Ayish, 2003). Among other things, the diffusion of Web-based communications in Arab societies has been viewed as a precursor for a new public sphere where individual citizens are empowered to take part in public debates on issues of concern to their communities (Lynch, 2005). As a conference on online journalism in the Arab world concluded, "online communications are likely to define the future of Arab media, especially with the acceleration of media convergence trends in the region" (College of Communication, 2005). It has also been noted that online media are likely to put more pressures on conventional media in the Arab world by virtue of their interactivity, diversity and accessibility. By the end of 2004, Internet diffusion rates in the Arab World were put at 25 million users, or 7.6% of the total population, compared to 50-70% in Western Europe and North America (Wheeler, 2004).

An outcome of Web communications developments in the Arab World is the emergence of online journalism as a defining concept of Internet-based news and public affairs media in the region. Since the historic 1995 launch of the electronic edition of the London-based *Asharqalawsat* Arabic daily, online journalism in the Arab World has come a long way.

Recent surveys show that almost all Arab world daily newspapers and weekly magazines maintain online editions either in PDF or HTML formats to carry news and commentary to audiences mostly on a free-access basis (Sadiq, 2005). Yet, the most remarkable trend in Arab online journalism has been the launch of dedicated news portals with a wide range of interactive and multimedia features. These include *Eilaf, Aljazeera, bbcarabic, cnnarabic*, Middle *East Online, Islamonline* and *Emirates Media Incorporated online.* Unlike the electronic editions of conventional newspapers, these specialized media outlets provide information offerings for exclusive online publishing. They employ permanent and freelance staff and use a range of interactive services and multimedia features in their Web sites.

Although online journalism derives its intrinsic value from its interactivity and multimedia capability, it is the immediacy of reporting the news that contributes to its popularity in a region where accelerating developments have marked public life. Political and military developments associated with the U.S.-led global war on terrorism have generated profound interest among Arab audiences, especially as those developments have come to bear more directly on their lives. Online media are generally unobtrusive, providing periodical news updates with multimedia features, and keep users abreast of ongoing developments. Studies have shown that the frequency of users' access to specific news portals increases in crisis times as a means of gratifying their needs for information about developments impinging on their lives (South, 1999).

Christopher Kelly, an Internet analyst, says that "every time an event like the 7/7 London bombing happens, people are motivated to try the Web" (*Sunday Times*, 2005). When America went to war with Iraq in 2003, CNN's Web site saw a 30% jump in weekly visits. The online edition of *Sunday Times* (2005) noted that "in the immediate aftermath of the July 2005 bombings in London, millions of people went online to seek information, analysis, discussion and witness accounts. Victims sent images snapped with mobile phones straight to the BBC. The government rushed out advice on its Web site dedicated to civil emergencies (www.pfe.gov.uk). None of this would have happened but for New York's tragedy four years ago today and the subsequent war on terror.

This chapter addresses how Aljazeera.net, the online organ of the Qatar-based Al-Jazeera satellite channel, handled the Anglo-American invasion of Iraq in March 2003. Based on an analysis of 170 Arabic news stories carried by Aljazeera.net during the period from March 17 to April 9, 2003, the study investigates how war developments were framed as an act of drama, not only with heroes and villains, but with spectators who demonstrated varied signs of disdain, shock, support, apathy, anguish and/or outrage at the decision to wage such a war. The writer argues in this article that Aljazeera.net, echoing public sentiments on the war, was apparently bracing for a David-and-Goliath confrontation in Iraq between what were described as "Anglo-American invaders" and Iraq. Popular Arab perceptions of the war were drawing on both mythical convictions and political views about an Armageddon-style showdown in the making. The long-awaited "Battle of Baghdad" (that never materialized) was envisioned to be the Armageddon of the 21st century, marking a dramatic plot that was to be resolved in tune with a what was upheld in the Arab world as a historically determined conflict. Aljazeera.net even injected mythical elements into the epic, arguing that "Sandstorms and Friendly fire fight alongside the Iraqis." But as Baghdad fell into the hands of the "invaders without resistance," an air of anti-climax seemed to dominate Aljazeera.net coverage of the conflict. On April 9, 2005, Aljazeera.net's coverage looked bleak and bordering on despair.

STORYTELLING IN ONLINE JOURNALISM

The rise of Web-based media outlets has called into question the viability and relevance of traditional linear and inverted-pyramid styles of news reporting in a new, visually rich, interactive communication environment where the audience itself can participate (Huesca, et al., 1999). While the conventional paradigm governing the relationship between mass media and audience was characterized by minimal audience control over a one-way communication process, the new Web-based communication environment has empowered users to engage in information selection and search from a wide range of multimedia elements converging into a single operational platform. Jonathan Dube (2005), publisher of Online Cyberjournalist.net, comments on this metamorphosis:

> Telling news stories online is exciting and challenging because of all the tools at our disposal. Online journalists must think on multiple levels at once: words, ideas, story structure, design, interactives, audio, video, photos, news judgment. TV is about showing the news. Print is more about telling and explaining. Online is about showing, telling, demonstrating and interacting. It's easy for online journalists, most of whom have been trained in traditional media, to stick to broadcast and print storytelling forms. But that would be a waste. In online journalism you have many more elements to choose from — so

use them. Combine the best of each world: Use print to explain; use multimedia to show; and use interactives to demonstrate and engage.

Paul and Fiebich (2005), who have done extensive research on digital storytelling, identify five elements in this process: *media, action, relationship, context* and *communication.* Media refers to the material(s) used to create the story package that should draw on four considerations: configuration, which is the relationship between media used in the story package; type, which identifies the medium or media used to tell the story; currentness, which indicates synchronous or asynchronous delivery; and time/space, which addresses editing of the content. According to Paul, action in digital stories comes as movement of or within the content, and movement required by the user to access the content.

On the other hand, context is defined as "that which surrounds, and gives meaning to, something else." Multi-nodal communication makes the online environment unique from previous media. While two-way communication allows the user to communicate with the content developer or other users, one-way communication does not allow the user to communicate digitally.

Nonlinearity is an outstanding feature of online news media. While nonlinearity contravenes the inverted-pyramid format in traditional journalism, its main function is to free users from time and space constraints and provides them with freedom of choice in handling different information elements. It draws on the concept of hypertext, which was coined by Theodore Nelson in the 1960s, describing it rather conservatively, as "no-sequential writing — text that branches and allows choices to the reader, best read as an interactive screen." Nelson saw hypertext format as "a series of text chunks connected by links which offer the reader different pathways" (Landow, 1992, 4). Hypertext theorists have pushed conceptual boundaries considerably, arguing that hypermedia turn story telling into a poststructuralist experience by opening previously closed texts (Bolter, 1991). According to Landow, hypertext creates an open-bordered story, a story that blurs "all those boundaries that form the running border of ... what we once thought this word [i.e., media content] could identify, i.e., the supposed end and beginning of a work, the unity of a corpus, the title, the margins, the signatures, the referential realm outside the frame, and so forth" (Landow, 1992, 61).

Another feature of online journalism that bears on Web-based storytelling is interactivity, which allows the audience to "feed on and respond to the past" through the stories themselves (Massey & Levy,

1999), using such capabilities as connecting to searchable archives or personalizing their news feed. Being interactive, online media once again come into head-on collision with the one-way communication model common in traditional media. In an interactive context, audiences also can, and do, interact with other humans, including journalists as well as other readers. Such active audience members are able to easily shape themselves into communities of interest rather than into social units based primarily on physical location that constitute the audiences of traditional mass media. Online journalism audiences can break the bonds of geography in order to both obtain information from and share interests with sources all over the globe (Singer, 1998). However, building avenues for interactivity into the news consumes time and resources, and many journalism sites deliver something closer to the one-way information found in a newspaper or on television (Roscoe, 1999).

In the Arab World, studies on online journalism are still scarce. However, research works presented at a November 2005 conference on online journalism in the Arab world show growing interest in this topic (College of Communication, 2005). Al Arabi (2005), in a survey of 600 online media users in the Riyadh area, noted that a majority of them make frequent visits to Web sites offering a range of information in Arabic, especially in the areas of news and current affairs. Mustafa (2005) observed that university faculty members believe online newspapers are credible sources of information that stand on the same footing as conventional newspapers. He concluded that online and conventional papers are likely to operate in parallel lines while sharing a common portion of readers. In Egypt, Ismael (2005) found positive correlations between the relative importance of online newspapers and the real existence of a critical mass point. He noted that issues of audience fragmentation, communication speed, access, computer literacy and virtual geographical space are major determinants of realizing a critical mass point of online newspaper readers in Egypt.

ALJAZEERA-NET: AN OVERVIEW

Aljazeera.net is the online version of the Qatar-based Aljazeera Satellite Channel (JSC) launched in January 2001 as the first mainstream Arabic news site, offering a range of news and other information to users around the world. In 2002, Aljazeera.net (Arabic) received more than 811 million impressions and 161 million visits, placing it amongst the 50 most visited sites worldwide (Aljazeera.net, 2005).

In September 2004, Aljazeera.net was re-launched with a new more integrated design offering visitors four sources of online information: *News, Knowledge, Channel* and *Business*. The four sites are integrated through a portal that shows the latest and most important content in each site. *News* is an Arabic news site, which offers comprehensive coverage of world affairs and developments. *Knowledge* offers an in-depth view of what goes on beyond the daily flow of news through analysis, research, and comprehensive studies. The *Channel* is Aljazeera's special site. It shows the channel's latest developments and keeps a complete record of what it produces in a huge database that is made available to the audience. *Business* is Aljazeera's electronic marketing tool selling Web services and the channel's various productions (Aljazeera.net., 2005).

Aljazeera.net's upgrade was accompanied by the launch of an English site that offers a versatile content of news and information, but it also aims to be more interactive. The new service defines its mission as to set up a more proactive relationship with our audience, where the audience is not simply a visitor at the other end of the line.

Aljazeera.net, as an extension of Al-Jazeera satellite channel, upholds a professional code of ethics drawing upon the journalistic values of honesty, courage, fairness, balance, independence, credibility and diversity — giving no priority to commercial or political considerations over professional ones (Aljazeera.net, 2005). The code affirms the service's endeavor to get to the truth and declare it in dispatches, programs and news bulletins in a manner that leaves no doubt about its validity and accuracy. It also provides for treating audiences with due respect and for addressing every issue or story with due attention to present a clear, factual and accurate picture, while giving full consideration to the feelings of victims of crime, war, persecution and disaster, their relatives and our viewers, and to individual privacy and public decorum. It also seeks to present diverse points of view and opinions without bias or partiality and to recognize diversity in human societies with all their races, cultures and beliefs and their values and intrinsic individualities.

Like its mother satellite channel, Aljazeera.net has come under fire from different governments for what was perceived to be an inflammatory and sensational reporting of events and issues, especially in crisis times. In August 2004, Aljazeera satellite channel's office in Baghdad was closed down by the interim Iraqi government that accused the news service of providing "a propaganda outlet" for terrorists. On April 2003, American forces killed JSC's correspondent in Baghdad, Tareq Ayoub, as they bombarded the Palestine Hotel area. In September 2001, FBI agents confiscated tapes and equipment at Infocom offices in Dallas, Texas, which hosted Aljazeera.net. In March 2003, Aljazeera.net site was hacked by anonymous pirates, leading to the disruption of services and the decline of the host company to continue its partnership with JSC a few days after the posting of pictures of U.S. troops captured in Iraq. In June 2003, an American Web designer named William Rasin disrupted access to Aljazeera.net by diverting visitors to "Let Freedom Ring" site. The most recent threat of JSC came in November 2005 when the London *Daily Mirror* disclosed that President G. W. Bush was planning to bomb the Qatar-based satellite channel, but was dissuaded from doing so by British Prime Minister Tony Blair.

ANALYSIS

The analysis of 170 Arabic news items carried by Aljazeera.net over 24 days from the declaration of the war (March 17) to the fall of Baghdad (April 9) is presented in three central themes: *villainy; heroism* and *spectatorship.*

The analysis starts with villainy because, according to Aljazeera.net account, the war was launched by "aggressors" in front of a global audience whose reactions to the unfolding drama ranged from outrage to anguish to shock to disdain to submission. The protagonist was Iraq while the antagonist was the President of the United States and his administration, along with the Blair-led British government (rather than the American or British people). This differentiation between antagonist governments and their people was essential for highlighting the anti-peace sentiments harbored by huge portions of American and British people. Aljazeera.net was very keen in fact to align American and British people with the global anti-War camp around the world. Although the analysis showed that U.S.-Anglo sources quantitatively dominated Aljazeera.net's coverage of the war, the author believes that empirical findings are incapable of capturing the full depth of the story. Therefore, this study draws on a qualitative approach to explicate how Aljazeera.net handled the Iraqi story during the invasion and the subsequent fall of Baghdad.

Villainy

In classical works of drama, villains or antagonists are the incarnation of the full evil. They do not exhibit the slightest sign of righteousness, and hence are not expected to work for the good of humanity. They are evil for what they think, say, or do. Their evil nature is indivisible.

When applied to framing the Bush administration in Aljazeera.net., the diabolic representation is so thoroughly conveyed to the extent that the outside observer would find no loopholes in the woven evil image. This evil framing takes place despite the fact that Aljazeera.net's coverage of the war accorded U.S. military and political sources 60% of news statements while Iraqis received no more than 33%. The news profile of the Bush administration as constructed by Aljazeera.net during the invasion of Iraq was that of global superpower with low morality and human empathy, always drawing on military might to subdue other nations regardless of the suffering and anguish inflicted on innocent civilians. Such perception of the Bush administration, in fact, marked global pubic opinion on the eve of the war on Iraq, as evident in UN opposition to military solutions and worldwide demonstrations against the idea of going to war. Iraq never attacked the United States or even threatened to do so. Neither the Iraqi people nor their government participated in the September 11 attacks.

Diminishing Political Morality: In the immediate post 9/11 era, it was widely perceived in the Arab world that the Bush administration was using the horrendous attacks on New York and Washington, D.C. as a pretext for carrying out a conquest of the Islamic world in the name of democratization and political reform. A few months before the invasion, Iraq repeatedly denied possessing weapons of mass destruction and having any connections with Al-Qaeda organization.

When President George W. Bush joined forces with former Spanish Prime Minister Jose Maria Aznar and British Prime Minister Tony Blair to declare war on Iraq in the famous Azores summit on March 17, 2003, the event was framed by Aljazeera.net as an act of belligerency ("war summit" as described by the online service) on the part of three world leaders. The final statement issued by the summit, titled "A Vision for Iraq and the Iraqi People," was viewed as a pretext for taking over an Arab country to use it as a launching pad for further domination of other neighboring countries.

The online news service focused on the summit as a call for war to rid Iraq of its weapons of mass destruction "should Saddam not decide to do it himself," in the words of President Bush. The Spanish Prime Minister was firm in declaring a war on countries "that harbor terrorism, possess weapons of mass destruction, and condone authoritarianism." The three-pronged strategy sponsored by the coalition — fighting terrorism, curbing weapons of mass destruction, and promoting democracy — marked a new phase of conquest that was envisioned to start a chain of deep transformations in the long-dormant Arab-Islamic world. This global agenda was presented by Aljazeera.net as a "recipe for disaster" because it was based on the use of force to achieve political goals.

In the summit, Bush affirmed that the Iraqi people deserve to be free of repression and authoritarianism. Aljazeera.net seemed cognizant of the need to strike a sensitive Arab nerve by noting that the new Bush agenda was conducive to promoting Israeli domination of Arab societies. Aljazeera.net quoted Iraqi foreign minister in Cairo as saying that Israelis were fighting alongside the U.S. forces in Iraq. On March 26, Aljazeera.net used a headline: "Future Ruler of Iraq is a Strong Supporter of Israel." The online news service even quoted the Iranian spiritual leader Ali Khamenie describing the U.S war on Iraq as a "form of a neo-Hitlerism," adding that "the U.S. launched its attack on Iraq with no respect for the most basic human principles, something that turns this war into the dirtiest in history."

Framing the Bush Administration as having low respect for international legitimacy and the peaceful solution of global conflicts was another aspect of the flawed political morality. Aljazeera.net presented U.S. attitudes towards dissenting voices as drawing on pressures and blackmail. President Bush's comment that "you are with us or against us" defined how the United States approached the formation of the international coalition in Iraq. The United States is presented as a "bully" that forces others to conform to its military ideology in the name of fighting international terrorism.

Such policy has not turned potential friends into enemies, but it has generated divisions among traditional U.S. allies like France and Germany. Aljazeera.net highlighted U.S. criticism of France and Germany as they opposed the use of force in Iraq while giving both countries considerable space and video time to express their views on this issue. President Chirac and French officials were allocated good visual space in the stories about the war as voices of reason and peace standing up to the voices of war and insanity. U.S. officials were reporting that more than 15 countries were willing to join the U.S.-led coalition in Iraq while 15 others remained committed to this mission, but officials refrained from publicly announced their positions. When Canada and Mexico refused to support the war in Iraq, former U.S. Secretary of State Collin Powell was very critical.

As the United States launched a worldwide campaign to expel Iraqi diplomats abroad, Aljazeera.net emphasized that several counties like Jordan, Egypt, Yemen, Russia, and France opposed such move. On March 23, Aljazeera.net reported statements by former Iraqi Vice President Taha

Yassin Ramadan criticizing the UN Secretary General Kofi Anan as a tool in the hands of the United States. He accused Anan of being a "State Department employee who did not act according to the spirit upheld by the majority of UN Security Council members."

Hiding Behind Military Supremacy: If the Bush administration lacked the moral foundations appropriate for a global power, then its supremacy on the ground was derived more from its military superiority and firepower. Aljazeera.net seemed keen on describing and presenting images of U.S. fighting equipment as the most advanced around the world. The online service featured complete paragraphs describing the U.S.'s cutting edge in warfare technologies as represented by Cruise missiles, B-52 bombers, aircraft carriers, field combat gear and crystal-clear imaging satellites.

The author has noted over 70 images of different war equipment used in attacks on Iraq with no showing of Iraqi military gear. Even the interactive links were devoted to highlighting superiority of U.S. firepower by providing some details on its arsenal of a wide array of weapons. An implicit assumption here is that the United States was waging this war with an arsenal of weapons of mass destruction rather than with a well-defined moral ideology. Apparently, Aljazeera.net wanted to give the impression that should the United States win the war, it would not be because of the righteousness of its "cause," but because of the destructive power of its war gear. Another important point that needs to be raised here is that Aljazeera.net gave detailed information about U.S. warfare technology perhaps to counter its claims that Iraq had weapons of mass destruction. It was believed that if Iraq had weapons of mass destruction, the United States had far more destructive weaponry unmatched by the Iraqi side.

Images about the war were also used to emphasize the U.S. possession of superior destructive weapons to be used as killing tools in Iraq. In one picture, U.S. soldiers were depicted loading a huge Cruise missile aboard the carrier USS Abraham Lincoln in the Arabian Gulf sea. The missiles were lined up and their huge size reflected their excessive destructive power. Another picture showed U.S. military officers fully engaged in work at the Central Command Center in Seiliya, Qatar, from which military operations in Iraq were commanded. Yet another picture showed British soldiers in the Kuwaiti desert with state-of-the-art combat gear. On March 23, Information Minister Mohamed Sahhaf accompanied media reporters to some sites destroyed by U.S. forces where he noted "that targeting civilian places is evidence that their missiles are not smart but testify to their criminal intentions and acts."

The emphasis on the technological superiority of the U.S.-led coalition forces was apparently meant to underscore two points. First, the United States and its allies were totally dependent on their sophisticated warfare gear rather than on an appealing morality to control another people. This attitude defies the logic of history, which testifies to the failure of coercive technology to achieve human welfare in social, cultural, economic and political spheres. Second, the exaggeration of the U.S. firepower was also meant to prove that even those superior military tools would fail to achieve their assigned military objectives. Hence, Aljazeera.net showed pictures of the assumed downing of a U.S. Army Apache helicopter by an old gun (which later turned to be a fabricated Iraqi story) and of Cruise missiles being shot down by Iraqi soldiers well before they arrived at their destinations. On April 5, Aljazeera.net featured pictures of cluster bombs being loaded into fighter plane with a caption stating that those bombs are prohibited by international law.

Demonizing the Bush Administration: Despite the fact that the Bush Administration's rationale for invading Iraq partly drew on human concerns for Iraqi people living under a dictatorial regime, and despite promises by U.S. officials that the invasion would bring freedom and democracy to Iraq, U.S. troops were never displayed in a humanitarian context. Soldiers were referred to as aggregate masses of regulars affiliated with certain divisions or brigades, fully engaged in fighting operations or in shooting or bombing civilians, loading weapons, carrying out air raids, driving huge tanks or destroying houses, and arresting Iraqi civilians. In cases of U.S. casualties, references were made to those injured in combat as numbers and those captured in the early phase of fighting were viewed as just partners in the invasion. Although the analysis noted that Aljazeera.net devoted over 65% of statement attribution to U.S. military and political sources, those quotations dealt with threats, military operations, and political maneuvering. There was no single statement dealing with humanitarian aspects of the conflict except those praising Iraqi people in their capacity as fighting for liberation from Saddam regime. All U.S. military personnel were shown in bloody combat operations despite the fact that many of them were reported to have offered humanitarian assistance to Iraqis.

The missing human touch on the U.S. side of the war on Iraq was represented by Aljazeera.net through featuring images of women and children maimed or smashed to death as a result of U.S. bombardment. This is perhaps used to repudiate claims about U.S. soldiers welcomed as liberators by Iraqi people. The huge amount of news space and interactive links devoted to the devastation inflicted on Iraqis by the U.S. war machines suggested that Aljazeera.net was trying to counter U.S. claims about Iraqi reconstruction in the post-war era. Over 25% of published pictures were of Iraqi cities immersed in inferno and devastation. There was apparently a message about the use of such weapons of mass destruction against a country that was attacked in the first place on the pretext of owning such weapons. The magnitude of devastation inflicted by the U.S. military on Iraqi cities was featured in Aljazeera.net coverage of the war developments. A good amount of coverage focused on the destruction of Iraqi infrastructure services like water supplies, medical centers and transportation facilities. There were 101 pictures shown during the coverage period of public and private buildings on fire as a result of air raids carried out on Iraqi cities. Fifty-five other pictures posted by Aljazeera.net dealt with civilians injured in the attacks, some of them were shown in miserable conditions with smashed skulls or bullet-rattled bodies. In one story posted on March 23, Aljazeera.net noted in a headline: "50 Iraqi civilians in Basra in British air raids on residential targets."

Heroism

If Aljazeera.net's handling of the Iraqi conflict suggests that the Bush Administration was the Goliath of the 21st century, Iraq was certainly its David. Iraq was much smaller and far less powerful than the United States; yet it was presented as possessing rich moral values, the most outstanding of which is the will to ward off invaders and preserve its political and territorial integrity. While the antagonist was presented as made up of a small political and military junta of conservative rightists and military adventurists, Iraq was presented as total indivisible entity with its political leadership, military commanders and people standing united in the face of the invaders. The concept of heroism was used significantly to define the positions of the Iraqi government and the Iraqi people. Heroism applied to political leaders, military commanders, as well as ordinary citizens. Iraq was framed by Aljazeera.net as a defiant voice in the wilderness of submission, ready to resist the invasion and offer unlimited sacrifices for its cause.

Defiance: Aljazeera.net was eager to highlight the defiant stands of Iraqi government leaders and citizens against U.S. and British threats. The decision taken by Saddam Hussein not to surrender to the Azores ultimatum received widespread coverage in text and visual forms. When Saddam Hussein was given an ultimatum to leave the country, he responded with a threat to fight the "invaders all over the world." Aljazeera.net showed a picture of Saddam chairing a cabinet meeting with a full smile on his face. Another headline read: "Iraqi Leadership Rejects Bush Ultimatum and Saddam Promises Victory for Iraqis." Under this headline, Aljazeera.net posted a two-column picture of Saddam Hussein brandishing a gun in a gesture of defiance. His Foreign Minister Naji Sabri noted that the statement issued by the Azores summit represented "arrogance and aggression," threatening to turn Iraq into "a graveyard for the invaders." In the meantime, Aljazeera.net highlighted statements by former President Saddam Hussein that Iraq would respect the rights of prisoners of war in accordance with the Geneva Conventions.

Aljazeera.net appeared to be intent on keeping its audiences informed that top Iraqi leadership was still surviving the war and leading the fight. On March 24, Aljazeera.net featured Iraqi Deputy Prime Minister Tareq Aziz as saying that Saddam was in control of the situation in Iraq. He denied U.S. reports of controlling Um Qasr, noting that resistance was continuing. On March 25, Saddam was featured urging tribes to resist the invasion as U.S. forces forced their way into Baghdad despite a sandstorm. Aljazeera.net showed Iraqis standing by a downed Apache and an Iraqi woman carrying a machine gun in a gesture of defiance for the invaders. Iraqi TV on March 25 showed footage of Apache crew. On March 30, Saddam said he was certain of defeating invading forces despite the huge devastation they inflicted and the military gains they have achieved. On April 1, Aljazeera.net showed a picture of Saddam meeting with his commanders and his two sons. On April 4, as battles got more fierce, Saddam Hussein met with his top aides and military commanders to review the situation on the ground. He looked quiet after he addressed the nation in two speeches read on his behalf by al Sahhaf. On April 4, Saddam was quoted as promising to fight back and kick the invaders out of Iraq. On April 4, Aljazeera.net quoted Information Minister Mohamed Sahhaf as saying that Iraq vowed to bury invading forces at Saddam airport. It also showed Saddam picture still intact in airport despite U.S. attack on airport. On April 6, Iraqi TV transmitted images of Saddam and his commanders. The next day, Aljazeera.net showed Saddam appearing on TV smiling in military uniform as he met with his sons and commanders with a message that all Iraqis should confront the invaders.

Resistance: Aljazeera.net devoted a good amount of space to news of Iraqi resistance of invading forces, especially in Um Qasr. Many quotes attributed to U.S. and British military commanders of hardships facing the invading forces received outstanding coverage. Also highlighted were news statements affirming Iraqi steadfastness and resistance as evident in the downing of an Apache helicopter by what was termed as an Iraqi farmer using an old gun. The showing of pictures of the downed Apache alongside simple Iraqi farmers was meant to affirm the fact that Iraqi will was stronger than the most sophisticated U.S. weaponry. The site carried news items detailing accounts of fierce battlefields.

Also news of losses on the Coalition side was featured in headlines (16 soldiers killed in Apache fall) to draw attention to the fact that the United States was suffering from this war. Although news was coming from the southern port city of Fao indicating its fall into British hands, Aljazeera.net continued to speak of resistance, drawing on JSC correspondents accompanying the invading troops as well as on statements attributed to Iraqi Defense Minister Sultan Hashem. Also highlighted was a statement by a Pentagon spokesman that U.S. forces were facing sporadic resistance as they advanced to major Iraqi cities. When referring to a statement by Donald Rumsfeld about the surrender of hundreds of Iraqi troops, Aljazeera.net used the word "claimed" rather than "affirmed."

Even when news about the fall of Basra and Naseriya was confirmed, Aljazeera.net was attributing statements to Naji Sabri affirming continued resistance to the invasion for 13 more years and calling for turning Iraq into a graveyard for invaders. In an updated posting on March 23, the headline reported the destruction of 16 U.S. tanks and the deterrence of invading forces near Najaf. Daily news briefings by Mohamed Sahhaf were carried by Aljazeera.net, especially his statement about resistance in different parts of the country. On March 23, three days into the conflict, Aljazeera.net continued to report resistance in Um Qasr, two days after the small port town was declared falling under British control. The online service quoted statements from a British commander who spoke of some form of resistance in the area by civilian persons using light weapons.

The daily press briefings carried by Sahhaf, in addition to statements made by former Iraqi Vice President Taha Yassin Ramadan about capturing U.S. soldiers, were accorded a good amount of space. On that day, Aljazeera.net reported some training marshes carried out by Iraqi soldiers in Tekrit and showed pictures of those soldiers in action. On the same day, the former Iraqi Vice President criticized Arab and Turkish governments for what was perceived as collaboration with the invaders.

On March 24, five days into the war, Aljazeera.net reported resistance continuing in Um Qasr and showed a picture of Saddam Hussein chairing a military meeting. On that day, there was a report of heavy U.S. losses and stiff Iraqi resistance. The spirit of resistance was reinforced as U.S. sources admitted the capture of two marines and the death of 25 others in combat operations across Iraq. John Abizaid told reporters, "Sunday, March 23, was the worst day for American forces." He was critical of Al-Jazeera Television's airing of pictures of U.S. hostages, describing it as "disgusting." On the same day, Aljazeera.net reported that Mosul was under heavy bombardment, quoting official reports denying any evacuation of residents. Aljazeera.net said, "Tens of thousands of residents and Ba'ath party members were roaming the city brandishing guns while Iraqi army units were stationed outside the city." The online service reported more resistance in Naserya in the south, but provided no concrete information on casualties on the American side.

March 24 was indeed a bad day for U.S. forces in their war on Iraq. A sweeping sandstorm, coupled with rejuvenated resistance, contributed to the highest number of casualties among Coalition troops. On that day, Saddam was featured in Aljazeera.net praising the Iraqis for their resistance and promising them victory. In a televised 20-minute speech, Saddam called on the Iraqis to stand up to the challenge and stop the aggression. On the same day, Aljazeera.net reported the downing of an Apache helicopter by a farmer in Naseryyah using a traditional rifle. The downed craft was featured in a wide picture with the farmer standing by its wreckage. On the same day also, Aljazeera.net ran a full story headlined: "Success of Iraqi resistance Raises Iraqi's Ability to Stand up to the Invaders." Under this headline, Aljazeera.net showed a photo of British soldiers lying in the shadow of a tank with a caption: "Exhausted British soldiers take rest near a tank in southern Iraq." The article read:

> As the war on Iraq enters new directions, and with the continuation of the popular and military Iraqi resistance of the invasion in the south and the north, and with the steadfastness of the Iraqi citizens in the face of intensive U.S. air raids, and with the Iraqi army achieving tangible new results, the most outstanding of which is the capture of several marines, the Iraqi citizen's morale has gone up and their spirit of defiance has risen, thus becoming more ready to embrace for the unexpected and the even the worse.

On the same day, another news update about Mosul noted that

> in the meantime, preparations are underway in Mosul to face the American-British invasion by digging ditches. Armed members of

Saddam Fedaeyyn are scattered across the city, threatening to kill Americans if they dare to enter the city. Iraqi citizens in Mosul followed up on the speech delivered by President Saddam Hussein in which he promised to inflict defeat on Americans and achieve victory for Iraqis, and took to the streets in public support for his policies.

Aljazeera.net was giving publicity to U.S. statements about potential hardships in the war to substantiate claims of stiff resistance. It quoted a U.S. field commander expecting a 3,000-casualty loss among invading forces, noting that the United States miscalculated the situation of the conflict. On March 25, a sub-headline ran by Aljazeera.net stated "Gallant Resistance" and the accompanying text noted that stiff Iraqi resistance hampered the advancement of invading forces and kept them from getting into the cities. Aljazeera.net quoted a military spokeswoman that U.S. forces were still unable to control the tiny town of Um Qasr. If Um Qasr was able to keep invaders for few days, then Baghdad would do it for years, it was believed. In an updated news release on March 25, Aljazeera.net featured a picture of Iraqi resistance men in a march of support for President Saddam Hussein. On March 26, Aljazeera.net reported that Shia leaders called on Iraqis to defend their country, running a story headlined: "On the sixth day of the invasion, Iraqi resistance continues and sandstorms fight invaders." On March 26, it was reported that Iraqis in Basra took to the streets to express their support for the leadership of Saddam Hussein.

Although Coalition forces were clearly forcing their way into Baghdad by the end of March, Aljazeera.net was keeping high publicity for resistance in the south. On March 30, the online service reported that U.S. forces fought fierce battles with Iraqi resistance in Naseryaeh, while some shooting and explosions were reported in Um Qasr. On March 30, Aljazeera.net reported a bloody day in Baghdad as resistance forced invaders to change their plans. On March 31, an Iraqi commander denied news he was captured, saying that fighting was raging in Basra. On the same day, British sources backed down on their claims saying the captured solider was of low rank. On April 1, Aljazeera.net reported Iraqi forces engaging in fierce battles with invaders on the Euphrates area as U.S. troops tried to control a bridge in the area to secure their supply lines. On the same day Aljazeera.net also reported that Iraqi tribesmen and Ba'ath members stifled a landing operation by coalition forces in Mosul, adding on April 2 that invading forces face still resistance in Naseryeh and Najaf. Aljazeera.net reporter said, "Iraqi forces near Naserya ambushed a convoy of U.S. Army."

Even as U.S. troops were advancing into Baghdad, Aljazeera.net was speaking of resistance in the tiny town of Um Qasr, which was reported falling on the first two days of the invasion. News of resistance at Najaf, Naweryya, Basra, Mosul and Baghdad Airport continued to feature highly on Aljazeera.net by April 5. On that day, Iraqi Information Minister Mohamed Sahhaf announced the eviction of U.S. forces from Baghdad airport, while U.S. sources said Coalition troops were already in Baghdad.

Sustaining Civilian Casualties: An important component of the heroic profile constructed by Aljazeera.net relates to the immense suffering inflicted on innocent Iraqi civilians by invading forces. The online news service seemed interested in focusing on children with smashed skulls and torn-apart bodies as evidence of U.S. barbarism while at the same time highlighting the human face of the Iraqis as "victims of an inhumane war of aggression on their country." The showing of Iraqi children at a Baghdad orphanage as missiles from sea, land and air rained the city was meant to highlight the ugly face of the war. United Nations' statements about setting up refugee camps for potential Iraqi refugees also received good attention at Aljazeera.net to expose the human cost of the U.S.-led war on Iraq. Some of the children were looking at the photographer with pure innocence and candidness as the specter of a grinding war came closer. Little Iraqi children were also shown at their house, which was "fortified with sand bags" in anticipation of a coming war.

As war broke out on March 20, Aljazeera.net reported warnings of serious civilian casualties as a result of the attacks. It showed a picture of an Iraqi child treated from injuries sustained in an American raid on Baghdad, quoting UN relief workers of an inevitable human catastrophe that would exacerbate humanitarian conditions long deteriorating from 12 years of sanctions. Another picture showed a refugee camp at the Turkish borders. On March 23, Aljazeera.net reported a story about civilian casualties in the war with a headline reading: "Over 80 killed in Basra, Baghdad and the North." The story carried a full image of one of the victims whose skull was smashed beyond recognition in air raids, while another picture below it showed General Tommy Franks discussing military plans with aides in the U.S. Qatar-based Seileya base. On March 23, a picture of civilian casualties was captioned: "Massacre against civilians."

The highlighting of Iraqi victims of U.S. air raids reached its peak on April 2, 2005, with the posting of several heart-breaking pictures showing Iraqi victims of war in maimed and bullet-rattled bodies and smashed skulls. They were ordinary men, women and children with bloody faces, broken abdomens, smashed skulls and broken bones, some of the little children were killed in their mothers' laps. The posted images represented agonizing dying experiences by civilians who had nothing to do with the war. On March 31, a headline noted: "Invasion forces perpetrate a massacre in residential suburbs in Baghdad." Accompany it was a picture of a broken skull. In another picture, a devastated school building was shown with children in the background, while a third showed Iraqi civilians taking shelter in Basra. On April 2, an Iraqi was shown wailing in anguish over the death of his little child. Aljazeera.net reported, "In continuation of the series of massacres, U.S. forces killed seven women and children who were driving in a car close to a checkpoint near Najaf." On April 1, "Aljazeera.net reported a massacre perpetrated by invaders in Najaf."

Spectatorship

The Iraqi battlefield in which the David-Goliath showdown took place was not an isolated local arena, but a global spectacle viewed by the whole world, with its political leaders, governments, and civil institutions and groups. Spectatorship was framed in terms of anger, anguish, disdain, and ambivalence. Spectators included a range of actors, including the Arab League, France and Germany, China, Russia, anti-war movements and anti-U.S. movements around the world.

Aljazeera.net highlighted the Arab League's regret over President Bush's ultimatum to Saddam Hussein to leave the country. Spectators also included members of Blair cabinet who resigned in protest over Britain's intention to join forces with the United States in waging the war in Iraq. The resignation of Robin Cook, Claire Short and other figures received good coverage in Aljazeera.net to highlight a proactive spectator attitude towards the war. The war spectacle also drew negative reactions within the United States, from the While House vicinity, the place where the war was originally conceived, where thousands of anti-war demonstrators gathered and shouted anti-war slogans.

Aljazeera.net devoted a good amount of pictures and video files to Arab world and worldwide demonstrations infuriated by the U.S. war on Iraq. News text, pictures and video files showed huge demonstrators in Jordan, Egypt, Yemen, Sudan and other countries in addition to international demonstrations in Russia, the United States, London and Italy — all condemning the decision to go to war. A fair amount of coverage was allocated to anti-war statements made by French President Jacques Chirac and German Chancellor Gerhard Schroeder. Chirac was quoted as saying that "disrespect for UN legitimacy and the use of force instead of law to resolve problems entails great responsibilities." Schroeder, on the other hand, was quoted by Aljazeera.net as saying that "the waging of war and the killing of thousands of innocent people is unwarranted. Many people around the world share this German position." Russia, China, India and the Vatican also reported similar anti-war statements. When the United Nations decided to evacuate its UNICOM teams from Iraq, Aljazeera.net suggested that such a move "would shed suspicions on the role of the UN as a neutral international organization created to resolve conflicts through peaceful means." A commentary posted in Aljazeera.net said:

> When Kofi Anan submits to the orders of the White House to withdraw UNICOM and relief staff from Iraq to create the appropriate context for a U.S. war on that country despite anti-war sentiments in the Security Council and the General Assembly, is Anan carrying out his assigned job or is he implementing instructions from Washington?

As fighting broke out on March 20, 2003, Aljazeera.net reported worldwide demonstrations against what it called the U.S. war on Iraq. Anti-war demonstrations were reported from Cairo, where several demonstrators were injured in clashes with police. Similar protests were reported from Australia, Indonesia and the United States itself. Aljazeera.net showed a picture of Indonesian demonstrators with a caption: "Thousands of Indonesians Pray for Iraqi Victory in Jakarta demonstrations." In another updated edition of the same story, Aljazeera.net reported more demonstrations in several countries in a story carrying the headline: "Demonstrations of Wrath Sweep Several World Capitals." The story included news of demonstrations in Germany and France. On March 21, a day after the launch of the attacks on Iraq, Aljazeera.net devoted a special photo section to highlight global protests against the war from Cairo, Paris, Washington, D.C., Tokyo, Geneva, Madrid, Ramallah, Seoul, Australia, Karachi and Kashmir. While some demonstrators carried slogans calling for ending the war, others shouted anti-U.S. slogans and burned U.S. and British flags. European Union official calls for keeping the territorial integrity of Iraq were allocated full coverage, featuring a full picture of Jafier Solana talking to journalists about the European position.

In a March 21 posting headlined "An International Day for Condemning the Aggression," Aljazeera.net ran a full story about Arab and international protests against the U.S. war on Iraq, showing pictures of demonstrators in Washington, D.C., New York and Paris carrying anti-U.S. slogans and calling for an end to the conflict. The reporting of anti-War demonstrations in the United States in particular was apparently meant to show that American people are not part of the villains' camp as they hold progressive ideas of peace and co-existence. The story included a statement by one of the self-chained demonstrators in San Francisco as saying: "The world should know that there is an organized opposition, and if this is to take place in every city, martial law would be declared and the war would come to an end."

On the same day, more pictures of demonstrators were shown from Jordan, Egypt and Palestine, and highlighting the bloody nature of the demonstrators showed the intensity of the showdown with security forces. This, again, is a suggestion that while Arab governments were taking an ambivalent position on the invasion of Iraq, the "Arab street" was decisive in its support for Iraq and condemnation of the U.S.-led war. Aljazeera.net even showed demonstrators carrying picture of Saddam Hussein in his military uniform while others were burning U.S. and British flags. In an updated March 22 news story, Aljazeera.net headlined a story: "Demonstrations Show the Depth of Gap Between Arabs and their Regimes." In that item, Aljazeera.net showed pictures of a Yemeni boy who was killed by police during anti-U.S. protests and another in Jordan showing Jordanians stepping on a U.S. flag in protest against the war on Iraq. On March 23, Aljazeera.net reported a statement by Arab League Secretary General Amr Mousa describing the U.S. war on Iraq as "an act of aggression that was likely to have serious repercussions for neighboring countries."

On March 23 and 24, Aljazeera.net came back to highlight the anger in the Arab street by reporting about more demonstrations in several Arab countries, especially Egypt and Jordan. The protests were marred by clashes with security forces that left some casualties. On March 25, Arab League head Amr Mousa was quoted as "praising Iraqi resistance of the invasion noting that Iraqi steadfastness has changed expectations about the war." On March 27, Aljazeera.net ran an interview with a former Egyptian defense official about Egypt not blocking U.S. military ships from using Suez Canal to reinforce the invasion. It was such an embarrassing interview for Egypt as the largest Arab country. On March 27 Aljazeera.net reported calls by the Mufti of Syria to carry out suicidal attacks on U.S. forces. Some of the spectators were military experts like Brigadier Mustafa Maher who was presented as a strategic expert. He commented on March 30 on the potential fall of Baghdad by saying:

Should Baghdad fall, it would be only through the use infantry divisions who would have to gain ground, neighborhood after neighborhood, and house after house, Baghdad will not collapse easily. The Iraqi forces are ready to receive them at the Baghdad borders. Regular Iraqi forces have not been engaged in the battle yet. What the (invaders) have seen are only militias and Fedayee Saddam and gallant tribal forces. The battle in Baghdad will be waged from house to house and from room to room. ... Iraq has a strong and well-trained army with deep experiences in warfare. Iraqi commanders are known for their wisdom and shrewdness and the ability to handle things with utmost efficiency.

DISCUSSION

The overall conclusions drawn from the quantitative aspects of the coverage suggest that Aljazeera.net was following a balanced approach to major actors in the Iraqi story. Since the war was launched by the United States, it was natural to see a considerable number of statements attributed to U.S. and British politicians and military commanders engaged in combat operations. On the other hand, Aljazeera.net was cognizant of the need to provide fair access to its Web site for former Iraqi government actors, including Saddam Hussein, Mohamed Al Sahhaf and other officials. The same balance was noted in reference to the use of online video clips and related links. This suggests that, from a professional point of view, Aljazeera.net was honoring its proclaimed vision of providing the "opinion and the other opinion."

Yet, from a qualitative perspective, this quantitative balance could be of less significance, since what matters are not the volumes of statements reported, but rather the quality of context provided for each actor. Hence, this author argues that it was more insightful to investigate the qualitative aspects of the coverage to gain an insight into how this online news service addressed the Anglo-American war on Iraqi. The main premise on which qualitative analysis draws is that the story of the war in Iraq was initially envisioned by Aljazeera.net as a David-Goliath confrontation before it turned into a painful tragedy as Baghdad caved in to invading forces.

For many observers, Aljazeera.net's coverage of the 2003 war in Iraq carried more than storytelling attributes; it was rather the epitome of a classical Greek-genre epic with tragic proportions. Iraq was portrayed as the physical arena of a bloody conflict sparked off by the evil intentions of a global power to subdue another nation long exhausted by ruthless sanctions. The epic began on March 17, not in Iraq or Washington, D. C., but in the Azores where the "Global Empire" made clear its intentions to conquer another country with disregard for international law and legitimacy. In the epic, the antagonist was omnipotent with far-reaching power to keep all nations lined up in its march to Iraq, sparing no hesitance in applying its huge power to ensure the minutest conformity. Among other things, this war mongerism has turned other nations into helpless spectators witnessing the appliance of the Empire's version of skewed justice on the last "surviving stronghold of Arab pride and unity. "At the onset of the conflict, Aljazeera.net was apparently embracing for a David-Goliath confrontation, but the sudden fall of Baghdad on April 8, 2004 seemed to have generated a mass-mediated version of a Greek-style tragedy. An air of anti-climax dominated the last-day coverage of the war events.

What was envisioned to be an Armageddon-style showdown in which Iraq, the David of the 21st century, was to defeat the U.S. invaders, the Goliath of the 21st century, turned into a nightmarish tragedy of agonizing proportions. Aljazeera.net, of course, was mirroring dominant Arab world sentiments on the whole issue of the Anglo-American invasion. That was exactly what Fox News and other U.S. television networks were doing in America during the war. Public perceptions of the showdown and the ensuing war were drawing on realistic as well as mythical interpretations of the conflict. Many people in the Arab world thought of the war as an epitome of the long-awaited Armageddon and Iraq was certainly to emerge as winner.

Because Aljazeera Satellite Channel, the mother organization of Aljazeera.net, was established to offer an Arab perspective of global and regional issues to counter Western views on Arabs and Islam, it was natural to see the online service more aligned with mainstream public sentiments on the war in Iraq. On the eve of the conflict, public opinion polls in the area revealed growing political stagnation in the Arab World induced primarily by unjust and biased U.S. policies. What is needed, however, is that the online service should have demonstrated more professionalism than sensationalism and patriotism in its handling of this issue.

REFERENCES

Al Arabi, O. (2005). Online journalism credibility among Saudi youth: A survey of Internet users in Riyadh area. Paper presented at the conference on Online Journalism in the Arab World, University of Sharjah, Nov. 22-23.

Aljazeera.net (2005). http://www.aljazeera.net.

Ayish, M. (2003). *Arab World television in the age of globalization*. Hamburg: Center for Middle Eastern Studies.

Bolter, J. D. (1991). *Writing space: The computer, hypertext and the history of writing*. Hillsdale, NJ: Lawrence Erlbaum Associates

College of Communication (2005). Conference on Online Journalism in the Arab World: Realities and Challenges. University of Sharjah, Nov. 22-23.

Dube, J. (2005). Online storytelling forms. [online] at http://www.cyberjournalist.net/ news/ 000117.php.

Huesca, R., et al. (1999). Inverted pyramids versus hypertexts: A qualitative study of readers' responses to competing narrative forms. Paper presented to the Association for Education in Journalism and Mass Communication, March 30.

Ismael, W. (2005). Exposure to online newspapers and audience fragmentation in Egypt. Paper presented at the conference on Online Journalism in the Arab World, University of Sharjah, Nov. 22-23.

Landow, G. P. (1992). *Hypertext: The convergence of contemporary critical theory and technology*. Baltimore: The Johns Hopkins University Press.

Massey, B. L., & Levy, M. R. (1999). Interactivity, online journalism and English-language Web newspapers in Asia. *Journalism & Mass Communication Quarterly*, 76 (1): 138-151.

Mustafa, S. (2005). The exposure to the e-newspapers and the printed newspapers: A field study on a sample of the Arab faculty members in the University of Sharjah. Paper presented at the conference on Online Journalism in the Arab World, University of Sharjah, Nov. 22-23.

Paul, N., & Fiebich, C. (2005). The elements of digital storytelling. A project of the University of Minnesota School of Journalism and Mass Communication's Institute for New Media Studies and The Media Center.

Sunday Times (Sept. 11, 2005). "How they Triggered War on the Web," at: http://www.timesonline.co.uk/article/0,,2103-1774033,00.html

Sadiq, A. (2005). Conventional and new applications in Arab online journalism. Paper presented at the International Conference on Online Journalism in the Arab World, University of Sharjah, Nov. 22-23.

Roscoe, T. (1999). The construction of the World Wide Web audience. *Media, Culture & Society*, 21 (5): 673-684.

South, J. (1999, June 11). Web staffs urge the print side to think ahead. *Online Journalism Review*. Available online at <http://ojr.usc.edu>.

Singer, J. B. (1998). Online journalists: Foundations for research into their changing roles. *Journal of Computer-Mediated Communication* 4 (1). Accessed March 28, 2002).online at: http://www.ascusc.org/jcmc/vol4/issue1/singer.html.

Wheeler, D. (2004). The Internet in the Arab World: Digital divides and cultural connections. Royal Institute for Interfaith Studies, London. Downloaded from: http://www.riifs.org/guest/lecture_text/Internet_n_arabworld_all_txt.htm

DISCUSSION QUESTIONS

1. To what extent did Al-Jazeera's online war coverage support or digress from the Social Responsibility model professed by Western journalism organizations?

2. How would American-based international media respond in their news coverage if America had been invaded by a powerful military from another country and culture? Would coverage have differed from Al-Jazeera's?

3. Who was the intended audience for the Al-Jazeera Web site and the underlying reason the site approached war coverage the way it did?

4. Do you agree or disagree with the writer's analysis of how Al-Jazeera "framed the war" for Arab and Western audiences, and what do you think are the lasting effects of those frames in the Arab World?

5. After reading this chapter, how would you assess the performance of Aljazeera.net during the Iraq War?

Part II

The Convergent Medias' Power to Mobilize

CHAPTER EIGHT

A PASSION FOR PEACE AND JUSTICE: INDYMEDIA, THE GLOBAL VOICE FROM BELOW

CARLOS FONTES

Throughout history international alternative media have sought to produce different content from mainstream media, create democratic processes of communication, and contribute to the development of a democratic society by being the voice of progressive civic groups, grassroots organizations and social movements. While alternative media have had palpable impacts at local levels (i.e., to educate, inform and activate small groups and communities around specific issues), they have been unable to reach general audiences or create a democratic system of mass communication open to the participation of large numbers of people.

The failure to develop such a global system can be traced to a large number of problems amply discussed in the literature: funding, difficulty training large numbers of people in media production, the professionalization of media activists who end up abandoning their causes, poor articulation between media activists and social activists, access to appropriate media technologies, and the perceived need of some media activists to produce programs aesthetically similar to those of mainstream media, a goal not usually achieved by grassroots producers.

This chapter describes the democratic characteristics, functioning and organization of Indymedia, (www.Indymedia.org), a coalition of Independent Media Centers (IMCs) located in cyber and geographical spaces that emerged in 1999 in the context of the Seattle protests against the Word Trade Organization (see Nogueira, 2002). I argue that the development of Indymedia in the run-up and prosecution of the 2003 Iraq War and its aftermath has moved the alternative media movement from the local sphere to a mass scale of development. I also argue that Indymedia's coverage of the peace movement and the war is the latest evidence that the network is the voice of the global movement against corporate globalization and that it poses a challenge to mainstream media and institutionalized powers.

ALTERNATIVE MEDIA

The history of alternative media can be traced to many historical events, including the use of the printing press to publish the Bible in vernacular languages during Reformation, the dissemination of pornographic publications ridiculing the nobility in the time leading up to the French Revolution, the array of pamphlets, fliers and newspapers that fermented the American revolution, the political posters and murals sprouting in Europe in the 19th century and used in full during the Chinese revolution, the workers' photography movement in Germany, and the songs chronicling the early years of the labor movement in the United States (Downing, 2001). Electronic media technologies since the early 1960s also fueled the development of the alternative media, enabling a growing number of marginalized people throughout the world to express themselves, document their struggles, and educate and organize their communities. From urban centers to small rural towns, media activists working in conjunction with a wide variety of citizen groups have altered social relations at a local level, forged democratic channels of communication based on access, participation and self-empowerment, and created local, national, and international alternative media organizations (Fontes, 1996).

This vigorous media activism is reflected in a relatively young but lively scholarly literature characterized by the continuous introduction of terms such as guerrilla video, pirate TV, tactical media, advocacy video, community media, process video, video product, participatory media, popular video, radical media, citizens' media and, of course, alternative media. This array of terms, often used interchangeably and without agreed-upon meanings, emphasize different aspects of alternative media — process of production vs. final product, citizens participation in media production vs. need to create "quality" media, focus on community vs. a wider social project — and betrays the difficulty that scholars have had theorizing the panoply of alternative media practices, its goals, strategies and impact on diverse sociopolitical contexts.

Addressing this issue, Rodriguez (2001) noted that alternative media theorists tend to fall into two main groups. The first group defines alternative media from a macro social perspective and focuses on its capacity for counter-information in a struggle with the mainstream for the hearts and minds of citizenry (Schechter, 1991), and its role in building a counter-hegemonic project of society. Spa (1979), for example, affirmed that it would be possible for video activists from grassroots organizations to replace the communicational power of the state and big economic groups, while Getino (1985) argued that alternative media had to be conceptualized by its role in an "historical political project of development" (p.34). By all historical accounts, alternative media have fallen short of these all encompassing goals, and because of that have been the subject of pessimistic assessments and severe criticisms. Echoing a theme first introduced by Matta (1983), Roncagliolo (1991) affirmed that:

> The word "alternative" is a dangerous one. It can easily become a synonym for poor quality, or — just as easily — for marginal: the efforts of a few tiny groups that have no effect on the great battles for control of the communications media…the so-called alternative to the extent that it is marginal and of poor quality, is not really alternative at all and is of no interest or importance. (p. 206)

The second group of theorists, in which Rodriguez includes herself, finds the binary oppositions of alternative versus mainstream media of limited theoretical utility. Instead they argue that alternative media practices help to change subjectivities and everyday social relations in micro social settings, and that the impact of alternative media can be detected cumulatively over time in the strengthening of grassroots organizations and the struggles of local communities. Addressing this issue, Downing (2001) asserts that alternative media build grassroots solidarities and contribute to social "eddies and ferments" in a "slow burn" fashion, and that sometimes they simply "keep alive the vision of what might be, for a time in history when it might actually be feasible" (p.9).

Defending the concept of citizens' media, Rodriguez (2001) argues similarly that the term:

> Implies first that a collectivity is *enacting* its citizenship by actively intervening and transforming the established mediascape; second, that these media are contesting social codes, legitimized identities, and institutionalized social relations; and third, that these communication practices are empowering the community involved, to the point where these transformations and changes are possible (p. 20).

While it is ultimately unproductive to examine alternative media solely in relation to their capacity to effect major social changes and challenge, reform or replace mainstream media, the refusal to draw distinctions between alternative media and mainstream media guts alternative media theory of analytical power and excuses it from developing prospective understandings of a different media landscape connected with a new project of society. Instead of viewing alternative media from either a micro or a macro perspective, I conceptualize it as a broad spectrum of practices that take place at the levels of small group settings, communities, specific public spheres, popular culture and mass diffusion. Despite the wide heterogeneity of practices and the various levels and contexts in which these practices take place, alternative media can be defined by a set of common goals and principles: focus on process, access to technology, participation in media production, democratic social relations and decision-making, diffusion of information neglected by mainstream media, constitution of communities and public spheres and an oppositional stance to oppressive power structures. This framework, outlined in the next few pages, allows us to understand Indymedia as an example of global alternative media.

PROCESS, PRODUCT AND PARTICIPATION

One the most enduring dualistic arguments about the use of media in small settings is whether it is more important for participants to focus on programming or to focus on the process of media production. The proponents of *process* as the most important aspect of alternative media activism believe that engagement with media — through writing, acquisition of technical skills, editing, or presenting a piece for public consumption — requires individuals and groups to discuss their social conditions (Kawaja, 1994), step into new roles, redefine their identities (Rodriguez, 1994), and organize for action around a particular issue (Protz, 1991). The focus on process characteristic of alternative media is also operative at a mass level in the Indymedia network in its symbiotic relationship with the multifaceted global movement for peace and justice.

A large number of alternative media theorists (Stuart, 1989; Tomaselli, 1989) have consistently emphasized that community members should have direct access to media technologies and participate in media production because this "allows people to speak for themselves" (Stuart & Bery, 1996, p.199). For some authors and activists working with small grassroots groups, participation is defined comprehensively as:

a process wherein people themselves control not only the media decision-making process and the content of the media productions, but also the means of production and the resulting media materials (Protz, 1991, p. 32).

People's participation in media production is important because it is the building block of media democracy and the democratic organization of any media system. Participation requires social relations around media use based on dialogue, shared power and democratic decision-making. In the case of Indymedia, this principle of participation has been put in practice through open publishing software architecture and a democratic stance that allows anyone to post news on Indymedia Web sites. The intricacies of this process will be discussed later. In reality not everyone will want or will be able to participate in all or any of the aspects of media production Protz outlined.

Nevertheless, it is fair to expect that any alternative media enterprise pursuing social justice, democracy and progressive social change at whatever level would be organized in a congruent way and strive — within its own context and preserving its own identity — to maximize the participation and shared control of any willing citizen. In this sense, I would argue that along with progressive content, the adherence to participation is the fundamental distinction between alternative and mainstream media.

COMMUNITY MEDIA

The analysis of alternative media in community settings reveals that alternative media are often used to constitute a community. Communities are often thought of as stable geographical entities devoid of competing views or internal strife. These assumptions seem to be the basis for the way in which a number of authors view community media as the voice of a community (Burnett, 1996), a source of needed information (Downing, 2001), an empowering tool of social struggle and a "small scale form of public communication within a neighborhood, village town or suburb" Hollander and Stappers (1992, p. 19). Different assumptions about the nature of communities lead us to recognize another less obvious role of alternative media.

Downplaying the geographical factor, some theorists have conceptualized communities as imagined entities (Anderson, 1983), held together by interrelated individuals (Mouffe, 1991) who have agreements regarding collective action (Melucci, 1989). A community, then, is an entity that is permanently being built on the basis of shared interests, cultural elements, and ways of interpreting the world (Dahlgren, 1995).

This perspective highlights the fact that community media often do not take place in established communities but, rather, are a means for the development of the dialogues, relationships and common identities that form the basis of a community. This constitutive role of alternative media is not limited to small communities but also takes place with larger groups of people. In his study of *e-zines*, Duncombe (1997) demonstrated that *e-zines* function as clubhouses for geographically isolated people and as maps for an underground bohemian scene geographically dispersed throughout the United States. Similarly, Atton (2002), in his study of alternative media and the environmental movement in England, found that the environmental press reflected the organizational structure of the environmental movement, "involved individuals and groups in reflexive practice" and "empowered activists in their communities of resistance" (p. 102). The analysis of the use of media at a community level shows that one of the functions of alternative media is to strengthen and develop small and large communities into an oppositional stance to oppressive power.

ADVOCACY VIDEO

If we shift the analysis to the level of the public sphere, it becomes clear that alternative media are also often used to construct a public sphere and project a community onto that public sphere. Nothing could be more illustrative of the power of advocacy video than Web sites that carried videos of beheadings and pleas for their lives from foreigners kidnaped by insurgents in Iraq.

The international conference of advocacy video organized by the Benton Foundation in Washington, D.C., in 1993 showed that alternative media practices are often part of a broader campaign with pre-defined goals and strategies. In the wake of identity politics, various authors (Fraser, 1993; Robbins, 1993; Dahlgren, 1995) argued that the public sphere is not a singular universal space of public dialogue but an arena fractured by power and constituted by different social groups in a multiplicity of spaces. Alternative media are also used to constitute specific public spheres that enable a community to give visibility to its interests and achieve its goals. Alternative media is used to create public spheres by forging dialogue and a Web of connections between people in different social locations, evidence that alternative media are not simply a means of communication within and between predisposed audiences of grassroots organizations and social movements (Kaplun, 1983), but that they also reach beyond these boundaries to constitute their own audiences.

POPULAR MEDIA AND POPULAR CULTURE

Alternative media are also a form of cultural production, influenced by grassroots culture and social dynamics and also by the wider terrain of popular culture. The placement of alternative media in the cultural terrain allows us to see that alternative media uses ideas, aesthetics, modes of production and technologies of the mainstream, but that it also affects mainstream media over time in diffuse ways.

The term *popular* as in *video popular* and *radio popular* has been widely used in the alternative media literature in Spanish and Portuguese and has been translated into English as *grassroots* or *popular media, video, radio* etc. Used in this context these terms have carried ideas of authenticity and purity, and the assumption that alternative media are a folk cultural production sealed off from the mass and pop cultures produced by the cultural industries. This assumption could not be farther from the truth.

As Latin American cultural theorists García Canclini (1995) and Martín-Barbero (1993) persuasively argued, grassroots cultures and pop cultures undergo a constant series of transactions and interpenetrations with mainstream culture, albeit in an unequal relation of forces. Cultural analysts have provided plenty of examples of the way underground and marginal cultures function as a source of new ideas and aesthetics for the mainstream, which then packages them without their original resistive dimension and sells them in the marketplace. We have only to think of images of Che and Mao in the market place, the overuse of the word revolution, the shaky video aesthetics of MTV adopted from video art and independent documentary or the degeneration of much hip-hop into misogyny, to detect this dynamic.

This process is also clearly visible in the interaction between culture jammers and advertisers. The culture jamming movement, whose flagship publication is the magazine *Adbusters*, undermines corporate values and discourses through the use of corporate aesthetics logos and key signs but change their meaning by setting them in a new critical context. An example is the use of the Nike logo and its accompanying caption *Just Do It* placed over a picture of a sweatshop with children workers. However, in turn, as Jordan (2002) reports, Nike has also used culture-jamming techniques by making fake jams of its own previous ads. In the concrete case of Indymedia, the transactions with the mainstream can be seen in the intermittent use of news and reporting styles originated in the mainstream media, and also in the use of Indymedia as a source of information for the mainstream. According to Kidd (2002):

Since the Seattle experience, the corporate media have used the IMC as a source of information at every new anti-globalization encounter, from Washington to Prague and from Quebec City to Genoa (p. 79)

Theorists have also consistently pointed out in various studies (Willis, 1977; Hebdige, 1979; Barbero 1993; Canclini 1995, Duncombe 1997) that alternative culture is both a form of resistance and of adaptation to hegemony. On one hand, alternative culture provides a mode of expression for subaltern classes, transitorily autonomous spaces for social interaction and mappings of a world yet to exist, but on the other, alternative culture can also sap resistive energy by allowing people to resolve real social issues in a symbolic imaginary way. As Duncombe (1997) argues, making a *zine* can be a stepping-stone towards political activism, but it is not the same thing.

The participatory nature and the focus on democratic process characteristic of alternative media provide additional means for proactive resistance. An example is TV Viva's-a Brazilian street television-production of a program about contraception and women's liberation that was shown in installments in public squares. True to the processes of hybridization inevitable in alternative media, TV Viva appropriated the format, the codes and the narrative structure of the telenovela but then created a program against patriarchy that was shown in the public square. This showing was followed, right then and there, with a public discussion that challenged the prevalent norms of machismo. Participants in Indymedia may certainly feel that they are doing their activist part by producing alternative news content, but their participation is also a form of activism because it contributes to the existence of a radically democratic form of social organization.

The interpenetrations between alternative media and mainstream media have impeded a number of authors from drawing clear distinctions between these two areas. Despite their overlaps and exchanges, alternative media and mainstream media are driven by very different social, political, and above all organizational logics that need to be explicated. Let us just say that it is difficult to imagine a time when mainstream media, whether corporate- or state-controlled, could be open to popular participation and consistently represent the range of views of the world seen from the perspective of the many voices from below. This is the mission of Indymedia and of other alternative media outlets at this historical time. As former Representative Cynthia McKinney pointed out in a speech given on July 31, 2003, at the Abyssinian Baptist Church in Harlem, about the difficulty of placing anti-Bush administration ads on mainstream media in the United States:

> At the top of the ad is a cartoon. It features the big corporate media being "played" from behind the curtain by the great big, huge, Wizard. Like in the Wizard of Oz. But there, ever so small, at the bottom of the cartoon, is Toto, the little dog, pulling open the curtain and exposing the truth about the big, corporate media-kinda like BAI does here. And the alternative media do all over our country. Well, in the cartoon, Toto is the alternative media — getting the truth out to the people (From Global Network Against Weapons & Nuclear Power in Space, http://www.space4peace.org).

INDYMEDIA: SOCIAL AND POLITICAL LINEAGES

In real life, Toto is no longer an insignificant factor but has now the potential to reach people at national and global levels with the development of Indymedia. The idea of alternative mass media has been an oxymoron in the alternative media literature. In the past, theorists have had a hard time imagining a democratic alternative mass medium, partly because alternative media have been conceptualized as local and small scale, and before the Internet's emergence there was no technological infrastructure that supported them. The other related obstacle to conceptualizing an alternative mass medium was of a social nature. Despite their ideological allegiance to democratic processes, many in the previous generations of media activists did not seem to have committed themselves heart and soul to collaboration, consensus decision-making and the creation of open decentralized forms of socio-media organization.

The antecedents of Indymedia include the Liberation News Service, which provided news to the alternative press during the Vietnam war, an alternative media center organized in Chicago in 1996 to cover the Democratic convention (Stockwell, personal communication, 2003), the community radio and public access TV movements, the e-zine movement with its emphasis on openness of content and do-it-yourself ethic (Meikle, 2002), and also Deep Dish TV, which is the first alternative media organization to distribute programming over the satellite. Starting in 1986,

Deep Dish solicited videos on specific social issues from video producers throughout the United States, compiled them into programs and broadcasted them two hours a week on a rented transponder to more than 200 U.S. community access stations. According to Cynthia Lopez (personal communication, 1994), program coordinator in the mid 1990s, Deep Dish also helped create links between local grassroots organizations and video producers, publicized and coordinated the local distribution of programs and organized audiences around the issues being broadcast.

Indymedia was also preceded by 30 years of sustained organizing work that resulted in the creation of alternative media organizations such as Videoazimut, the Video Olympiads, Zebra Network, Alternative Media Asia, the Next Five Minutes (N5M) — to name a few. Through their ebbs and flows, these organizations tried to share resources and organize alternative media activism at local national, regional and global levels (Fontes, 1996). Even though these organizations succeeded in creating alternative news and distributing their programs over large geographical areas, the social, political, intellectual and technological conditions for the creation of a radically democratic alternative mass medium were not yet present. The advent of the Internet, the influence of the Do-It-Yourself (DIY) punk ethic, the eruption of geek and hacker cultures producing open free source codes, as well as the emergence of a vigorous anti-corporate global movement guided by anarchist principles, finally provided the right confluence of forces to enable the emergence of Indymedia as the first de facto alternative mass medium.

In fact, Indymedia's maxim is: "Don't hate the media, become the media." That lesson was not lost on a host of Middle East Web sites during the buildup and wake of the 2003 Iraq War.

INDYMEDIA: AN OVERVIEW

The first Independent Media Center in Seattle was set up from scratch in a donated space in just a few days by local "techies" who, in turn, were supported by Rob Glaser, a former Microsoft executive who contributed technical expertise and the latest streaming technologies (Kidd, 2003), and also online by Mathew Arnison in Australia. Arnison, along with Gabrielle Kuipper, created Active, the open code software used to set up the first Indymedia site and many other subsequent sites.

By Nov. 30, 1999, the Indymedia site was getting a million hits, more than CNN, because their coverage was showing the rubber bullets on the streets when the mainstream media reported the official line that no such bullets were being used (Stockwell, personal communication, 2003). Since then, the number of IMCs have grown rapidly and unexpectedly throughout the world — 119 at the time of this writing — in close connection with the protest movement for peace and against corporate globalization. One of these sites (www.Indymedia.org) is the global site of the Indymedia network and features articles originated from IMC centers throughout the network. While the largest concentration of IMCs is in the United States and Europe, there are a significant number of IMCs in Latin America, Africa, the Middle East, Asia and the Pacific region.

Each IMC functions autonomously with its own level of organization and connection with local entities, but all IMCs are connected through Web links, a philosophy of solidarity and a set of shared Principles of Unity featuring nonhierarchical relationships, democratic decision making, inclusion, open access and participation in the production of content. Each center is staffed by volunteer grassroots reporters — and technicians wherever know-how exists — who provide the news and maintain the digital infrastructure of each center and of the network as a whole. IMCs with a critical number of activists are usually organized in subgroups for each medium or function such as video, print or techs. Each of these subgroups may has its own listservs, hold meetings, and participate in the larger meetings and listservs of the whole network (Halleck 2002). Some IMCs have their own physical meeting space, while others share space with kindred organizations, while still others, like the Western Mass IMC to which I belong, meet wherever it is possible.

Each IMC site has variations in color, types of banners and local style but, with a few exceptions, they all share a common structure that includes the IMC logo, a newswire on the right-hand column constituted by self-published articles and a link to a self-publishing page supporting print, audio, photo and video files, a center section of news features selected from the newswire postings by volunteer editors, and a left or bottom column with links to all other IMCs in the network as well as links to archived material, discussion lists and other backstage areas of the Indymedia process. Many sites also have sections or links to a calendar page publicizing local events. A few IMCs also have their own hard copy newspapers, wall postings and radio programs.

Since its inception in 1999 the IMC network has been part of a larger collaborative Web with akin alternative media organizations that exchange programming resources and technical expertise. During its first days in Seattle, IMC produced videos were shown over the satellite by Deep Dish TV and Free Speech TV, while Web radio programs were retransmitted on many low power and community radio stations (Halleck, 2002). This collaboration has taken different forms over time:

> In some places Indymedia has fostered the emergence of other alternative media while in other communities it became part of an already established Web of alternative radio and newspapers (Stockwell, personal communication, 2003)

This synergy is an important factor in the development of the alternative media movement, because it may contain the seeds of a loose decentralized macro alternative media network.

INDYMEDIA: THE ALTERNATIVE MASS MEDIUM

Indymedia is more than the sum of its parts. It is not just a collection of connected independent media centers, but rather a global network organized in a democratic and participatory fashion. Let us then analyze the configuration and the democratic features of the Indymedia network.

The Indymedia network is expressed both socially and technologically. It is constituted as an all-channel open network in which every node/center is able to communicate directly and autonomously with any other node in the network. Each node/center is itself a smaller network of people connected through face-to-face meetings, and also through listservs and Internet Relay Chats (IRC) — real time text based discussion rooms in cyberspace. Some IMCs, like Brazil IMC and Italy IMC, are constituted by smaller independent groups of IMC activists located throughout the country, who post on a common Web site. Some IMCs also form loose regional associations such as those from Europe, Latin America and the Southern Cone. The hardware infrastructure of the network is composed by a number of computer servers, each hosting a number of IMC sites. IMC activists are trying to train more technical people and increase the number of servers to further decentralize the infrastructure.

The network is also bonded by a set of shared Principles of Unity (http://docs.Indymedia.org/view/Global/PrinciplesOfUnity) that was adopted in 2001 and required to be subscribed by all new centers seeking to be part of the network. These principles set forth a common vision based on equality, social diversity, decentralization, local autonomy, open publishing and access to information, use of open source code, democratic process and consensus decision making and being not-for-profit. The whole network is coordinated by a dense but decentralized communication process that includes between 500 and 600 active listservs addressing a large numbers of issues, projects, common interests and subgroups within the network. About a million messages exchanged weekly across the network, with 10 or more IRC chat rooms open at any given time bringing together people from throughout the network as well as exchanges of resources and technical expertise between the south and the north, exchanges between sister IMC centers and 22 Global Working Groups at the time of this writing (e.g. video, audio, IMC process, tech, finance, database, translation etc.).

Social relations based on trust, solidarity, inclusion and open process also hold the network together:

> The commitment to function in a democratic way is part of the ideological ethic and the very fabric of Indymedia. Ideologically, Indymedia is about open process, democratic process, collective and consultative process. But is more than an ideological commitment. It is also a commitment that is felt deep down. People do feel that way and respond viscerally to any attempts to redirect from that democratic process. This is the reality factor that keeps the network healthy (Norman Stockwell, personal communication, 2003).

The democratic organization of the whole Indymedia network is anchored on the articulation between local IMC centers and global working groups (groups working on issues affecting the whole network) through agile and effective processes of decision making that maintain shared control of the network at the local level.

The democratic organization of Indymedia is also put into effect through transparency, open publishing, the use of open free source code, autonomy of each collective, organic development of the democratic process, shared resources and the use of multiple languages. All of the decisions, documents, e-mail discussion and work proceedings developed throughout the network are archived and open to anybody with access to the Internet. Given that information is power, this degree of transparency enables and invites anybody to participate on an equal footing in any area of the network. Anyone can publish video, audio, photo or text on the newswire section of any Indymedia center, but not all of the postings get the same treatment by Indymedia activists. Each center has a group of volunteer editors (anybody who is a regular member of an IMC can be an editor for that site) who review postings to the newswire on a regular basis and choose some to be featured in the center column. Every center also has its own editorial policy; with varying levels of elaboration-to guide the procedure for hiding or deleting offensive material such as child pornography or Nazi propaganda. One of the current debates in the network is precisely about the limits of open publishing and whether this principle allows the deletion of any posting.

The democratic functioning of Indymedia extends to the nature of its software. Whenever possible, Indymedia activists use open and free source code software, because it can be designed collaboratively, used freely, and tailored to serve the particular needs of each center. Unlike proprietary software, open code allows multiple autonomous expressions through its various versions. Besides the requirement to abide by the Principles of Unity, each IMC collective is an autonomous entity that can organize and link up with any other organization as it sees fit. Local autonomy is a crucial principle of democratic functioning because it maintains decision making at a local level and contradicts any movement towards centralization of the network.

The democratic organization of Indymedia is not pre-established by a number of "brains" but emerges organically from the concrete needs, situations and interactions of the participants. This is exemplified in the development of the principles of unity. Up until 2000 new IMCs approached the global tech group in order to become part of the network because the tech group had the expertise to make that happen on a technical level. Realizing that their decisions were affecting the network as a whole, the tech group stopped adding collectives to the network and asked the Indymedia community to create a set of guidelines to direct their own development. This process culminated in the development of the principles of unity.

Indymedia is guided by a sharing ethic that is translated in the allocation of money to centers with the most difficult access to resources, the free exchange of technical expertise. Resource sharing is a fundamental tenet of democracy. Indymedia activists discuss openly the fact that asymmetric resources can lead to asymmetric relations of power between those who have most and those who have less within the network. Thus, they engage in the process of resource sharing with an explicit awareness and determination to avoid reproducing colonial relationships.

Even though English is the dominant language, Indymedia is making an effort to function in a multilingual environment. This is plain in the existence of the translation working group, the translation of important documents in several languages, the posting of news on the global site in several languages-although the featured articles are mostly in English-and the simultaneous translation of IRC meetings into the languages of those attending them. These efforts runs counter to the hegemony of the English language on the planet and reveal a commitment on the part of activists to function democratically at the various levels of the network.

This does not mean that Indymedia is a perfect system. It continues to face the challenges of decentralizing its infrastructure and protecting it from right-wing hacker attacks, resolving the tension between the principle of open publishing and the political will to be a means for the expression of progressive voices from below, of developing an ever more supple articulation between local autonomy and global decision making and coordination, of minimizing concentrations of power in those activists with the biggest social capital and knowledge base, and of diffusing the central positions of the United States, the northern hemisphere and the English language in the network. Despite these challenges, Indymedia is at present the most sophisticated example of an alternative mass medium functioning in a participatory democratically coordinated network.

INDYMEDIA: VOICES FROM BELOW

Alongside being the first alternative mass medium, the Indymedia network is a significant historical development because it is also articulated with the global movement for peace and justice and against corporate globalization. This articulation is visible in the participation of many Indymedia activists in organizations composing the global movement, in the similar modes of social organization — both Indymedia and the global movement organizations tend to reach decisions through consensus and are organized as decentralized networks of autonomous groups with shifting links and configurations — and in Indymedia's coverage of the Iraq War.

To be precise Indymedia covered not just the war but also the context of the war. An analysis of the coverage on the global site-archived at http://www.indymedia.org/archive/features/current shows that, taken as a whole, Indymedia's articles provided a contextualized analysis of the motivations for the war from national and international perspectives, drew connections between the war, imperialism, oil and corporate globalization, highlighted the idea of continuous war, criticized mainstream media coverage, and above all accompanied closely the development of the global peace movement. One could say that Indymedia's coverage of the war started on Jan. 14, 2002, with an article titled "Enron, 'Big Oil' and the New World Order" which pointed to "the capture of the white house by big oil" in a "time of war" and the emergence of a new international order. This article was followed by another on Feb. 23 that denounced the rise in the government's propaganda effort to link Iraq with terrorism, and explained that an expanded war on terrorism would bring an eventual "friendly government" in Iraq and a boon for the multinational oil and gas corporations well represented in the government. On March 19, 2002, Indymedia published an article asserting that mainstream media was continuing to produce questionable news and commentary on a "war against terror" and that the FCC was paving the way for a new wave of mega media mergers.

The coverage of the peace movement started on March 11, 2002, when Indymedia reported that on the six-month anniversary of the attacks on the Twin Towers, New Yorkers were gathering on Union Square to mourn the victims of the attacks and ask the Bush Administration — which had killed 3,000 people in its invasion of Afghanistan — to stop the spread of "infinite war on the world." Another article of April 20, 2002, on the first peace march in Washington reported that the protesters "linked the struggle for self-determination to resistance against global capitalism and the U.S.-led 'war on terror' that now extends around the planet from Colombia to West Africa, to Afghanistan, to the Philippines." It is clear from the examples above that Indymedia reported the first noticeable peace activities and set them in the wider context of globalization. On April 14, 2002, Indymedia announced that after months of discussion throughout the network and unanimous decision the global site had been restructured to automatically include news featured by local IMCs. This architectural change enabled a more agile inclusion and accessibility of international perspectives on the global site and contributed to the ensuing representation of the multiple voices of the global peace movement on their own terms.

As the peace movement grew and succeeding protests against neo-liberal policies and corporate globalization increased throughout the world, Indymedia systematically covered the wide span of events and drew a lucid picture of the new geostrategic world order and the growing resistance against it. In an article published on Sept. 23, 2002 — titled "Global Justice Movement Gears Up for D.C." — Indymedia reflected on the "expansion in both breath and depth" of the global justice movement over the previous year in the United States and abroad, drew a connection between authoritarian international economic policies and the war on terrorism, and urged the global justice movement to "fuse a strong anti-war message with its criticism of corporate globalization." This article and the fact that such fusion did indeed occur illustrate the articulation between Indymedia and the global justice and peace movement.

The coverage of the peace movement was marked by reports of large events like the half million people who demonstrated in London on Sept. 28, 2002, but also of smaller actions like citizens weapons inspections at army bases in the Netherlands or protests at the Pine Gap U.S. base in Australia. Each Indymedia report typically included — and still does — hot links to related articles posted on local centers throughout the world. This type of coverage reflected the breath and the depth of the movement.

CONCLUSION

Indymedia has been criticized for biased reporting in favor of the global movement for peace and justice. This criticism is disingenuous because overlooks the fact that all reporting has built-in biases. Unlike the barely concealed bias of the mainstream, Indymedia's bias is open, honest and explicit. Indymedia's coverage also has the unique merit of not being skewed by profit or economic interests and of allowing a multiplicity of voices from below to speak for themselves.

REFERENCES

Anderson, B. (1991). *Imagined communities: Reflections on the origin and spread of nationalism.* New York: Verso

Atton, C. (2002). *Alternative Media.* Thousand Oaks: Sage.

Barbero, J. M. (1983). Comunicación popular y los modelos transnacionales. *Chasqui, 8,* Octubre-Diciembre, 4-11.

Burnett, R. (1996). 'Voice of the voiceless' and other well known clichés. *Zebra News, 27* April 10-12.

Canclini, N. G. (1995). *Hybrid cultures: Strategies for entering and leaving modernity.* Minneapolis: University of Minnesota.

Dahlgren, P. (1995). *Television and the public sphere: Citizenship, democracy and the media.* Thousand Oaks: Sage

Downing, J. (2001). *Radical Media and Rebellious Social Movements .* Thousand Oaks, CA: Sage Publications.

Duncombe, S. (1997). *Zines and the politics of alternative culture.* New York: Verso.

Fontes, C. I. (1996). Alternative video at a crossroads: Towards a strategy of extended participation. UMI Dissertation Abstracts.

Fraser, N. (1993). Rethinking the public sphere: A contribution to the critique of actually existing democracy. In B. Robins (Ed.) *The phantom public sphere* (pp1-32). Minneapolis and London: University of Minnesota Press.

Getino, O. (1985). La importancia del video en el desarollo nacional. In J. Tello (Ed.). *Video, cultural nacional y subdesarollo* (pp. 23-35). Mexico City: Filmoteca de la ONAM.

Halleck, D. (2002). *Hand-held visions: The impossible possibilities of community media.* New York: Fordham University.

Hebidige, D. (1979). *Subculture: The meaning of style.* New York: Methuen.

Herman, S., & McChesney, R. (1997). *The global media: The new missionaries of global capitalism*. London: Cassell.

Hollander, E., & Stappers, J. (1992). Community media and community communication. In N. Jankowski, O. Prehn, & J. Stappers (Eds.), *The people's voice: Local radio and television in Europe* (pp. 7-15). London: John Libbey.

Jordan, T. (2002). *Activism! Direct action, hacktivism, and the future of society.* London: Reaktion Books.

Kaplun, M. (1983). Comunicación popular, alternativa valida?. *Chasqui*, 7, Julio-Septiembre, 40-43.

Kawaja, J. (1994). Process video: Self-reference and social change. In P. Riano (Ed.), *Women in grassroots communication* (pp.131-148). Thousand Oaks, CA: Sage.

Kidd, D. (2002). Indymedia.org: The development of the communications commons. *Democratic Communiqué, 18*, 65-86.

Kidd, D. (2003). Indymedia.org: A new communications commons. In M. McCaughey & M. D. Ayers (Eds). *Cyberactivism* (pp. 47-69). New York: Routledge.

Matta, F.R. (1983) Comunicación Alternativa: Respuesta de compromiso político. In F.R. Matta *Comunicación alternativa y busquedas democraticas*

Martín-Barbero, J. (1993). *Communication, culture and hegemony: From the media to mediations.* Thousand Oaks, CA: Sage.

Meikle, G. (2002). *Future active: Media activism and the Internet.* New York: Rutledge.

Melucci, A. (1989). *Nomads of the present: Social movements and individual needs in contemporary society.* Philadelphia: Temple University Press.

Mouffe, C. (1991). Democratic citizenship and the political community. In Miami Theory Collective (Eds.) *Community at loose ends.* (pp.70-82). Minneapolis and Oxford: University of Minnesota Press.

Nogueira, A. (2002). The birth and promise the Indymedia revolution. In B. Shepard, & R. Hayduk (Eds.). *From Act-up to the WTO* (pp. 290-297). New York: Verso.

Protz, M. (1991) Distinguishing between "alternative" and "participatory" models of video production. In N. Thede, & A. Ambrosi (Eds.), *Video the changing world* (pp. 31-39). Montreal: Black Rose Books.

Robins, B. (1993). Introduction: The public as a phantom. In B. Robins (Ed.) *The phantom public sphere* (pp. 1-32). Minneapolis and London: University of Minnesota Press

Rodríguez, C. (1994). A process of identity deconstruction: Latin American women producing video stories. In P. Riano (Ed.), *Women in grassroots communication* (pp. 149-160). Thousand Oaks, CA: Sage.

Rodriguez, C. (2001). *Fissures in the Mediascape.* Hampton Press: Cresskilll, New Jersey

Roncagliolo, R. (1991). The growth of the audiovisual imagescape in Latin America. In N. Thede, & A. Ambrosi (Eds.), *Video the changing world* (pp. 22-30). Black Rose Books: Montreal

Schechter, D. (1991). The globalvision experience. In N. Thede, & A. Ambrosi (Eds.), *Video the changing world* (pp. 110-116). Montreal: Black Rose Books.

Spa, M. (1979). El trabajo teórico y la alternatives a los "mass media". In J. Vidal-Beneyto (Ed). *Alternativas populares a las comunicaciones de masas* (pp. 63-82). Madrid: Centro de investigaciones sociológicas.

Stuart, S. & Bery R., (1996). Powerful Grass-roots Women Communicators: Participatory Video in Bangladesh. In Servaes, J., Jacobson, T. & White, T. *Participatory Communication for Social Change* (pp.197-212). Thousand Oaks CA: Sage

Stuart, S. (1989). Access to media: Placing video in the hands of the people. *Media Development*, 36(4), 8-11.

Tomaselli, K. (1989). Transferring video skills to the community: The problem of power. *Media development*, 36(4), 11-15.

Willis, P. (1977). *Learning to labor: How working class kids get working class jobs*. New York: Columbia University Press.

DISCUSSION QUESTIONS

1. Why did Indymedia grow from a protest organization focused on a single topic to a far-reaching social movement, albeit essentially a virtual one?
2. Why do you think an organization like Indymedia has a predominant left-leaning and socialist predilection? What, if anything, does this tell us about mainstream media?
3. To what extent do you agree or disagree with the author's assertion that Indymedia empowers the powerless?
4. How does or does not Indymedia follow a "Revolutionary Concept" of the press? Explain what happens to "revolutionary media" once it's goals have been achieved.
5. Could Indymedia have achieved its global reach by means other than the Internet? Explain.

Chapter Nine

Connecting the Local and the Global During War: A Case Study of the St. Louis Independent Media Center

Lisa Brooten

Saint Louis is asleep, everybody. Quietly lulled into a comfort zone through geographical isolation and historical backwash, the windows to the outside world have been painted shut. There are those who are wired through the underground networks, though. We need a source of independent thought and information here. Those of us working together on this project can aid in disseminating these amazing ideas through the Web, in the Confluence *newspaper and in the streets. Then, this sleeping giant will stand with the other rogues on the frontlines of love and revolution.* —From "a little more about us" on the St Louis Independent Media Center Web site

March 9, 2003

This evening was my first visit to the St Louis Independent Media Center at 3026 Cherokee Street, a place they call "CAMP," short for the Community Arts and Media Project. This building, which houses the IMC and a handful of other activist groups, is a large, three-story building in South St. Louis.

Arriving a bit early for the evening's meeting, I walked into the entrance to the building (one of three facing the street) that seemed the most lit and active — at the far left of the building. The room was rather chaotic, with a line of several computers that didn't look too set up sitting on tables along one wall. There was stuff all over — furniture, boxes, pieces of wood and various building materials, assorted odds and ends, and stacks of the alternative newspaper, *Confluence*. Two men looked up at me curiously as I entered and somewhat hesitantly returned my "hello." When I asked if this was where I'd find the IMC, they said that this was the building, but that the meeting would be held in an upstairs room, which the younger guy said was his "place." He introduced himself — "Andy" — and offered to show me where the meeting would be. We went back outside, and he led me to the next door and up a set of stairs.

The stairway walls were covered in brightly painted designs of purple, blue, pink and green. At the top of the stairs, Andy opened a door to the left, which led into a room with walls painted in bright reds, greens and oranges. A circular table sat in the middle of the room, with many mismatched chairs gathered around it — many covered in splatters of paint. Some looked like dentist chairs. It turns out they are from the old hair salon once housed in the ground-floor room I'd first walked into, the one Andy told me will eventually house the St. Louis IMC newsroom.

INTRODUCTION TO THE ST. LOUIS IMC

During that first meeting, which marked my introduction to the St Louis Independent Media Center (StLIMC), it became clear that while the group's members were concerned with the imminent war, they were at least equally concerned with events locally. They discussed at that meeting the preponderance of anti-war features on their Web site (www.stlimc.org), and how this was potentially detrimental, pursued at the expense of locally focused or more motivating news. They also discussed the features they would be working on in the coming weeks, including an anti-war rally planned for the end of the month.

They were concerned about the Patriot Act, and how people deemed by the government to be members of terrorist groups could possibly be stripped of their citizenship rights, become stateless, and then be subjected to the same vulnerabilities as those who have already been arrested and are being held on charges of terrorism. One person pointed out that there were already some activist groups that had been identified as terrorist organizations by the government, with the implication that IMC could meet the same fate. They discussed locally based corporations, such as Monsanto and Boeing, and their culpability for global problems, including the war.

Yet, even as they discussed the possibility of war and the resultant political climate, they also planned a feature about a rally against police brutality in St Louis, and someone who I learned later was a founding member of the StLIMC summarized a central goal of the group: to help bring the city of St Louis together, especially in the area of race relations.

What became clear during my subsequent visits to the St. Louis IMC and my research on the global IMC network of alternative media collectives is that the activists involved are especially concerned with demonstrating how the situation at the local level, from the day-to-day actions and choices of individuals to the operations of locally based businesses, are linked in important ways with the global maneuvers of governments and multinational corporations, including the war in Iraq. While this is perhaps most obvious in the repression against anti-war dissent at the local level, the IMC also brings the local-global connection into the neighborhoods where people live, through both its reporting by the network's local chapters and through its global Web page (www.indymedia.org).

By detailing the experiences of a specific local chapter of the Independent Media Center within the larger context of the global IMC network, this research answers calls to explore the connections between anti-war and globalization protesters (Fisher et al., 2005) and, in doing so, to better understand the relationship between the local and the global online. This research, which draws on data obtained through participant observation of the StLIMC, interviews with StLIMC members, and examination of StLIMCWeb content during the war, demonstrates how corporate media representations of war are challenged by the IMC through protest and beyond protest, forcing people to recognize the connections between global realities and their local communities. The StLIMC demonstrates how the distinction between local and global is spurious, and how the most effective way to fight for global justice is to begin in one's own backyard. This local-to-global analysis characteristic of Indymedia reporting remains virtually invisible in corporate media news.

THE IMC: CONNECTING THE VIRTUAL AND THE VISCERAL WORLDS

Despite philosophical musings on war as an unreal event in cyberspace, the real-world experiences of the war and responses to it by anti-war protesters around the world made the use of the Internet by activists a reaction to visceral, lived realities as well as a cyber experience. The newest communication technologies became means of showcasing connections between and expressing outrage against what anti-war protesters were seeing and experiencing, not only from the U.S. government in its global maneuvers but also from local police authorities in repressive reactions against dissent and from their locally based companies in contributing to the war. Police overreactions to dissent in St. Louis, for example, brought home to the predominantly white StLIMC activists the realities African-Americans have faced in their city for years, and reinforced further the connections these activists had already been making between aggressive actions locally and globally. The IMC challenges the role of the corporate media in forming public understandings and opinions of these events.

The IMC, or Indymedia, emerged during the protests against the World Trade Organization (WTO) in Seattle in late 1999 to provide alternatives to the information found in corporate media, which rarely provide adequate context about social movements and their goals for audiences to understand the complex issues involved (Ackerman, 2000; Gamson and Wolfsfeld, 1993; Gitlin, 1980; Giuffo, 2001; McLeod and Hertog, 1999; van Zoonen, 1992). The network has grown quickly since then, with more than 200 chapters throughout the world, in Europe, North America, Latin America, Asia, and Africa. The IMC challenges mainstream journalistic practices, blurring the boundaries between producers and audiences, by urging people to "be the media," and providing an open-publishing platform where anyone can contribute (Brooten, 2004a, 2004b).

The network has no central governing body, operating as a decentralized network of collectives committed to the nonhierarchical, nonsexist, and nonracist practices found in its Principles of Unity. The IMC operates using consensus-based processes of decision making. Local IMC editorial groups draw many of the features posted to their local Indymedia homepage from writings posted to the open-publishing newswire generally found in a column to the right of feature stories on local sites. These local features then feed into a global newswire from which an international editorial group working online draws the features found on the global feature page (www.indymedia.org).

The IMC network has experienced a pattern of suppression since its founding and has worked to show the connections between the actions of police, paramilitary, and military groups at the local and global levels. The IMC has faced harassment, arrests of its journalists, legal challenges, and confiscation of its materials and tools (Morris, 2004). The network's increased visibility has made it a target of not only hate mail and spammers, but also national and international security agencies such as the

FBI (Kidd, 2003a, 2003b). Several IMC sites have been shut down, and others systematically hacked (Kidd, 2003a). In October 2004, the U.S. Justice Department, reportedly working with the Swiss and Italian authorities, seized Indymedia's hard drives from the network's Web hosting company, shutting down about 20 of the then more than 130 IMC Web sites. The drives were returned on October 13, but "the particular legal framework under which the seizures took place is unknown" and Indymedia has no confirmation of who ordered the seizures, who took the servers and why, or whether it might happen again ("International Outcry," 2004).

It did happen again, this time in June 2005, when police seized the Bristol Indymedia's server in an attempt to identify someone who had posted a message to the open publishing newswire. Since September 11, 2001, there have also been attempts to identify the more radical elements of the global justice movement as terrorists (Morris, 2004). In response to these moves, a central theme of Indymedia reporting is the connection between military maneuvers globally, including the Iraq War, and the suppression of dissent locally, both in police response to protest actions and through attempts to intimidate Indymedia participants.

But the connections made between local and global events are not all negative, and IMC chapters have often emerged from already existent networks of activists who have been working to identify how, as the global justice movement puts it, "another world is possible." Their efforts include the building of global solidarity between local groups. The IMC network is itself a powerful tool for connecting like-minded people, serving as a connection point and often a place to stay for activists who travel to protest actions or to network among other activists. This movement of people is a powerful means of globally connecting local places, and such physical realities demonstrate that the IMC is much more than a Web site.

Rather than conceptualizing the Independent Media Center (IMC) as a "macro" public sphere that enables debate and discussion between geographically dispersed participants in opposition to a "micro" public sphere that is more local in nature (Haas, 2004; Keane, 1995), the IMC must be more broadly understood as working to incorporate local sites and experiences into its transnational work. As such, the IMC is a tool in the effort of people around the world to demonstrate how local events affect and are affected by what happens globally. Although literature about Internetworked Social Movements (ISMs), such as the IMC, suggest that their methods developed as a direct result of the Internet (see Langman, 2005), in many cases these methods were embedded in already existent local struggles. Research has demonstrated how uses of new information technologies are socially constructed rather than embedded in the technologies themselves (Castells, 1996), so that the "technology in use and the social world are not seen as separate—they coconstitute each other" (Kling, 2000, 220). The incorporation of nonhierarchical and radically democratic values throughout the IMC network is a result of activist practices that preceded the Internet.

In addition, as Castells (1997) suggests, resistance networks of social movements are a reaction against the "deterritorialization" of control and command characteristic of the globalized capitalism made possible through the new information technologies. For the StLIMC, this resistance is accomplished through an insistence that people attend to the local manifestations — what happens in actual places to actual people — of this deterritorialization. In radically internationalizing the issues in their own backyard (Atton, 2003), members of the StLIMC also maintain that the alternatives to global problems must begin with one's own life and community.

FOUNDING THE ST. LOUIS IMC

From its inception, the StLIMC features and public events have pointed out connections between global and local events, and patterns of aggression, exploitation and repression around the world. This was obvious with the first story with which the StLIMC went online in April 2001 — an account of the Midwest convergence in Kansas City to protest the drafting of the Free Trade Area of the Americas (FTAA) at the Summit of the Americas in Quebec City. IMC activists Vishal Singh and Molly Pocket wrote this opening article for the St Louis IMC Web site, decrying the "undemocratic and overall exploitative nature of this trade agreement." This was followed by stories about the World Agricultural Forum (WAF) hosted in St. Louis, which made connections between local agribusiness giants such as St. Louis-based Monsanto, "the leading producer and marketer of genetically altered seeds," and the plight of family and peasant farmers around the world. There was then an article connecting the North American Free Trade Agreement (NAFTA) with thousands of jobs lost to the state of Missouri. This pattern of coverage has continued.

Throughout its short history, the St. Louis IMC has identified ways in which these local and global connections are maintained through a hierarchical global system of rule that is at base sexist and racist, and has focused on the ways privileged whites in the United States both benefit from and perpetuate this system of global inequities. Art Friedrich describes his early and gradually increasing involvement with the StLIMC as a very easy and natural process, since he was finding "all these people from my same demographic with similar concerns about social justice ... and [interested] in looking at the effects of classism and racism and imperialism, and wanting to keep all of these things in mind with whatever we were doing." For him, the IMC is a tool for connecting many different struggles, such as police brutality, environmental concerns, and anti-war activities, because "it's a place for dialogue, it's a place for people to educate themselves" (personal communication, June 24, 2003).

From the start, its core members conceived of the StLIMC as a means of facilitating communication within St. Louis as well as globally. Andy Jones, for example, describes his initial enthusiasm as inspired by conceptions of the IMC "as this public chalk board ... Most of what it is, is what people who use the site bring to it" (personal communication, June 23, 2003). Art Friedrich finds the discussions and debates the most compelling reading, such as when "someone puts up this really strong, opinionated piece, left wing or right wing, and then people are just discussing it and commenting on it, and reading all these discussions" (personal communication, June 24, 2003).

Betsy Resnicek at times posts messages to intentionally provoke a lively discussion, like the time she posted a photograph of Jefferson Barracks, one of the oldest local burial sites for soldiers, and "put like 'those who have fallen as martyrs' or something kind of broad ... just to try and get discussion going." She wanted to stimulate discussion of the Iraq War using an image that was thought provoking and from the local area, rather than "opposed to something" pulled from the global IMC Web site (personal communication, July 3, 2003). For many of the StLIMC activists, then, the Web site aspect of their work allows for an invaluable diversity of opinions and sources of information on issues of concern to those working to promote social justice both locally and globally. War (or the possibility of war) has been a focus of this discussion, especially since 9/11.

9/11 AND THE BUILD-UP TO WAR

The St. Louis IMC did not produce a feature on the New York and Washington attacks of September 11, but there was active discussion and analysis of the events on the open-publishing newswire, with posts commenting on the attacks, their implications for the Left and for the possibility of war. StLIMC features around this time continued to focus on local issues of concern to activists, virtually ignoring the attacks. The first StLIMC feature after the attacks appeared on September 12, and focused on the push for a Civilian Oversight Board to provide a watchdog group against police brutality in St. Louis. The weeks that follow continued to include no discussion of 9/11 in the features but included a feature interview with a local African-American feminist activist and a report on the October 22 National Day Against Police Brutality. The first explicit mention of the 9/11 attacks in the StLIMC features appeared in a November 15 report about a peace protest, "Women in Black Mourn the Fallen, Stand for Peace." The feature states that seven local women "of various faiths and ages" stood in black holding signs "stating that our grief over September 11 is not a cry for war." Other anti-war news and features began to appear before the bombing of Afghanistan in the aftermath of 9/11, and again later, well before the bombing of Iraq began in March 2003.

The 9/11 attacks stimulated local social justice activities as well as discussion on the StLIMC Web site's open publishing newswire. Andy Jones and Art Friedrich began rejuvenating their work with the group Food Not Bombs after 9/11. As Andy describes it, he and Art had formed the Food Not Bombs chapter in St. Louis and had been distributing food leftover from the weekly farmer's market in University City to shelters and food kitchens each week. But it was not until the Sunday after 9/11 that they took the work a step further and prepared the food to pass out to people on the street for free. Andy explains: "What we were saying was we were going to put the 'Not Bombs' back into 'Food Not Bombs'" (personal communication, June 23, 2004). Andy described this work as a way to "call attention to the wastefulness of society and then also our skewed priority in putting all this money into the military, and to doing sketchy stuff in other countries when we haven't even solved the problem of hunger, which should be a pretty easy thing to solve" (personal communication, June 23, 2003).

For IMC member "LL," the onset of war in response to 9/11 was a personal catalyst for becoming politically active, and it was her focus on global events that led her to explore the IMC, first through the global site, and then, locally, once she realized there was a St. Louis chapter. But it was her personal contact with people in St. Louis as she began to meet IMC activists at local protest events that led her to see many of the connections between problems she was learning about locally and globally. She joined IMC as a means of countering the type of denial or ignorance she saw among the students in the university she attended and among her upper-middle class family and friends.

> People really don't want to have to critically think about their world and their worldview and their country and their lifestyle and their livelihood, their president and all of that. It's so much easier to think we are the good guys, you know, we're justified in doing whatever now because they killed our people. (personal communication, Aug. 3, 2003).

For many StLIMC activists in the aftermath of 9/11, the IMC provided an outlet to counter the misleading and partial picture painted by mainstream media, and the resulting rise of U.S. nationalism they saw around them. Andy, for example, describes mainstream media coverage as "one-sided, speaking whatever the administration would say, repeating over and over and over, not being analytical, not being critical, never talking about why. Never talking in a serious way about why terrorists would want to bomb the World Trade Center and the Pentagon" (personal communication, June 23, 2003). LL began to recognize that what the people involved in the anti-war and global solidarity movements were saying "was never on the corporate media ever, ever, ever" (LL, personal communication, Aug. 3, 2003). The StLIMC offered a means of countering this deficiency.

CONNECTING MILITARISM AND SOLIDARITY AT HOME AND ABROAD

> Fighting for equality and justice in the United States and against war in Iraq are both important and related struggles. Going to these rallies and talking with people helps me make the connections between racism, oppression, war, consumerism, oil, over-consumption, capitalism, and militarism. I am more determined now to oppose this war, but also to continue the other struggles, that will continue until we can create a more free, just and egalitarian society. — post by LL to St. Louis IMC, Jan 20, 2003.

> After we stop this war, we will stop all other U$-sponsored wars, from Colombia to Israel to the Philippines to the streets of this city. We will grasp the giant triplets of materialism, militarism and racism at their roots. — post by Mike Schaefer to the St. Louis IMC, Jan 19, 2003.

Anti-war protests in St. Louis, while organized and conducted locally, emphasized the connections between St. Louis and the rest of the world, including the building of global solidarity between local groups around the world. Betsy Resnicek described the simultaneity of globally organized protests as especially motivating, such as the Feb. 15, 2003, global day of protest against the expected U.S. attacks on Iraq. "There are marches going on everywhere, you know, but you still get to do it locally" (personal communication, July 3, 2003). Local anti-war rallies also brought home to white activists their privilege vis-à-vis those living locally who are less fortunate.

After the rally ended, a few people gathered inside Soulard to warm up. I had picked up some signs that were left behind, including one that said, "No War for Oil!" One woman wearing a head scarf came up to me and thanked me, just for being there and holding up my sign. I am able to stand there and voice my dissent because I am not afraid of being arrested and deported, as a white, U.S. citizen. Though I could still be harassed, even imprisoned for my dissent, I know my rights of assembly and free speech (despite Ashcroft's efforts to strip me of them) are more protected as a U.S. citizen, and as a white woman. The woman who thanked me, however, has fewer luxuries. She is easily identified as a Muslim woman, and I'm guessing probably an Arab woman. I cannot even imagine how much harassment she endures on a daily basis. Is she taunted and threatened by uber-patriots? Does she have to pay an immigration lawyer hundreds of dollars to make sure her visa is still valid? Do her male relatives have to "register" with the INS? — From first hand account of anti-war rally at Soulard market by LL 5:11p.m., Monday, Jan 20, 2003.

Evidence of local efforts at global solidarity was visible as organizers of a March 30 anti-war protest in St. Louis arranged to fly the flags of those countries that opposed the war, but this protest was also a wakeup call to St. Louis activists regarding local police brutality. The anti-war group Instead of War spearheaded the anti-war rally. At the end of the rally, a group of about 30 young activists decided to form a breakaway, unauthorized march nearby to express a more radical view than that expressed during the main rally. They wore masks and banged on buckets like drums, but there was reportedly no violence or destruction. After a few minutes, however, police on motorbikes, yelling at them to get off the street, suddenly surrounded this group. Betsy Resnicek witnessed the scene, where at one point she reports counting 20 squad cars. She recalls an unprofessional and brutal police response, in which officers were yelling and cursing at activists while manhandling them violently.

> I watched as they took my friend and slammed him so hard against the back of the cop car his head bounced, and I was thinking "oh my god, what the hell?" I watched as this girl was tackled by two or three male officers and a female officer. There were dogs all around. It was just a scene from an awful movie. They were macing the air, so you could like see it in the air, and smell it, and I remember some kid saying, "Devon's hurt! Devon's hurt! He can't see." This kid, his face was beet red and he couldn't open his eyes, he was in massive pain and a girl that we had known happened to be driving by and stopped far enough back and ran up to see what was going on, and actually carried him back to her vehicle, turned around and took him immediately to the hospital. I was very grateful for that. (personal communication, July 3, 2003)

By the end of the march, many people had been hurt, two sent to the hospital, and seven arrested. For Betsy, the police violence during this anti-war march demonstrated the connections between major local issues: police brutality in St. Louis and the lack of attention by the city's whites. She says that while she wishes this violence had never happened, she is also grateful for the insight it gave her. She recalls a conversation she had with Jamala Rogers, an activist with the St Louis Coalition Against Police Crimes and Repression (CAPCR).

"I told Jamala Rodgers one time, 'I'm ashamed. I never would have thought about CAPCR. It wouldn't have crossed my mind, until this happened.' She had just finished saying that 'when the white folks want police brutality to end, it is going to end.' And here we had it on tape, you know, we were good American, suburban, youth" (personal communication, July 3, 2003).

> White groups often choose to work on issues that are more global, but never link them up to local issues. Because then you have to reach out into communities that are not your own, and I think people don't think about that, or if they do, they think those communities are by and large inferior. It really is a white skin privilege piece that we need to put squarely on the table and talk about, and those people who are

consistent in that behavior need to continue to be struggled with. —
Jamala Rogers, quoted in an interview on St. Louis IMC, Nov. 8, 2001

KEEPING IT LOCAL WITH ᴸCAMPꜞ

For most of the core StLIMC activists, the Web site is a secondary concern
in the struggle to fight injustice and militarism. Perhaps more effective,
many of them feel, is the effort to open access to new information
technologies and, more importantly, their potential among a larger base
of local users. This involves the physical space in which the StLIMC is
housed, the Community Arts and Media Project, or CAMP. In Fall 2001,
about half a year after the founding of StLIMC, its members joined with
several other activist groups to discuss the possible purchase of a building
that could be developed into a community center.

This initial vision eventually resulted in the Spring 2002 purchase of
the Randall Building in south St. Louis as the home of the new
Community Arts and Media Project. Since its purchase, the building has
been significantly renovated using recycled materials and donated labor,
including the volunteer labor of a licensed architect. Its core supporters
conceive of the nearly renovated CAMP building as an open space,
available for all kinds of community projects, arts workshops, skill-
sharing sessions, and whatever educational, political, or outreach projects
the community chooses to use it for. Andy Jones moved into CAMP and
has been central in managing major renovations. He says, "We were
talking in IMC about the need for a physical space, to make it bigger than
the Web site, because ... there are class issues with being able to access
the Web. It could be so much more if it was a physical thing" (personal
communication, June 23, 2003). Art Friedrich, who also lives in the
building and has been central to its rehab, believes CAMP will "bring the
IMC even more into the real, physical world" (personal communication,
June 24, 2003).

While the accomplishment of buying and working to renovate a
building was motivating for many IMC activists, this process along with
other events during the Spring of 2002 resulted in a period of burnout for
the core group of IMC activists. As a result, while the StLIMC's open
publishing newswire remained active that summer, the group held no
meetings and very few features appeared. It was the rumblings of war that
Fall, however, as George Bush began talking seriously about attacking
Iraq, that reinvigorated the core StLIMC working group. They started
holding regular meetings again, and features began appearing after the
summer hiatus.

The re-energized StLIMC began once again to interrogate the connections between the global move toward war and social injustice in St Louis. Before, during and after the attacks on Iraq began, StLIMC features included news of various anti-war rallies; actions against Boeing's "war profiteering" through production of "weapons of mass destruction," including a blockade at the local Boeing missile plant; reports on the "human face of war" with activists writing accounts direct from Baghdad; concerns over increasing restrictions on civil liberties, including a University City resolution against the U.S. Patriot Act and the detention of a local Muslim activist; and efforts to combat police brutality in St. Louis that made direct reference to its connections with the war against Iraq.

The strength and consistency of such connections in StLIMC reporting reinforces the argument that protesters at global events are engaged citizens primarily working to connect locally-based actions with international issues while only periodically engaging in transnational protest events (Fisher et al., 2005; Tarrow, 2005). For the StLIMC, the emphasis on reporting the connections between the local and the global continues, as does the rehab work on the building that the StLIMC calls home.

February 5, 2005

I drove up to CAMP tonight to attend a fundraising party for the IMC with the theme Possessed/Dispossessed, a theme which was intended to explore the many ways in which we are all complicit in the act of dispossessing others as we work to possess things. ... The party was in part a celebration of the progress made on the CAMP building, and was held in the newly renovated downstairs space. Gone are the piles of building materials, broken computers, and other junk that filled the room the first time I entered it. Gone, in fact, are portions of the walls that separated each of the three downstairs rooms, which are now connected, creating a much larger space than before, capable of accommodating a big party like the one held tonight. People filled the room — mostly young and white, but also a few young African-American men and women from the neighborhood. ... Art, Andy and other IMC folks showed newcomers around proudly. They described plans for the space in the coming summer months — skill-sharing workshops, a "zine" library, independent film screenings, more work on the garden in the backyard, and especially exciting, the bike workshop, which the summer before had begun drawing large numbers of neighborhood kids. Donated bikes and bike parts are used to repair old bikes and build new ones, which the kids can then ride home. The bike workshops had become a success in their eyes, not only for the alternatives that a bike culture provides to our country's dependence on foreign oil, but also for the chance it gives these activists to work together with and get to know people from the neighborhood. Eventually, too, the plans for the space include a computer lab, in which free training classes will be offered by a non-profit organization with multiple labs across St. Louis. The goal is that neighborhood people will be able to access the Internet, surf the Web, and create their own media.

As Andy explained to me, CAMP is the real-world place in which the local meets the global, and the militaristic culture of war can be challenged.

> I have a vision of communities, communities that work, communities that communicate within themselves, that are able to identify their needs and address those, and take into account how they effect other communities too, without screwing other people over or destroying resources. I think that it's just so essential, and I feel like in a lot of ways we're living in the opposite of that, we're living in the belly of the beast, you know, America in the 21st century, this militaristic superpower with subtle repression at home, and really violent policies abroad.... We lack creativity, and we need a culture of people who are thinking about stuff, and who are active, and who feel empowered to change their surroundings. And being able to create media rather than just being a media consumer... you know, it's really important, and empowering. (Andy Jones, personal communication, June 23, 2003)

REFERENCES

Ackerman, S. (2000, January/February). Prattle in Seattle: WTO coverage misrepresented issues, protests. *Extra!* Retrieved from http://www.fair.org/extra/001/wto-prattle.html

Atton, C. (2002). News cultures and new social movements: radical journalism and the mainstream media. *Journalism Studies*, 3(4): 491-505.

Atton, C. (2003). Reshaping social movement media for a new millennium. *Social Movement Studies*, Vol. 2, No. 1, 2003

Brooten, L. (2004a). Digital deconstruction: The Independent Media Center as a process of collective critique. In R.D. Berenger (Ed.), *Global media go to war: The role of news and entertainment media during the 2003 Iraq war*. Spokane: Marquette Books.

Brooten, L. (2004b). The power of public reporting: The Independent Media Center's challenge to the "corporate media machine." In L. Artz & Y. R. Kamalipour (Eds.),

Bring 'em on! Media and politics in the Iraq war. Lanham: Rowman & Littlefield Publishers.

Castells, M. (1996). *The rise of the network society, the information age: Economy, society and culture.* Cambridge, MA: Blackwell.

Castells, M. (1997). *The Power of Identity, The Information Age: Economy, Society and Culture.* Malden, MA: Blackwell Publishers.

Fisher, D., Stanley, K., Berman, D., & Neff, G. (2005). How do organizations matter? Mobilization and support for participants at five globalization protests. *Social Problems,* 52 (1): 102-121.

Gamson, W., & Wolfsfeld, G. (1993). Movements and media as interacting systems. *Annals of the Academy of Political and Social Science,* 528: 114-125.

Gitlin, T. (1980). *The whole world is watching: media in the making and unmaking of the new left.* Berkeley: University of California Press.

Giuffo, J. (2001, September/October). Smoke gets in our eyes: The globalization protests and the befuddled press. *Columbia Journalism Review,* 40 (3), 14-17.

Haas, T. (2004). Alternative media, public journalism and the pursuit of democratization. *Journalism Studies,* 5(1): 115-121.

International outcry against Indymedia hard drive seizure. (2004, Oct. 13). Retrieved from the FreePress Web site http://www.freepress.net/global/update.php?id=65 on Jan. 13, 2005.

Keane, J. (1995). Structural transformations of the public sphere. *Communication Review,* 1(1): 1-22.

Kidd, D. (2003a). Become the media: the global IMC network. In A. Opel & D. Pompper (Eds.), *Representing resistance: Media, civil disobedience, and the global justice movement* (pp. 224-240). Westport, CT: Praeger.

Kidd, D. (2003b). The Independent Media Center: A new model. *Media Development,* XLX(4): 7-11.

Kling, R. (2000). Learning about information technologies and social change: The contribution of social informatics. *The Information Society,* 16:217—232

McLeod, D. and Hertog, J. (1999). Social control, social change and the mass media's role in the regulation of protest groups. In D. Demers & K. Viswanath (Eds.), *Mass media, social control and social change: A macrosocial perspective.* Ames: Iowa State University Press, pp. 305-330.

Morris, D. (2004). Globalization and media democracy: The case of Indymedia. In D. Schuler & P. Day (Eds.), *Shaping the network society: The new role of civil society in cyberspace.* Cambridge: The MIT Press.

Tarrow, S. (2005). Rooted Cosmopolitans and Transnational Activists. In *The new transnational activism.* Cambridge: Cambridge University Press.

van Zoonen, E. A. (1992). The women's movement and the media: Constructing a public identity. *European Journal of Communication,* 7:453—76.

DISCUSSION QUESTIONS

1. The St Louis Independent Media Center is just one link in a worldwide chain of similar Web sites that have coalesced around opposition to war, big business, globalization, and in favor of wealth distribution, protection

of natural resources and other environmental concerns. To what extent has the StLIMC contributed to the organization of a new global Left in terms of ideology?

2. The re-elections of George W. Bush and the Republican-dominated Senate and House and their support of the Iraq War seemed a central concern of IMCs around the world, which argued that, because of newsroom tradition, ethical restrictions, or favoritism toward elites, mainstream media are not doing a proper job of informing the public. How valid are those arguments, and do IMCs fill the alleged information void?

3. Roland Robertson coined the term "glocalization" to refer to digital media behavior that localize global issues. To what extent do IMCs like the one in St. Louis support Robertson's notion?

4. Indymedia Centers theoretically can be a force in energizing and mobilizing like-minded individuals. How successful was the St. Louis IMC in supporting this concept in the run-up to the Iraq War?

5. Often IMCs like the one in St. Louis offer links to mainstream news Web pages, thus acting as "gateway" sites. But how do the IMC "gatekeepers" decide which stories will be linked and which will not? What role do the gatekeepers play in schema development of their users by the selection of these links?

CHAPTER TEN

MoveOn.org Goes to the Movies: A Case Study in Contemporary Anti-War Activism and Base-Building

Jon R. Pike

MoveOn.org has come far in five years since Berkeley-based computer entrepreneurs Joan Blades and Wes Boyd (who are married) launched an online petition to ask Congress to censure President Clinton but not impeach him. The original name of the organization was "Censure and Move On." When the House of Representatives voted to impeach, Boyd and Blades decided to see if they could help vote out pro-impeachment incumbents. This is when MoveOn.org became noticed, according to Kush (2000). The new political organization gained notice

> largely because it transcended its Internet confines by attracting the attention of the news media and successfully gathering millions of dollars to dispense to the campaigns of congressional candidates running against pro-impeachment incumbents (p.242).

After the impeachment issue played out, the organization found other issues to rally around, including one that put MoveOn.org back in the national headlines. MoveOn.org was successful in mobilizing support for the McCain-Feingold campaign finance reform legislation. Harnessing the power of the Internet, MoveOn.org delivered 15,000 e-mails to Congress in one day. A news release from the organization quoted some of the e-mail messages. For example, Aaron Kincer of Georgetown, Kentucky, wrote: "As long as companies are dropping millions in your pockets, I don't feel I can EVER trust any of you" (cited in 'Constituent e-mails flood Congress in support of McCain-Feingold bill. 15,000 messages delivered today,' March 22, 2001).

Taken together these two cases demonstrate that while members of MoveOn.org wanted to change the system, they clearly believed in the system and sought change from within via elections and legislation. MoveOn.org was attempting to build a platform for national issues, and the organization had definitely moved out of the Bay area and into the political consciousness.

SETTING AN AGENDA BY BUILDING THE BASE

Agenda setting has been a staple of political communication studies since McCombs and Shaw (1972) found evidence that media set the public agenda in the 1968 presidential campaign. Since then, multiple wrinkles have been put into agenda-setting theory.

A German study, for instance, examined how nonelite media made the public aware of issues. In the early 1980s, a newspaper associated with the German counterculture helped increase public resistance to a German national identity card (Mathes & Pfetsch, 1991). Although a counter-cultural medium initiated the resistance, establishment media picked up on the issue as part of their content. The issue flowed from those who were involved in fighting this issue, to the alternative media, to the establishment German media, to the public. First there was a movement, and then there was a medium that appealed to this movement and believed their struggle was important enough to report. It became a part of the public agenda when the establishment media reported on it and gave it legitimacy. But it became a public issue initially because there was a movement to give the issue a voice.

In more recent work, McCombs, Weaver and Shaw (2004) have thought more expansively on agenda-setting. They now say that the transmission of cultural values is also a part of the agenda-setting process. An example of this was the rise of the culturally conservative right wing in the 1980s. Activist Richard Viguerie took almost 20 years to build this movement through computer-assisted direct mail (Freidenberg, 1998, p. 134). Viguerie understood the values of the people who formed the base he wanted to build. He kept mailing them, over and over, and his supporters grew until other institutions, including the mass media, could no longer ignore their numbers. Viguerie's efforts paid dividends in the 1980 election of Republican Ronald Reagan and the defeat of three liberal Democratic icons, Senators Birch Bayh of Indiana, George McGovern of South Dakota and Frank Church of Idaho. More than merely an electoral success, the careful cultivation of Southern voters by using alternative media (direct mail) resulted in moving their "Solid South" voting bloc from the Democratic to the Republican column, where it resides today.

Social movements have taken to cyberspace to promote their causes and mobilize their bases out of the reach of more traditional power brokers with contacts in the establishment media. A 2002 analysis showed that while constituents and others sought substantive information about their federal representatives on the Internet, they discovered their members of Congress were using Web sites primarily as promotional tools for candidacies (Congress Online Project, 2002). Those wanting substantive information about issues had to look elsewhere.

What people find when they turn to the Web for information on issues are Web sites sponsored by organizations that have bypassed the more traditional gatekeepers of political information, like traditional news media. Owens and Palmer's 2003 study of anarchist Web sites, which sprang up after the 1999 WTO protests in Seattle, found that these groups could define their own visions of themselves without waiting for the establishment media to do it for them.

What online social movements also apparently understood, which politicians didn't, was the importance of interpersonal communication. This was probably understood best by movements that had tried to build public interest before the Internet era. They understood that you had to listen to people as well as talk to them. In framing this from a public relations perspective, Taylor, Kent and White (2001) suggest that "dialogic" features can be built into social movement Web sites. They include:

- sending messages to the organizations;
- voting on issues;
- requesting information updates;
- completing opinion surveys.

To be successful, social movements must show they care. Joan Blades claims that the organization she helped create falls in to this category:

> We have a forum in which people can post comments and those comments can be rated so we get a sense of what tens of thousands of people feel most passionately about. We also do surveys when we're trying to figure out the right thing to do (quoted in McNally, 2004, para. 13).

Social movements that use Web sites to build their base and establish a public-policy agenda often have an advantage over establishment efforts because the former are less hierarchical. Nonhierarchical organizations can be more spontaneous, flexible and faster in their communication responses. This was demonstrated by numerous anti-war organizations that quickly responded to the Bush administration's plan to launch a pre-emptive war against Iraq. The Feb. 15, 2003, international antiwar protest was the first global pre-emptive protest in the history of social movements. Social movements had organized people quickly and spontaneously. In *The Nation,* Andrew Boyd (2004) said that the group United for Peace and Justice simply put fliers on its Web site urging people around the world to take to the streets in protest of the coming war. Other Web sites followed the lead and posted the flier. The result: Millions were mobilized to attend nearly 800 protests worldwide on every continent, including 200 in the United States and Canada.

Computer media are equally good at communication between individuals and groups of people and vice versa. Myers (2002) said that individuals might belong to more than one organized social movement that could seem unrelated but nonetheless might share overlapping membership, such as proponents of gay rights might also be active in the anti-nuclear power movement. If a group is organized as an ideological umbrella for people who share some of the same activist agendas, then those people could get in touch with each other, and seek each other out with relative ease over the Internet.

Sunman and Reilly (2004) argue that the features found on such Web sites, like e-mail lists and databases, are so deeply ingrained into the online world of activism that they become "the building blocks of these movements" (para. 24). A media principle that MoveOn.org seems to understand well is the "two-or-multi-step flow" of communication and its benefits for building a base that can press agenda. According to Vivian (2004), people are less motivated to act by the public agenda or the media, *per se*, than they are by other people whose opinion about what is reported on the public agenda they respect. These people share their opinions and people listen to them. (p. 375). MoveOn.org depends upon this complex Web to build its base.

CASE STUDY METHODOLOGY

A case study was used to examine MoveOn.org's anti-war activism. Case studies are a "real-life" methodology; they seek to describe "events in such a way as to enhance our understanding and bolster our insights in ways that other methods could or normally would not do" (Sypher, 1990, p.4). Case studies are particularly useful for studying new phenomena. According to Yin (1984), case studies are particularly valuable in situations where there might be a fuzzy boundary between a phenomenon and its context. Virtual organizations, by their very nature, blur the distinction between context and phenomenon. Yin also advocates case studies when multiple sources of data are used. However, case study observations must be complete as it reconstructs and analyzes a particular case. It also should incorporate the views of the actors (Zonabend, 1992). The approach should be holistic.

This current study used a grounded theory approach. Frey et al. (1991) describe this methodology for the reconstructed case. They argue that grounded theory case study analysis should not only be descriptive but "identify appropriate strategies that were used or that could have been used to solve problems experienced in that particular situation" (pp. 209-210). In other words, not only must a case study follow certain steps and be grounded in research and theory from the relevant field, it must also highlight solutions that were used in problems that arose in the case, or suggest strategies for solving those problems.

Case studies have been used in law, business, education and public policy. In these types of investigations "merely quantitative techniques tended to obscure some of the important information that the researchers needed to uncover" (Tellis,1997, para. 9). So case studies are important when there is an evaluative component necessary to a study. The agent who must do that sort of evaluation is the researcher, who cannot divorce him or herself completely from the analysis.

One of the first things needed for this study was evidence. This study focused on how MoveOn.org is building a base and attempting to influence the public agenda through a unique strategy of distributing films to people's houses and having them discuss these films in a social setting. The study needed informants who had also been participant observers and could talk about these particular strategies from an insider's point of view. The Internet search engine Yahoo! turned up a group of MoveOn.org members who participated in this very event. This group, from San José, California, had set up a Web site with a listserv as one of its features. The researcher subscribed to the listserv and posted messages soliciting comments and opinions about MoveOn.org's organizational strategies.

This researcher also studied MoveOn.org for its perspective on its own strategy. MoveOn.org's Web site features an extensive collection of its own news releases and news stories about the organization. These provided valuable evidence for reconstruction of the case and analysis of the organization and its methods. In terms of analyzing this data, both the interviews and the analysis of the news articles and news releases focused on the research question. Interview statements and analysis of the documents provided evidence of how MoveOn.org used both the interpersonal capabilities and mass communication capabilities of computer-mediated communication to build a base for future electoral action.

THE CASE OF MOVEON.ORG

In 2002, while the Bush administration was making its preliminary case for war with Iraq, MoveOn.org was making its first foray into foreign policy, with member Eli Parriser leading the way. Parriser and MoveOn.org publicized their case against the impending war and called for an international response to Iraq that would allow UN weapons inspectors to continue their work in Iraq (Hara & Estrada, 2004). Before the Bush administration ordered the invasion, MoveOn.org's stance focused entirely on working within the system to carry out its members' agenda.

At that time the emphasis was on lobbying members of Congress (Congressional Offices across the Nation Visited by Internet Activist Group to Oppose Rush to War in Iraq, 15 September 2005). The lobbying efforts even extended into the increasingly Republican South, where Greenville, S.C., members of MoveOn visited the offices of their local representatives (Buchanan, 2003). MoveOn.org had not yet taken the next step: advocating global opposition to the coming war, civil disobedience or any form of direct action.

It is not surprising then, that MoveOn.org's activism since the invasion of Iraq remained largely focused on education. This trajectory naturally led MoveOn.org to the case that is the focus of this particular study. MoveOn.org helped finance Robert Greenwald's documentary about this subject, *Uncovered: The Whole Truth About the Iraq War.* MoveOn.org then short-circuited the normal distribution process, which could have taken months to get the independently produced movie into theaters. Instead, MoveOn.org used its Web site to ask members to host a movie viewing and discussion party in their homes, all on the same day. MoveOn.org posted a list of homes where the film would be shown and matched the hosts with those who wanted to see the film and participate in discussion groups.

According to journalist Don Hazen, MoveOn.org members are not shy about spreading their feelings or recruiting family and friends, "They know that communication from a trusted friend or colleague is far more influential than an advertisement or a direct market appeal" (para. 18). MoveOn.org attempts to turn its membership into opinion leaders, people who will go out an communicate with others about the issues and try to advance their agenda. Additionally, as Saco (2004) says, a paradox of today's Internet is that relationships can develop on the Internet between people around the world, when they don't even know their neighbors. MoveOn.org seems to be dedicated to resolving this paradox by bringing people who are geographically close together for the purpose of national political action.

MoveOn.org's anti-war campaign is to educate its own membership about the issues via movie showings and discussions and then having these people and go out and talk to others. They are attempting to build the sort of critical mass necessary to influence the public agenda. At least this was the hope expressed by movie director Robert Greenwald:

> What's unusual about this film is that it's being seen in "real time" the same debates about the ramifications of Bush's Iraq war policies debated in the film, are taking place everyday, at work places, in the media, and will surely be a key topic in the 2004 election (Greenwald, cited in Hazen, 2004, Dec. 3, para. 4).

Greenwald could not have been more transparent. He was building a base for future action at the ballot box.

The story picks up for a group of people from San José when Pattie Bossert came across the page soliciting places to hold the film screening. Bossert, a Quaker, had been involved with social activism for quite some time. Bossert said that, as a Quaker, she had been involved in Northern California groups like the Mid-Peninsula Peace Center and has been active in war tax resistance and has been a frequent contributor to letters-to-the-editor pages. She says that when she saw the house party page, she brought it up to members of her monthly meeting and she was given the go ahead. "We were all upset about the war in Iraq and wanted to educate people about the truth and speak truth to power" (Personal Interview, Sept. 7, 2004). This underscores the educational component that MoveOn.org sees as essential to its anti-war activism. Bossert combined this with the Quaker mandate to confront the powerful with the truth. Though she was not a member of MoveOn.org, Bossert went ahead and put a posting on the house party board.

She said the results astonished her. Her goal was to get 50 people in three days for the viewing party. Bossert started e-mailing her "compadres" about the house party and then those people forwarded the e-mail to others. She said that they didn't have any trouble "selling out" the event. The response overwhelmed the Quaker meeting. "All we had was one 20-inch TV," Bossert said. "My husband figured out a way to connect two TVs so people could be more comfortable and we hooked up speakerphones for the discussion afterwards." The discussion provoked a reaction from the audience.

"People were excited by the film," said Bossert, "They were upset. They wanted to know what they could do." The talk immediately turned to keeping this particular group together. This is where another MoveOn.org activist came into the picture. Au Nguyen, who Bossert did not even know prior to this meeting, offered to set up a list-serv, which led to a Web site (http://moveon-friends.org). The list-serv and Web site provide a political and social forum for the group.

Nguyen received one of the forwarded e-mails that Bossert had sent out. He said he was not even sure from where he received an e-mail message to participate in MoveOn.org activities. "I guess it hit me at the right time I was feeling frustrated with the direction our country was going at the time" (Personal Interview, Aug. 24, 2004). That was what he said motivated his decision whether to keep the forwarded e-mail or delete it. The year 2004 was really the first year that Nguyen got actively involved in politics. He was involved in the Howard Dean presidential campaign and then kept being involved in Dean's "Democracy for America" political action group. Nguyen says that he "dragged" his wife and a friend to the house party. As for the house parties he says:

> It's a great icebreaker. Complete strangers can come together. It inspires them. People can follow up with what happens at the house parties. It's much more concrete. You see real people. Then people can start using usenets. People can then talk about things that weren't mentioned that happened at the house parties.

Nguyen said the Internet has significantly lowered the cost of being involved politically as people can access Web sites and list-servs easily. One of those people who accessed the Internet so easily was Ariel Imrie, who admits her political activism was at a pretty low level prior to getting involved with MoveOn.org. She says that while she voted in every presidential election, she sometimes passed on the mid-term elections. Although she did not consider herself a politically involved individual, before her more recent involvement with MoveOn.org, she actually had heard of MoveOn.org's before either Bossert or Nguyen, "I actually signed the original online petition in 1999. I don't remember where I got the e-mail from. But I certainly didn't think we needed to be dragged through the mud. I just thought we should censure [Bill Clinton] and not impeach him." But her political activism lay fallow until the e-mail invite to the house party.

Imre said says thinks that activism events like the movie house parties that MoveOn .org has put together are ideal for people like her, who were not necessarily involved in politics but want to get involved. She says she definitely believes that MoveOn.org's use of the Internet "lowers the bar" for political involvement and makes it easier for people to be involved. But she adds that the interpersonal aspect that has been brought to the fore with the house parties and the discussions after the movies has been important also. She calls it "uplifting." She said that unless you see other people united in the same place discussing the same things, "You don't feel that you can make a difference, otherwise. You're more engaged. A lot of that is missing from the political. It really puts a face on the whole process." Imrie credited this initial involvement with getting herself on other listservs, such as those for Tom Paine.com and for the ACLU.

MoveOn.org has continued to use movies and home-based discussions for its activities. The documentary that takes FoxNews to task, *Outfoxed,* has never been screened theatrically, but is available as a DVD and has been shown in people's homes with Moveon.org facilitating house parties for people to view the film. Robert Greenwald also put this film together. The success of Michael Moore's film, *Fahrenheit 9/11,* prompted MoveOn.org to use a successful theatrical release in much the same way. MoveOn.org helped put together house parties that shared in a teleconference and Internet hook-up with Moore on June 28, 2004. Keeping in line with the organization's use of interpersonal communication, MoveOn.org volunteers solicited participants in the town hall-type meeting with leaflets outside of movie theaters, as well as via the Internet (Michael Moore Will Star in MoveOn.org Town Hall Meetings, June 22, 2004). We've seen through the previous case how MoveOn.org attempted to build a base for future political action through online mass and interpersonal communication via the Internet through organizing movie watching house parties.

DISCUSSION

Since it's beginning, MoveOn.org has worked within the system to achieve its goals. It was born out of a petition drive, and MoveOn.org has always focused on lobbying and motivating people to vote in elections. And when their preferred candidates seem to be out of favor, they focused on educational initiatives.

The national leadership of MoveOn.org seems committed to building and maintaining a base. It also seems committed to the strategy of trying to capture the National Republican Party. Although the interviews for this research focused on MoveOn.org's anti-war activity, the interviews, which were conducted in September and October, did address the fact that MoveOn.org members were working hard to defeat President Bush.

MoveOn.org went to the movies to build its base in 2004 and brought the movies to the people. The case of MoveOn.org speaks to the interpersonal and mass communication aspects of computer media. It brought people in to build a base and now it remains to be seen how well it keeps that base. It has built enough of a base that the media are paying attention to it now the group has to make its agenda the public's agenda.

References

Boyd, A.A. (2003, July 17) The Web Rewires the movement. *The Nation.* Retrieved Dec. 14, 2004, from http://www.thenation.com.mhtml?i=20030804&s=boyd.

Buchanan, M. (2003, Jan. 21). Local activist urge no rush to war. Retrieved Dec. 14, 2003,from http://greenvillonline.com/news/2003/0121/2003012183.htm

Congressional Offices across the Nation Visited By Internet Activist Group to Oppose Rush to War in Iraq. (2004). Retrieved Dec.14, 2004, from http://www. moveon.org/press/ pr/release012103.html.

Congress Online Project. (2002). Assessing and improving Capitol Hill Web sites. Retrieved from Dec. 14, 2004, from http://www.congressonlineproject.org/ congressonline2002.html

Constituent Emails Flood Congress in Support of McCain-Feingold Bill 15,000 Messages Delivered Today (2001, March 22). Retrieved Dec. 14, 2004, from http://www.moveon.org/press/pr/release032201.htm.

Frey, L. R., Botan, C. H., Friedman, P. G., & Kreps, G. L. (1991). *Investigating communication: An introduction to research methods.* Englewood Cliffs, NJ: Prentice-Hall.

Friedenberg, R.V. (1998). Narrowcast media and political campaigns: Trends and implications. In J.S. Trent (Ed.). *Communication: Views from the helm for the 21st century.* Boston: Allyn and Bacon, pp. 133-137.

Hara, N., & Estrada, Z. (2004). Hate and peace in a connected world: Comparing MoveOn and Stormfront. *First Monday, 8.* Retrieved July 22, 2004, from http://www.firstmonday.org/Issue8_12/hara/index.html.

Hazen, D. (2003, Dec. 3). Bringing down the house. Retrieved Dec. 14, 2004, from http://alternet.org/story/173080/ on.

Kush, C. (2000). *Cybercitizen: How to use your computer to fight for all the issues you care about.* New York: St. Martin's Griffin.

Mathes, R., & Pfetsch, B. (1991). The role of the alternative press in the agenda building process: Spillover effects and media opinion leadership. *European Journal of Communication, 6,* 33-62.

McCombs, M.E., & Shaw, D.L. (1972). The agenda-setting function of mass media. *PubliOpinion Quarterly, 36,* 176-185.

McCombs, M.E., Weaver, D., & Shaw, D.L. (2004). Agenda-setting research: Issues, attributes and influence. In L.L. Kaid (Ed.) *Handbook of political communication.* Mahwah, NJ: Lawrence Earlbaum.

McNally, T. (2004, June 25). MoveOn as an instrument of the people. Retrieved July 24, 2004, from http://alternet.org/story/19043/.

Michael Moore Will Star in MoveOn Town Hall Meetings (2004, June 22) Retrieved Dec. 14, 2004, from: http://www,oveon.org/press/pdfs/mooremtgs.pdf.

Myers, D.J. (2001). Social activism through computer networks. In O.V. Burton (Ed.). *Computing in the social sciences and humanities.* Urbana: University of Illinois Press. Retrieved July 24, 2004, from http://www.press.uillinois.edu.edu/epub/books/burton. ch06.html.

Owens, L., & Palmer, L.K. (2003) Making the news: Anarchist counter public relations on the worldwide web. *Critical Studies in Media Communication, 20,* 335-361.

Surman, M., & Reilly, K. (2004, Spring). Appropriating the Internet for global activism. Retrieved July 24, 2004, from http://www.yesmagazine.org/29globalhope/surmanreilly.htm

Sypher, B. D. (1990). *Case studies in organizational communication.* London: Guilford.

Taylor, M., Kent, M.L., & White, W. J. How activist organizations are using the Internet to build relationships. *Public Relations Review, 27.* Retrieved from http://www.sciencedirect.com/science?_ob=ArticleURL&_udi=B6W5W-441n5DM-2&user=513528&_handle=B-WA-A-AU-MsSAYWW-UUA-AUEAZDBUVC-AUYEWCBYVC-CUBDEDZVU-AU-U&_fmt=full&_coverDate=07%2F01%F2001&_rdoc=2&_orig=browse&_srch=%23toc%236581%232001%23999729996%23265238!&_cdi=6581&view=c&_aact=C000025359_version=1&urlVersion=0&_userid=513528&md5=39e84307a75cdeb9af7596bda232e572

Tellis, W. (1997). Introduction to case study. *The Qualitative Report, 3.* Retrieved July 24, 2004, from http://www.nova.edu/ssss/QR/QR3-2/tellis1.html.

Yin, R.K. (1984). *Case study research: Design and methods.* Newbury Park, Ca: Sage.

Zonabend, F. (1992,). The monograph in European ethnology. *Current Sociology, 40*(1), 49-60.

DISCUSSION QUESTIONS

1. Moveon.org used movie showings in people's homes and other small venues to help build a political agenda against the Bush administration and the Iraq War. What are the advantages and drawbacks to this strategy?

2. What aspects of Internet communication are the most effective in helping to create a social movement organization? Cite examples.

3. Why would social movement organizations that use the Internet for mobilizing want to have interpersonal communication within the

organization instead of staying totally online?
4. Imagine you are a coordinator for a social movement organization. How would you use the Internet to organize social activities to advance the agenda of your group?
5. What steps should a social movement organization take to move its agenda beyond the Internet and activities within the organization so that it can have a greater impact on the society?

CHAPTER ELEVEN

E-MOBILIZING THE PEACENIKS DOWN UNDER

SHAUN PETER CANNON

Melbourne Peace Rally, Feb. 14, 2003, 5:00 pm.

S ome in the crowd stood out more than others. For one rally participant, her appearance suggested that she had been frozen in time. Her clothing indicated that she had been one of the 100,000 protesters who on March 8, 1970, marched down Bourke Street, Melbourne, during the first phase of the Vietnam Moratorium.

It was as if, when her fellow protesters departed on that day and accepted the evolutionary transition towards late modernity, she did not go with them; but, rather, she went into an icy isolation from which she would not return for more than three decades. A red bandana protruded deep beyond her forehead, almost to her eyebrow line. Her hair, partly covered by the bandana, was long and free. Aside from the biker-style headpiece, a patchwork bra was the only form of clothing she wore from the waist up. The letters P-E-A-C-E spread across her stomach. A love heart had been painted just above the cleavage on her chest. Two smaller hearts decorated her cheeks. Her blue denim hipsters were tight at the top and flared at the bottom. Her belt, although purely decorative as it served no functional purpose, consisted of a chain of circular peace symbols linked together. She hoisted a placard, NO HOWARD, high above her head. The letters N, O, W, A and R had been painted red to reinforce the reasons behind her attendance. From the tips of her wrist to the point of her shoulder, anti-war slogans were painted in blue along her bare arms. Content to stand still, she chanted as other protesters shuffled by.

Despite her appearance the unknown protester could not possibly have been an activist in the 1960s or the 1970s. The 70s were the decade in which she was most probably conceived judging by her youthful looks. Our bandana-clad activist was, in other words, a "gen-Xer" rather than a "boomer." Although not universal, there was definitely a retrospective flavor to many of those who attended the Feb.14, 2003, Melbourne Peace Rally, hereafter referred to as "the rally." The Lennon inspired "give peace a chance" mantra was back in the public domain. The rally was not, however, simply a case of history repeating. While the past might have brought with it the peace ideal, it was the present that provided the means for mass mobilization.

This paper suggests that the transnational peace movement that unfolded in response to the looming war in Iraq was as much a product of cyber activity as it was of circumstances in Iraq. An analysis of the Victorian Peace Network (VPN), a coalition of interest and geographically localized groups that merged towards the end of 2002 under the banner of peace, is included. Lacking in tangible assets or exposure in traditional media outlets, the VPN exemplifies the ways in which "virtual" networks are able to circumnavigate conventional corridors of power.

This chapter is based on exploratory research that used relevant literature to posit some broad theoretical themes aimed at encouraging a shift in debate away from traditional concerns about *who* and *how many*, towards questions of *why* and *how* alternate methods of social integration have emerged. The chapter combines both qualitative and quantitative research methods. Although not restricted to a specific research design, phenomenological and case study methodologies were principally employed in the collection of data. Documents were gathered, interviews, focus groups and questionnaires were conducted, and results were collated and analyzed.

9/11, SADDAM AND CYBERSPACE

The origins of the 2002/2003 transnational peace movement can be traced to the Sept. 11, 2001, Al-Qaeda terrorist attacks in America. From the moment United Airlines Flight 175 crashed into the South Tower of the World Trade Center, the world held its breath waiting for Americas reaction. The international community was aware that the ramifications of America's response to terrorism on home soil would extend well beyond national borders.

While this paper does not to enter into the debate as to whether or not 9/11 provided a convenient "window of opportunity" (Chomsky, 2003; 2003b) for the neo-conservatives within President George W. Bush's Republican administration to accelerate foreign policy initiatives that were already underway, we can be certain that 9/11 dramatically influenced Americas foreign policy objectives. It heralded the arrival of the so-called

"Bush doctrine" (Coulon, 2003; Dumbrell, 2002; Marks, 2002), a policy initiative with pre-emption at its core. The enforced overthrow of regimes hostile to America and American interests was foreshadowed. American and presidential unilateralism was internally legitimized. Indeed, Shuja argues that the "bellicose attitude" America now displays is directly related to the "intense anger and humiliation" Washington experienced in the wake of the 9/11 attacks (2004:30-1). Inevitably, it was never a question of if, when or how America would retaliate, but rather whom it would target first.

Subsequent to the partially successful military incursions into Afghanistan targeting the ruling Taliban regime during the closing months of 2001, the Bush Administration set its sights on Iraq and its President, Saddam Hussein. In line with the Bush doctrine of pre-emption, during the second half of 2002 the Republican administration began the political process of generating a U.S.-led international military support, the "Coalition of the Willing," for the forceful removal of the Baathist regime if necessary.

While the Blair government in Britain supported the coalition, agreeing to provide British resources and personnel, other European nations, including France, Germany and Russia, did not. Cracks in trans-Atlantic relations began at first to appear, then widen, as America remained committed to what continental Europe perceived to be President Bush's unilateralist agenda (Daalder, 2001; Gordon & Shapiro, 2004; Walker, 2001/2).

Closer to American domestic borders, Mexico and Canada also opposed U.S. military intervention in Iraq. And, despite America's potentially persuasive monetary incentives, even weak African and Asian nations were reluctant to commit to any conflict without sanctioning from the United Nations Security Council (UNSC). The international coalition Bush had hoped for to legitimize war in Iraq was failing to materialize. Trans-Pacific ties were tested.

Since 9/11, the Australian government led by Prime Minister John Howard has been steadfast in its support for President Bush and America's pre-emptive ambitions in Iraq. The Australian governments commitment to the U.S.-led coalition was, however, widely condemned by Australian oppositional political parties, former politicians, military personal and members of the general public. Opposition the war was centered around three key arguments. First, the government's uncritical embracement of the U.S.-Australian military alliance was detrimental to Australia's long-term security interests. Secondly, the invasion would bring undue death and destruction to Iraqi civilians. Thirdly, pre-emptive and unilateral action undermined the democratic values that are a necessary condition of international institutions such as the UN. Indicative of widespread public opinion, eminent Australians, including former defense chiefs and Prime Ministers from both side sides of politics, took the unusual action of writing an open letter urging the Howard government not to be part of any military attack on Iraq without UN Security Council backing. Published in newspapers across the country, the letter read:

UN authority a must for action
We, the undersigned, are a former governor-general, prime ministers, leader of the opposition, chiefs of the defense force and other holders of senior military office, including the current president of the Returned and Services League of Australia. We either represented opposing sides of politics or were appointed to our positions by governments of differing persuasions. We would hold varying views on many issues in the public arena, but we join in writing this letter because we share deeply held convictions on a matter that we believe is of the most profound importance. We put this conviction directly and unequivocally: it would constitute a failure of the duty of the government to protect the integrity and ensure the safety of our nation to commit any Australian forces in support of a U.S. military offensive against Iraq without the backing of a specific UN Security Council resolution.

Bill Hayden, governor-general, 1989-1996; E.G. Whitlam, prime minister 1972-75; J.M. Fraser, prime minister 1975-1983; R.J. Hawke, prime minister 1983-1991, John Hewson, opposition leader 1990-1994; General Peter Grafton, chief of the Defence Force 1987-1993; Admiral Alan Beaumont, chief of the Defence Force 1993-1995; Admiral Mike Hudson, chief of the naval staff 1985-1991; Major Peter Phillips, national president, RSL. (*The Age*, Sept. 26, 2002).

Despite international condemnation, the Bush Administration was resolute in its push for regime change in Iraq. On Feb. 5, 2003, U.S. Secretary of State Colin Powell addressed the UN in New York outlining reasons why a pre-emptive attack on Iraq was necessary. During his submission Powell produced satellite photos that he said indicated the presence of active chemical munitions bunkers. He argued that Iraqi scientists had been banned from participating in interviews conducted by UN weapons inspectors, that Iraq had mobile production facilities for biological weapons, and that Iraq remained committed to acquiring nuclear capabilities. Furthermore, Powell alluded to Iraq's links with terrorist organizations, suggesting it had acted as a safe haven for Al-Qaeda operatives (Powell, 2003).

In spite of the allegations, the Security Council remained unconvinced of the legitimacy of any pre-emptive attack on Iraq. Despite America's call for haste, the international community wanted more time to make certain that allegations relating to Iraq's links with weapons of mass destruction and terrorist organizations were indeed correct. Ultimately, international consensus on an appropriate course of action to take in Iraq was not achieved. When hostilities in Iraq commenced on March 20, 2003, only British, Australian, Spanish and Polish forces were engaged in active conflict along side their American allies.

Prior to the commencement of war in Iraq an alternate nonmilitary coalition had, however, been forming under a "no-war" agenda. The emerging transnational peace movement provided a stark contrast to the unilateralist based military coalition. Citizens from around the world had been inspired to become peace and political activists. Although their unity may have been temporary, a truly international social movement had been created. The culmination of peace activists efforts came on the weekend of Feb.14-16, 2003, when demonstrations on varying scales took place in over 600 cities across the globe. Estimates put the number of participants as high as 10 million (Lawson, 2003).

The weekend of global protest signified civilian mobilization on a massive scale. The simultaneous unity of so many people across so many borders succeeded in unveiling a new force within the geo-political system. The unprecedented display of transnational synchronization would simply not have been possible prior to the "e-revolution." The emergence of accessible information and communication technologies (ICTs) has drastically reconfigured the way in which social movement activists operate. Thus, in assessing the February 2003 weekend of global protest or activist groups such as the VPN, *cyberspace*, rather than simply *space* itself, needs to be factored into any analysis.

E-MOBILIZING AND THE VICTORIAN PEACE NETWORK

In the Information Age, social movements have the potential to be powerful agents for social change and offer a counter balance to state power on a number of fronts (Foley & Edwards, 1996). First, their presence demonstrates the existence of transnational networks. Secondly, they provide opportunities for marginalized groups to seek influence on the global stage. Thirdly, they bring together individuals and communities that would otherwise have relatively weak infrastructure levels. Fourthly, they generate local discourse around global problems. Finally, social movements are now no longer dependent on being tied to a particular geographic area. Political action, in other words, is not bound by locality. It is in these regards that the link between the cyberworld and mass mobilization is best represented.

The ability of mass movements to create spaces in which the ideologies they adhere to can be easily accessed are now limited only by human imagination. Time-space compression has been a notable derivative of ICT's continuing to identify new opportunities for social cohesion (Brunn-Leinbach, 1991; Foucault, 1986; Graham, 1998). Increasingly, it is through cyber activities that acts of resistance are taking place. In other words, acts of dissent need no longer be limited to the street. Before proceeding though into the depths of ICT analysis, a word of caution. Despite the partial de-localization of our experiences, geography remains a fundamental determinant in shaping human identities. That is, we continue to be bound in many ways by both time and place. It is important, therefore, that we do not ignore the grassroots realities that underpin our "virtual" encounters. The Victorian Peace Network or VPN, for instance, provides one such example of how a geographically localized activist group became an additional node within a transnational network connected in cyberspace.

Established in September 2002, the origins of the VPN extend no further than a small group of individuals united by a concern over the possibility of war in Iraq. Determined to register local resistance to what had become a transnational conflict, the Melbourne based VPN set about organizing a grassroots campaign to merge with those already underway in distant horizons. At first, the steering committee of the then embryonic VPN set about targeting established organizations that have histories of campaigning on issues related to social justice. As such, various church, trade union, political and environmental groups were approached to become VPN affiliates.

During the second wave of network-building, efforts were made to construct local geographic groups that were prepared to be active around issues related to peace. When hostilities in Iraq commenced during March 2003, more than 60 groups or organizations from various ethnic, religious, political, environmental, humanitarian and labor backgrounds were VPN affiliates. Indicative of the diversity of the VPN's support base, affiliates included the Australian Jewish Democratic Society, Islamic Council of Victoria, Buddhist Council of Victoria, Refugee Action Collective, Oxfam

Community Aid Abroad, Vietnam Vets for Peace, Women for Peace: No Weapons No War, Young Labour Left, Resistance, Medical Association for Prevention of War, Psychologists for Promotion of World Peace, Earth Worker and Friends of the Earth. In addition, more than 50 regional and suburban activist groups formed in contrasting geographic localities such as Inverloch (population: 2,100; distance from Melbourne: 84miles South East), Bairnsdale (11,000; 144 miles East), Shepparton (28,000; 108 miles North), Ballarat (84,000; 66 miles West) and Warrnambool (30,000; 156 miles South West).

Lacking in many of the tangible resources private and government organizations take for granted, the VPN has proven nonetheless to be a highly effective source of information and facilitator of mass mobilization. Between September 2002 and the end of that year, it is notable that the VPN had only one paid employee, an office coordinator working approximately three days per week. During the three-month period spanning January to March 2003, the VPN created only one additional paid position. At the height of the VPN organizational activities, the extent of paid labor emanating from the offices of the VPN amounted to approximately eight days paid labor per week (McClellan, 2004). As a substitute for paid labor, the VPN relied on individuals and affiliates making substantial time, skill and financial commitments to the networks operations. Volunteers eager to contribute to the movement carried out activities such as photocopying, preparing posters, distributing informational leaflets, fund-raising, answering the office telephone and so forth.

It is, however, the transportation of information across networks that we are unable to see that is of particular interest for the present discussion. The task of collectively keeping the VPN's affiliates, activists and interested individuals informed and in touch with each other is administered largely through the VPN's Web site. Maintained by voluntary labor, the regularly updated Web site provides extensive information on any number of issues related to the VPN and the peace movement more generally. Sub-headings on the VPN's Web page include such matters as *Actions*, *Coming events*, *Make your voice heard*, *Posters and Downloads* and *Donate*.

In addition, the Web page is able to place acts of local resistance within an international framework. Issues related to the *Middle East*, *Asia Pacific*, *Weapons & Disarmament* and *War & Intervention* are publicized through a variety of links emanating from the VPN Web page. So to are an array of international opinion pieces by noted social commentators. As at October 2004, articles that could, for example, be accessed via the VPN

Web page include: Tariq Ali (2004) "This is not sovereignty," Robert Fisk (2004) "Restoration of Iraqi Sovereignty — or Alice in Wonderland," Naomi Klein (2004) "Shameless in Iraq," George Monbiot (2004), "Apocalypse please," and Noam Chomsky (2003d) "Dominance and its dilemmas."

In addition to the Web page, the VPN also has an e-mail database consisting of about 2,000 individuals who receive regular information and updates about forthcoming events in the form of an online newsletter. VPN announcements are used to promote rallies, public lectures, weekly vigils, affiliate activities, fund-raising campaigns and the like. The VPN Web page and e-mail announcement list are fast, efficient and cost effective. It is through the use of cyber communication mediums such as e-mail and the Internet that the reach of the VPN is able to exceed what its limited tangible resources would otherwise permit.

"If News has Anything to do with What's New"

While cyber activity is important in facilitating the rapid exchange of information and removing barriers associated with distance and cost, more tangible expressions of social movement activism are required at times to propel the movement's agenda into more mainstream domains. During January 2003, A.C. Nielsen surveyed 1,431 Australians about their attitude towards the war in Iraq. The results showed that 92% of those surveyed were opposed to the war in Iraq; 6% supported Australian military involvement without UN backing; 62% indicated that Australia should only be part of the war as a part of a UN force; and 30% indicated that Australia should not be involved in war (Dodson, 2003).

The Howard government's decision to commit troops to the Iraqi conflict had angered large sections of the Australian public. Pre-war polling indicated that for the majority of Australians, the most important decision an elected government can make — the decision to commit national citizens to a foreign conflict — had been made without their consent. Deciding to deploy the most visible expression of power social movement organizers have at their disposal, the VPN committed to staging a mass rally on Feb. 14, 2003. The rally needed to be a success if the burgeoning peace movement was to maintain its momentum. Pre-rally publicity would be paramount. The role of the media would be decisive.

The relationship between social movements and the media is somewhat of a poisoned chalice. The relationship can, of course, be mutually beneficial. The news agency gets a story while the movement receives exposure to mainstream audiences. Yet the relationship between the two can be soured because each often views the other with degrees of mutual cynicism. For the mainstream media, war is the biggest news story there is (Muller, 2003).

War stories are given top billing for obvious reasons: They contain violence, action, danger, political ramifications and new and dramatic events occur with unusual frequency. Needless to say, international media agencies were well prepared to deliver their own "shock and awe" campaign to news audiences around the world when hostilities in the Middle East finally commenced. What the Australian media hadn't prepared for, though, was the groundswell of anti-war sentiment within the Australian public. Gay Alcorn, a senior investigative reporter with *The Age*, Melbourne's highest selling broadsheet daily newspaper, and one of the few mainstream journalists within Victoria to investigate the peace movement (Alcorn 2003a; 2003b; 2003c), suggests that the print and televised media's reluctance, in general, to provide detailed analysis or coverage of social movement activities stems from a belief that activists are not representative of popular opinion. The argument being that social movements are supported by individuals and organizations that Alcorn suggests the media refer to disparagingly at times as the "usual suspects." Summing up media coverage prior to the rally, Alcorn concludes:

We (*The Age*) didn't cover it in a serious way and I was trying to think why that was. Generally we do cover protests, "Iraqi's protesting outside the U.S. embassy or something" and we do a little piece. It's quite often a junior reporter and well take a picture. Often what were looking for, although we wont actually say it, is if it turns violent, if it somehow turns into something very dramatic. If it is a little protest we don't actually cover it much at all, or, well do a little picture story where you don't have enough words to explain what the hell is going on ... When I first went to say Id like to do a feature on the peace movement, the reaction was "Why would we do a feature on the peace movement? Very cynical. Eventually the editor said you can do it, but don't just talk to the "usual suspects." The usual suspects comes at us a lot, which means that "peace movement" is almost a hangover term, a Sixties, Seventies term, its irrelevant now, that it is the usual kind of people that would be doing it; socialist alliance, some trade union groups, some resistance groups. The view is why should we give them publicity for an extremist view. We were pretty slow I think to pick up that it wasn't, that it was actually quite a mainstream movement or whatever you want to call it (Alcorn 2003d).

Thus, in the absence of exposure from traditional media outlets, the task for rally organizers was to manufacture their own pre-rally publicity. They needed to, as Boyd (2003) suggests, come up with "a grassroots answer to the consolidation of (mainstream) media." Consequently, rally organizers turned to a mixture of old and new campaigning practices. In combination with entrenched mobilizing tools such as manning sidewalk stalls, handing out fliers, hanging posters and organizing public meetings, efforts also turned to occupying the open and uncensored expanses of cyberspace. Fears that VPN messages of peace and activism were only being heard by those already converted proved to be unfounded. A mixture of grassroots organizing, communications extending across distant horizons and widespread and deeply felt public anger over Australia's involvement in the war in Iraq, delivered 250,000 Victorians onto the streets of Melbourne. Similar acts of resistance around the world were equally as impressive. Much to the pleasure of the peaceniks down under, and capturing the essence of the transnational movements, the late edition of the *New York Times* headlined with "From New York to Melbourne: Cries for Peace" (McFadden, 2003).

David Spratt, a member on VPN steering committee and the person responsible for maintaining the VPN's Web page and e-mail announcement list, suggests that the link between cyber activity and the success of the February rallies is deservedly strong. He says,

> The fact that there was mobilization simultaneously around the world was probably entirely due to the Internet. If it had been letters going out it just wouldn't have happened. I think the fact it was worldwide, same day, same time, is entirely due to the Internet. It just would not have been possible in other circumstances. And given the success in a sense of its world wideness, then that makes all the difference in the world ... I don't think its everything, but it certainly helps ... It makes networking easier and cheaper and more effective for movements without money (Spratt, 2003).

The weekend of global protest dramatically altered the focus of the war. Conflict analyses now needed to extend beyond weapons of mass destruction, liberation of the Iraqi people, oil or alleged U.S. imperial ambitions. E-mobilizing and the actions of 10 million peace activists had transcended the immediate military conflict. Schell (2003) described the movement as the "other superpower," suggesting that "if news has anything to do with what is new, then this campaigns birth and activity are the real news." What emerged, he says, was "a portrait of a world in resistance."

CONCLUSION

Cybermedia and those responsible for its administration went to battle over the war in Iraq. They emerged victors of sorts. The weekend of global protest, for instance, provided the most compelling example seen thus far of the possibilities that are available to social movement activists when they engage the cyber world in their organizing endeavors. Internet traffic in form of e-mails, chat rooms, bulletin boards, petitions and so forth have the ability to channel activist energies across transnational borders in previously unaccustomed ways. It is the dynamics of the cyberworld that make possible the apparent seamless integration of place-based groups with movements that are trans-boundary in character.

Social movement practitioners have been obvious benefactors of the ICT revolution. On the other hand, despite activists' best intent, the war went ahead. Pitted against formidable opponents that included the might of the U.S. military and monetary machines, the peace movement, not to the mention the thousands of war casualties, came off second best. Guns, money and political power ensured that the legacy of the peace movement's ideological victories would be limited. In Australia, for instance, despite widespread public condemnation to the war during 2003, the Howard Liberal/National coalition has recently been re-elected to government with an increased majority. The challenge of converting a popularly supported political protest into effect political results was not fulfilled. Ultimately, groups such as the VPN who campaigned against the war and those that supported it, have little choice beyond viewing the 2002/2003 transnational peace movements with mixed emotions. Although difficult to view the non-attainment of core goals and the loss of life in any favorable context, the peace movement succeeded nonetheless in capturing a number of positive experiences. It is these experiences that will be its legacy.

The high tide that we saw with the Feb. 14 rally has left shells dotted on the shore that are there to be picked up in the future. The tide has receded but the high tide has left memories, has left experience, and has left some organizational legacies that will be vital for the rest of the decade. Memory and experience are important in this. Emotion is a very important part of it. It's very intangible. Very difficult to categorize. But a lot of what made VPN work was the emotion and the experience. People had a good time doing it. People felt alive doing it. That's an important part of social movement activity. There is a layer of dedicated activists who do the slog and they do the boring stuff, but there was a lot of young people who got a buzz out of it, and they enjoyed that buzz, and they will search for that buzz again, at other times in history (McClellan 2004).

REFERENCES

Alcorn, G. (2003a, Jan. 18). Back to the barricades. *The Age.*
Alcorn, G. (2003 b, March 22). For protesters, a sense of bewilderment, despair and failure. *The Age.*
Alcorn, G. (2003c, April 15). Giving peace (another) chance. *The Age.*
Alcorn, G. (2003d, Oct. 2).. Personal interview, recorded 2 October 2003, Melbourne, Australia.
Ali, T. (2004, June 28). This is not sovereignty. *The Age.*
Batty, M. (1993). The geography of cyberspace. *Environment and Planning B: Planning and Design,* 20:6, 615-61.
Boyd, A. (2003, Aug. 4). The Web rewires the movement. *The Nation,* 277:4
Brunn, S., & Leinbach, T. (Eds.). (1991). *Collapsing space and time: Geographic aspects of information and communication.* London: Harper Collins.
Castells, M. (1996). *The information age: Vol.1: The rise of the network society.* Oxford: Blackwell.
Castells, M. (1997). *The information age: Vol.II: The power of identity.* Oxford: Blackwell,.
Castells, M. (1998). *The information age: Vol.III: End of millennium.* Oxford: Blackwell.
Castells, M. (1999). Grassrooting the space of flows. *Urban Geography,* 20:4, 294-302.
Castells, M. (2000a). Toward a sociology of the network society. *Contemporary Sociology,* 29:5, 693-699.
Castells, M. (2000b). The network society in D. Held, & A. McGrew (Eds.). *The global transformations reader: An introduction to the globalization debate.* Cambridge: Polity Press
Chomsky, N. (2003a). Wars of terror. *New Political Science,* 25:1, 113-127.
Chomsky, N. (2003bMay/June). What lies ahead for Iraq and the anti-war movement? *Canadian Dimension,* 37:3.
Chomsky, N. (2003c, Nov. 17). One man's world, *New Statesman.*
Chomsky, N. (2003d, Oct. 14). Dominance and its dilemmas. *Sydney Morning Herald.*
Coulon, J. (2003). How unipolarism died in Baghdad. *European Foreign Affairs Review,* 8:4, 537-541.
Daalder, I. H. (2001 Summer). Are the United States and Europe heading for divorce? *International Affairs,* pp.553-567.
Dijk, J. van (1999). *The network society: Social aspects of new media,* SAGE Publications, London.

Dodson, L. (2003, April 1). Backing for the war rises. *The Age.*

Dumbrell, J. (2002 July). Unilateralism and America first? President George W. Bush's Foreign Policy. *Political Quarterly,* 73:3, 279-287

Fisk, R. (2004 June 29) Restoration of Iraqi Sovereignty - or Alice in Wonderland. *The Independent*

Foley, M., & Edwards, B. (1996). The paradox of civil society, *Journal of Democracy,* 7:3, 38-52.

Foucault, M. (1986 Spring). Of other spaces. *Diacritics.* 16, 22-27.

Gordon, P., & Shapiro, J. (2004). *Allies at war: America, Europe, and the split over Iraq.* New York: McGraw-Hill.

Graham, S. (1998). The end of geography of the explosion of place? Conceptualising space, place and information technology. *Progress in Human Geography,* 22:2, 165-185.

Klein, N. (2004 July 12). Shameless in Iraq. *TheNation.*

Lawson, V. (2003 Feb. 17). With one voice the world says no. *The Age.*

Marks, R. (2002). Defining America's brave new world, *Cambridge Review of International Affairs,* 15:2, 329-343.

McClellan, N. (2004). Personal interview recorded January 30, 2004, Melbourne. *Nic McClellan was previously employed as the VPNs Office Co-ordinator.

McFadden, R. D. (2003 Feb. 16) From New York to Melbourne, cries for peace, *The New York Times.*

Monbiot, G. (2004 April 20). Apocalypse please. *The Guardian.*

Muller, D. (2003 March 23). War is the biggest story there is.*The Age.*

Powell, C. (2003 Feb. 5). Remarks to the United Nations Security Council, New York, Retrieved Sept. 20, 2004, from http://www.state.gov/secretary/rm/ 2003/17300.htm

Rheingold, H. (2003). *Smart mobs: The next social revolution.* Cambridge: Perseus Publishing,

Ronfeldt, D., & Arquilla, J. (2001 Oct. 1). Networks, netwars, and the fight for the future. *First Monday,* 6:10.

Schell, J. (2003 April 14). The worlds other superpower. *The Nation.*

Shuja, S. (2004 Summer). The Bush doctrine and the emerging new world order, *National Observer,* 59, 30-40.

Spratt, D. (2003). Personal interview recorded 21 January 2003, Melbourne. *David Spratt is a member of the VPNs Steering committee.

VPN (2003). www.vicpeace.org/aboutvpn

Walker, M. (2001/2 Winter). Post 9/11: The European dimension, *World Policy Journal,* xv111:4, 1-10.

Wellman, B. (1999). A Network Community: An introduction. In B. Wellman, (Ed.). *Networks in the global village: Life in Contemporary Communities.* Boulder, CO: Westview Press.

Wellman, B. (2001). Physical place and cyberspace: The rise of personalised networking. *International Journal of Urban and Regional Research,* 25:2, 227-252.

Discussion Questions

1. While millions of people were mobilized via Internet Web pages for the February 2003 anti-war protest, news coverage of the organizational efforts was minimal, if not hostile. Why did the mainstream media give scant attention to the large numbers of anti-war protesters and failed to follow-up with "second-day" stories?
2. What reasons could governments supporting the war give to justify ignoring protesters mobilized around the anti-war issue?
3. How were "amateur" demonstration organizers able to mobilize such large crowds across several continents around the world for a day of protest? Why were the organizers successful?
4. What characteristics do Australians seem to possess that made mobilization of anti-war protests effective? Could lessons learned from the Victoria Peace Network be replicated elsewhere?
5. What are the differences and similarities of "virtual communities" and "real communities" and do these differences or similarities explain how social movements can be sustained?

CHAPTER TWELVE

IRAQ'S CYBER-INSURGENCY: THE INTERNET AND THE IRAQI RESISTANCE

IBRAHIM AL MARASHI

The Internet is relatively new to Iraq, previously forbidden by Saddam Hussein's government (Human Rights Watch, 1999). Various elements of the Iraqi insurgency used the Web to send messages to audiences inside Iraq and abroad about their efforts to expel U.S. forces after the regime fell in May 2003.

The Internet was a powerful weapon for Iraqi insurgents to report and glorify their operations and to promote their ideologies. Their Web sites featured news, images and slogans of a struggle in Iraq, embellished with photos and videos designed to intimidate their enemies and inspire their sympathizers. The Web allowed insurgents to post statements and videos and to claim responsibility for their attacks — essentially creating an "e-jihad" in a virtual world. While Web sites served the practical purposes of indoctrination, mobilization and recruitment, these portals also include instructional videos and manuals on making explosives to firing weapons, as well as advice on how to attack Coalition and Iraqi forces. As American forces attacked Iraqi insurgent havens in towns such as Falluja, Samarra and Ramadi, these groups found their virtual bases in cyberspace also under attack. Internet sites were either hacked or shut down, but popped up in other places, just as the insurgents were able to reemerge in various areas of Iraq after their bases were destroyed by U.S. and Iraqi government forces.

Numerous Web sites reflected the proliferation of insurgent groups after the 2003 Iraq War. The vast majority of the Web sites were affiliated with Al-Qaeda, the Jordanian national Abu Musab al-Zarqawi, or created by their sympathizers. These portals displayed the religious or nationalist leanings of those who supported the insurgency. An examination of the content and images of those Web sites reveals a unique discourse and symbolic world that has emerged since the beginning of this conflict. The common theme in most of the Web-based discourse is the glorification of a struggle to expel the occupying powers from Iraq. By analyzing these Web sites, one can gain insight into how the insurgents envision a virtual Islamist Iraqi nation, or virtual Ba'ath nation — a nation they endeavor to turn into reality.

ROOTS OF THE CYBER INSURGENCY

The Saudi national, Yusuf al-'Ayyiri, could be considered one of the first "e-jihadists" in Iraq's cyber-insurgency. He authored a 263-page book titled, *The Truth of the Neo-Crusader War*, which could be obtained in PDF format from the Web. In the book, al-'Ayyiri outlined al-Qaeda's tactics for a jihad in Iraq, from ambushes and remote-controlled bombings to suicide attacks, months before the actual 2003 Iraq War began in March 2003. It is believed that he also served as the secret Webmaster of the al-Qaeda-affiliated site of "The Center for Islamic Studies and Research." The original domain disappeared in July 2002 and continued to change Web addresses until May 2003 (Halden, 2003). The Saudi Arabian authorities pursued al-'Ayyiri for planning the bombing of a Riyadh apartment complex in May 2003, and, soon after, he was killed in a battle with police in the town of Ha'il, an event that also resulted in the virtual death of the Web site. He emerged as a virtual martyr on Salafi Muslim Web sites and mailing lists, where even al-Zarqawi referred to him as "The Vanquisher of the Crusaders, Shaykh Yusif al-'Ayiri, God's Mercy on him" ("Al-Zarqawi Claims Attack," April 26, 2004).

There were three main factions involved in Iraq's insurgency and its "cyber insurgency." The first consists of former Ba'athists, that emerged immediately after the 2003 Iraq War, including groups such as "The Return" (*Al-'Awda*), which was made up of former Iraqi security service members and soldiers of the armed forces determined to bring their former leader back to power. However, after Saddam Hussein's arrest in December 2003, the group's stated goal seemed unattainable as he was in U.S. custody. Despite Hussein's capture, many of these forces are still active in posting statements glorifying their attacks in the name of the Arab Socialist Ba'ath Party and their "glorious, leader-hero, Saddam Hussein."

A few months after the war, elements in Iraq emerged that had no desire to fight for the return of their former dictator. Their attacks against Coalition forces were specifically directed towards ending the American occupation of Iraq. These groups can be categorized as the second faction, the Iraqi nationalists, where most of their fighters are recruited from Iraqi towns, such as Falluja, Ramadi and Samarra — commonly referred to as the "Sunni Arab Triangle" — which are sympathetic to this faction's tactics. However, there is no evidence to link the Webmasters with the actual parties involved in the fighting.

The third faction can be traced to a shadowy organization known as "The Soldiers of Islam" (*Jund al-Islam*), which emerged in September 2001. It was made up of Kurdish Islamists who tried to seize control of several villages near the Iraqi town of Halabja in northern Iraq in order to establish a mini-state similar to the Taliban's Afghanistan. The organization accepted Al-Qaeda fighters fleeing Afghanistan in October 2001. In December 2001, the group changed its name to "The Supporters of Islam" (Ansar al-Islam). After U.S. Special Forces and Kurdish militias destroyed their main base during the Iraq War, members of *Ansar al-Islam* scattered over Iraq itself and most likely to Iraq's neighboring countries.

Abu Musab al-Zarqawi, a Jordanian national, was believed to play a key role in directing the *Ansar*, although he was not declared its leader. It was reported that in late 2003 *Ansar al-Islam* changed its name to "Army of the Supporters of the Sunna" (*Jaysh al-Ansar al-Sunna*). The relationship to another organization, "The Unity and Jihad Group" (*Jama'at al-Tawhid wa 'l-Jihad*), which is also believed to be led by al-Zarqawi, is unclear ("Al-Zarqawi deceased top aid," Nov. 30, 2004). To make matters even more confusing, this group assumed a new name, "The Al-Qaeda Organization for Holy War in the Land of the Two Rivers" (*Tandhim Qa'ida Jihad fi Bilad al-Rafidayn*), indicating al-Zarqawi's allegiance to Osama bin Laden's organization. These insurgents have stressed the importance of the Internet in spreading their message and have described it as the best forum to spread information. "If you cannot publish it on the Internet for some reason, you may send it to another person who would publish it for you, or send it to *mujahidin* sites" ("Zarqawi group threatens prime minister," July 14, 2004).

The United States and the interim Iraqi government have attributed much of the violence in Iraq to foreign Arab fighters linked to the aforementioned organizations. However, Iraq analysts have argued that the numbers of the foreign fighters pales in comparison to the numbers of Iraqis involved in the insurgency. One of the Islamist Web sites, "The Pulpit of the Sunna and Community," gave a breakdown of 67 "martyrs" killed in battles with American and Iraqi security forces and revealed where most of these foreign fighters originate ("Forum posts 'martyrs' in Iraq," Dec. 30, 2004). Examining the list offers a sample of origins of the foreign fighters allied with al-Zarqawi. Out of the 67 killed, 24 were from Saudi Arabia, by far the largest group, and 12 were from Syria. Other fighters came from Lebanon, Jordan, Yemen and Libya. Nevertheless, nine Iraqis were also killed fighting for this organization, indicating a level of local cooperation with the foreign fighters ("Forum posts 'martyrs' in Iraq," Dec. 30, 2004).

Besides the Zarqawi-linked factions, there were other Islamist insurgent groups who also utilized the Web to glorify their "struggle." Such factions included "The Mujahideen Battalions of the Salafi Group of Iraq" (*Kata'ib al-Mujahidin fil-Jama'a al-Salafiyya fil-'Iraq*), which claimed its spiritual mentor as the deceased, 'Abdallah 'Azzam (bin Laden's mentor in the Saudi Arabia and later Afghanistan). The other faction included the "Islamic Army in Iraq" (*Al-Jaysh al-Islami fil-'Iraq*); however, it is unclear if the organization is made up of Iraqis or foreign fighters.

Overview of the Web Sites

One of the difficulties in examining Web sites affiliated with the insurgents in Iraq is the temporary and transient nature of the portals, as their Web sites change addresses frequently, closed by their Web hosts or hacked. Perhaps the most valuable repository of their Web sites is the online U.S. government Open Source Center (OSC; formerly known as the Foreign Broadcast Information Service[FBIS]), which devotes an entire section to collecting what they term "jihadist Web sites." Similarily, *Islam in the Digital Age* is a Web site dedicated to tracking portals of these natures and maintained by the scholar Gary R. Bunt.

The al-Zarqawi-linked factions did not maintain their own Web site, but relied on several portals to post their statements, usually signed by his spokesman Abu-Maysara al-Iraqi. Al-Iraqi insisted that his statements were only posted on the *Al-Ansar al-Islam* bulletin board, a password-protected site that did not accept new registrants. Only then could members on all other Islamic jihadist bulletin boards copy his statements. ("Forum posts 'martyrs' in Iraq," Dec. 30, 2004). The Web sites of the "Fortress" (*al-Qal'a*), the "Movement for Islamic Reform in Arabia," the "Faithful," and the "Faith Restoration Network" often displayed messages issued by al-Zarqawi. The *al-Anbar* forum named after a province in Iraq where Falluja lies, posted communiques from Zarqawi's *Jama'at al-Tawhid wal-Jihad* group, as did the "Global Islamic Media Center" and the "Islamic Renewal Organization" forum. "The Lion's Den" forum is dedicated to the promotion of al-Zarqawi's *"jihad,"* as is the *al-Saqifa* Web site. "The Islamic Magazine" (*al-Majala al-Islamiyya*) has a special section called the "'Usama Islamic Forum," which carried posted messages from al-Zarqawi after he declared his allegiance to Osama bin Laden, as has the "Islamic Dialogue Open Forum."

The Ansar al-Sunna Army (ASA) maintained its own Web site, although the domain names changed frequently. The group's links to Zarqawi were illustrated by the fact that the Jordanian has used the ASA's Web sites to post his messages as well. Their first Web site was found at <www.al-ansar.biz>, which was passworded and inaccessible to nonmembers. The group later used the following domain at <www.ansar-sonnah.8m.com> and then changed to a new URL at <www.ansarnet.ws/vb>. There was no evident change in the appearance of the Web site and its forums, but it dropped its password requirements to make it more accessible to a wider audience. The group's online Arabic magazine, *Ansar al-Sunna,* could be downloaded from the site in PDF format.

Other less numerous Web sites posted messages from Iraqi insurgent groups independent of Zarqawi's control. The "Crow" (*Al-Uqab*) Forum, for example, issued a statement by an alliance of "resistance groups" in Iraq. The "Islamic Advantages Network" and the "Arab Dialogue Forum" posted messages from Iraqi insurgents or their sympathizers. The Baghdad al-Rashid forum at carried statements from Iraqi Sunni insurgent groups, as well as contains a link to a Ba'athist Web site. The pro-Saddam "Iraq Patrol" Web site also featured statements issued by the Ba'ath.

SYMBOLISM IN ISLAMIST AND BA'ATHIST WEB SITES

Religious Terminology

The symbols and rhetoric of insurgent Web sites revealed the groups' ideologies and political orientations. Factions loyal to Al-Qaeda and Zarqawi tend to justify their actions in a religious context, while the discourse of pro-Ba'athist sites glorified its struggle with Iraqi nationalist slogans, albeit with a sprinkling of Islamic terminology.

Religious symbols dominated the Web sites devoted to the actions of Zarqawi, who was usually referred to as a "prince" (*amir*) or "religious leader" (*shaykh*). Each of Zarqawi's messages posted on the Internet followed a specific format. They began with the invocation, "In the name of God, the most Merciful, the Most Gracious," followed by the number of their communiqué. Afterwards, the statement was opened by a verse from the Quran, such as,

> Then when the sacred months have passed, then kill the polytheists wherever you find them, and capture them and besiege them, and lie in wait for them in each and every ambush ("Al-Zarqawi group claims responsibility," May 6, 2004).

Such a verse usually gave a religious sanction to the text of the message, outlining attacks against Coalition and Iraqi security forces. The verse was followed by an injunction to God and a greeting to the Prophet Muhammad,

> Thanks to God, God of the universe, and prayer and peace be upon the leader of the *mujahidin*, our Prophet Muhammad, and upon his followers and decisive and blessed companions ("Al-Zarqawi group claims responsibility," May 6, 2004).

The text of the message usually began with the date of an attack according to the Islamic calendar and the intended target:

> In the early morning of Thursday, 17 Rabi' I, 1425, the *mujahid* hero Abu-Mat'ab from the land of the two holy sites, God's mercy be upon him, departed in a car loaded with 600 kilograms of TNT for the main headquarters of the occupying forces and their apostate quislings, known as the Republican Palace. It was a successful operation, in which the brother was granted the chance to harvest many of the infidels and the apostates ("Al-Zarqawi group claims responsibility," May 6, 2004).

These statements were usually signed by the organization, in this case The Military Wing of The *Tawhid* and *Jihad* Group ("Al-Zarqawi group claims responsibility," May 6, 2004).

This faction's struggle was carried out in the name of restoring the "Islamic nation" (*umma*) and the fighters and battles in this cause were labeled with a standard set of euphemisms. Fighters linked to Zarqawi were usually referred to as "holy warriors" (*mujahadin*), "lions" (*asud*) or "knights" (*fursan*). Their brigades included titles such as the "Martyrdom-seeking Brigade" or were named after heroes of the Islamic conquest, such as Khalid Ibn al-Walid, otherwise known as "The sword of God" (*Sayfallah*); Hamza, the Prophet's uncle and accomplished swordsmen; Tariq Bin-Ziyad, who invaded Spain in 711; and Salah al-Din, who liberated Jerusalem from the Crusaders in 1178. In reward for these fighters' sacrifices, the Web messages promise that the *Hur al-Ain* (beautiful virgins in paradise) would be waiting for those "martyred" in battle ("Al-Zarqawi's deceased top aide," Dec. 30, 2004), and one message stated how these fighters "race each other to win the *huri*s in Paradise" ("Ansar al-Sunni claims attack," Jan. 7, 2005).

The Neo-Crusaders

The portrayal of the United States as a neo-Crusader entity in the heart of the Islamic world has proven to be a dominant symbol in the Web-based discourses. In some of the poetry accompanying the messages, references are made to the battles of the Crusades:

> There is no option other than *jihad*, a blow of fate, with immeasurable consequences. O stallions of death, get ready for *jihad*. Hittin, thou war shall go on ("Al-Zarqawi group claims responsibility for attack on Iraqi national guard," July 17, 2004).

The battle of Hittin, in 1177 was a reference to Salah al-Din's defeat of a Frank army during one of the Crusades. The battle in this case refers to the United States, whose goal is to "raise the Cross in the lands of Islam" ("Al Zarqawi claims responsibility for al-Basra port attack," April 26, 2004). While some messages accuse the United States of invading Iraq to control its oil, this faction argues that the real motivation is an American plan to counter "the increasing Islamic expansion" ("Al-Zarqawi group claims operation in Iraq," April 6, 2004). One *mujahadin* statement said that this goal was even more important to the United States than acquiring Iraq's oil ("Interview with foreign Mujahadin," Dec. 1, 2004).

These groups also developed a specific terminology to describe a "Zionist conspiracy" to occupy Iraq, which, they said, was controlling the American occupation from behind the scenes. For example, a new Iraqi flag had been designed to replace the old flag, which the United States and interim Iraqi authorities associated with the old regime. The new flag, which featured a blue crescent in the middle of two blue lines was deemed by many Iraqis as too similar to the Israeli flag, which had a Star of David in place of the crescent. This design convinced many of the insurgent Web sites of such a conspiracy to control Iraq. *Al-Basrah Net* featured an image of the new Iraqi flag morphing into the shape of the Israeli flag. The Iraqi Ba'ath Party posted a detailed statement to *Al-Basrah Net* deriding the

Iraqi Government for changing the flag, especially for taking out the "God is Great" script from its middle and dedicated its operations to the "flag and its banner" ("Al-Zarqawi, Ba'ath Party claim responsibility," June 24, 2004). Messages also stressed that the Israeli intelligence agency Mossad was omnipresent in Iraq. For example one statement in reference to the leader of the Patriotic Union of Kurdistan said:

> Ask the American-Zionist agent Jalal Talabani about the death squad, affiliated with the Mosad, which resides on Al-'Adnaniyya Street in the center of Kirkuk and which is trying to swiftly liquidate the symbols and cadres of al-Sunna ("Al-Zarqawi claims operation in Iraq," April 6, 2004).

The Collaborators

The Web-based texts indicated how the insurgents, many of whom happened to be Arab Sunni Muslims, considered Iraqi Kurds and Shi'a as "collaborators" with the United States and the "Zionists." Those collaborators with the Iraqi government are accused of selling "their religion, honor, and land cheaply for few *darahim* [Iraqi currency]" ("Al-Zarqawi group claims responsibility for North Baghdad attacks," June 7, 2004). Prominent Shi'a cleric, Ayatollah Ali al-Sistani, was also branded as one of these collaborators and was referred to as "the Imam of infidelity and atheism." *Al-Basrah Net* posted a message issued by the "Mujahidin Brigades" (*Kata'ib Al-Mujahidin*) stating that al-Sistani was part of a "Zionist-American plan." Another statement on the Web site concluded that he has "helped his Anglo-Zionist God and deprived the Iraqis of their victory." Shi'a Muslims, even those who were not directly linked to the occupation, were considered apostates and were usually referred to as "rejectionists" (*al-rafida*), a label used by Salafi groups to deride the sect as "unbelievers." Al-Zarqawi had declared that the Shi'a doctrine conflicted with the Islamic faith, giving examples from history on Shi'a support for Christians and "the enemies of Islam." Members of the Iraqi Shi'a parties were referred to as "traitors" as demonstrated in the following statement: "Yusuf, the traitor and apostate general and the Interior Ministry undersecretary, who belongs to the Islamic Da'wa Party," referring to the Shi'a party that played an active role in the interim Iraqi Governing Council and that fared well in the January 2005 elections.

Symbols employed in pro-Ba'athist Web sites shared some similarities with the Islamist portals. The pro-Saddam *Iraq Patrol* Web site also threatened Iraqi "collaborators" or "agents" and still referred to the Ba'ath as the "legitimate leaders of Iraq." Their statements also portrayed Iraq as being occupied under "Zionist, colonialist pretexts." However, while religious symbols were scattered throughout Ba'athist discourse on the Web, the site claimed the struggle was still in the name of "Unity, Liberty and Socialism" — the official slogan of the Party when it was in power ("Post says suicide bombing suspect in U.S. camp," Dec. 22, 2004). Despite Saddam Hussein's incarceration, he was still referred to as the "struggling leader of the Party."

The Fortress Web site posted an audio recording by al-Zarqawi, which demonstrated the interplay between these labels. Al-Zarqawi considered interim Iraqi Prime Minister 'Iyad 'Allawi a "traitor" and a "tool of the 'tripartite Satanic and infidel alliance,'" which consisted of the United States, who are the "bearers of the Cross"; the Kurds, who are "injected with Jews"; and the Shi'as, derogatorily referred to as "rejectionists" ("Al-Zarqawi releases new recording," Sept. 13, 2004). He added,

> The barking dog, 'Iyad 'Allawi, thought that his pack of rabid dogs that he calls the Rapid Deployment Forces would settle the battle with the glorious lions of the victorious sect and would extricate him and his masters from the rotten quagmire — an impossible dream to achieve.

Often the leaders in Iraq were compared with the Pharaohs, pre-Islamic leaders known for their blasphemy and iron-rule: "Such infidels will follow on the path of those who preceded them, such as Pharaoh's soldiers, Nimrod and Abu-Jahl" ("Al-Zarqawi group issues video of beheading of Japanese hostage," Nov. 2, 2004). Threats against Iraq's leaders were invoked in the name of God:

> We bring to you the good tidings of what will hurt you, 'Allawi, for even though you escaped from the rockets of death that dropped fireballs on your house, with God's grace, our quiver is still full of the arrows of death. And if an arrow missed you, soon, by the grace of God, another arrow will penetrate your heart ("Al-Zarqawi group threatens Iraqi prime minister," July 14, 2004).

Messages demonstrated how the insurgents played on words to express their views. For example, the Iraqi Shi'a Party, the Supreme Council for the Islamic Revolution in Iraq (SCIRI) has a militia called the Badr Corps. One Web site referred to it as the "Treason Corps," alleging it "participated in the killing of Muslims and the raping of Muslim women in Al-Falluja" ("Ansar al-Sunnah gives curfew, warning," Dec. 29, 2004). In some cases, the White House was referred to as the "the Black House." Another statement played on the notions of the West as the "civilized world":

Leading armies of sodomites and idiots who don't even know what they are fighting for. The civilized world came to the birthplace of civilization as we know it and have shown to the world how uncivilized they are ("Al-Zarqawi group claims assassination," Jan. 10, 2005).

The Minister of the Environment is referred to as Mishkat al-Kufr (*Al-Kufr* is Arabic for infidelity, the antonym of the minister's real name, which is al-*Mu'min*, which means the "believer") ("Al-Zarqawi group claims assassination attempt against Iraq enviroment minister, Aug. 24, 2004). When referring to the Qatar-based Arab news channel Al-Jazeera, one Web site says, "The suspicious role that the 'piggish' television channel and other secular channels play to frustrate Muslims and revive rotten nationalism is revealed, day after day" ("Al-Zarqawi's Al-Tawhid group claims responsibility for Iraq assassination," May 18, 2004). "Piggish" or *al-Khanzira* appears to be a play on the name Al-Jazeera.

THE GOALS OF THE INSURGENCY

While those behind the violence in Iraq were portrayed as a monolithic movement in the Western media, the Web sites revealed often-contradictory goals of the factions that form the insurgency. For example al-Zarqawi used the Web to appeal to constituents in the *umma*, calling on this "nation to wake up." The message said the West fears that the "Islamic giant" will wake up and reach the gates of "Rome, Washington, Paris, and London" ("Al-Zarqawi group claims operation in Iraq," April 6, 2004). His factions are using Iraq as a battleground in the process of establishing a greater Islamic *umma*, ruled by a Caliph, as mentioned in one statement attributed to Zarqawi:

Lastly, we make our vow to God and his messenger to be the cutting swords of the heads of apostates, traitors, and spies, and to remain the highly drawn, high in the sky swords, to raise the banner of God is Great, and establish the Caliphate. We warn each and everyone not to govern with but what has been enacted by God. We will be standing alert" ("Mujahadin brigades in Iraq and Syria," Oct. 28, 2004.

The first step in establish the Caliphate is the striking at the United States, which protects the Arab regimes and impedes the unity of the *umma*:

These operations herald imminent victory to eliminate the Crusader and Jewish hegemony on Muslim countries and overthrow apostate and despotic regimes in Islamic states (Sawt Al-Jihad article highlights 'jihad's success,' Nov. 1, 2004).

These organizations believe that the Soviet Union collapsed due to the actions of the *mujahadin* in Afghanistan, and the fighters in Iraq aim to bring about the collapse of the United States in a similar fashion. One al-Zarqawi linked site declared that they were well prepared for an impending American attack on Al-Fallujah in November 2004, and that this assault would usher in the collapse of the United States in the same way the USSR had collapsed previously ("Interview with foreign mujahadin from Al-Fallujah," Dec. 1, 2004). The *Ansar al-Sunna* Army said in one Web site, "We do not want to drive it (the United States) out of Iraq, but rather bring about its downfall inside its (Iraq's) borders. If it stays, it collapses, and if it leaves, it loses everything" ("Interview with foreign mujahadin from Al-Fallujah," Dec. 1, 2004).

The *mujahadin*'s actions in Iraq were part of a greater struggle in bringing about the collapse of the United States and restoring the Caliphate, a persistent theme expressed by Osama bin Laden as well. One statement remarked that al-Zarqawi's pledge of allegiance to bin Laden "represents the unification of jihad in the world and the beginning of the announcement of an Islamic Caliphate." It also added, "The fighting in Iraq is not for liberation ... instead it is for the establishment of the Islamic Caliphate" ("Interview with foreign mujahadin from Al-Fallujah," Dec. 1, 2004). Even bin Laden himself, in an audio speech, reminded his audience that Iraq was once the seat of the Caliphate, during the Abbasid period and perhaps it can take up this role again. He greeted the Iraqi people as "our patient kinfolk in Baghdad, the house of the Caliphate and its environs" ("Bin Laden message on Iraq," Dec. 28, 2004).

While these fighters explicitly stated their desire to establish Iraq as the seat of the *umma*, or bring about the return of Saddam Hussein, the Web-based discourse indicated that another goal of their struggle was to redress the "humiliation" endured by the Iraqi people under an American occupation. For example, one site said, "The *mujahidin* build with their skulls the glories of their religion. They are sick of and hate the life of humiliation." Another statement said, "Praise be to God the Compeller, who humiliated the infidels and inflicted pain on them day in and day out" ("Abu —Mus'ab al-Zarqawi group claims responsibility," June 5, 2004). An Islamist militant site declared the effectiveness of their tactics:

> Muslims are capable of attacking the largest force, no matter how equipped and qualified, because guerrilla warfare does not depend on the size of the military operation alone, but also on its impact and the humiliation it can cause the enemy" ("Al-Zarqawi's group claims responsibility for attack on Baghdad convoy," June 15, 2004).

In reference to the situation of Iraqi prisoners, *Al-Basrah Net* posted the 21st edition of online journal, titled "The Call for Resistance" *(Nida'a al-Muqawamah)*, which was issued by the Iraqi National Alliance, a coalition of insurgent groups. One article featured the headline, "Only Eradication of the Perpetrators Will Erase the Iraqis' Humiliating Scandal" ("Al-Zarqawi group claims responsibility for North Baghdad attacks," June 7, 2004).

UTILITY OF THE WEB IN THE IRAQI INSURGENCY

The Internet served as an effective tool of not only challenging the occupation powers but also for countering the news channels that refused to air the insurgent media. While the Iraqi government had accused the Arabic news channel, Al-Jazeera, of supporting the Iraqi insurgency, the insurgents criticized the channel for taking orders from the United States. For example, *Al-Basrah Net* posted a statement issued from the outlawed Iraqi Ba'ath Party accusing Al-Jazeera of taking orders from U.S. diplomats and the Iraqi government:

> It is necessary to direct and turn our attention to the Arab news stations with Al-Jazeera at the forefront. Al-Jazeera abides by controls that the occupation authority placed on orders from Nabil Khoury, a State Department official.

The party alleged that Khoury ordered Al-Jazeera not to broadcast any of their statements or even to refer to the party ("Iraqi Ba'athist Party accuses U.S. diplomat of blocking media efforts," Nov. 15, 2004). The *Al-'Izah* bulletin board posted a statement from The Islamic Army in Iraq Media Branch announcing that every employee of the Dubai-based Al-Arabiyya station is a target of the Group ("Al-Zarqawi's group issues statement, posts video on operations," Oct. 12, 2004).

The al-Zarqawi factions stated on another Web site,

Al-Arabiyya TV channel should be hit. The station and all who sustain it help in the killing of Muslims. The station and its staff mislead and hide the crimes of the United States and its barking agent Allawi. We pray to God to speed up the strike ("Kuwait's Mujahadin threaten 'collaborators,'" Jan. 10, 2004).

Some of the insurgent groups criticized the Arab news channels for not broadcasting their statements. A group calling itself Saddam's Fidayin in the Northern Region posted a statement on the *Baghdad al-Rashid* forum, stating that they had sent information about their attacks against the Americans to Al-Jazeera but the station refused to air it ("Saddam's Fedayeen issues list of operations in Mosul," Nov. 16, 2004). One Islamist Web site stated that to overcome such obstacles, there was a need for "a jihadist satellite station that will take upon itself the responsibility of spreading jihad education within the *umma*" ("Al-Zarqawi group video on Haifa Street," Nov. 26, 2004).

While the Internet domain illuminated the goals and motivations of the insurgents, they also served as an effective tool of religious indoctrination. Web sites often posted religious guidance and ruling from clerics, who justified violence against U.S. forces. For example, a *fatwa* (an Islamic ruling) by 'Abd al-Sattar al-Kubaysi, a member of the Iraqi Muslim Scholars Council, was posted on the "Fortress" Web site stated: "It is lawful to kill Arab and Muslim troops if they enter Iraq." He also warned that "the Iraqi people and the resistance will consider any Arab or Muslim armies that enter Iraq to be occupation armies, and thus the shedding of their blood is permitted" and "any Arab or Islamic government that agrees to send troops to Iraq is an agent of America" (Al-Zarqawi group claims killing of SCIRI commander," Aug. 11, 2004). The *Ansar al-Sunna* Army Web site offered information on how to organize resistance cells but included religious guidance on undertaking this task:

There should be *Shari'a* (Islamic law) basis for the establishment of jihadist cells, including but not limited to the following: Definition of religious basis and regulations for each individual in the cell. There should be a religious authority to review decisions taken before any operation. It is preferred that a cell has several such individuals to form a small *Shari'a* council ("Iraqi 'resistance" groups claim Al-Zarqawi killed," April 9, 2004).

Islamist Web sites proved useful in the dissemination of online literature and manuals. The Al-Qaeda-affiliated online magazine *Voice of the Jihad* (*Sawt al-Jihad*) speaks of the "jihadists achievements" in Iraq and Saudi Arabia ("Sawt Al-Jihad article highlights 'jihad's successes,'" Nov. 1, 2004). One issue featured an article entitled "Illuminations on the Path of Jihad, The Road to the Battle Ground" by the deceased Yusuf al-'Ayyiri. The *Minbar Ahl al-Sunnah* forum posted about 61 English-language weapons and military training manuals as zip files or in PDF format, including U.S. Army field manuals, the CIA's *Improvised Sabotage Devices*, *The Mujahidin Poisons Handbook*, and *The Mujahidin Explosives Handbook*. The Web site had been offline since mid-September 2004 but it reappeared later in December ("Participants post audio tape of attack on U.S.Consulate in Jedda," Dec. 14, 2004).

Their portals serve as message boards to announce developments and alliances in the evolution of the insurgency. Perhaps the most significant event that was announced through this medium was Oct. 17, 2004, when Abu Mus'ab Al-Zarqawi's pledged his allegiance to bin Laden:

> We deliver to the nation the news that both Jama'at al-Tawhid wal-Jihad's Amir and soldiers have pledged allegiance to the *shaykh* of the *mujahidin*, Osama bin Laden and that they will follow his orders in jihad for the sake of God so there will be no more tumult or oppression, and justice and faith in God will prevail ("Al Zarqawi's group pledge allegiance to Bin Laden," Oct. 17, 2004).

After that date, an announcement was made by and the *Al-'Izah* bulletin board by Abu-Maysara al-'Iraqi that the group had changed its name from *Jama'at al-Tawhid wal-Jihad* to Al-Qaeda of Jihad in the Land of Two Rivers.

While the Web has proven useful in declaring allegiances, it has served a valuable role in distancing the various insurgent groups from another. U.S. authorities in Iraq have stated that former Ba'ath insurgents were cooperating with the Islamists in sowing violence in Iraq, but in the virtual realm, in fact, they were rivals and often criticized each other. For example, in the "Fortress" forum, an audio message from al-Zarqawi to the *umma* blamed the United States for alleging "the remnants of the defunct regime and the elements of the infidel Ba'ath are the ones who are waging resistance operations" (Al "Zarqawi claims operations in Iraq," April 6, 2004).

Another Web site also listed the enemies of al-Zarqawi, among which included the Ba'ath:

I bring to you the good news that your brothers in Al-Falluja are doing well, especially our beloved leader Abu-Mus'ab, who has baffled the Americans, Zionists, and Ba'ath elements ("Posts on Zarqawi group downing U.S. 'spy plane,'" Dec. 20, 2004).

In fact, both factions competed with each other on the Internet for the claim of leadership of the Iraqi resistance. Al-Zarqawi's group and the Iraqi Ba'ath Party claimed in separate online statements responsibility for attacks against U.S forces in June 2004. Al-Zarqawi's group used the *Al-'Izah* Web site to release their claim of responsibility for an attack, while the Ba'athist posted their claim on Al-Basrah Net (Al-Zarqawi, Ba'ath Party claim responsibility for 24 June attacks," June 24, 2004).

The Internet also served as a tool for the insurgents to threaten the Iraqi elections that took place on Jan. 30, 2005. On Nov. 4, 2004, the Ba'ath party posted threats on the *Al-Basrah Net* Web site against any Iraqis who voted in the elections and to target any election employees and candidates, claiming that the United States would rig the process to promote pro-American candidates. It stated,

> boycott and reject the election farce ... to oppose it by different means and make it fail ... because that will mean the downfall and failure of the enemy and its agents ("Ba'athist threat to elections," Nov. 4, 2004).

The *Ansar Al-Sunnah* Army Web site also posted messages to deter Iraqis from going to the polls in January. They justified the call for a boycott since the elections would legitimize an "infidel and apostate government" that rules with "infidel man-made laws." The accused "the infidel agent government" of giving the Iraqi "people the illusion that they are free and that they are electing their president and their government in a 'democratic and free' manner." According the *Ansar al-Sunna* Army, such a process is sacrilege since, "Democracy means, according to its gods and creators, the rule of the people by the people" ("Ansar al-Sunnah army threatens Iraqi elections," Nov. 18, 2004) and not the rule of God himself. The statement ended with the threat:

> Our jihadist brigades will kill every candidate that runs in the election conspiracy. His destiny and that of his family will be bitter death, and his house will be blown up with them inside.

They claimed that they would destroy election centers and that anyone who participated in the process would be considered to be "spies, traitors, and agents." In reference to the list system that was used in the election process, they said:

A special list will be issued with the names of those who participated in this wicked conspiracy, the elections, and they will be eliminated within 48 hours of the appearance of this list ("Post says suicide bomber informant in U.S. camp," Dec. 22, 2004).

While the violence on Jan. 31, 2005, was relatively minimal by Iraqi standards, the use of the Web prior to the election day demonstrated how the insurgents have used this medium to serve as a tool to intimidate Iraqi from taking part in establishing an Iraqi government.

CONCLUSION

Since the beginning of the Iraqi insurgency in April 2003, the evolution of this conflict has been mirrored in a virtual world. One of the insurgent's primary aims has been to broadcast their cause to an Iraqi, Arab and global audience. The cyber-insurgency has been an integral part of this campaign. The Iraqi insurgency has proven adept in manipulating the media to broadcast their struggle, inspiring its sympathizers while creating a mass-mediated fear into Iraqis who may consider working or cooperating with the interim authorities.

To compliment these tactics, the Web's ability to disseminate videotaped attacks and beheadings have given the insurgents an ability to circumvent the mainstream media, especially when Arabic satellite channels such as Al-Jazeera and Al-Arabiyya fail to air their statements and activities. These portals reveal an insurgency with little central coordination and often-contradictory goals. Analyzing the Web-based discourse reveals that while some insurgents may be content with causing American forces in Iraq to withdraw, other factions will not stop their struggle until a Talibanesque state is established in Iraq, indicating the violence could continue in this nation indefinitely.

Zarqawi was killed after an American aerial attack near the city of Baquba on June 7, 2006. Yet the cyber-jihad has proved resilient. Despite the death, the Web continues to serve as a means to perpetuate the jihad.

References

"Abu-Mus'ab Al-Zarqawi group claims responsibility for 5 June Baghdad ambush," (FBIS) GMP20040606000014, June 5, 2004.

"Al-Qaeda-Affiliated Sawt al-Jihad posts 28th issue of online magazine," (FBIS) GMP20041102000217, Nov. 2, 2004.

"Al-Zarqawi-affiliated group claims responsibility for attack on coalition headquarters in Baghdad," (FBIS) GMP20040506000218, May 6, 2004.

"Al-Zarqawi, Ba'th Party claim responsibility for 24 June attacks," (FBIS) GMP20040624000272, June 24, 2004.

"Al-Zarqawi claims responsibility for Al-Basrah port attack," Foreign Broadcast Information Service, (FBIS) GMP20040426000227, April 26, 2004.

"Al-Zarqawi claims responsibility for attack on Iraqi Interior Ministry official," (FBIS) GMP20040522000175, May 22, 2004.

"Al-Zarqawi claims operations in Iraq, calls for more attacks," (FBIS) GMP20040406000026, April 6, 2004.

"Al-Zarqawi's deceased top aide Al-Shami eulogized in video," (FBIS) GMP20041213000005, Nov. 30, 2004.

"Al-Zarqawi group claims assassination attempt against Iraqi Environment Minister," (FBIS) GMP20040824000082, Aug. 24, 2004.

"Al-Zarqawi group claims responsibility for attack on Iraqi national guard," (FBIS) GMP20040718000153, July 17, 2004.

"Al-Zarqawi claims responsibility for Al-Basrah port attack," (FBIS) GMP20040426000227, April 26, 2004.

"Al-Zarqawi group claims responsibility for North Baghdad attacks; Iraqi cleric questions legitimacy of new govt.," (FBIS) GMP20040607000286, June 7, 2004.

"Al-Zarqawi group issues video of beheading of Japanese hostage, statements," (FBIS) GMP20041102000262, Nov. 2, 2004.

"Al-Zarqawi group video on Haifa Street; Al-Fallujah Shura Council statement," (FBIS) GMP20041126000216, Nov. 26, 2004.

"Al-Zarqawi releases new recording," (FBIS) EUP20040913000069, Sept. 13, 2004.

"Al-Zarqawi's Al-Tawhid group claims responsibility for Iraqi assassination," (FBIS) GMP20040518000261, May 18, 2004.

"Al-Zarqawi's group claims assassination of Dep. Police Chief, posts videos of raid on police station, U.S. transgressions," (FBIS) GMP20050110000297, Jan. 10, 2005.

"Al-Zarqawi's group claims responsibility for attack on Baghdad convoy," (FBIS) GMP20040615000222, June 15, 2004.

"Al-Zarqawi's group issues statement, posts video on operations; Islamic Army in Iraq threatens Al-Arabiyah employees," (FBIS) GMP20041012000291, Oct. 12, 2004.

"Ansar Al-Sunnah Army threatens Iraqi elections; Tips on ambushing U.S. helicopters," (FBIS) GMP20041118000268, Nov. 18, 2004.

"Ansar al-Sunnah claims attack on joint US-Iraqi patrol; 'Mujahidin of Iraq' announces rebuilding of Army," (FBIS) GMP20050107000240, Jan. 7, 2005.

"Ansar al-Sunnah gives curfew, warning on military targets, elections; Al-Zarqawi group claims assassination attempt on SCIRI leader," (FBIS) GMP20041229000213, Dec. 29, 2004.

"Ba'th threat to elections; Al-Zarqawi group on Japan; Martyr with Al-Shami," (FBIS) GMP20041104000306, Nov. 4, 2004.

"Bin laden message on Iraq, Al-Zarqawi; processing plans," (FBIS) GMP20041228000079, Dec. 28, 2004.

"Forum posts names of 'martyrs' in Iraq," (FBIS) GMP20041230000232, Dec. 30, 2004.

Halden, Phillip. (2003, Dec. 13). Salafi in virtual and physical reality. *ISIM Newsletter*, p. 38.

Human Rights Watch (1999). *The Internet in the Mideast and North Africa: Free expression and censorship.* New York: Human Rights Watch.

"Interview with foreign Mujahidin from Al-Fallujah, solicitation for jihad posted," (FBIS) GMP20041201000327, Dec. 1, 2004.

"Iraqi Ba'th Party accuses U.S.diplomat of blocking media efforts, Offers rewards for killing US, Iraqi soldiers," (FBIS) GMP20041115000249, Nov. 15, 2004.

"Iraqi 'resistance' groups claim Al-Zarqawi Killed; Basic planning for jihadist cells posted," (FBIS) GMP20040409000240, April 9, 2004.

"Kuwait's Mujahidin threaten 'collaborators'; Posts claim Al-Qaeda plans attacks in US, threaten Al-Arabiyah, election workers," (FBIS) GMP20050110000284, Jan. 10, 2004.

"Mujahid claims to have seen Al-Zarqawi; Al-Basrah net postings denounce Al-Sistani ," (FBIS) GMP20040825000257, Aug. 25, 2004.

"Mujahidin brigades in Iraq and Syria issue statement; Al-Zarqawi's group claim responsibility for attacks," (FBIS) GMP20041028000317, Oct. 28, 2004.

"Participants post audio tape of attack on U.S.Consulate in Jedda, military manuals," (FBIS) GMP20041214000334, Dec. 14, 2004.

"Post says suicide bomber informant in U.S.camp; Ba'th Party threatens elections," (FBIS) GMP20041222000255, Dec. 22, 2004.

"Poster confirms Al-Zarqawi's group changes name; Ba'th warns U.S.against trying Saddam," (FBIS) GMP20041022000215, Oct. 22, 2004.

"Posts on Zarqawi group downing U.S.'spy plane'; Ansar al-Islam of Bahrain Web site," (FBIS) GMP20041220000310, Dec. 20, 2004.

"Saddam's Fedayeen Issues List of Operations in Mosul," (FBIS) GMP20041116000241, Nov. 16, 2004.

"Sawt Al-Jihad article highlights 'jihad's success' during Ramadan," (FBIS) GMP20041112000233, Nov. 1, 2004.

"Zarqawi Group claims killing of SCIRI Commander; Post: Attack US, EU Sudan NGOs," (FBIS) GMP20040811000282, Aug. 11, 2004.

"Zarqawi group threatens Iraqi prime minister, claims Al-Ramadi operation," (FBIS) GMP20040714000238, July 14, 2004.

WEB SITES:

Al-Anbar Forum. www.anbaar.net.
Al-Ba'ath Al-'Arabi. www.albaathalarbi.org.
Al-Saqifa. www.alsakifah.org/vb.
Al-Uqab. www.alokab.com/forums.
Ansar al-Sunna Army. www.ansarnet.ws/vb.
Arab Dialogue Forum. www.hdrmut.net
Baghdad al-Rashid forum. www.baghdadalrashid.com.
Center for Islamic Studies and Research. www.alneda.com.
Faith Restoration Network. www.alpalsam.com.

Faithful. www.ekhlas.com/vb.
Fortress. www.qal3ah.net.
Global Islamic Media Center. www.alhesbah.net.
Iraq Patrol. www.iraqpatrol.com.
Islam in the Digital Age. www.virtuallyislamic.com.
Islamic Advantages Network. forum.fwaed.net.
Islamic Dialogue Open Forum. www.openforum.ws/vb.
Islamic Magazine. www.almjlah.com.
Islamic Renewal Organization Forum. www.tajdeed.net.
Lion's Den Forum. www.alm2sda.net/vb.
Movement for Islamic Reform in Arabia. www.islah.tv/vboard.
Open Source Center <www.opensource.gov>.
Voice of the Jihad. <www.hostinganime.com/neda5/sout/>.

DISCUSSION QUESTIONS

1. Given that fewer than 5% of the population in the Middle East was connected to the Internet during the Iraqi insurgency that erupted after the 2003 Iraq War, who were these Web sites trying to reach?
2. Why did the primarily secular Ba'athist Web sites employ essentially the same symbolism as the Islamcist Web sites?
3. How did the insurgency Web sites use traditional propaganda techniques to further their religious/nationalistic goals? To whom would these techniques appeal?
4. Some of the insurgency Web sites used message boards. How effective are message boards in supporting or detracting from general themes featured on the Web sites?
5. Could the Iraq insurgency have sustained its momentum in an earlier era of traditional media and person-to-person discourse? Has the Internet prolonged the insurgency?

Part III

How People Used
New Media During the War

CHAPTER THIRTEEN

INFORMATION WARFARE: E-MAIL AS AN INSTRUMENT OF PROPAGANDA DURING THE 2002-2003 IRAQ WAR

EMMANUEL ALOZIE

The need to find a secure and instantaneous vehicle for relaying missile telemetry information at the height of the Cold War in the 1960s led to the development of the Internet. Developed by the Advanced Research Projects Agency (ARPA) of the Department of Defense, the primary use of the Internet was to transfer large databases using file transfer protocol (FTP). However, in addition to transferring data, researchers and contractors in different parts of the United States began to use the network to send personal communications to their colleagues. These activities marked the genesis of the Internet and the e-mail protocol (Dominick, Sherman & Messere, 2000; Kayany, 2001).

The vehicle remained within the military for more than 20 years until it grew into civilian and commercial use in the mid 1980s. The evolution largely transformed the way societies interact, conduct business, compete in the international market, deal with social welfare issues, and set agendas. It contributed to macro and micro structural changes in the economic system that led to the economic boom, sociocultural and political changes of the 1990s (Alozie, 2001). By 2005 the Internet was projected to generate about $269 billion in sales and influence another $378 billion in offline sales (Kayany, 2001). However, the demise of many high technology firms in the late 1990s made these estimates questionable (Alozie, 2001). Even as the Internet became a force for good, it has also become a force for ill will as well (Lefevre, 1997; Albarran & Goff, 2000).

Recognizing the diffusion and persuasive power of the Internet, entities of all strides employed the technology as an effective propaganda tool. They relied on it to campaign for their objectives. Of all the forms of utilities available on the Internet, e-mail has become the most widely used medium for campaign in favor or against an issue, a policy and an entity. As a propaganda tool, there is a growing recognition of e-mail as an important vehicle for mobilizing the public in support, or against government policies as in the case of the 2002-2003 Iraq crisis and war (Weaver, 2004; Webb, 2003). Prior to the invasion of Iraq in 2003, the George W. Bush Administration used the technology to galvanize domestic and international support for its intention to invade Iraq and overthrow Saddam Hussein's regime.

The administration also employed e-mail as a weapon of war to stir an Iraqi rebellion against the regime. Beginning in early 2003, the U.S. government launched an *agit prop* e-mail campaign to encourage and mobilize the people of Iraq to overthrow Saddam Hussein and prepare for an invasion by American and British forces. That campaign was acknowledged as the first use of e-mail as an offensive information operation. The practice is known as information warfare (Delio, 2003). Just as the U.S. government was using these new information and communication technologies to advance its policies, national and international groups that supported or opposed those policies also used e-mail as a mobilization vehicle to advance their causes before, during and after the 2003 Iraq War. This exploratory study, the first of its kind, will use interpretative approaches and interviews and will draw upon information and propaganda theories to explore the following subjects:

- How U.S. officials framed the e-mail messages as offensive operations to incite Iraqi officials and the public to rise against the Hussein regime. The study examines how the Iraqi regime reacted to the campaign. An attempt will be made to examine the role and effectiveness of e-mail as a weapon for information warfare.
- How groups supporting or opposing the Bush administration policies framed their messages to advance their goals by analyzing their contents.
- Examine the effectiveness of using e-mail as a propaganda vehicle through a combination of surveys and focus group interviews of recipients of pro- and anti-Bush e-mail campaigns.

REVIEW OF LITERATURE

Garrison (2004) observes that new media technology has often been studied within the context of the uses and gratifications theoretical approach. He explained that research based on this approach focuses on various uses of a new or existing technology as well as the intended gratifications and psychological needs an individual derives from using the technology. He stated that the wide acceptance of e-mail utility seems to follow the classic concept of diffusion, which offers research opportunities that focus on the audience and their use of e-mail and its role in an ever-evolving communication environment.

Studies (Black, Bryant & Thompson, 1998; Kayany, 2001; Garrison, 2004; Albarran & Goff, 2000) attributed the growing penetration of e-mail to a number of factors.

- Convenience and ease of use (replacing fax machines because it is faster, more reliable, personalized and does not require paper).
- Asynchronous communication. Users do not have to communicate in real time in order to send or receive a message.
- Information networking among users. It permits electronic conferencing via a listserv, whereby users can send messages simultaneously to several people in different locations.
- Cheaper than facsimile or long-distance telephone calls.

E-mail represents an effective way to communicate and monitor public opinion about current events and issues. It enables the exchange of information and views about news stories with potential sources, gatekeepers and the public. It is used for distribution of press releases, texts of speeches, tip sheets, announcements, graphics and press conference notifications to target specific recipients. Researchers employ it to chase down information, confirm acts, monitor distribution lists and discussion groups, exchange information with other news researchers and subscribe to alert services. It creates an interactive communication with audiences and they often value reader feedback.

Distinct and like-minded bodies worldwide, including citizens' groups, pressure groups, non-governmental organizations, trade unions, political parties, and consumer activists, have recognized the ease and convenience of e-mail provides them an opportunity to generate greater dialogue, organize, cooperate, draw attention to their issues and establish a consensus of view. By developing Web sites, listservs and other Internet protocols, the paradigm of protests against government policies and business entities have been complemented and shifted from street demonstrations to electronic protests (Aikat, 2000; Klopfenstein, 2000). E-mail offers an avenue for supporters of an idea, subject, individual and entity to muster, organize and demonstrate support (Weaver, 2004, Webb,

2003). Electronic protests provide an avenue for inexpensive, far-reaching and influential medium for groups to organize and disseminate information about the consequences of government policies and actions. It also offers consumer activists an avenue to expose flaws and trade secrets. At the same time, the government uses e-mail for propaganda and as a weapon for war, while business entities use it as a powerful vehicle to fight back (Whillock, 2000).

Despite its advantages, reliance on e-mail does pose some problems: It can be used to attack or support government policies and other issues without exploring both sides. It can be used as a propaganda tool by one government against another without justification. "E-mail bombing" has been used to interfere with national sovereignty when governments or entities from different countries use it to disrupt or destroy sites they oppose. As an information warfare mechanism, e-mails have been used for intrusion into government and industrial Web sites. Cyber-terrorists have used e-mail to relay information that alters relations among nations and to disrupt the conduct of business (Aikat, 2000; Whillock, 2000; Black, Bryant & Thompson, 1998; Kayany, 2001; Garrison, 2004; Albarran & Goff, 2000). It is a favorite tool terrorists employ to communicate with each other and campaign for their causes.

E-mail can also be used to destroy the reputation of companies and individuals by disgruntled elements. Marketing companies increasingly utilize online information services for marketing, generating junk mail that clogs the network. It represents a vehicle for invading privacy. For example, businesses sell personal information and employers use it to monitor the activities of employees. It should be noted that businesses lose money when employees spend inordinate amounts of time on their e-mails. E-mail has become a favorite tool for initiating financial scams. Junk e-mail or spamming clogs networks, thus increasing costs, and reducing productivity; prompting calls for legislation to curtail spamming because it has become a nuisance (Aikat, 2000; Whillock, 2000; Kayany, 2001; Gershon, 2001; Albarran & Goff, 2000; Damon, 2004). Attempts to control spamming have remained unsuccessful, but filters have been developed to protect users. E-mail is used to convey worms that cripple the networks.

As Garrison (2004) stated, the growing penetration and application of e-mail for a variety of purposes, good or bad, provides researchers opportunities to examine the role of the Internet from different theoretical perspectives, as this study does with its focus on the role e-mail as a vehicle for propaganda and information warfare.

THEORETICAL FRAMEWORK

As a mechanism for altering attitudes and opinions and spurring actions, propaganda historically has been used for religious conversion, political reorientation, promoting national unity and development, and war mobilization, as well as for promoting goods and services and changing lifestyles (Severin & Tankard, 2001). Propaganda employs values, symbols, emotional appeals and cognitive content to achieve a given goal (Alozie, 2004).

Whether propaganda works in the interest of the targeted group, or for the benefits of propagators, remains a subject of debate. Some argue it depends on the aim of the campaign. Some argue that when propaganda is used to promote a common good, it serves the interest of the targeted group and society, but when it is used for self-serving aims, it serves the interests of the propagators — usually a small group with a narrow interest. Others contend that any message that is manipulative and fails to appeal to rational reasoning must be discouraged because it leads people to act emotionally and irrationally. Irrational action, they argue, hardly promotes the welfare of a society. It remains a subject of controversy and debate to ascertain when propaganda has not been manipulated, even when it could be argued that it is being used for the good of the society (Ionesco, 1968).

Given these contradictions, Lasswell (1927, p. 9) defines propaganda as any activity that "refers solely to the control of opinion by significant symbols, or, to speak more concretely and less accurately by stories, rumors, reports, pictures, and other forms of social communication," while Brown (1958) describes it as a "symbol manipulation designed to produce action in others" (p. 299), aimed at achieving an "action which is the goal of the persuasive effort will be advantageous to the persuader but not in the best interests of the persuadee" (p. 300).

Lasswell (1927, 1937, p.195) identified four objectives of propaganda: (1) to mobilize hatred against the enemy; (2) to preserve the friendship of allies; (3) to preserve the friendship and, if possible, to procure cooperation of those that are neutral; and (4) to demonize the enemy. To achieve these goals, propagators employ a variety of devices, including name-calling, glittering generality, transfer, testimonial plain folks, card-stacking and bandwagon (Severin & Tankard, 2001).

Lasswell (1927, 1937) and Ellul (1965) noted that propaganda is used dominantly in times of crisis and war to maximize power and support through subordinating or disparaging enemies, while minimizing the material and physical cost of power. Since the end of the Vietnam of War, when thousands of Americans lost their lives, the American public has been reluctant to support and send their wards to war where high casualty is expected. Since then, most administrations have recognized that reluctance and have employed a variety of strategies to keep American military losses at the barest minimum to inoculate Americans from suffering casualties.

That recognition and the lukewarm domestic and international support may have accounted for the Bush administration's decision in early 2003 to use information warfare to undermine the Iraqi administration. Borne out of the spectacular development in information and communication technologies, Fogleman (1995) stated that information warfare consists of activities that deny, exploit, corrupt, destroy, or protect information. Means of conducting information warfare include psychological operations, electronic warfare, military deception, physical attack, and various security measures. If coupled with traditional warfare techniques, information warfare is designed and aimed at achieving advantages over military adversaries (Goldberg, 2003).

Goldberg (2003) defines information warfare as "the offensive and defensive use of information and information systems to deny, exploit, corrupt, or destroy an adversary's information, information-based processes, information systems, and computer-based networks while protecting one's own" with the goal of achieving advantages over military or business adversaries. The concept has also been described as the use of information or information technology during a time of crisis or conflict to achieve or promote specific objectives over a specific adversary or adversaries; however, not everyone shares the view that is limited to the realm of traditional warfare because information warfare is being applied in other contests such as economic, political, and public affairs debate (www.cogsci. princeton.edu/cgi, 2004, Nov. 1).

This study attempts to discern the role, effectiveness and impact of e-mail as an instrument of propaganda aimed at altering attitudes and opinions during the 2002-2003 Iraq crisis and war. A goal of the study is to uncover the propaganda techniques opponents and proponents of the Bush administration's Iraq policies used to achieve their respective goals. It will rely on surveys and focus group interviews to determine the effectiveness of the campaign.

METHOD: AN HERMENEUTIC APPROACH

This pilot study, which aims at determining the value of e-mail as a propaganda instrument, strives to achieve two main goals: (1) use critical textual analysis of the contents to determine the frames being cultivated and (2) use a combination of surveys and focus group interviews to explore the role or impact those communications played in decision-making and actions of recipients. To accomplish the goals, the analysis, which examines a variety of aspects and characteristics of e-mail communication including content, reactions, feedbacks and impact it elicited, is hermeneutic in nature because it applies a variety of research techniques and critical insights (Alozie, 2003; Costello & Moore, 2004; Hudson & Ozanne, 1991).

Emphasis is placed on critical-interpretation of the texts of the e-mail, reports and surveys and focus group interviews for data collection. Since it was manifestly impossible to access and analyze every e-mail raised in support of or against Bush's 2002-2003 Iraq policies or those U.S. military officials used for their information campaign, data for this study was generated from the following sources: direct e-mail the analyst received, those his relatives received, and e-mails received by participants in the study as well as accounts published or broadcast from reputable media outlets. Data is also gathered from surveys and focus group interviews of available samples of members of a senior comprehensive university community in the American heartland. The analyst developed the survey and focus group questions and instruments based on the aforementioned aspects and issues being explored.

The study used the critical-interpretative approach to analyze the contents of e-mail texts, reports and responses obtained from the surveys and focus group interviews to gain insights about the role and reliance on e-mail as a propaganda vehicle. As a form of social criticism, the critical-interpretative approach calls for thoughtful examination of texts and/or subjects under review based on personal and direct experiences (Newcomb, 1974; Vande Berg, Wenner & Gronbeck, 1998). The experience may come from an analyst's personal contact with the texts (such as e-mail solicitations received to join a cause or those sent to others), information extracted from the mass media, or from participants who had contact with texts on the population the analysts surveyed or interviewed. It is assumed that direct experience allows the analyst to explore the characteristics and underlying meanings by exploring the surface, intended and ideological messages a text conveys in an attempt to discern their contents and implications.

It should be noted that when applying the critical-interpretative approach, an analyst can use surveys and interviews to extract micro- and macro-information surrounding the texts, issues and the audience. The interpretation is aimed at discerning the contours of patterns of communication from the data obtained from the population; discovering broad categories with regards to similarities and differences of perception and practice interaction; discerning the meanings, and implications from the group(s); and the responses of those who received a message developed and acted on (Schroeder, 1999).

Costello and Moore (2004) observed that there are obvious risks in a technique that depends on individuals to report or express their own experiences in an informal manner. An analyst is not unable to affirm if the subjects are getting the complete truth from their sources; nor can they be certain if their interpretation of the data is accurate. In view of these shortcomings, they stated that the findings cannot be generalized and are not predictive. However, Costello and Moore (2004) state that the technique allows the researcher to look at the "rough edges, special cases, and subtle peculiarities" of real experience (Lull, 1990, p. 30), and to discern how meanings and influences are created, negotiated, and dispersed throughout society (Fiske, 1988, p. 248).

The critical-interpretative approach enables the analyst to overcome these shortcomings through deconstruction. Deconstruction of texts involves organizing, describing, analyzing, and evaluating symbols and contents, relationships and patterns to cultivate an informed perspective about texts and responses from the population (Vande Berg, Wenner & Gronbeck, 1998; Berger, 1995; Alozie, 2003). To do so, the analyst develops categories by identifying basic structural elements within a text or among groups of texts as well as the response of the individual surveyed or interviewed. It also offers insights into understanding past, present and future sociocultural values and orientation that influences members of a society. Past studies that have employed the approach have classified communicative acts based upon the type of manipulation strategies used, the kinds of situations in which communicative acts occurred or were initiated, the apparent purpose of the these communication acts, their similarities and differences, as well as the reactions elicited, as this study does (Chesebro & Hamsher, 1974; Bitzer, 1968; Wilson & Arnold, 1976, Wrage, 1947; Bush, Bush & Boller, 1994).

Analysis and Findings

The findings and discussion that emerged from this study were gleaned from textual and interpretative analyses of (a) e-mails U.S. military officials employed to seek to galvanize support from Iraqis to turn against the Hussein administration and reports about their efficacy; (b) anti- and pro-Bush administration Iraqi policies e-mails; and (c) results of surveys and focus group interviews of recipients of anti- and pro-Bush administration Iraqi policies.

The Bush Administration and Use of E-mail to Overthrow the Saddam Hussein Regime

U.S. Information Warfare Campaign: Beginning in January 2003, the U.S. military periodically sent e-mails to Iraqi military, government officials, and the public aimed at persuading them to rebel against the Hussein administration. The e-mails, written in Arabic, marked the first time the United States launched information warfare. Four dominant themes emerged from the analysis of the e-mail texts used in this psychological information campaign. The e-mails:

- urged Iraqis to protect their families by helping UN inspectors and turning away from Saddam Hussein;
- advised Iraqis to disobey any orders they may receive to deploy chemical, biological or nuclear weapons;
- pleaded with them to identify instead the locations of such weapons to inspectors or to destroy the weapons, and
- painted the Hussein administration as inhuman, corrupt and intransigent.

Iraqi Government Reactions: At the time, e-mail and Net connectivity in Iraq was only officially available through the government-owned, heavily censored (uruklink) net services. However, some users — mostly scholars, scientists and government officials — assumed their access to the Net and e-mail communications through their home or work computers was private, without government intervention, because they paid $50 a year fee for subscribing to (uruklink). Nonetheless, the government monitored Internet activities. Due to strict government control, the Iraqi public could only get online at about 36 Internet centers across the country. Despite efforts to restrict public access, it was not difficult for anyone with a phone line, a government ID card and cash to establish e-mail accounts with Yahoo and Hotmail (Delio, 2003).

However, accessing the Internet does not connote Iraqi subscribers could surf as much as they wanted. Access remained unreliable because of the constant disruption of service due to poor infrastructure, power failures and other steps the government undertook to regulate and monitor Internet access and communication. By monitoring Internet activities, Iraqi officials were able to block access to e-mail they objected.

For example, reports indicated that within 15 minutes of the arrival of U.S. information campaign e-mails in inboxes, uruklink would go down while the contents of mailboxes were deleted. Using content-filtering software from 8e6 Technologies, an American company, Iraqi government restricted or completely blocked access to vast portions of the Internet (Delio, 2003).

Effectiveness of the U.S. Information Campaign: Judging the effectiveness of the campaign is based on public reports and records about the reaction of the Iraqi public and officials. Based on those reports — and the fact no major insurrection against the regime was evident — it could be argued that the campaign was largely ineffective. There were no known reports of demonstrable reactions and defections of Iraqi government officials or public unrest as the e-mail campaigns urged. However, the names of those who reacted favorably to the campaign by providing information, defection, or taking action per the advice of the information might have done so privately or might not have been disclosed for security purposes by U.S. officials, thus remaining an official secret of the U.S. military officials and government.

On the other hand, the ineffectiveness of the campaign to produce significant open reactions and defections could be attributed to a number of other factors. These include the fact that most Iraqis were not computer literate. In a country where the monthly salary is about $120, where the cost of a computer is about $500, where it costs about 15 cents to send or receive a message and $1 to access the Web for an hour, access to the Internet remained the privilege of a few, not the masses (Delio, 2003). Fear among users that government monitors might spot, arrest and deal harshly with anyone reading and responding to e-mail from the U.S. military officials might also have been a factor. Also, constant service disruption kept people fearful and ambivalent from connecting to the Internet often, thus affecting the effectiveness of the campaign. Earlier Iraqi government campaigns that called the Internet a vehicle for ending civilization, impugning traditional cultures and ethics, and a tool of Western domination have taken hold among Iraqis, forcing them to develop a skeptical view of information they receive from the Internet (Delio, 2003).

It should be noted the Hussein administration used Western technology to establish Web sites where people can access and receive government propaganda. Iraqi government initiated e-mails within and outside its borders to counter the United States.

Anti and Pro-bush Administration Iraqi Policies

To discern the frames and stance the e-mails conveyed regarding the Bush administration's call for invasion of Iraq, the study attempted to answer the four basic questions Entman (1991) suggested an analyst should explore when reading a text. These include scrutinizing the problem being debated, the cause, consequence, and who to praise or blame.

Anti-Bush Policies: E-mails that opposed the Bush policies and invasion of Iraq focused on making the case against a war and consequences of a U.S. invasion. The themes that emerged in opposition of the Bush policies and physical invasion of Iraq oriented around the following frames:

- The United States must not act alone; acting alone will isolate the United States.
- Loss of American and Iraqi lives will be enormous.
- Cost of war will be exorbitant.
- Hussein has been contained, and cannot invade other countries.
- Iraq does not support or harbor terrorism.
- Iraq was not involved in 9/11.
- Military action should be the last resort; diplomacy should be allowed to work.
- George W. Bush is avenging his father's failure to overthrow Hussein in 1991.
- Invasion of Iraq will instigate hatred of Americans.
- Invasion of Iraq will increase racism.
- American Middle East policy is unfair and one-sided.
- Invasion will instigate instability in the region.
- America is acting of out selfish interest to control Iraqi oil and economy.
- America plans to install a regime pliant to Israel and the West.
- America wants to establish a military base in the region
- Iraq does not possess weapons of mass destruction.

Pro-Bush Policies: If the anti-invasion e-mails focused on making a case against war, pro-invasion e-mail conveyed the rationale for immediate military action to overthrow and disarm the Hussein administration. The following themes were gleaned from their contents:

- Overthrowing the Hussein administration would liberate Iraqis and promote democracy.
- Overthrowing the Hussein administration would promote free market.
- Overthrowing the Hussein administration would secure world trade and economy.
- Overthrowing the Hussein administration would keep America, the West and allies in the regions   safe.
- Overthrowing the Hussein administration would curtail terrorism and keep the homeland safe by focusing the attention of militants in the region.
- Invading Iraq would project American power to other dictators and force them to behave.
- Overthrowing the Hussein administration would curtail the spread of weapons of mass destruction.
- Overthrowing the Hussein administration would promote human rights in the region.
- Invasion must take place because the Hussein administration has ignored diplomacy and failed to comply with UN resolutions.

Surveys and Focus Group Interviews about Bush Administration Iraq Policies

Results of Surveys and Focus Group Interviews: The results of the surveys and focus group interviews produced a variety of orientations, including the impact of e-mail, what actions the e-mail campaigns suggested and spurred, and the effectiveness of e-mails as a propaganda tool. The results also outlined problems associated with e-mail campaigns that interfere with its effectiveness, and what the respondents suggested should be done to improve the effectiveness of future e-mail campaigns.

Whether anti-or pro-Bush Iraq policies, respondents in the survey and focus group interviews stated that the e-mails campaign reinforced their beliefs and motivated them to action. They stated the e-mail prompted them to learn more about the subject, enhancing their knowledge and awareness of the complexity of international dispute. They stated that the e-mail campaign forced them to share and debate the policies with their families, friends and colleagues. It should be noted some of the respondents stated they did not recall receiving e-mail on the subject. This might be a result of conducting the surveys and interviews almost a year after the crisis began and over six months after the physical invasion of Iraq by the United States and the coalition of the willing. About half of the respondents indicated that some of the actions the e-mails told them to undertake ranged from organizing street protests and marches to sharing information, raising and donating money and engaging in distribution of materials and texts. Some also stated that the e-mail campaign motivated them to get involved in local political activism. The respondents stated by providing links and directing them to those links they sought more information about the policies and events.

However, the other half seemed to be ambivalent about the effectiveness of the e-mail campaigns because of the problems they encountered. They identified the clutter of e-mails they received made it practically impossible to read most. They indicated that they read only e-mails from friends, families and known organizations. Some respondents stated most of the e-mail they received lacked diversity of opinion because they came from like-minded activists. The respondents said that, when they sought answers, the failure to receive feedback made it difficult to clarify rumors and obtain answers to questions that affected their ability to reach personal consensus. This is one of the confounding findings of the surveys and focus groups because the Internet is viewed as an interactive medium where people are able to communicate and share information instantaneously. Respondents complained that the e-mails clogged their computers and attracted worms that disrupted the use of their computers. They pointed out some of the Web sites the e-mail directed them to in order to receive further information were inactive. Such failure produced reluctance and frustration.

To overcome these and other problems associated with the e-mail campaign, respondents suggested areas of improvement, including finding means of improving interactivity, as well as providing instant feedback and active Web sites where one can be directed to seek out more information. They called on campaigners to keep text information short and simple and to provide directed information. The respondents stated that they were more likely to respond to e-mails that came from individuals and groups known to them. The respondents indicated personalizing e-mail with regard to source and content information makes the protocol a more effective campaign vehicle. Most respondents stated presenting both sides of an argument is more effective than making only a one-sided argument.

OBSERVATIONS AND CONCLUSIONS

This study found that U.S. information campaigns as well as e-mail campaigns of groups that opposed or supported the Bush administration's policies of invading and overthrowing the Saddam Hussein administration combined two forms of propaganda devices: card-stacking and name-calling. Name-calling instigates ill perception about a person, organization or issue in order to influence people to reject and condemn the subject, idea and entity without thorough examination. Card-stacking involves the selection and use of facts or falsehood, illustration or distraction, and logical and illogical statements to make the best or worst correlation for an idea, program, or individual.

Name-calling and card-stacking have one common element — they are often one-sided. They do not necessarily include facts that may help a person engage rational thoughtful elaboration of both sides of an issue. For example, anti-Bush e-mails hammered the ill consequences of U.S. physical invasion and occupation of Iraq. Their one-sided arguments concentrated on the arrogance of the Bush administration and consequences of invading a sovereign nation without UN sanction. They condemned the Bush administration for its unilateral foreign policy, adding it has made America a pariah in the world, produced world hatred for America and doomed to destabilize the region and fail. They argued that the cost would be enormous and described government officials as having been corrupted with greed in their quest to work in the interests of huge oil companies. Anti-Bush e-mails omitted the arguments the Bush administration advanced for seeking the invasion of Iraq as such a liberating Iraq and overthrowing regime that has flouted UN resolutions and posed danger to its neighbors having instigated two wars in two decades.

On the other hand, the pro-Bush policy e-mails underscored the need to remove from power the Saddam Hussein administration because of the danger and instability it posed to the region and the world. Their one-sided arguments concentrated on the evils of the Hussein administration and his failure to comply with UN inspections as demonstrated earlier. The contents of their e-mail campaign reflected the Bush administration as resolute and as a guardian and promoter of human rights, democracy values and free market. However, they failed to present information regarding the cost of the war, human and material losses, and the failure of the Bush administration to garner international support for immediate military action. While stressing the fact that the Hussein administration disrupted the work of UN weapons inspectors, they failed to indicate that the inspectors asked for more time to work, a request the Bush administration rejected.

Nevertheless, the respondents in the surveys and focus group interviews might not have found name-calling and card-stacking as effective e-mail campaign techniques because they were primarily one-sided. The respondents indicated that they would like to have received e-mails that presented both sides of the arguments for invading, or not invading Iraq in order to learn more about the issues involved so as to reach informed decisions.

The respondents also identified other problems that hampered the effectiveness of the e-mail campaign. They pointed out that the e-mails did not adequately elaborate on the issues involved in the crisis by explaining the argument the opposite side made, or was making. Thus, if one agrees or opposes the policies, the e-mail campaigns tended to reinforce those beliefs. They did not shift minds or win new converts. The subjects stated they started treating e-mails dealing with the campaign as junk, trashing most except those sources they recognizes or interacted with in the past. They pointed out some attachments were difficult to open and some links to other sites did not work.

However it must be noted that e-mails helped galvanize some people to act. The large worldwide February 2003 demonstrations of groups that opposed the invasion indicated that e-mail campaigns made significant contributions. Recipients donated money to groups they supported. However, the e-mail campaign's modified success could be argued because organizers complemented their e-mail activities with traditional forms of mobilization, including mass media, advertising, door-to-door solicitation, human contact, speeches and posters, among others. Pro-invasion groups conducted scattered marches in support of Bush policies to counter those anti-war groups sponsored. In addition to helping raise money for either group, the surveys and focus group interviews demonstrate it could be argued that the other key role e-mail campaigns contributed related their offers of advice and directions on what, where, when, and how to do something or take action. At the same time, it must be stated some respondents indicated the campaign did not spur them to do or act.

The Bush administration's reliance on name-calling and card-stacking as propaganda techniques in its information warfare effort of rallying Iraqi officials and public to disrupt the Hussein administration can be summed up as having produced an "ambivalent outcome." The attempt, aimed at avoiding the physical invasion in order to placate reluctant Americans who were afraid of loss of American lives and to assuage a skeptical international community failed to establish known tangible results. Despite studies that have found propaganda techniques do work to mobilize people (Severin & Tankard, 2001), the paucity of public reports and records about demonstrable responses of Iraqi's public and officials indicated the technique might not have worked as the administration had hoped judging from public reports. However, without surveying and interviewing Iraqis who received the information, or having access to secret American and Iraqi information, the observations noted about the impact of information campaign among Iraqis must be viewed as advisory, not concrete evidence.

Several factors may account for the lack of reports indicating demonstrable responses: Fear that exists among Iraqis who lived under Hussein's brutal regime for more a generation. They might have been afraid of the administration's reaction if they were caught responding to the campaign. Thus, the U.S. government might have kept most response from Iraqis secret. The failure of the United States to assist the 1991 Shi'ah uprising and rebellion against the Hussein regime after the Americans had encouraged them to do so, might well have resulted in distrust of the U.S. government's e-mail campaign this time around. The former Bush administration stood by as Saddam's regime brutally squashed the Shi'ah uprising, killing thousands.

One could argue that the Iraqi administration took concrete and effective steps to disrupt the flow of messages from reaching its public through jamming and disruption of services. Lack of access due to poor penetration of the Internet among Iraqis may be a factor. Skepticism among Iraqis about American intention in the Middle East might have contributed (Khoury-Machool, 2004). Like the Bush administration, the Hussein regime employed propaganda to counter America's. The regime's effort might have been more effective than the Bush administration's, especially among those in the international media and governments predisposed toward disliking the Bush administration's application of hegemonic power for political ends. However, it must be noted that observations and conclusions regarding the effectiveness of Bush's information warfare campaign were based on observations of the author, not surveys or interviews of the government officials who sent the message, or Iraqis who received them. A future study in this regard is important to fully discern the role and effectiveness of e-mail as a weapon of war.

These observations make it difficult to ascertain the effectiveness of e-mail as an instrument of propaganda and mobilization. But it must be pointed that the vast and instantaneous global reach will continue to be used as an instrument of propaganda. More studies are needed to understand their effectiveness. Campaigners must keep in mind their target groups are asking for contrasting views instead of drumming a one-sided message. Offering advice and direction on what to do to a targeted group represents the most useful aspect of employing e-mail as a propaganda tool and information warfare vehicle. It has proven to be an effective vehicle for calling attention to issues, raising money and getting the public and government official to act.

REFERENCES

Aikat, D. (2000). Of online news and "rogue" Web sites: Impact of the Web on the private section. In A.Albarran & D. Goff (Eds.), *Understanding the web: Social, political and economic dimension of the Internet*. Ames, Iowa: Iowa State University Press, pp. 49-71.

Albarran, A., & Goff, D. (Eds.), *Understanding the web: Social, political and economic dimension of the Internet*. Ames, Iowa: Iowa State University Press, pp. 49-71.

Alozie, E.C. (2001, Fall/Winter). Review: Understanding the web: Social, political and economic dimension of the internet. *Transnational Broadcasting Journal* 7. Retrieved Nov. 19, 2004, from http://tbsjournal.com-alozie.html.

Alozie, E.C. (2003). Critical analysis of cultural values found in Nigerian mass media advertisements. *Studies in Media & Information Literacy Education*. 3:4. Retrieved Nov. 19, 2004, from www.utpjournals.com/jour.ihtml ?lp=simile/issue12/aloziefulltext.html.

Alozie, E. C. (2004). African perspectives on events before the 2003 Gulf war. In R.D. Berenger (Ed.), *Global media go to war: Role of news and entertainment media during the 2003 Iraq War*. Spokane, WA: Marquette Books, pp. 39-55.

Berger, A. (1995). *Cultural criticism: a primer of key concepts*. Thousand Oaks, CA: Sage.

Bitzer, L. (1968). The rhetorical situation. *Philosophy and Rhetoric* 1:1-14.

Black, J., Bryant, J., & Thompson, S. (1998). *Introduction to Media Communication*, 5th ed. Boston:McGraw Hill.

Brown, F. (1958). *Words and things*. New York: Free Press.

Bush, A., Bush, V., & Boller, G. (1994). Social criticisms reflected in TV commercial parodies: The influence of popular culture on advertising. *Journal of Current Issues and Research in Advertising* 6(1):67-77.

Chesebro, J., & Hamsher, C. (1974, Spring). Communication, values, and popular television series. *Journal of Popular Culture* 8:589-603.

Costello, V. & Moore, B. (2004, August). *TV Fans as ' outlaws': An examination of audience activity and online fandom*. Paper presented at Association for Education in Journalism and Mass Communication, Toronto, Canada.

Damon, D. (2004, July 17). Table turns on Nigeria's e-mail conman. *Vanguard*. Retrieved Nov. 19, 2004, from http://www.vanguardngr.com.

Delio, M. (2003, Feb. 13). U.S. tries e-mail to charm Iraqis. Retrieved Nov. 7, 2004, from http://www.wired.com/news/conflict/0,2100,57648,00.html

Dominick, J., Sherman, B., & Messere, F. (2000). *Broadcasting, cable, the Internet, and beyond: An introduction to electronic media*, 4th Ed. Boston: McGraw Hill.

Ellul, J. (1965). *Propaganda: The formation of mean attitude*. New York: Vintage Press.

Entman, R. (1991). Framing U.S. coverage of international news: Contrasts in the narratives of the KAL and Iran Air incidents. *Journal of Communication* 41(1):6-27.

Fiske, J. (1988). Critical responses: Meaning moments. *Critical Studies in Mass Communication* 5 (3):246-250.

Fogleman, R. (1995, April 25) Remarks as delivered by Gen. Ronald R. Fogleman, Air Force chief of staff, to the Armed Forces Communications-Electronics Association, Washington. Information Operations: The Fifth Dimension of Warfare Volume 10, Number 47. Retrieved Nov. 19, 2004, from www.iwar.org.uk/iwar/resources/5th-dimension/iw.htm.

Garrison, B. (2004, Spring). Newspaper journalists use e-mail to gather news. *Newspaper Research Journal* 25:58- 69.

Gershon, R. (2001).*Telecommunication management: Industry structure and planning strategies*. Mahwah, NJ: Lawrence Erlbaum Associates, Publishers, pp.141-163.

Goldberg, I. (2003, Oct. 27). Glossary of information warfare terms. Retrieved Nov. 1, 2004, from www.Psycom.net/iwar.2/html.

Hudson, L. & Ozanne, J. (1991). Alternative ways of seeking knowledge in consumer research. *Journal of Consumer Research* 14(4):508-521.

Ionesco, E. (1968). *Fragments of a journal*. J. Stewart, Translator. London: Faber.

Kayany, J. (2001). The Internet. In R. Gershon, (Ed.) *Telecommunication management: Industry structure and planning strategies*. Mahwah, NJ: Lawrence Erlbaum Associates, Publishers, pp.141-163.

Khoury-Machool, M. (2004). Propaganda and Arab audiences: Resisting "hearts and mind" campaign. In R. Berenger (Ed.), *Global media go to war: Role of news and entertainment media during the 2003 Iraq War*. Spokane, WA: Marquette Books, pp. 313-320

Klopfenstein, B. (2000). The Internet phenomenon. In A. Albarran & D. Goff (Eds.), *Understanding the web: Social, political and economic dimension of the Internet*. Ames, IA: Iowa State University Press, pp. 3-22.

Lasswell, H. (1927). *Propaganda technique in the World War*. New York: Peter Smith.

Lasswell, H. (1937). Propaganda. In E. Seligman & A. Johnson (eds.), *Encyclopedia of the Social Sciences* 12. New York: Macmillan, pp. 521-528.

Lefevre, G. (1997, March 27). The Internet as a god and propaganda tool for cults. CNN Interactive. Retrieved Nov. 19, 2004, from http://www.cnn.com/TECH/9703/27/techno.pagans.

Lull, J. (1990). *Inside family viewing: Ethnographic research on television's audiences*. New York: Routledge.

Newcomb, H. (1974). *TV: The most popular art*. Garden City, New York: Doubleday/Anchor.

Schroeder, K. (1999). The best of both worlds? Media audience research between rival paradigms. In A. Pertti (Ed.), *Rethinking the media audience: The new agenda*. Thousand Oaks, CA: Sage, pp. 38-68.

Severin, J., & Tankard, J. (2001). *Communication theories: Origin, methods and uses in the mass media*, 5th Ed. New York: Longman.

Vande Berg, L., Wenner, L., & Gronbeck, B. (1998). *Critical approaches to television*. Boston: Houghton Mifflin.

Weaver, J. (2004, April 1). Iraq war a "milestone" for Web news: More than half of Internet users turn to news sites. MSNBC Interactive. Retrieved Nov. 19, 2004, from ww.msnbc.com/news/894028.asp

Webb, C. (2003, March 11). The war on the Web: Mobilizing online against war. Washingtonpost.com. Retrieved Nov. 19, 2004, from at www.washingtonpost.com/ac2/wp-dyn?

Whillock, R. (2000). Age of reason: The electronic frontier confronts aims of political persuasion. In A. Albarran & D. Goff (Eds.), *Understanding the web: Social, political and economic dimension of the Internet*. Ames, Iowa: Iowa State University Press, pp. 165-191.

Wilson, J & C. Arnold (1976). *Dimensions of public communication*. Boston: Allyn & Bacon.

Wrage, E. (1947). Public address: A study of social and intellectual history. *Quarterly Journal of Speech* 33:451-457.

www.cogsci.princeton.edu/cgi (2004, Nov. 1). Overview for "information warfare." Retrieved Nov. 1, 2004, from www.cogsci.princeton.edu/cgi-bin/webwn. Posting date is unstated.

DISCUSSION QUESTIONS

1. The U.S. government used a variety of electronic warfare techniques prior to the 2003 Iraq War to destabilize the Saddam Hussein regime. Why didn't the techniques work? Or did they?

2. One of the electronic techniques used in the pre-war period was e-mail. What were some of the reasons this technique failed in its goal to overthrow the Iraqi regime by insurrection?

3. What are examples of two popular propaganda techniques, "card stacking" and "name calling," that were used extensively by war supporters and opponents. Give examples of each.

4. People with which kinds of socioeconomic factors are most likely to be susceptible or resistant to "one-sided" propaganda messages? How were the most susceptible people targeted?

5. Can you think of examples where e-mails can mobilize large groups of people to a common cause? Be specific.

CHAPTER FOURTEEN

INTERNET USE BY ELITE EGYPTIAN YOUTH DURING THE 2003 IRAQ WAR: A USES & GRATIFICATIONS STUDY

DINA HUSSEIN AND NAGLAA HASSANIEN

While the Internet has been around since 1969, it did not come into popular use until 1993, two years after the 1991 Gulf War, with the creation of the World Wide Web and improved computer Web browsers. The World Wide Web, the most popular portion of the Internet, allows for the display of text, graphics and other media and connects all of these documents via hypertext links (Hunter, 1997). The Internet promises to have a more serious impact on society than the introduction of television.

Television, primarily involves only leisure time, [but the] Internet will affect work, school, and play [as well as develop] personal, family and business relationships (Ebersole, 2000). Global audiences still depend mainly on TV for news, if television is available and affordable. However, during the 2003 Iraq War online news audiences jumped to record levels (Hamdy & Mobarak, 2004, pp. 247-248). In fact, reliance in the Internet increased after the September 11 attacks in the United States.

> At the time of the 9/11 attacks, only 3% of online Americans said that the Internet was their primary source of Information about the attack. However, now 17% of online Americans said that the Internet was their main source to get the news [in the opening days of the war] (Rainie, Fox, & Fallows, 2003).

The Internet is perceived to be just as accurate and dependable as television, although Internet users still think that television news is up to date (Gallup Organization, 2000).

Realizing the importance of the Internet, the Pew Center for the People and the Press released a study early in 2002 which indicated that network television viewership had decreased in the previous three years. That trend continued in 2004 with 75 million Americans seeking information on the U.S. presidential election from the Internet, more than double the users from 2000 (Rainie, Cornfield & Horrigan, 2005).

To analyze this situation, journalists and media analysts attributed the decline, especially among young people, to "lack of time and lack of relevance in TV news stories." In general, younger Internet users tend to have more favorable opinions about online news (Rainie, Fox & Fallows, 2003).

The Internet is a significant global medium. "Computer-mediated communication (CMC) has increased our informational and interactive capabilities in unimaginable ways" (Angleman, 2000). This is especially true during a crisis. During the 2003 Iraq War, an unprecedented number of users sought information on the Internet in the first few hours of the war (Dimitrova, Kaid & Williams, 2004). The 2003 war the first to be fought in cyberspace as well as on the ground and in the air (Berenger, 2004, p. xxxiii). Both opponents and supporters of the war went online for war information and news. Users also went into chat rooms and sent e-mail to communicate with others, compare opinions and thoughts, or share prayers.

Ever since 9/11, the Internet has been under the microscope of researchers. The increasing dependency on the Net for news has been escalating since this crisis. In fact, this dependency was especially noticeable during the Iraqi war in March 2003.

Significance of the Study

This study was undertaken to counter the paucity of research in the area of Internet usage during crisis situations in the Arab World and, specifically, in Egypt. The Internet affords us a rare opportunity to study an important medium in its infancy, which could help us better understand its properties and possible impact on users.

To that end this chapter will examine the how university students in the world's largest Arab country used the Internet during the 2003 Iraq War, and what they got out of that experience. Once we understand the motives people have for using such a medium during crisis, we can enhance the medium to better satisfy its users during crisis situations. This is a short step in that direction.

Theoretical Framework

Ever since the Internet and the World Wide Web appeared, the innovation has rapidly diffused around the world, first quickly in the developed world, and more slowly in developing countries. Despite the Internet's remarkably swift penetration, there are actually only few working theories to explain the Internet phenomenon (Angleman, 2001). Most of the research exploring the uses of the Internet is still in the development stages. Understanding why and how people use the Internet and to what effect is important. Therefore, the uses and gratifications approach would be useful in exploring the intended uses of the Internet and the expected and latent gratifications.

During the 1940s, researchers seldom looked at any correlation between "observed gratifications and psychological origins of the satisfied need" (Angleman, 2000, p. 1). Twenty years later, the situation had not changed much. Researchers then focused on the intended gratification and not the gratification actually received. In the 1970s, researchers recognized that the cognitive state of the users influenced media usage. If researchers could identify the various needs of users involved, it would be beneficial to understanding why a person chooses a particular medium over another.

Schutz (1966) suggested three interpersonal needs affecting all aspects of communications: affection, control and inclusion. Then, in 1998, Flaherty, Pearce and Rubin observed that individuals use computers to satisfy three major needs: interpersonal needs (inclusion, affection, relaxation and control), traditional needs associated with the media (social interaction, passing time, information, habit, entertainment), and new media needs (time shifting, meeting other individuals).

Recently, Papacharissi and Rubin (2000) identified three other factors that influence the usage of the Internet:

- Contextual age (opposite to the limitations of the chronological age).
- Unwillingness to communicate due for instance to low self-esteem.
- Media perceptions i.e. the lack of social presence of the Internet, informational and Interpersonal benefits.

All of these needs interact to motivate the user's behavior. Understanding why the Internet is used can certainly shed light on the Internet's effect.

The importance of the media escalates during crisis situations. The 9/11 attacks in the United States left the nation shocked, confused and angry. Many turned to the media for answers. Not only did people turn to traditional or legacy mass media such as television and radio, but to the Internet as well. While mature U.S. audiences still favored the older media in percentage terms, international audiences anecdotally seemed to follow the story over the new media.

In fact, the 9/11 crisis was a great opportunity to test how well the Web could handle sudden and massive traffic. In the first few hours after the attack, major news sites were heavily overloaded to the extent that people couldn't access them. However, when these sites dropped the photographs and graphics, the situation was resolved.

> The Internet itself handled massive traffic well on September 11. The Internet also handled e-mail very well allowing many people ... to contact family and friends (Carey, 2002, p. 205).

Researchers also examined the functions and use of media in people's lives. Research in that area answers questions such as: What media do people use during crisis situation? What is the strength of each medium in satisfying the informational and emotional needs of the citizens (Carey, 2002, p. 201)? Because of this apparent shift in media dependency because of 9/11, the University of Mississippi initiated a grant for new professors to research how people use the media and how the media affects them during crisis times. The pilot study sought to assess the relationship between "perception of threat in times of social crisis, the degree to which audiences feel dependent on mass media for information about the crisis and the degree to which audiences change behavior in regard to the crisis" (Gordon, 1).

It was deduced from the research findings that the more fearful people were after the 9/11 attacks, the more dependent they were on mass media. Moreover, it was also deduced that the greater one feels dependent on an information source, the more one feels that this source must be trusted i.e. "greater dependency leads to greater effects" (Gordon, 1).

INTERNET USES DURING THE 2003 IRAQ WAR

The dependency on the Internet for news skyrocketed during the run up and prosecution of the 2003 Iraq War. A study by Lee Rainie, Susannah

Fox and Deborah Fallows of the Pew Internet and American Life Project assessed Internet dependency during the war. The study was based on a daily tracking survey on Americans' use of the Internet. The data were collected through telephone interviews conducted between March 20 and 25, 2003. Their sample was a random digit sample of 1,600 adults, 18 and older.

Their report noted the growth of the Internet as a news source. According to the results of the study, 77% of those Americans online used the Internet in connection to the war. They were going on line for a variety of reasons such as:

1. To get information about the war
2. To share opinions about the war
3. To send and receive e-mails about the war
4. To offer prayers and express their own views.

The study found that of the nation's 116 million adult Internet users, 55% of them have gone online for matters relevant to the war and 56% used the Web to get war news. In addition around 14% were going online more because of the news (Rainie, Fox & Fallows, 2003, p. 2). Dependency on the Internet was very clear during the war period. The study reported a dramatic increase in the size of online news audience between March 19 and in the immediate days after the hostilities was started.

On each of the five days after the war began, more than 33% of U.S Internet users went on line to get news. And on line news interest was even higher in the days immediately before the war broke (Rainie, Fox & Fallows, 2003, p. 3).

In general, the Internet performed well in rapidly informing the public about the war and provided minute-by-minute coverage. The Web proved to be an essential medium through which people got news information, exchanged views with others through forums and even stored news information for later use.

RESEARCH METHOD AND QUESTIONS

The Internet has experienced incredible growth over the past few years. The emergence of the World Wide Web has led millions of people in throughout the world to "plug into" the Internet's vast information resources.

Coinciding with this remarkable growth has been the development of the Internet in Egypt's educational community in 1994. In the nine years since its deployment, Internet use exploded at the American University in Cairo (AUC), an upscale private liberal arts institution, arguably the most prestigious — and expensive — Western-style university in Egypt. Checking e-mail and surfing the Web have become integral parts of the daily routine of most AUC students, staff and faculty.

Although Internet use at AUC has grown rapidly, little is known about how or why Egyptians use the Internet, especially in times of crisis. In essence, we know that students are using the Internet, but we don't know the dynamics of how or why they use the Net, which increasingly is taking on functions and appearance of a new mass medium. For a medium to be a functional mass medium, its use must be motivated by similar needs.

Prior research indicates that television viewing is used primarily for relaxation and entertainment, followed by passing time and obtaining information. Viewers are basically passive. Internet usage, however, includes various services and is rarely related to relaxation. Users are active. This study tried to identify the uses of the Internet resources available at AUC, especially during the 2003 Iraq War, and answer three research questions:

RQ1: How are AUC Egyptian students using the Internet?

RQ2: What gratifications are AUC Egyptian students seeking and receiving from using the Internet, and what factors motivate the selection of the Internet as a medium that will give satisfaction?

RQ3: As a new mass medium, how did AUC Egyptian students utilize the Internet during the 2003 Iraq War crisis?

Three main sets of variables were present in this study. These variable sets are: uses variables, gratification variables, and demographic variables.

Uses Variables

All uses variables identify the functions of electronic mail, Usenet, and World Wide Web uses. These questions were derived from the characteristics of each of these Internet applications. For example, questions about e-mail use generally focus on its ability to facilitate communication between individuals, whereas questions about the World Wide Web refer more to its entertainment and research characteristics.

Gratification Variables

These variables try to identify the gratifications sought and acquired from Internet use, especially during crisis situation. Gratification variables are measured with questions that were derived from the distinctive characteristics of electronic mail, Usenet, and the World Wide Web.

Demographic Variables

Several demographic variables were included to see if Internet use patterns during crisis vary among students. These variables were also useful in classifying users by age, class level, and major and for correlations. Sex and age are the primary variables within this section.

SAMPLE AND DATA COLLECTION

The initial sampling method used a database provided by The American University Academic Computer Services Center. The database included 300 randomly drawn active Egyptian student e-mail addresses. Active student accounts were determined by current semester enrollment status and totaled about 5,000. Requests to complete the questionnaire online were sent to all addresses provided.

A survey was used to collect data because it was found the most cost-effective way to reach the respondents. A pretest of the questionnaire was administered to an undergraduate class of about 18 students. From their responses ambiguous questions were identified and corrected. Researchers created an online Web survey. The Hypertext Markup Language (HTML) was used to create the online survey. This Web design allows respondents to select answers in their computer screen by clicking on the appropriate "button" with a mouse and to respond to open-ended questions by writing answers in text areas. An e-mail was sent to the sample explaining the purpose of the study. A hyperlink was included that enabled them to link to the online Web survey. Unfortunately, the university rules did not allow sending e-mail reminders.

Limitations

Five major limitations of the study were apparent:

- Sampling methods restricted the research to a small population. Larger samples from the target population (active Internet users)

certainly would have been preferable.
- Time limited this research, as by the time the 2003 Iraq War was taking place students were preparing for their final exams.
- Sampling was limited to college students who might or might not have established Internet habits.
- Scarcity of research in this area forced this study to be more exploratory in nature than analytical.
- After making requests for participants, it appeared that many students used e-mail address outside of the university server and did not regularly check school-provided e-mail accounts.

Sample Demographics

By the end of the survey period, 100 students responded, producing a return rate of 33%. The female-to-male ratio was closer than expected for the AUC population. About 55% of the student sample was between the ages of 19-23, with the remaining 45% between the ages of 24-28. Thirteen percent of students were freshman, 15% sophomores, 27% juniors, 20% seniors, and 25% graduates.

Forty-five percent were from the School of Business, Economics, and Communication, 35% from the School of Humanities and Social Sciences, 15% from the School of Sciences and Engineering, and 5% undecided.

RESEARCH FINDINGS

The typical respondent has been going online for an average of more than three years. Twenty-five percent reported going first online two years ago, 30% since three years ago, and 45% for four years or more.

In an average week, 2% of students had accessed electronic mail for 25 hours, 25% for 12 hours, 18% for 10 hours, 18% for 7 hours, 12% for 6 hours, 20% for 5 hours, and 5% for 3 hours. Five percent of the students chatted in an average week for 40 hours, 10% for 38 hours, 18% for 20 hours, 25% for 15 hours, 10% for 12 hours, 15% for 10 hours, with the remaining 17% chatting for 3 hours.

As for browsing the Internet in an average week, 3% of the students browsed for 32 hours, 10% for 30 hours, 20% for 20 hours, 15% for 15.5 hours, 25% for 10 hours, and 27% for 4.5 hours.

Nearly 40% of the sample's spent four hours or more online daily, 25% spent three hours or more but less than four hours, 20% spent two hours or more but less than three hours, and 15% spent one hour or more but less than 2 hours. Sixty-eight percent of the students stated that most of the time they logged on with a specific task in mind, such as searching for information, and/or checking e-mail. On the other hand, the remaining a third (32%) said they "just log on." Moreover, 66% of the students paid a lot of attention to the task they are doing, while 34% paid some attention.

Nearly 25% of students accessed the Internet in their homes. Thirty-five percent stated they accessed the Internet on campus. Forty percent reported accessing the Internet from both locations.

Attitudes Toward the World Wide Web

Several questions were designed to determine the students' affinity for the WWW. The responses were operationalized on a five-point Likert-scale, with results ranging from strongly agree to strongly disagree.

For example, 80% of the students strongly agreed with the statement, "Using the WWW is very important to me," and 76% agreed with the statement, "Using the Internet is one of the most important things that I do." Furthermore, 78% of the sample agreed with the statement, "I would feel lost without the WWW," and 68% strongly disagreed with the statement, "I could easily do without the Internet for several days."

Several other questions attempted to explore the students' beliefs about the WWW, especially its value as a source of information, entertainment, and as a means of communication. As a source of information, 60% of the students rated the WWW "excellent," 30% "good," 8% "fair," and 2% "poor." As a source of entertainment, 57% of the students rated the WWW "excellent," 31% "good," 8% "fair," and 4% "poor." As a means of communication, 53% of the students rated the WWW "excellent," 33% "good," 11% "fair," and 3% "poor." Based on these responses, students rated the WWW highest for information, followed by communication, and then entertainment. Eight out of ten students said the WWW is most like audio/visual-television, with remaining 20% equating it with printed books or magazines.

Most students evaluated their overall skill at using computers as "excellent" (66%), followed by "average" (22%), "good" (10%), and "below average" (2%). Moreover, four questions assessed the sample's skill at using the WWW. Seventy percent strongly agreed that they were very skilled at using the WWW, 22% agreed, and 8% neutral. Ninety-two percent of the students strongly disagreed with the statement indicating that they know less about using the WWW than most users, and 8% were neutral. Sixty-seven percent of the students strongly agreed that they consider themselves knowledgeable about good search technique, 28%

agreed, and 5% disagreed. Finally, 70% of the students strongly agreed that know how to find what they want with a search engine, 20% agreed, and 10% neutral.

The most useful site on Web was the search engine Google (50%), followed by Yahoo (15%), CNN (15%), Hotmail.com (15%), and Download.com (5%). In addition, Al-Jazeera (25%), BBC (20%), CNN (15%), Reuters (10%), MSN(10%), and Supercars.com(10%), and newscientist.com (5%)were listed by the sample as their favorite sites.

Reasons for Using the WWW

One question addressed the reasons why students might choose to use the WWW. Because of the paucity of research in uses and gratifications on use of WWW as a mass medium, a list of "use statements" is used to classify these use statements into categories. The categories are: "for research and learning," "to communicate with other people," "for access to material otherwise unavailable," "to find something fun or exciting," "for something to do when I'm bored," "for sports and game information," and, "for shopping and consumer information."

Student WWW utilization appears to significantly satisfy three functions. Fifty-five percent of the students reported using the Web for browsing, 30% for entertainment, and 15% for academic research. One function increasingly associated with Web is its ability to promote commerce. However, fewer than 10% of students reported shopping online.

Correlation Analyses

Following the independent-sample *t* tests, Pearson correlation coefficients were computed among the eight WWW-use scales and three variables measured at the interval level. The three variables that were correlated with the WWW usage categories were class standing, affinity for the WWW, and skill level at using the WWW. Both affinity and skill are positively correlated with all WWW usage categories identified by this research.

Of the students in the higher class standing (mostly juniors, seniors, and graduates), 72% said they use the WWW for access to material otherwise unavailable. A significant positive correlation was obtained between class standing and affinity for the WWW. This suggests that as respondents increase in age and class standing, they become more fascinated with the WWW as a source of information. Another significant positive correlation detected was between class standing and skill.

Internet Vs. Traditional Media Use During the Iraqi War

Eighty-eight percent of the sample used the Internet for issues related to war in Iraq. They went online to acquire information about the war, to learn and share the various opinions about the conflict, to send and receive e-mails where they discuss the current events, express their opinions and offer prayers. Furthermore, e-mail was used by 66% of the students to mobilize others and gain support for their views about the war.

Seventy percent of the students utilized e-mail in one way or another to communicate or learn about the war, and 60% have used the Web to get news, general information, and comments (supporters and opponents of the war) on numerous Web sites discussing the war.

Forty-five percent of the Internet users stated they are using the Web more during the war period to seek news. However, most of the respondents (75%) got most of their news about the war from television, especially satellite television news channels (50%) such as Al-Jazeera, BBC World and CNN International. In other words, a fourth of the Egyptian students said the Internet was their main source of information about the war. In addition, more female respondents (40%) accessed the Internet for war news more than male respondents (32%).

E-mail and the War

Sixty percent of the sample used e-mail to discuss the war with family and friends. Forty percent of the respondents communicated with someone about the war using instant messaging. Male respondents (30%) were more likely than female (25%) to use e-mail to get news alerts. Female respondents (30%) were more likely than men to use e-mail for prayer requests.

Internet and the War

Sixty-six percent of the students sampled went online to seek news about the war and information about the country and people of Iraq. Many (70%) used the Internet to sign a petition online for or against the war in Iraq, and 35% read or posted comments about the war in an online group or a bulletin board.

Twenty percent used the Internet to get information about how to get involved politically, while 50% looked for information about how to prepare for a possible terrorist attack. Only 10% used the Web to get information about the reaction of financial markets. Forty-five percent of the respondents stated that the war was a normal part of their online groups or e-mail lists' discussions. Ninety percent of the students stated that all their online activities did change their opinion about the war.

The Sites They Use

Sixty-five of the respondents indicated they used news organizations in other countries as their primary online source for news, followed by American television networks' Web sites (15%), groups that oppose war (10%), Weblogs posted by individuals about the war (5%), and organizations thought of as sources of nontraditional news (5%).

Why Students Went Online for News

Many students (80%) mentioned that it was "very important" to them when they were online to get up-to-the-minute news and information from a variety of sources about the war. Moreover, when online, the majority of students (75%) mentioned that it is important to them to seek points of view that are different from traditional news sources and official government source. Sixty-six percent of the sample stated that when online it was "not too important" for them to exchange e-mails or instant messages with others about the war

Twenty-two percent said they usually went to Web sites that shared their point of view, while 33% went to those that offer alternative perspectives; and the remaining 45% went to both types of Web sites.

How the Internet Helped Them

Students valued their skill in using the Internet to keep up to date on events. Two-thirds (66%) of the sample said their use of the Internet kept them updated on developments and events in the war.

Seventy percent stated that using the Internet has helped them shape their views on the war. Sixty-six percent said the Internet helped them related their views about the war to others either by e-mail or instant messaging.

The Online World vs. The Traditional World

Toward the end of our survey, we asked respondents whether the use of the Internet gave them points of view that are not available in newspapers and TV. Only a third of the sample said that going online gave them different points of view. Seventy-seven percent said the points of view online were pretty much the same as those in newspapers and TV. About half of those who said they are relying most on the Internet for news said the Internet is different from traditional media.

DISCUSSION AND CONCLUSIONS

Results of this study indicated that the American University in Cairo students, who overwhelmingly come from the Egyptian elite classes, used the Internet to exchange information and ideas. The vast majority of AUC students used e-mail and 60% used e-mail to discuss the war with family and friends. Moreover, 40% of the respondents communicated with someone about the war using instant messaging. E-mail was also utilized by 66% of the students to mobilize others and gain support for their views about the war. In addition, two-thirds (66%) used both e-mail and/or instant messaging to make their views on the war known to others.

The Internet also was used daily by students for three other purposes: browsing (55%), entertainment (30%), and academic research (15%).

The research and the entertainment functions of Web use can be regarded as an extension of the browsing function. By surfing the Web, users seem to be experiencing the excitement of discovering a new world, which is part of the entertainment function. In the exploration process, students find pages that address their interests, which also satisfy the research function. A reasonable explanation why the browsing function was the higher reported Web use is that because of its rapid growth there is no site that has a comprehensive index to the entire Web. Sites like Yahoo! and Google attempt to index all of the sites out there; however, they are still unable to keep pace with the Web's vastness and growth. In other words, users are obligated to browse to find exactly what they are looking for until a comprehensive system is devised to keep track of all of its sites.

That students are using the Web for academic purposes is a very promising sign for the medium. This finding indicates that the Internet is fulfilling one of its important intended functions as a mass medium, which is dissemination of information.

Students' using the Web for entertainment purposes is another sign of the medium's potential. In the Web's short history, it has developed a vast amount of entertaining content with the assistance of new interactive technologies such as Java, streaming audio, and streaming video; thus, strengthening the Web's competition with other mass media's entertainment content.

Since students turn to the Internet for research information, entertainment, communication and browsing, it was interesting to explore its potential as a mass medium during crisis. The findings of this research study indicate the Web's increasing importance to Egyptian students, because it provides them with better and easier ways to access information including current news during the war. Forty-five percent of the students said that they used the Web more during the war period to seek news.

Students stated that the Internet kept them updated on developments and events in the war. Eighty-eight percent of the sample under study used the Internet in issues related to war in Iraq, and 60% have used the Web to get news, general information, and comments (supporters and opponents of the war) on numerous Web sites discussing the war. Moreover, 70% stated that using the Internet has helped them shape their views on the war. In addition, 70% used the Internet to sign a petition online for or against the war in Iraq, and 30% read or posted comments about the war in an online group or a bulletin board.

Most of the respondents (75%) got most of their news about the war from television, especially satellite television news channels (50%). However, 33% of the sample said that going online gave them different points of view than those offered by newspapers and television.

Future research should investigate questions relating to how Internet use affects a student's traditional media use patterns. More questions relating to how students use traditional media during crisis would help to provide a comparative base with Internet use. Answers to these questions could help explain why students are not completely turning to the Internet as an alternative to traditional media. They would also offer a more comprehensive picture of media/technology use during crisis in the university environment.

This study represents a first step in identifying the functions of Internet use during crisis in Egypt among elite Egyptian students. Being exploratory in nature, the scope of the study prevented a more sophisticated analysis. Future research into the functions of Internet use should begin with national or regional representative sample in non-academic environment. Results generalized to the entire Egyptian youth population would be beneficial.

REFERENCES

Angleman, S. (2001). Uses and gratifications for Internet profiles: A factor analysis: Is Internet use and travel to cyberspace reinforced by unrealized gratifications? Paper presented at the Western Science Social Association 2001 Conference held in Reno, NV. Retrieved May 23, 2005, from http://wssa.asu.edu/pdf/2001abstracts.pdf

Angleman, S. (2000 December). What does it mean to dwell in cyberspace and why do we go there? A look at theories and definitions. Unpublished manuscript, Arkansas State University, Jonesboro. Retrieved June 1, 2005, from <http://www.jrily.com/LiteraryIllusions/TheoryResearchPaper Index.html>

Berenger, R.D. (2004) Introduction: Global media go to war. In R.D. Berenger (Ed.), *Global Media Go to War: Role of news and entertainment media during the 2003 Iraq war.* Spokane, WA: Marquette Books, pp. xxxvii-xxxiv.

Campbell, D. (2003 February 11). Internet brings together Americans against war. *The Guardian.* Available at: http://www.guardian.co.uk/antiwar/story/0,12809,893245,00.html

Carey, J. (2002). Media use during a crisis. *Prometheus, (3),* pp.1-6.

Dimitrova, D.V., Kaid, L.L., & Williams, A.P. (2004). The first hours of online coverage of "Operation Iraqi Freedom". In R.D. Berenger (Ed.), *Global media go to war: Role of news and entertainment media during the 2003 Iraq war.* Spokane, WA: Marquette Books, pp. 255-263

Ebersole, S. (2000). Uses and gratification of Web among students. *Journal of Computer-Mediated Communication.* Retrived May 5, 2005, from http://www.ascusc.org/jcmc/vol6/issue1/ebersole.html.

Flaherty, L. M., Pearce, K. J., & Rubin, R. R. (1998). Internet and face-to-face communication: Not functional alternatives. *Communication Quarterly, 46*(3), 250-268.

Gordon, M. (Undated). *The response of the media.* News release. Retrieved from http://www2.msstate.edu/~meg21/lowrey.html

Gore, A., & Allman, B. (May 1994). Bumpy ride on the info highway. *Harper's Magazine,* (288), pp.25-26. Accessed May 3, 2005, at: http://search.epnet.com/direct.asp? an=9405242205&db=aph

Hamdy, N., & Mobarak, R. (2004). Iraq war ushers in Web-based era. In R.D. Berenger (Ed.), *Global Media Go to War: Role of news and entertainment media during the 2003 Iraq war,* pp. 245-254. (Spokane, WA: Marquette Books).

Hunter, C. (1997 April 21). The uses and gratifications of Project Agora. Retrieved May 7, 2005, from http://www.asc.upenn.edu/usr/ chunter/agora_uses/index.html

Pacharissi, Z., & Rubin, A. (2000 Spring). Predictors of Internet use. *Journal of Broadcasting and Electronic Media,* 175-196.

Rainie, L., Cornfield, M., & Horrigan, J. (2005, March 6). The Internet and Campaign 2004. Washington: Pew Internet and American Life Project. Retrieved June 1, 2005, from http://www.pewinternet.org/pdfs/ PIP_2004_Campaign.pdf

Rainie, L., Fox, S., & Fallows, D. (2003 March) The Internet and the Iraq war: How online Americans have used the Internet to learn war news, understand events and promote their views. Washington: Pew Internet and American Life Project. Retrieved May 5, 2005 from http://www.pewinternet.org/pdfs/ PIP_Iraq_War_Report.pdf

Sadow, J., & Karen, J. (1999). Virtual billboards? Candidate Web sites and campaigning in 1998. Paper presented at the American political Science Association annual meeting, Atlanta, GA. Retrieved May 5, 2005, from http://www.uis.edu/~sadow/cwsp/swpsa00.htm

Sadow, J. (2000). The uses and gratification theory of Internet campaigning. A paper presented at the 2000 annual meeting of the American Political Science Association, Washington, DC.

Schutz, W.C. (1966). *The interpersonal underworld.* Palo Alto, CA: Science and Behavior Books.

Surfing the Warblogs for news from the front (2003 April). *Maclean's* (116) 14, p. 28 Accessed May 3, 2005, at http://search.epnet.com/direct.asp? an=9415936&db=aph

The Gallup Organization, Poll Analysis (2000 Nov. 30). Available at: http://www.gallup.com/subscription/?m=f&c_id=9954

TV News and the Net (1996 July). *Christian Science Monitor, (88)*, p. 20. Retrieved May 1, 2005 from http://search.epnet.com/direct.asp? an=960823285&db=aph

DISCUSSION QUESTIONS

1. While the Internet worldwide is still a male domain, according to many students, what socioeconomic or cultural factors could contribute to this study's findings that Egyptian females used the Internet more than men to get information about the Iraq War?

2. What role do "place or proximity" play when it comes to intensity of Internet use?

3. The study found that of thee-mails sent by students at one Middle Eastern university, two-thirds were used for "mobilization." What broad inferences can be drawn, in light of other chapters in this book, about the power of e-mail to coalesce public opinion and encourage participation?

4. Almost half the students reported using SMS text messaging to pass along information about the war to friends and relatives. In what new, unstudied ways does mobile communication technology contribute to a "Two-Step Theory" of public opinion?

5. The importance of international satellite channels (such as BBC, CNN and Al-Jazeera) cannot be understated. Given the bilingual nature of the students studied, which satellite channels would you think they found more credible and why?

CHAPTER FIFTEEN

IDENTITIES UNDER CONSTRUCTION: A STUDY OF THE PERSONAL HOME PAGES OF ARAB YOUTH IN CONFLICT ZONES

LAMYA TAWFIK

Personal home pages, some researchers argue, are the first truly digital genre (Dillon & Gushrowski, 2000, p. 202). It is common for the Internet to borrow genres from the print world and to package them for the online audience. Online newspapers, for instance, use styles similar to that of its paper format to help users identify it and browse with ease. E-books also follow a chapter-by-chapter format that is similar to their print counterpart.

Personal home pages may seem to fall under the autobiographical genre, yet their owners, unlike those who pen printed autobiographies, capitalize on the medium's unique feature of interactivity and often encourage visitors to provide feedback. The main similarity between autobiographical writers and personal home page owners is the way in which both engage in a level of deep introspection on their life and personas. This is particularly true in times of conflict, such as the 2000 Palestinian Intifada (uprising) and the 2003 Iraq War and its bloody aftermath.

But what is really meant by a personal home page? A hard and fast definition is provided by researcher Nicola Döring (2002): "A personal home page (personal Web page; private home page) is a Web site published and maintained by an individual who may or may not be affiliated with a larger institution." Most personal home pages usually follow a similar formula: an introduction or welcome message, information about the owners' interests, views, biography, favorite links and pictures of his/her family, friends and places visited. Thus, personal pages have become somewhat predictable in content and sometimes even in design.

As any emerging media, personal home pages have been at the receiving end of both critics' praise and reprimands. Some criticize the sometimes "trivial or even tasteless, amateurish and superfluous products of narcissism and exhibitionism." But advocates shun critics and emphasize "the emancipatory and self-reflexive potential of autonomous portrayals of individuals in the public space of the Web" (Döring, 2002). Web surfers have already begun producing their own media through establishing their presence on the World Wide Web. However, personal home pages may be a form of "branding," having evolved from a somewhat "exotic hobby to a professional and civic necessity" (Killoran, 2003, p. 67).

What are the apparent motives for the construction of the Web sites? This is the main question this paper seeks to answer.

ARE YOU TALKING TO ME?
ONE-ON-ONE COMMUNICATION

Before looking at the functions of the personal home page, its important to first establish the major differences between social interaction and interaction over the personal home page. Unlike, real-time conversational exchanges, home-page authors struggle with lack of visual information and resort to monologues that puts them in a position of presenting themselves without "validating cues, as if in response to questions that nobody really asked" (Killoran, 2003, p. 77).

Adaptive as humans are, Internet users utilize emoticons (a word itself a convergence of "emotion" and "icon") to express various emotions. Feelings as complex and obscure such as cynicism or embarrassment are made possible by these graphical representations. The lack of physical contact may also efface psychological barriers and encourage home-page authors to present themselves without the fear of being judged.

But, according to social theorists, "physical bodily interaction with objects and people is necessary to develop a sense of self. Therefore, eliminating physical contact by socially interacting in electronic space, raises the issue of how people present themselves to each other" (Barnes, 2000, p. 169).

Because of the illusory cyberspace, as Barnes puts it, the hypertext self emerges. "The Web has the ability to present lots of pieces of information linked together in complex ways with no necessary order or hierarchy. By using this, people can present many aspects of themselves simultaneously (or at least non-hierarchically), or their extended selves, or themselves as nodes within an extended community" (Miller & Mather, 1998). This electronic form of the self is what is presented through personal home pages.

Erving Goffman's *The Presentation Of Self In Everyday Life* (1959) drew an analogy between impression management in daily interactions and a dramatic performance. It is argued that home-page authors engage in a similar form of self-presentation as they try to encapsulate their true essence in a one shot, although multi-layered, self-description.

> One of things people need to do in their interactions with others is present themselves as an acceptable person: one who is entitled to certain kinds of consideration, who has certain kinds of expertise, who is morally relatively unblemished, and so on ... . Goffman sees embarrassment as an important indicator of where people fail to present an acceptable self, and an important motivator (Miller, 1995).

Miller continues to describe home pages as a "locus for electronic self" and says that "there's even more possibility for misrepresentation than in e-mail, because Web pages are carefully set up before presentation to the world, and are only slightly interactive."

CLASSIFICATION OF PERSONAL HOMEPAGES

The literature review for this paper indicated that there are two ways to classify personal home pages. One is according to their "form of existence (home page not available: "nominal home page" versus home page available: "actual home page") and their construction status (advance notice of a home page: "projected home page" versus home page with substantial content: "realized home page")" (Döring, 2002).

The second is according to content. The first category retains "basic format listing the author's name and standard information (age, sex, occupation). A second type of home page is shaped around a narrative account of the author's life. The third kind of home page is arranged topically around the hobbies, interests, and affiliations of the creator. Some pages use a mixture of all three formats" (Walker, 2000, p. 101).

AVENUE FOR DEMOCRACY

The fact that newmedia are offering communication powers to a larger part of the world's population is seen by some analysts to be a trend that is "contributing to increased political democratization" (Ghareeb, 2000, p. 396). The basic argument is that the Web has empowered common people to have the potential to disseminate information and ideas to the net citizens, hence making it the new political structure. Acknowledging that developing countries need to jump onto the Internet wagon as they seek further development, analysts feel that it's more than having the technological know-how that is needed to bring about true empowerment. The most beneficial IT strategy is seen to be one that "facilitates the active involvement of citizens at all levels in economic, social and cultural development" (Hudson, 2000, p. 363).

> The Internet ... is the technological tool and organizational form that distributes information power, knowledge generation and networking capacity in all realms of activity. Thus developing countries are caught in a tangled Web. On the one hand, being disconnected, or superficially connected to the Internet is tantamount to marginalization in the global network system. Development without the Internet would be the equivalent of industrialization without electricity in the industrial era (Castells, 2001, p. 269).

The counter-argument questions the notion of the Internet's power to bring about democracy. Some say that this is a myth that is "propagandized especially by those benefiting from this development like Bill Gates" (Kirchner, 2000, p. 138). Yet, in the Arab world, where the national media fall under the local political umbrella, Internet citizens, through their Web pages, still act as agents of change that can transmigrate from virtual public sphere to real political action.

"IT" IN THE ARAB WORLD

According to the 2003 Arab Human Development report issued by the United Nations Development Program, the number of Internet users in the Arab world reached 4.2 million in 2001, making it a part of the lives of 1.6% of the Arab population as opposed to just 1% in the year before. "A considerable increase even through Internet penetration in the Arab region is still limited in a comparative context" (AHD Report, 2003, p. 64). Penetration of the Internet by 2004, fueled by rapid acceptance in the Gulf region just prior to the war and skyrocketing in Iraq after the war, has been estimated at nearly 4% today (Berenger, 2005). Other reports indicate that the number of Internet connections in the Arab World is only

10% of those in Southeast Asia and only 5% of those in the industrialized societies (Hudson, 2000, p. 369).

Optimism about use of the Internet in the Arab world also is tempered by the fact that many areas have limited telephone service and access to computers. "[S]ome Arab countries have succeeded in improving their infrastructure [of telephone networks], while still lagging behind international levels. The number of lines in Arab countries is about 109/1,000 persons, while it amounts to 561 in developed countries. There is only one telephone for every 10 Arab citizens, while in developed countries the ratio is 1/1.7 persons" (AHD Report, 2003, p. 63). In addition, there is a severe shortage of computer availability throughout the Arab world. "There are less than 18 computers per 1,000 persons in the region, compared to the global average of 78.3 computers per 1,000 persons" (AHD Report, 2003, p.64).

In short, the AHD Report contends, "people do not have sufficient access to the media and information technologies, compared to world rates and to other countries in the region, and in proportion to the population of the Arab World" (AHD Report, 2003, p. 64). However, the time will come when the Internet will be firmly embedded in Arab societies, perhaps within the next few years. Ghareeb (2000) contends the Arab Diaspora has been instrumental in Arab presence in cyberspace. Arabs living around the world have brought their identities to the online world.

PURPOSE OF THE STUDY

What this study aims to do is to assess the level of political expressiveness of Arab youth who are located in conflict zones: their self-presentation and interests as projected by their Web pages.

Researchers have indicated that late adolescence and early adulthood are the years of forming a distinctive "personal outlook to politics" which in effect "remains essentially unchanged through old age." The critical years are between the ages of 15 and 17. If these years are in fact formative, then neither the years preceding nor following are decisive in the formation of self-identity (Rintala, 1974, p. 17), if not political orientation, although the latter point is arguable since life experiences play an important role in determining how an individual perceives the world politically. What is not arguable is that crises often shape political perspectives of young people.

Thus, the main hypothesis of this research is that

H1: Personal home-page owners of the youth in conflict zones of the Arab world will carry more political sentiments on their pages than youth in nonconflict areas.

The second hypothesis is that

H2: Personal home-page owners of the youth in conflict zones will also actively promote their countries and will exhibit several symbols of their countries more than pages in nonconflict areas.

To test these hypotheses, 88 personal home pages of young Arabs from Algeria, Lebanon, Iraq, Palestine and Sudan were gathered by looking through several personal lists directories (Yahoo, Geocities, Albab, Bareq, Hahoaa, Internet 4 arab, 4arabs, Arabo, arabcastle.com). Sites were excluded if they were commercial, touristic in nature, purely political in nature, shared by groups of people, part of academic institutions, and created by people older than 35.

This purposive sampling was adopted since as previous researchers have indicated there seems to be a problem in establishing a sampling strategy for research like this (Miller & Mather, 1998). Not "enough is known about what the sample base of personal home pages is to allow anything very systematic" (Arnold & Miller, 1999)

Five main aspects were coded and analyzed: data about the Web site owner, the main design feature, the purpose of the Web site, the main content features of the site and finally, how well the coders felt they knew the Web site owner. Two coders, both graduate mass communication students at an English language university in Egypt, were trained extensively prior to the study to ensure that the study was well understood. A coding instruction sheet was also given to them for further assistance. In addition, the researcher also served as a third coder. The original sample was 102 Web sites. However, sites that were deactivated and were not coded by all three coders were removed from the study's sample. This reduced the size of the study's sample to 88 personal home pages. The intercoder reliability of the study when the Holsti formula was applied was 0.82.

RESULTS AND DISCUSSION

Of the 88 personal home pages that were studied, 75 belonged to males and 13 belonged to females. Most of the Web sites (28) belonged to

Palestinians (a conflict area), which was followed by Lebanese owners (26, nonconflict), Iraqi owners (14, conflict), Sudanese owners (12, nonconflict) and Algerian owners (8, nonconflict).

Out of the 51 who identified their age or date of birth, 14 were from 21-25, 13 were aged from 26-30, 12 were aged from 31-35, 11 were aged from 16-20 and one owner was 12 years old.

From the sample, only 28 identified their educational level: 16 were college students, 6 were high school students and another 6 were postgraduate students. Fewer than a third of the sample identified their occupations: 13.6% were working in computer-related jobs 12.5% worked in engineering, 4.5% worked in the media, 3.4% worked in the medical field and another 3.4% worked in research.

A large portion of the sample used English as the main language of the Web site (89.8%), and 9.1% used Arabic as the main language and only 1.1% used French. Media scholars have asserted that the Internet is a challenge to those who are not proficient in English (Alterman, 2000, p. 22), and the sample in this study seemed to reinforce this notion as only a small percentage opted to create their pages in Arabic and many of those who opted for English wrote in bad grammar, the coders concluded.

According to the 2003 Arab Human Development Report, a greater effort is needed to promote the Arabic language online. "The Arabic language is undoubtedly the most prominent feature of the Arab culture. If the knowledge society, as delineated in the current report, is the source of hope for Arab human development, the Arabic language system is one of the decisive underpinnings for building that society and shaping its success" (AHD Report, 2003, p. 122).

A significant number of respondents (18.2%) lived in countries such as the United States, the United Kingdom, Australia, Canada, South Africa and Greece. This reinforces Alterman's observation that "most of the Internet activity involving the Middle East is carried out by Middle Easterners residing overseas rather than in the region itself" (22)

The way a home-page owner decides to design his or her page is as important for first impression management as is one's style of clothing when meeting another person in real life situations. However, while the wardrobe could offer a wide variety of mixing and matching, the ability to do the same in the World Wide Web is determined by the extent of the user's reliance on ready-made templates that only need to be filled with data. From the various prominent design features that were coded, 51.1% of the Web sites included advanced animations in the home page. However, 18.2% had broken links on their sites. Brown (1998) better explains this phenomenon:

About three months after the page has gone up, they realize that these links still don't go anywhere, because its much easier to decide what should go on a site than it is to put it there ... . It's as if books were published that contained a table of contents, a couple of chapters, and then increasingly random notes until, somewhere around chapter eight, the pages became completely blank. But the binding would be lovely (p. 39).

Almost three out of ten (29.5%) had the picture of the home-page owner on the main page. Another 13.6% included the flag of the owner's country of origin in the main page. However, throughout the various pages of their site, 55.7% of the owners had their picture placed, 40.9% had their country's flag, 31.8% of the sites had pictures of the owners' families, and 26.1% had pictures of their friends and colleagues placed.

Establishing the psychological reasons for creating the Web pages need a separate study due to its wide and sophisticated nature (Döring, 2002); however, the apparent reason for establishing the Web sites was identified by the coders. The Web site's purpose was stated explicitly by only 69.3% of the sample and was implicitly understood by the coders in 28.4% of the sample. Almost 35.2% created the Web site to promote their culture or their country of origin, 19.3% to display their hobbies and interests and 18.2% to display their qualifications. Of the political features shown on 32 Web sites (36.4%), 17% spoke about the Israeli-Palestinian crisis and only 5.7% spoke about the war on Iraq, a surprisingly small percentage given the timing of the study, and the general Arab opposition to the war and the Bush administration detailed in other chapters of this book.

Nearly 27.3% of the sites included some form of religious feature, 40.9% of the Web sites displayed interests and hobbies of the owners, 14.8% introduced the pop culture of the owner, and half the sites promoted the touristic features of the owners' respective cities or countries.

As Miller (1995) said about personal home page: "Show me what your links are, and I'll tell you what kind of person you are." The favorite links that are displayed on the Web page reveal the owners' interests and indirectly indicate a certain a part of his identity.

The favorite links included in the Web pages were mostly for newspapers or other media outlets (44.3%), followed by entertainment sites (42%), and also included country-related Web sites (29.5%), links to other personal home-page owners, (nearly 28.4%), Islamic Web sites (20.5%), computer-related Web sites (19.3%) and the least some all political Web sites (1.75%), again a small number considering the events going on at the time.

Although 55.7% of the Web sites included some form of welcome message, a large majority (90.9%) included e-mail addresses for the owners, and 62.5% of the sites included a guest book for visitors to sign. As Dominick (1999) points out:

> In order for self-presentation to be most effective it must be tailored to the perceived values and preferences of the target. As expected, authors of personal Web pages go to great lengths to find out about who actually visits their pages in an apparent attempt to find out more about their targets (655).

One of the methods of finding out how many visits they received is the use of hit counters. In this study, nearly 34.1% of the sample had hit counters on their pages. Counters can reveal the popularity of the site to visitors (Walker, 2000, p. 105), or even encourage home-page commitment to keep the site updated (Döring, 2002).

Over 18% of the site owners included a formal curriculum vita or resume and 13.6% gave a descriptive biography of themselves. Only 6.8% of the sites offered visitors introspection into their owners' personalities.

Finally, coders were also asked to indicate how well they felt they knew the Web site owners. Half of the owners were coded with "somewhat well," and 39.8% were coded with "not at all."

Before looking at the gender differences in the results it's important to note that the number of female owners in the sample was only 13. While not representative of female Web site owners' possible difference with male users in this survey because of the small sample size, the results seem to support previous studies that show that like most of the world more men considerably more men than women go online in the Middle East.

> Despite recent trends that suggest more older people and more females are using the Internet, home pages are still the domain of young males who are either students or white collar workers with jobs that have something to do with computers (Dominick, 1999, p. 654).

Nevertheless, a comparison is worth mentioning. With regards to the main design elements, researches conducted in the past show that female Web sites are more "feminine" and tend to use more floral images (Arnold & Miller, 1999). This was also found in this research with 23.1% of the female sites using pastels as opposed to 1.3% of the males' sites; 7.7% of the sites used floral images compared with 1.3% of the males' sites.

Both males and females used such features as advanced animations (50.7% males and 53.8% females). The interesting features of the site however was that 15.4% of the female owners had their pictures as a main design element of the site and 46.2% had their pictures somewhere on the site. This was unexpected given the conservative nature of Arab cultures. Some studies have indicated that "females are less likely to post photos of themselves" (Killoran, 2003, p. 69). Researchers have attributed this to "aspects of objectification and male gaze" and "the way the dominant culture problematizes self-portraits for women and abuse by men" (Miller & Mather, 1998).

With respect to the displaying qualifications, as indicated by previous research which shows that "for men what they do is who they are" (Arnold & Miller, 1999), more males than women tended to display their qualifications (20% males and 7.7% females) and while 9.3% of the males displayed their works (IT related) on their sites, none were displayed by the women and instead 15.4% of the women included their poetry.

COUNTRY-SPECIFIC DIFFERENCES

Looking at the differences of the results between youth from various countries revealed different motives for constructing their sites.

For example, long denied access to the Internet before the war, Iraqis were eager to promote their country (50%) over their own qualifications (21.4%). For the Palestinians, which share a nationality without a formally recognized country, the top reason was also to promote their would-be country (50%), followed by a need to discuss the Israeli-Palestinian political crisis (35.7%). The top purpose of constructing sites for the Lebanese also was for promoting the country, with displaying qualifications and displaying interests coming in second (each 23.1%).

But, as expected, the Sudanese and Algerians did not place political reasons on the top their agenda, which, for the Sudanese, was headed by displaying interests and getting to know others with similar hobbies for the Sudanese, and, for the Algerians, displaying interests and promoting their country. These findings provide partial support for the first hypothesis — that personal home-page owners of the youth in conflict zones of the Arab world would carry more political sentiments.

Overall, only 13.6% of the sample had political reasons as part of the chief reason behind their pages, even though 36.4% of the sites featured some form of political sentiment. Also, 13.6% of the sample posted their country's flag as their sites' main feature and a total of 40.9% of the sample had the flag somewhere on their site. Thus, the data also provide only partial support for the second hypothesis — that the owners will also actively promote their countries and will exhibit several symbols of their countries.

RECOMMENDATIONS AND CONCLUSIONS

While the research produced some significant findings, the study was not without limitations. One of the limitations faced was the paucity of personal home pages of Arab youth from the selected countries. The other was the deactivation of some of the sites before all coders could get the chance to code them. This led to a drop in the sample size.

Future researchers should consider downloading the sample so that the pages are available offline for coders. Also, the sites' owners should be contacted to find out their perspectives and why they decided to set up personal home pages in the first place.

While the Arab world is abuzz with scholars warning of the domination of Western media artifacts, without solid media research into the effects of the new media there is little firm ground to unsubstantiated claims of that dominion. More effort is needed in raising awareness among Arab populations at how the new media could empower them as citizens.

Youth — which now make up nearly three-fourths of the Arab world — should be encouraged to use the World Wide Web to express their political sentiments. The Internet should be viewed by these youth as more than merely a venue for amusement or entertainment. While all the personal home pages served the owners as contact ads, they still needed to be supported with more cultural context to create worldwide awareness to the particularities of the Arab world.

REFERENCES

Alterman, J. B. (2000, January). The Middle East's information revolution. *Current History.*

Alterman, J.B. (2000, Summer). Counting nodes and counting noses: Understanding new media in the Middle East. *Middle East Journal.* 54:3.

Arab Human Development Report 2003. United Nations Development Programme: New York.

Arnold, J., & Miller, H. (1999, March 28-31). Gender and Web home pages. Paper presented as a poster at CAL 99 Virtuality in Education Conference, the Institute of Education, London. Accessed at http://ess.ntu.ac.uk/miller/cyberpsych/cal99.htm.

Barnes, S. (2000). Developing a concept of self in cyberspace communities. In S.B. Gibson & O. Oviedo. (Eds.) *The emerging cyberculture: Literacy, paradigm, and paradox*, Cresskill, NJ: Hampton Press.

Berenger, R.D. (2005, Oct. 10). Personal communication with the author.

Brown, A. (1998, Oct. 2). Awful sites. *New Statesman,* p. 39.

Castells, M. (2001). The Internet galaxy: Reflections on the Internet, business, and society. New York: Oxford University Press.

Dillon, A., & Gushrowski, B.A. (2000, Jan. 15). Genres and the Web: Is the personal home page the first uniquely digital genre? *Journal of the American Society for Information Science and Technology*, 51:2.

Dominick, J. (1999, Winter). Who do you think you are? Personal home pages and self-presentation on the World Wide Web. *Journalism and Mass Communication Quarterly*, 76:4.

Döring, N. (2002, April). Personal Home Pages on the Web: A Review of Research. *Journal of Computer-Mediated Communication*, 7:3.

Ghareeb, E. (2000 Summer) Newmedia and the information revolution in the Arab World: An assessment. *Middle East Journal.* 54:3.

Hudson, M. (2000, Summer). A pan-Arab virtual think tank enriching the Arab information environment. *Middle East Journal.* 54:3.

Killoran, J.B. (2003, Winter). The gnome in the front yard and other public figurations: Genres of self-presentation on personal home pages. *Biography.* 26:1.

Kirchner, H. (2000). Internet in the Arab World: A step towards 'information society'? In L.A. Gear & H.Y. Hussein (Eds.). *Civic discourse and digital age communications in the Middle East.* Stamford, CN: Ablex Publishing.

Miller, H. (1995, June). The presentation of self in electronic life: Goffman on the Internet. Paper presented at Embodied Knowledge and Virtual Space Conference, Goldsmiths' College, University of London.

Miller, H. & Mather, R. (1998, March). The presentation of self in the WWW home page. Paper presented at IRISS '98 Conference, Bristol, UK.

Rintala, M. (1974). Generations in politics. In A. Esler (Ed.) The Youth Revolution: The Conflict of Generations in Modern History. Lexington, MA: Heath.

Walker, K. (2000). It's difficult to hide it: The presentation of self on the Internet home pages. *Quantitative Sociology*, 23:1.

DISCUSSION QUESTIONS

1. What do personal home page design and content tell us about their innermost concepts of the world around them, and what can we infer from young adults' worldview?
2. Based on your understanding, how do American or British Web pages by young people differ from Arab youth's? What significant differences, if any, would there be?

3. Surprisingly little political discourse was carried on Arab youth home pages, given the purported intensity and unity of opinion about the Iraq War and the Palestine-Israel conflict. Why do you think is the reason for this apparent lack of politicization?
4. While the Internet is global in reach with universal information potential, Arab youth's home pages tended to be more nationalistic and promote their countries of origin as a *raison d'être*.. Why do you think Arab youth think such a strategy is important?
5. In what ways do male and female home pages differ, and what do the pages tell us about gender preferences?

CHAPTER SIXTEEN

CLUELESS ON THE HOME FRONT, OR WHILE IRAQ BURNED

ELAINE CARDENAS

The 1995 film, *Clueless*, based on Jane Austen's 1815 novel, *Emma*, depicts the antics of a group of wealthy, popular teenagers attending Beverly Hills High. The girls, led by Cher, Emma Woodhouse's counterpart, exist in a social whirlwind of dating, shopping, hanging out, talking about relationships, and trying on clothes at the mall.

So what does that fantasy world, remote from terrorist threats and international power politics, have to do with real life and with real teens?

The purpose of this study is to answer that question through an analysis of online diaries of youths aged 14-19 maintained at www.FreeOpenDiary.com on March 19, 2003, and the weeks following. This Web site is part of the *Women's Forum* and one of an estimated 500,000 host sites for online diaries. At the time of the study, it had more than 250,000 diaries, most of which were maintained by teenage girls, the heaviest users of online diaries and instant messaging. Anyone 14 or older can create a diary on the site by completing an online questionnaire similar to a market segmentation form and by choosing an anonymous name, a location and a diary title.

The diaries are maintained as long as the diarists continue to make regular entries. Diarists can choose whether to make their diaries public and whether to accept comments from readers. An interesting feature of the site is that it is interactive. Readers can (if the diarist permits) respond to diary entries, thus initiating a dialogue with the diarist and others. Diarists also can personalize the sites with graphics, photographs, music and pop-up screens.

Examination of the diaries and communication with diarists suggests that the diaries represent a valuable source of information about people's most private thoughts and feelings, surpassing other sources of information such as personal interviews as a means of obtaining insights into people's daily lives. With that in mind, this study was conducted to determine how the war in Iraq was affecting English-speaking teenagers, and what their thoughts and feelings about the war might be.

A total of 203 online diaries from teenagers aged 14-19 were selected for analysis. Most of the diaries were selected randomly. However, there were so few mentions of the war in the randomly selected diaries that a purposive strategy was adopted to increase the likelihood of finding diaries that mentioned it. Most of the mentions of the war in the diaries were found using this strategy. Although there is no way of knowing how representative the online diaries are of all youths, they are nevertheless revealing about what was going on with America's youth the day the United States invaded Iraq and the weeks that followed.

FINDINGS

The overwhelming finding from the analysis of teen diaries was that the teens seemed, in fact, to be either oblivious to the war or uninterested in it. Table 16.1 summarizes the major topics discussed in the diaries.

The pages are filled with the minutiae of a teen's life — preparations for the prom, a paper that is due, what to wear to an upcoming dance, a trip to the mall, hanging out with friends, and eating pizza. Like the girls in Angela McRobbie's landmark ethnography of a working class girls' club, the online diarists describe in their diaries spending time "invariably doing nothing except hanging about, talking in groups of two, three or four, listening to [music] or flicking through magazines" (McRobbie, 1991, p. 39). Although they come and go to events, to the mall and to restaurants, they move about in "the safe, secure environment of the home, the [internet] and the school ..." (p. 37).

In page after page of the diaries, girls disclose their interest in certain boys, tell of friends who have started having sex, express their misery at the break-up of a relationship, and speculate about whether a boy knows they like him, and what his behavior means. For example, one exults that "the best thing happened ... Brian called me this weekend.!!!" (BigMac22, April 23, 2003). Another says that "at first it was really weird cuz my X was there and I hadn't seen him since I dumped him but we started talking and it was cool" (Megorian7, 2003, n.d.). Diary after diary tells of a break-up: "I broke with Matt today." "Two days ago me and Culver broke up." "Okay ... I miss brian (sic). We broke up sometime towards the end of April" (Megorian7, Stupidgirl007, and Still_Star_Dust, 2003, n.d.). Boys talks about relationships, too, especially about wanting "to find someone" or about getting a girl's number at a party. However, of the 203

TABLE 16.1

SUMMARY OF MAJOR TOPICS DISCUSSED IN DIARIES

Topic	Percent of Total (n=203
Love interest (male or female) (n=72)	35%
Hanging out with friends (n=43)	21%
Hassles from parents (usually mother) (n=13)	6%
Spring break (n=12)	6%
Prom (n=7)	3%
Drama—participation in school play (n=7)	3%
Death of a friend or close family member (n=5)	2%

diaries, males maintained only 23.

Of the 203 diaries, 62, or fewer than a third, mention the war, often very obliquely, alluding, for example, to a school trip or travel plans canceled because of the war or an anti-war rally that obstructed traffic. The day the United States invaded Iraq, one vowed to write about war in a list of future diary topics, saying "War (resist the urge to say 'ugh') what is it good for?" She never mentioned war again. The second, a 17-year old girl who calls herself "hobbits sweetheart," began her entry titled "an attack of pessimism" with a comment about homework on the Russian Revolution, then mentioned war as one of several social ills, comparing the United States to the Roman Empire:

> Another country that I feel like is on the verge of self destruction is the United States involved in wars we should avoid, we eat things like blue ketchup and fried twinkies, the public education system is in shambles, we're racking up a gigantic national debt, other countries hate us. This is beginning the slow crawl towards collapse. ... Pax Romana is what started Rome on its downward spiral. I'm telling ya, we may not be an empire in the true sense of the word, but we're headed for destruction ... Bush is our Nero. (Hobbits sweetheart, SPAM1, 2003, n.d.)

Seven diarists make connections with school history assignments. One makes a comparison to her lessons on World War I and speculates on how it will seem to her 25 years from now when she will be looking back on it and telling her children about it (Forgotten Tearz, Ramblings of Randomness, 2003, n.d.). Another quotes a Vietnam era song, and writes of "fear and blood," "pointless death," "stupid war," "above all oil." (Deleriums Escort, Requiem For A Nightmare, 2003, n.d.). Oil is a common theme in the diaries, often appearing in blank verse poems. One poem called "Oil War" goes "I won't carry guns for an oil war. As-salamu alaikum, wa alikum assalam. Peace to the Middle East." (glamour, My World, 2003, n.d.).

Here is what a 16-year-old teen from the UK who calls himself "001" said in an unusually long entry about the war on March 20, 2003:

> Iraq.
> i suppose it's time i aired my controversial political opinions- everyone else is.
> i think that this war is wrong and unjustifiable- i think that the UK and to a greater extent the U.S. are being hit with astronomically high amounts of propaganda, and so i choose not to except the media opinions.
> i think Bush is a very very stupid and moronic man, and possibly a racist trying to commit genicide and ethnically cleanse arab nations-like hitler really, although i'm not sure he's clever enough for that- he may just be stupid. i also think that Tony Blair- my own PM- is a very stupid very short sighted moron who has absolutely no interest in democracy.
> i thing Saddam Hueissain should be removed from power, is a tyrant, and is a liar- but i don't think that bombing a country will do it- why not send in clever SAS assasins? they've been there for 2 years!
> i see a very grave future where America oppresses and rules the whole world, and any who defy them are destroyed. i'm not anti-american. i'm not pro-saddam. i'm not a muslim. i'm actually not anti-war. just in this instance i think war is NOT THE WAY FORWARD. and that is my contraversial political view (001, loving Jesus, Iraq, March 20, 2003).

Surprisingly, there is no indication (other than references to school history assignments) to suggest how the diarists developed their opinions about the war, or what might have influenced them. There is no mention of discussions in the classroom, with friends or with parents. Strong expressions of opposition to the war frequently elicit angry responses to diary entries, but one is left with the impression that the youths have formed their opinions in isolation and are testing them out in their diaries. They do, however, mention watching the news, sometimes with parents, and reading about the war in the newspaper. Most of their comments about the news have to do with their irritation at seeing Bush on TV, or their anxiety about people affected directly by the war who have been profiled in the news. One could speculate that the youths' opinions reflect what they have been hearing at home and at school. However, youths often seem to use the diaries as a place to explore opinions that diverge from their parents' opinions. Other studies of diaries have shown that youths often object in their diaries to their parents' negative attitudes towards homosexuality and present their own more tolerant opinions (Cardenas, 2003).

DIARY ENTRIES ABOUT THE IRAQ WAR

In many cases, the comments on the war sound a little tentative, as if the youths are trying out their ideas. Indeed, earlier research on online diaries suggests that one of the primary ways in which youths use online diaries is to try out new identities (Cardenas, 2003). Judith Butler hypothesizes that people become entrenched in sexual identities through repeated performances or what she terms "performativity":

> [T]here is no power, construed as a subject, that acts, but only, to repeat and it is the power of this citation that gives the performative its binding or conferring power (Butler, 1993, p. 225).

The same sort of "performativity" seems to exist as youths test out political positions. One of the few diaries that really expressed deep personal feelings about the war was from a girl who mentioned her father's experience as a soldier. She said her father had been in the Gulf War and returned very changed, and mentioned that he still had bad memories and dreams.

Otherwise, the diarists make only oblique references to events that may be connected to the war, such as attendance at church vigils or participation in a "support America" rally. Now and then a diarist ends an entry that has been all about friends, school, and the usual routine with a comment like "GOD BLESS OUR TROOPS!!!"

Of the 62 diarists who mentioned the war, only nine were males; three of those were from the UK. Table 16.2 summarizes the types of comments teens made about the war.

Interestingly, the likelihood of mentioning the war seems to have some connection with the ways in which diarists use their diaries. Some write in them only infrequently about special events in their lives; some use

Comment	Percent of Diaries that Mentioned the War (n=62)
Make no clear declaration of opposition or support for war or president (n=33)	53%
Oppose war and Bush (n=22)	35%
Support war and Bush (n=7)	11%
Mention watching news about the war on TV (n=7)	11%
Express support for troops (whether or not opposed to the war) (n=6)	10%
Married or engaged to someone serving in Iraq (n=6)	10%
Talk about effect of war on relationship (n=5)	8%
Mention oil as motivation for war (n=4)	6%
Know someone serving in Iraq (n=2)	3%

them therapeutically (often on the advice of a therapist) as a place for "venting" or dealing with difficult situations; some use them as a forum for communicating with friends; and others use them as a daily record of everything going on in their lives. As a result, searches for war-related entries among diarists who make infrequent entries about special events revealed almost no mention of the war. Surprisingly, the diarists with the most entries — hundreds, with multiple entries each day — also yielded hardly any mentions of war, possibly because these diarists were using the diaries to communicate with friends, not to record thoughts or document their experiences.

The strategy that ultimately yielded the largest number of diaries with mentions of the war was one that searched entries for people with several entries per week. These individuals seem to be using the diaries to document their daily lives, and they are fairly meticulous in mentioning all of the significant things going on in their lives, including the war. Of the 62 diaries that mentioned the war, at least 50 were identified using this search strategy.

In addition, a targeted search was conducted to locate diaries with names indicative of an opinion or relationship to the war — e.g., names with the words "war," "soldier," "marine," "Saddam," "Iraq." The first diaries to surface were several by youths adopting the persona of Saddam or Osama fans. The few diaries of this type had only one or two brief entries, usually with some obscenities directed at the United States and statements of support for America's enemies. Many of the other diarists' expressions of opposition to the war seem like performances. It seems as though these diarists are trying on unpopular personas. It is hard to tell, because the text is fragmentary and incoherent, especially in contrast to the others. For example, the diarist Iraqi_Hotness says "Osama ain't your momma. He's my babies fatha. Best recognize." Not surprisingly, these entries elicit very hostile responses from readers.

From the perspective of communication during the war, the most revealing online diaries are possibly those of the wives waiting at home for their husbands, fiancés and boyfriends to return. The search located several diaries by women who label themselves in relationship to a soldier — e.g., Soldier's Daughter, MLRSsoldierswife, and .loving.a.soldier. (Indeed, a separate study of the diaries of soldiers' wives would be interesting, as many older wives maintained diaries during the war, apparently as a way of dealing with their fears and anxiety.) What distinguishes these diaries from the others, even though they are written by girls of the same age, is that they mention the invasion and the deployment of troops. The wives copy speeches they found inspiring on their sites and share advice about how to support the men (i.e., what to send, where to mail things). They all watch the war on TV, especially CNN. In fact, several of the older wives advised against watching the news. One wife in her 20s advised a young bride as follows:

> The best thing to do really is to take it one day at a time and keep really busy. The more stuff you have to do the less time you have to worry. Also write to him and put together packages and making a scrapbook is sometimes helpful and would make a nice gift for him when he returns. Oh and don't watch the news too much because it could make you worry to much limit yourself to only one hour a day. (Ghetto Navy Wife, response to MLRSsoldierswife, 2003, n.d.).

One wife talked about "going insane imagining all of the things that could be happening to him" and the problems of communicating with him during the war. "Before he left we got to talk everyday and ... we could console each other." She gives a different meaning to the word clueless, when she says "I have no clue what's going on" (MLRSsoldierswife, 2003, n.d.). Another said, "Trying to understand everything going on. Nothing is understandable anymore" (love my soldier, A Soldier's

Fiancee, 2003, n.d.). The overwhelming sense of these diaries is of waiting — waiting for news, waiting for a soldier to return home. This is further evidence in support of Elaine Showalter's claim that women spend their lives waiting.

Although the diaries provide insight into the feelings and emotions of the wives and girlfriends of soldiers during the war, it is interesting to note that the focus, even of these diaries, is not on the war, but on its effect on relationships. It is apparently true that the women express their pride in their husbands and say that they wish Americans would support the soldiers, but most of the text of their diaries is about missing them, worrying about what they'll be like when they return, wondering (if they are not married) if the soldier will return to them. One talks mostly about a wedding she is planning when her fiancé returns, and about the criticism of friends who have told her she is too young to marry and hasn't known her fiancé long enough. One typical entry (for a teen) says,

> Bradley left. He is now in Iraq. A week ago, he e-mailed his girlfriend and told her that things were over between them. I am very happy about this, but I just wonder what will happen when he comes back home. Will he want to date me or her. He asked my mother for permission to date me like a month ago and she told him not until I was 16 and yeah I am almost 16 now. I hope he still wants to try something because I think that he is just amazing (loving.a.soldier, Waitin' for him to come home, 2003, March 21).

In a diary posted by the researcher for the specific purpose of raising questions about how diarists were reacting to the war, a question was posed about why people were not commenting on the war. Several people responded that they were concerned about the war but tired of thinking about it and had so many other things going on in their lives they just didn't want to deal with it any more. Were they perhaps suggesting that they see the diaries as a place where they can escape from troubling events?

CONCLUSION

This paper began by comparing the online diaries of teenagers with the lives of teens portrayed in the movie, *Clueless*. What is interesting is how the diaries reflect the same preoccupation that seemed to consume people when Jane Austen wrote her novels in the early 1800s. Like Emma Woodhouse, many of the girls who write online diaries are absorbed with matchmaking, attracting the interest of a young man, getting in with the right crowd (or club), and sometimes meddling in other people's relationships. Major political events, such as the Iraq War and its aftermath, are not central to their lives. Perhaps this is one of the reasons there was so little active opposition to the war in Iraq.

REFERENCES

Amandalyn007, And so it begins. . . at http://wwwfreeopendiary.com

Butler, J. (1993). *Bodies that matter: On the discursive limits of "sex."* New York: Routledge.

BigMac22, (2003, April 21). Unusual as Usual,at http://www.freeopendiary.om, "HeyHeyHey".

Cardenas, E. (2003). We are all pawns. *Politics and Culture,* Issue 3, Retrieved August 30, 2003 from http://aspen.conncoll.edu/politicsandculture

Deleriums Escort, Requiem For A Nightmare (2003, n.d.) at http:/www.freeopendiary.com

Ghetto Navy Wife, response to MLRSsoldierswife (2003, n.d.) at http://www.freeopendiary.com "How am I supposed to deal with this?"

Forgotten Tearz, Ramblinhgs of Randomness (2003, n.d.) at http://www.freeopendiary.com

glamour, My World (2003, n.d.) at http://www.freeopendiary.com

Hobbits sweetheart, SPAM1 (2003, n.d.) at http://www.freeopendiary.com, "An Attack of Pessimism" Iraqi_Hotness, All You Saddam Haters at http://www.freeopendiary. com, "Osama ain't your momma."

love my soldier, A Soldier's Fiancee (2003, n.d.) at http://www.freeopendiary.com, "Constant CNN. . Constant thoughts.

loving.a.soldier .Waitin' for him to come home (2003, March 21). At http://wwww.freeopendiary.com,

McRobbie, A. (1991). The culture of working class girls. In *Feminism and youth culture: From "Jackie" to "Just Seventeen."* Boston: Unwin Hyman.

Megorian7, Stupidgirl007, and Still_Star_Dust (2003, n.d) at http://www.freeopendiary.com

Mirror, The last piece of my mind (2003, March 20) at http://wwww.freeopendiary.com,

MLRSsoldierswife (2003, n.d.) at http://www.freeopendiary.com "How am I supposed to deal with this?"

Pew Internet & American Life Project (2003). Retrieved September 3, 2003, from www.pewinternet.org/reports

Why not me, Life goes on (2003, n.d.) at http://www.freeopendiary.com.

001, loving Jesus, *Iraq,* (2003, March 20). http://www.freeopendiary.com

DISCUSSION QUESTIONS

1. What seems to be the primary motivation for young people to create, use, maintain and visit online diaries?

2. Are online diarists, who have a need for belongingness, more or less susceptible to Elizabeth Noelle-Neumann's "spiral of silence" theory, where unpopular speech is muted if it goes against majority opinion?

3. In a traditional sense, diarists express their innermost personal thoughts in private. Even though they assume a *nom d'Net*, what individual needs are satisfied by sharing their feelings with potentially the entire Internet community?

4. To what extent do online diaries contribute to consensus development concerning the U.S. military involvement in Iraq?

5. How do online diaries contribute to our understanding of those on the "home front" of the 2003 Iraq War — primarily young women with boyfriends or husbands at war — and their understanding of the geopolitical implications of armed conflicts? Are they interested observers, participants or victims of U.S. foreign policy?

Part IV

Blogging during the War: A New Journalistic Form or Trivial Self-Expression

CHAPTER SEVENTEEN

BLOGS OVER BAGHDAD: A NEW GENRE OF WAR REPORTING

MELISSA A. WALL

From William Howard Russell's first reports of the British involvement in the 19th century Crimean war, war reporting has held a special position within the news establishment. Covering war has long been considered a rite of passage for foreign correspondents. Characterized as more intense and more dangerous, war reporting was the place where reputations could be built and lives could be lost (Berenger, 2004). Yet today's war reporters have been described as less equipped to report on wars, often seemingly unable "to say something meaningful about the nature of modern warfare" (McLaughin, 2002, p. 4). Indeed, the reporting of the 2003 Iraq War has been described as among the most managed of all wars ever, covered by embedded reporters capable of providing only de-contextualized snippets of the war (Allen & Zelizer, 2004; Tumber & Palmer, 2004). Taking those criticisms into account, this study considers the role of a potentially new kind of journalist involved in covering war: bloggers.

This author has previously argued that news-oriented bloggers are changing our notions of journalism. Warblogs were sometimes black market information sources — providing a wider diversity of views than mainstream media but not always dependable in terms of credibility (Wall, 2004, 2005). On the other hand, Kaye and Johnson (2004) found that readers of warblogs believed their bloggers to be more credible than mainstream media.

NEWS MANAGEMENT SINCE VIETNAM

It is a common myth within the U.S. military and the public that the mainstream media "lost" the Vietnam war, even though research documents that public opinion turned against the conflict before the media truly challenged the powers that be (Hallin, 1986). Nevertheless, this belief resulted in a perceived need to control media access to and reporting of any conflict the United States has been involved in since.

Following the British approach established during the Falkland Islands war in 1982, the U.S. military adapted and honed the model of controlling access through news blackouts, information pools and other forms of news management throughout the 1980s and 1990s wars with Grenada, Panama, Iraq and Serbia. The same tendencies were evident in coverage of the second Gulf War, except that government control was more sophisticated and more widespread than ever (Allen & Zelizer, 2004; Tumber & Palmer, 2004). In general, most research suggests that war reporting is far from the critical watchdog model the press so admires. Instead, it tends to be reliant on elites — usually governmental, military — sources and leaves out the voices of ordinary people. The tone also is jingoistic and supportive of the home country's position, and it fails to provide historical background and in-depth coverage of the conflict.

Purpose of this Study

If these are the characteristics of typical war reporting, then the question of interest here is whether this new cultural form — the warblog — reported news any differently. The overall research question was: How do warblogs compare with traditional war reporting?

A set of blogs was chosen for analysis through theoretical sampling in which the units were selected to represent a range of types (Altheide, 1996). Once selected, each blog was examined using frame analysis techniques that aimed to discover if the discourses employed reflected the qualities of war reporting outlined above. Pan and Kosicki (1993) argue that focusing on the following elements can best assess news discourse: Syntax (What agency was identified in the headlines? What background information was included?); Script (How were the stories organized? Who were the main actors/sources? What were the actions? Datelines?); Themes (What were the main themes?); Rhetoric (What metaphors, catchphrases, and other rhetorical devices were used?)

Warblogs

Five warblogs were selected for examination. These included blogs run by an independent professional journalist, three grassroots bloggers (an anonymous armchair warrior, a U.S. soldier, and an Iraqi architect who also worked as a translator), and a mainstream media blogger. Each blog was downloaded during March 2003, just as the Iraq War's combat phase began. An assessment of their discourses follows.

Kevin Sites

Kevin Sites was a CNN correspondent who started his blog independently of that organization, which forced him to shut it down because CNN said the blog was a conflict of interest. Sites later re-started his blog in Iraq and achieved some fame as the reporter who shared the video clip of a U.S. soldier shooting a captured rebel in Fallujah during the fall of 2004.

In terms of the discourse devices, the "headlines" used on Sites' blog entries often lacked a subject and were so brief that they generally failed to convey what the post was about. Sites' storytelling style relied on conveying snippets of information that provided not so much a complete report as fragments or slices of what he saw, and, in this way, perhaps more clearly reflected the nature of reporting from a conflict zone. After each snippet was a link for readers to comment on the post. Sites did not link to other sources of information to support his reports. This was likely because the information there was all being directly reported from the Middle East as opposed to being culled from different Web sites as is typical of many warbloggers.

Although the site provided a bit of color and detail, this really could not be construed as background. One of the main actors was Sites himself, and he devoted much of the blog to describing the difficulties of reporting from the region. Other actors include journalists. The subjects of his photographs were always ordinary people (for example, a grandmother walking, two young boys playing in the street). The central themes were on the power of the blog as a journalistic tool and the act of war reporting itself.

Sites wrote, "This experience has really made me rethink my rather orthodox views of reaching folks via mass media" (Sites, 2003a, para 1). Thus, his blog is reflexive in nature. The rhetoric reinforces these themes, as he writes of "glory" in going to Baghdad to report (Sites, 2003b, para. 2) but notes he doesn't know if he is headed "toward the fires or toward the glory" (Sites, 2003b, para. 4).

Tacitus

Named for a Roman historian, Tacitus is the anonymous creation of a blogger who works as a federal employee in the Washington, D.C., area, and who remains anonymous because he feared retribution from his co-workers because of his blog's support for the war.

Like Kevin Sites' site, his headlines tended to be brief, sometimes only one word. This meant they did not contain an agent for actions and, indeed, often contained no verbs (e.g., "Legacy," or "Quotation"). Tacitus also included almost no background. The story he told stayed focused on the war as it unfolded, which he often conveyed with the enthusiasm of a sports fan watching the home team. For example, following U.S. troop movements, he writes that the "7th Cav is making an epic dash up the Euphrates-Tigris valley" (Tacitus, 2003a, para. 3).

Like many news-oriented bloggers, he did not collect his own information first hand but relied on mainstream news media reporting and on other blogger sites. From their reports, he aggregated information on which he posted comments or summaries on his blog. Each post also offered readers the opportunity to respond, and Tacitus himself sometimes participated in the reader discussions. The main actors were the military, Bush, Saddam, mainstream media and other bloggers. The only mention of ordinary people beyond bloggers was a peace activist who was mocked and belittled. The only time he gave a sense of where he was based was when he mentioned that the war might bring another terrorist attack to people, who like himself, lived in U.S. cities. The themes of the blog were the justness of the war, and the "stupidity" and "wrong-headedness" of those against it. He writes that Bush is "freeing enslaved people" (2003b, para. 6) which "makes you proud, really" (The latest and greatest, para. 9).

L.T. Smash

L.T. Smash was a reserve officer in the U.S. military deployed to the Gulf whose blog name was inspired by a character on the TV show, "The Simpsons." (When he returned home, he renamed the blog, Citizen Smash, and used it to rally conservatives in his hometown of San Diego.)

As with the other bloggers mentioned, his headlines tended to be two or three words long with no subject or agency. The blog provided no background and also had no links to outside sources. One of the main actors was the blogger and the other was Saddam Hussein, whom he tended to personalize, such as when he writes "Saddam fired a couple of those Scuds he doesn't have at me this afternoon" (L.T. Smash, 2003a, para 1) or "goodnight Saddam" (L.T. Smash, 2003b, para 4). Other actors were Bush, military personnel and military families. The storytelling form here did not rely on outside information sources, as Smash did not link to other news or blogger sites within his posts. The information was thus a diary-like account of his activities or his own comments, humor, etc.

Readers were able to comment on posts and Smash occasionally replied to their responses, sometimes including information readers have provided within his own posts. The actions here involved his being a soldier, detailing his interactions with superior officers, and how he carried out other activities as a military officer. The theme of the blog was that the army was mismanaged even though the United States was fighting a just war to defend itself from Iraq. He wrote, "we will not forget," a reference to the 9/11 terrorist attacks that the U.S. government claimed were linked to Iraq, and about fighting "as long as our freedom and safety is threatened" (L.T. Smash, 2003c, para. 9).

Where Is Raed?

Where Is Raed? was the blog of an Iraqi architect who blogged from Baghdad throughout the war. Initially anonymous, he later became a blogger for the U.K.'s *Guardian* newspaper, an author of a book under his nom d'blog, "Salam Pax," and an independent film producer.

His headlines were merely the date of the post, which did not provide any cue for the information that followed. His site did include background and read at times like an insider's guide based on Salam's knowledge of his country, its religious traditions, ordinary life under a dictator, and other particulars about life as an Iraqi. In one post he explained what is shown in an aerial photo of Baghdad found on the Internet:

> the road to the right of it is called Zaitoon (olive) Street, it has lots of olive trees obviously. On the green side of that street (the green area is a residential area called Harthiya) live many big wigs, don't bother you CIA types reading the blog, they are empty now. The yellow area is the Zawra public garden, you see it here during the renovation period ... The blue square is a building that has been hit twice (desert storm and desert fox) after desert fox they decided to do a redesign since it hit really bad (Salam Pax, 2003a, para. 2).

The blog was more of an eyewitness diary than a news report, yet its information was new to most readers who wrote in the comments section that they learned things about Iraq unreported elsewhere. Salam sometimes responded to his readers on the main page, apologizing for his lack of personal messages, and thanking those who support him. The primary actors were Salam, his friends and family, and Saddam Hussein.

All of the action took place in Baghdad where Salam lived and worked as a "fixer" (a native speaker who arranges interviews for journalists) for visiting journalists such as Peter Maas, sometimes inside his home, sometimes on the streets of Baghdad. The action mainly focused on what was happening in the lead-up to the war:

> The radio plays war songs from the 80's non-stop. We know them all by heart. Driving thru Baghdad now singing along to songs saying things like 'we will be with you till the day we die Saddam' was suddenly a bit too heavy (Salam, 2003a, para 3).

The themes of the blog were that, despite Iraqi hatred of Saddam Hussein, war was bad, and this was coupled with a sense of hopelessness. He writes, "how could 'support for democracy in Iraq' become to mean 'bomb the hell out of Iraq'?" (Salam Pax, 2003b, para. 2).

ML Lyke

This blog was the only one hosted by a mainstream news organization. Lyke was an embedded reporter based aboard the carrier, USS Abraham Lincoln. Unlike the other blogs, her blog featured fuller headlines: "Interview, mess hall restrictions lifted" (Lyke, 2003a, para. 1). The storytelling form was again a diary of her personal experiences as a professional reporter. Unlike most blogs, this one lacked both links to other sources of information as well as a place for readers to comment.

Her blog provided little background about the war. The primary actors were herself, the naval crew and other journalists. The action took place onboard a ship, and the scenes she described were generally small and personal, such as making a junk food run with other reporters, thinking wistfully about her daughter, and observing sailors loading weapons, sleeping, and playing games. The themes were that her time onboard had not resulted in much real reporting. She writes, "We're in the thick of it, knowing precious little ... It's confusing and anti-climatic for many aboard" (Lyke, 2003b, para. 2). Indeed, Lyke was reflexive about her role, revealing that she was reading Evelyn Waugh's *Scoop*, a parody of foreign correspondence, which she noted revealed that reporters tend to make up information when lacking any real news.

The rhetoric was not jingoistic, but it was not critical of the war either. She seemed bemused at the military and shipboard life, calling sailors "kids" and reporting on concerns about her personal appearance such as wearing a gas mask strapped to her waist and leg, or as when getting off a helicopter she noted, "I'm an air-ruffled, twitterpated (sic), helmet-hair mess" (Lyke, 2003c, para. 1).

CONCLUSION

Research suggests that war reporting tends to reflect elite, governmental voices; be unquestioningly supportive of war; and fail to provide enough background to adequately understand the conflict at hand. With the introduction of news-oriented blogs, the question becomes whether blogs are contributing to a new form of war reporting that might overcome these weaknesses in the mainstream news media. This chapter suggests that warblogs potentially offer new ways of reporting war that might even provide stronger support for a government's war propaganda.

In terms of new or different ways of reporting war, blogs can provide details and interpretations missing from mainstream reports. Salam Pax, for example, explained the effects of war on ordinary Iraqis and detailed a nuanced explanation of their fears and anger. L.T. Smash provided a window onto ordinary soldiers' lives as they executed a war. On M.L. Lyke's blog, the voices of ordinary sailors were given more space than their commanders and the more distant voices in official Washington. Interestingly, these first-person accounts were less reliant on elite sources. Salam Pax and Smash, for example, were ordinary people who spoke for themselves. For mainstream news media, blogs might provide an opportunity to break out of their patterns of reliance on status quo sources. Yet elite voices and players were not absent on the blogs. Those that relied particularly on links for their information, such as Tacitus, were in fact often relaying the elite voices found in the mainstream news media.

Due to the nature of their posts — short fragments of a sentence or two — it is difficult to find background about the war on nearly all of these sites nor did the bloggers tend to link to background information that could provide context. It is unclear whether nonjournalist bloggers did not know where to find background, did not have the time to locate it, or simply did not think it necessary to report. Even the professionals included little background, despite the argument that cyberspace offers so much more capacity to expand information. Salam Pax was an exception, describing religious ceremonies and providing detailed information about Baghdad.

As for jingoistic language — some bloggers such as LT Smash and Tacitus — were megaphones for the government-inspired patriotic interpretation of events. Their examples suggest that elite voices could well seek to manipulate blogs — providing information in order to make it appear as if it was coming from grassroots sources such as blogs (this technique is employed with the Drudge Report, which purports to be an alternative voice but actually is a frequent mouthpiece for the Republican party and other conservative groups [Alterman, 2003]). Other sites (e.g., Salam Pax) that did not support the war were not jingoistic. Interestingly, mainstream journalists seemed less chauvinistic than is often associated with war reportage. This raises the question of whether patriotic reporting found on some U.S. media outlets since Sept. 11 has been the result of editors', producers' or other managers' influence and not reporters' own decisions.

Ultimately, these blogs suggest that war journalism is changing with the possibility of old information hierarchies being both challenged and reinforced. At their worst, bloggers are simply amplifiers for propaganda, adding a level of emotion and lack of accountability for what is being reported. The excesses of this were later seen in some of the reporting on the U.S. presidential campaign. But the blogs also offer promise.

Blogging technology offers an opportunity for mainstream reporters operating under constraints imposed by profit-oriented media managers and owners to report more honestly and to do so with a closer connection to their audiences. The blogosphere might also change war experiences for audiences. Readers become less passive with the lack of headlines and other obvious cues on how to read what will follow. In some cases, audience members have become more active participants in constructing the meaning of information through comments and connections established via the blogs.

Ideally, a more involved audience could provide outspoken mainstream journalists with the support to report unpopular news that challenges rather than sustains the status quo. (Before he became a blogger, would Kevin Sites have shared the controversial video clip of the shooting of a captured rebel? Or did the knowledge that he had an audience of personal supporters give him the cover and the courage to share the tape?) Whatever the case, blogs have introduced new practices and new possibilities to the world of war correspondence.

REFERENCES

Allen S., & Zelizer, B. (2004). Introduction. In S. Allan & B. Zelizer (eds.) *Reporting war: Journalism in wartime* (pp. 3-21). New York: Routledge.

Alterman, E. (2003). *What liberal media? The truth about bias and the news*. New York: Basic Books.

Altheide, D. (1996). *Qualitative media analysis*. Newbury Park: Sage.

Berenger, R.D. (2004, Fall/Winter). Book essay: War correspondent memoirs personalize conflict. *Transnational Broadcasting Studies Journal*, 13. Retrieved May 12, 2005 from http://www.tbsjournal.com/Archives/ Fall04/bookessay.html

Hallin, D.C. (1986). *The uncensored war: The media and Vietnam*. Berkeley: University of California Press.

Kaye, B.K., & Johnson, T.J. (2004). Weblogs as a source of information about the 2003 Iraq War. In R. Berenger (ed.), *Global media go to war: Role of news and entertainment media during the 2003 Iraq War* (pp. 291-303). Spokane: Marquette Books.

L.T. Smash, (2003a, March 20). Is that it? Retrieved March 22, 2005 from http://lt-smash.com.

L.T. Smash, (2003b, March 21). In the air tonight. Retrieved March 22, 2005 from http://lt-smash.com.

L.T. Smash, (2003c, March 19). For Robert. Retrieved March 22, 2005 from http://lt-smash.com.

Lyke, M.L. (2003a, March 17) Interview, mess hall restrictions lifted. Retrieved March 25, 2005 from http://www.seattlepi.nwsource.com/lincoln/journal.

Lyke, M.L. (2003b, March 20) We're in the thick of it, knowing precious little. Retrieved March 25, 2005 from http://www.seattlepi.nwsource.com/lincoln/journal.

Lyke, M.L. (2003c, March 27) I'm an air-ruffled, helmet-hair mess. Retrieved March 30, 2005 from http://www.seattlepi.nwsource.com/lincoln/journal.

McLaughlin, G. (2002). *The war correspondent*. London: Pluto Press.

Pan, Z. & Kosicki, G. (1993). Framing analysis: An approach to news discourse. *Political Communication*, 10, 55-75.

Salam Pax. (2003a). Tuesday, March 18, 2003. Retrieved March 25, 2005 from http://dear_raed.blogspot.com.

Salam Pax. (2003b). Saturday March 15, 2003. Retrieved March 25, 2004 from http://dear_raed.blogspot.com.

Sites, K. (2003a, March 17). It's good to be in the blogosphere. Retrieved March 25, 2005 from http://kevinsites.net.

Sites, K. (2003b, March 17). Whispers of war. Retrieved March 25, 2005 from http://kevinsites.net.

Tumber, H. & Palmer, J. (2004). *Media at war; the Iraq crisis*. Thousand Oaks: Sage.

Tacitus. (2003a, March 21). Legacy. Retrieved March 22, 2005 from http://www.tacitus.org

Tacitus. (2003b, March 21). The latest and greatest. Retrieved March 22, 2005 from http://www.tacitus.org

Wall, M.A. (2004). Blogs as black market journalism: A new paradigm for news. Berglund Center for Internet Studies. Retrieved April 3, 2005 from http://bcis.pacificu.edu/journal/2004/02/wall.php.

Wall, M.A. (2005, May). Blogs of war: Weblogs as news. *Journalism: Theory, Criticism and Practice*, 6(2), 153-172.

DISCUSSION QUESTIONS

1. What characteristics do warblogs possess that makes them different from other Weblogs, aside from their concentration on coverage of conflicts?
2. Does blogging technology "empower" journalists to report on the net differently than they would for a mainstream media organization?
3. What are the advantages or disadvantages of unmediated coverage, especially during times of war?
4. Mainstream media (and the Weblogs associated with them) tend to support the prevalent power structures and do not stray too far from the middle of the road in news coverage, especially during a war. How do warblogs challenge this news tradition?
5. In what ways did the warblogs "set the agenda" for mainstream media during the 2003 Iraq War?

Chapter Eighteen

Is this Mic On? Celebrity Use of Blogs to Talk Politics During the War in Iraq

Kaye D. Trammell

C elebrities often have attempted to exert their political influence and power to persuade. The War in Iraq was no exception. For instance, actor Sean Penn traveled to Baghdad on a self-promoted "peace trip" (Baker, 2002) and more than 100 celebrities wrote and signed a letter to President George W. Bush urging him to avoid military action against Iraq (Breznican, 2002).

Even when celebrities are not exerting their arguable political force, as in the cases of Penn and the anti-war petition, they sometimes make political statements. The Dixie Chicks, an all-girl country music band, stands as an example. Natalie Maines, a singer in the band, spoke out against the president during a concert in London (AP, 2003). This act of political expression led to a firestorm of media attention against the band and celebrity politicking in general (AP, 2003).

Although celebrities often make news when they make political statements, they cannot count on international media to disseminate their entire messages without mediation (i.e., commentary and criticism). But, like other people, celebrities can communicate an unfiltered version of their politics regarding the war in their official weblogs, or blogs. And many of them do that.

Blogs are often topical Web pages that are frequently updated and the content is arranged in reverse chronological order (Blood, 2002). Many bloggers create online journals and archive their highly personal and opinionated prose. As such, blogging has become a more popular phenomenon to express one's online self and talk politics (Blood, 2002; Rice, 2003).

In this study, the "celeblog" bridges the two most common blog genres: diary and political blogs. The diary-like blog is noted to be the most prevalent type of blog today. In these more personal blogs, the author writes from his or her own perspective in a manner similar to a diary. These blogs sometimes don't even bother to explain people, places, or events to the audience when telling a story (Trammell, Tarkowski, Hofmokl & Sapp, 2006). The political blog is arguably the most publicized blog by media accounts. These blogs offer analysis, reactions, and criticism to current news and public affairs. Political bloggers can be likened to editorial columnists as they offer political commentary similar in spirit to that found on the editorial pages of newspapers.

Unlike other people, celebrities cannot reinvent themselves online without having the virtual world bleed over into their real world. For celebrities online, there is no real "off time" from their projected image, and, therefore, anything said online attributed to their identity will be rolled into the whole of their public persona. Trammell (2004) suggests that when one reads a celebrity-written blog post, the reader may process it as an interpersonal encounter (similar to a message from a friend) as opposed to a distanced attempt at persuasion. While this study does not attempt to assert effects of messages, other studies show celebrity blog readers do not avoid political content on celeblogs (Trammell, 2004). Therefore, the exact nature of these political messages should indeed be examined.

RESEARCH QUESTIONS

This research examines political messages being disseminated on blogs maintained by celebrities during the 2003 Iraq War. This investigation seeks to reveal characteristics of political messages in posts, comments, and trackbacks on these Internet pages. More specifically, it will attempt to answer four questions: (1) How often do celebrities make political statements in their blog posts? (2) How often do they discuss the War in Iraq? (3) How do readers of celebrity blogs respond to the celebrity political messages? (4) How often do they use hyperlinks and where are they connected?

METHOD

This study employed a quantitative content analysis of a 10-month sample of celeblogs during the 2003 Iraq War. Blog posts, comments, and trackbacks were the units of analysis. At the time this research was conducted, there were 46 known celebrity-run blogs on the Internet. Only blogs that were seemingly run by the celebrity (not a spoof site or publicists writing posts) were included and archived from February through November 2003 for analysis. During this time, the United States and a coalition of numerous other nations were at war with Iraq and the race to the Democratic presidential nomination was well underway.

The 46 archived celeblogs yielded 31,678 cases, comprised of posts (n = 5,099; M = 115.25 for each celebrity; SD = 319.46), comments (n = 25,901; M = 4,316.83 for each celebrity with comments), and trackbacks (n = 678; M = 339 for each celebrity with trackback). Five celeblogs in the sample include "comments" and two enable "trackbacks."

A stratified sample based on the post was created. Using a randomized number table, 10% or 10 posts (whichever was greater) for each celebrity were identified for analysis. For each of the posts identified for analysis, the researcher checked for the associated comments or trackbacks. Comments and trackbacks associated with a post were then sampled in the same stratified manner as the posts themselves. This sampling method ensures that all of the elements connected with a post were analyzed (the post and it's comments and/or trackbacks).

Using this stratified sampling method, 701 total posts were identified for analysis. The comments (n = 530) and trackbacks (n = 48) associated with these posts were also analyzed. Therefore, a total of 1,279 cases were analyzed.

The main base for creating categories in this content analysis comes from the established Webstyle method (Banwart, 2002; Bystrom, et al., 2004; Trammell, 2004). Using an abridged version of this method for analyzing political content on the Web, this study focused on topics discussed and hyperlinking strategy. For topics, the content analysis coded for the presence of political statements, mention of the war, and author expression thoughts or feelings. When items were determined to have mentioned the war in Iraq, they were further analyzed to determine level of support for the war (support, indifferent, oppose); mention, support, and criticism of American President George W. Bush; mention, support, and criticism of another political leader. Finally, hyperlinks were analyzed by first counting the number of hyperlinks within each item. Additionally, hyperlink destination was analyzed for the presence of hyperlinking to media articles, government Web sites, special interest groups, or blog posts on a different (external) blog. Determining if the hyperlink contained background information to the item being discussed or facts to support the viewpoint measured the concept of intertextuality.

Intertextuality looks at how readers construct meaning from fragments (e.g., text in posts, text in comments, text accessed through hyperlinks) of information that is brought all together.

Four trained coders content analyzed the sampled items. All coders were familiar with blog content, content analysis, and mass communication. Coders were instructed to code a post and then related elements (comments, trackbacks) in one sitting so that the relationship between the related element and the original post was considered. Intercoder reliability was established in the coder training and throughout the coding process. Reliability ranged from .78 to 1.0.

RESULTS

On celebrity blogs, there are two main types of voices: the celebrity who maintains the blog and the active reader who responds to the celeblog post in either comments or trackbacks. Celebrities start the conversation with the post and readers are able to respond on the Web site when comments and trackback are enabled. Because blogs are noted to be semi-conversational and said to create a community among readers, both of these voices are analyzed here.

The first research question asked how often celebrities make political statements in their posts. This question is answered by analyzing only the post (n = 701). In this sample, 60% of the celebrities analyzed made political statements. Table 18.1 lists these celebrities. Overall, celebrities make political statements 18.8% (n = 241) of the time on their blogs.

The second research question asked how often such political statements on celeblogs discussed Iraq. This question was answered by investigating that section of items (18.8%) that were political statements. Table 18.1 lists the celebrities who posted items about war during the sample. Data show that 42.4% of these political statements were about the War in Iraq. This finding makes the war the most talked about political issue among celebrities on their blogs.

A nonparametric chi square test found that such statements about the war are likely to be discussed in terms of the author's feelings and thoughts (p < .001). Coders were asked to determine if these statements about the war were in support or opposition and found that 75% (n = 30) of the war statements could be classified as opposing the war, 20% (n = 8) were indifferent, and only 5% (n = 2) supported it. This finding is statistically significant (p < .001).

When celebrities discussed the war, President Bush was mentioned

TABLE 18·1
FREQUENCY OF POLITICAL STATEMENTS AND WAR DISCOURSE ON CELEBRITY BLOGS

Celebrity	Occupation	Political Statements	War Discussed
Dave Barry	Columnist	23	4
Adam Curry	MTV Veejay	18	9
Moby	Musician	12	9
Barbra Streisand	Actress, Singer, Director	10	9
Michael Moore	Director	9	8
Neil Gaiman	Musician	7	1
Flea	Musician	6	-
Bill Maher	Comedian	6	1
George Takai	Actor	5	3
Wil Wheaton	Author, Actor	4	-
Jeanette Winterson	Author	4	4
Margaret Cho	Comedian	3	-
Douglas Rushkoff	Journalist	3	1
Jann Arden	Musician	4	1
Al Roker	Journalist	2	-
Brendan Fehr	Actor	2	1
Jeff Bridges	Actor	2	-
RuPaul	Entertainer	2	-
Gillian Anderson	Actor	1	-
Jenna Elfman	Actor	1	1
William Gibson	Author	1	1
Nina Hartley	Actor	1	1
Marilyn Manson	Musician	1	-
Steve-O	Actor	1	-
Penn Gillette	Comedian/magician	1	-
Glenn Phillips	Musician	1	1
William Shatner	Actor	1	1
Bill Tush	Journalist	1	-

21.2% of the time. This discussion was overwhelmingly critical (90%). Other political leaders were discussed 16.7% of the time and such discussion was more critical than supportive. Celebrities mentioned American Vice President Dick Cheney, Iraqi dictator Saddam Hussein and even the Iraqi Minister of Information, Mohammed Saeed Al-Sahhaf (known in the media as "Baghdad Bob," and to some commentators as "Comical Ali" for his wildly inaccurate statements about the war).

The third research question asked how readers who leave comments and trackbacks respond to these political messages. This question was answered by identifying any comment or trackback associated with one of the political message posts (n = 241). As earlier stated, only five celeblogs in this sample featured the comment system and two enabled trackback. Overall, 71 items were left as a comment (n = 70) or trackback (n = 1) in response to a post with a political message.

Of these responses to political messages, 36.6% (n = 26) also made political statements. A majority of the readers' political statements discussed the war (69.2%; n = 18). When coders were able to determine level of support for the war among these responding readers (n = 7), results indicate much lower level of opposition (14.3%) and more overall support for the war (85.7%). Readers did not mention Bush in the comments or trackbacks, but there was some criticism of UK Prime Minister Tony Blair and Saddam Hussein.

The fourth research question asked about the destination of hyperlinks on celebrity blogs. Overall, 34% of the entire sample contained hyperlinks. Each unit contained less than one hyperlink (M = .75) across all of the items analyzed. Predominately, hyperlinks went to media articles (42.0%), external blog posts (15.4%), and special interest groups (12.6%). Hyperlinking was much more prevalent in items that discussed the war (M = 3.27). The destination trends in war items mirrored that in the overall sample, but at a greater level: media articles (51.4%), external blog posts (17.1%), and special interest groups (17.1%).

The final research question asked if hyperlinking practices supported intertextuality. Overall, 58.9% of the hyperlinks contained background information about the topic being discussed and 28.2% presented facts on the page that was linked to. Among items that discussed the war, 71.4% of the items used hyperlinks to explain background information and 57.1% contained facts. A nonparametric chi square test showed that items with hyperlinks that mentioned the war were statistically significantly more likely to contain background information in the hyperlink than not (p < .01). Indeed, hyperlinking on celeblogs does support intertextuality. Intertextual hyperlinking strategy is greater when discussing a top political issue, such as war.

DISCUSSION

This study aimed to understand the messages disseminated by celebrities on their blogs. An integral part of the inquiry revolved around the presence of political messages and war discourse in an effort to identify the types of messages and content communicated from these unlikely political spokespeople. Such research adds to the initial understanding of this particular genre of Web content, the trend of celebrities making political statements, and the overall understanding of political conversation on blogs.

Political Statements and War Discourse

A majority of the celebrity blogs analyzed indeed made political statements. Even so, among these celebrities there was a difference in the frequency of such statements. The celebrities who have been known to make political statements (e.g., Barbra Streisand, Moby, Michael Moore, Margaret Cho, Bill Maher, Dave Barry) continue this trend on their blogs when speaking to their interested publics. Perhaps of greater interest here are those celebrities who are not known for making political statements but are so compelled to make them during the war. It is the study of these celebrities that deserves the most examination to determine what drives them to make such statements and how their publics receive them.

Within the group of out-of-character political statements, some celebrities acknowledged that their publics might not be interested. Such was the case with adult star Nina Hartley who, knowing her audience may be turned off by political messages, wrote the following advisory in bold face font in the middle of her post to warn readers about the content in her April 20, 2003 post titled "La Dolce Vita":

> ADVISORY: Political comments to follow. Those who don't wish to hear my thoughts on some topical subjects can skip down a few paragraphs.

Hartley then discussed the war in Iraq and the alleged looting of the national museum in Baghdad for several paragraphs. Upon completion of her political statement, she posted another advisory in bold advising her readers she was returning to her normal content. This visually set apart her political statement from her normal content, and illustrated how the celebrity was cognizant of the perceived appropriateness of political messages.

Others decided not to say anything. Some time after the war started, Wil Wheaton stopped making political statements but never discussed his change in content. While his intentions are unconfirmed, Wheaton also turned off the ability for his readers to comment on his posts immediately after the war started. Such a move sends a message that in politically heated times Wheaton was not interested in the feedback from his readers and preferred only one-way, non-political communication. After the sample time period for this study, Wheaton announced on his blog that he had been posting under a self-enforced, privately agreed upon moratorium of political discourse on his blog. In ending this moratorium, Wheaton posted a political rant that he claimed he could not hold in any longer. It can be assumed that Wil Wheaton believed in the power of celebrity influence and, during times of war, decided to not actively use it or attempt to persuade his readers.

The celebrities best known for their political statements continued doing so on their blogs. The finding that war discourse was wrapped in discussion of feelings and thoughts is especially key for this group. It can be assumed that such statements would not take a regular reader aback, as the media have pegged many of these celebrities as activists known for making such remarks. For this group, criticism of the war and political forces leading it, were much more pointed (expressing feelings) and focused on specific issues or people (expressing thoughts).

Director Michael Moore, known for his political outspokenness and his Bush-bashing cinematic polemic, *Fahrenheit 9/11*, wrote an expressive rant illustrating his dissatisfaction with the government and Bush on March 17, 2003, in a post titled "A Letter from Michael Moore to George W. Bush on the Eve of War":

If you really want to stand up for America, please send your twin daughters over to Kuwait right now and let them don their chemical warfare suits.

Another example of this is seen in author Jeanette Winterson's blog in an April 3, 2003 untitled post:

There is no excuse and no justification for this war. It is wrong. We all know that Saddam is a murderer, a torturer and a bully, but I am very nervous about the new American policy of pre-emptive war. Where are we going next? Korea? Pakistan?

With these examples it is obvious that even if celebrities did not post political messages often, the messages contained very strong wording when they did occur. In other cases, celebrities incorporated personal stories about their own experiences and relate it to the larger political statement. Together, these two types of political messages display the use of thoughts and feelings.

Incorporation of thoughts and feelings with the political statements make political statements on blogs stand out. Where political candidates have to announce their support for a particular political endorsement, blog statements can use a stealth, interpersonal political communication model. That is, celebrities can wrap political statements inside of stories about their lives, experiences, or families in their posts. Therefore, a reader may think that the post is about a day trip to visit a loved one in jail, when in reality the post is a political criticism of the country's prison system.

Reader Reactions

It is logical that reader reactions would stay "on topic" and discuss the war, as the feedback for 69.2% of the political statements in comments and trackbacks did. Somewhat contrary to the argument of celebrity influence, though, is that the readers disagree with the fundamental theme. That is, readers supported the war when the celebrities did not. However, only a handful of such statements actually went as far as revealing support in manifest content for coders to identify, so more work must be done in this area before generalizations can be made.

Stepping away from the linear reader reaction to the celebrity political posts lies the interesting finding that feedback is not a symmetrical conversation. That is, readers don't always respond to the post and stay "on topic." Rather, they use comments as an area to draw the conversation in other directions, talk amongst themselves, and even sometimes start up new conversations altogether. Again, such feedback elements are currently understudied and future research must investigate these preliminary findings.

Hyperlinks and Intertextuality

While many popular press reports herald the hyperlink as the essential element of blogs, such claims seem to overestimate their presence as found here. Indeed, other blog scholarship notes similar findings (Herring, Sheidt, Bonus, & Wright, 2004; Trammell, 2004; Trammell et al., 2004). Even so, the role of the hyperlink on blogs set the medium apart from others (Trammell & Gasser, 2004).

Interestingly, hyperlinking was more prevalent in items that contained political statements. Here, hyperlinks frequently led to media articles. Some posts, such as those by columnist Dave Barry and actress-singer Barbra Streisand, centered on hyperlinks to the point where the post would have no meaning without hyperlinks. The purpose of Dave Barry's posts was to share links to news items or games.

Streisand's blog posts were much the same in regards to hyperlinks in that she often compiled lists of media articles she agreed with and posted them for readers. While political content was discussed in hyperlinks, links rarely led to established institutions like government or political parities. Rather, the hyperlinks sent readers to presumably credible news organizations. This shows a strong reliance on source material for supporting or explaining topics discussed.

Such findings contribute to the overall support for the idea of intertextuality found here. This analysis found that hyperlinks led to other Web pages providing a deeper discussion of the background on the topic. This provides quantitative evidence to the popular claim that the hyperlink is an integral part of the blog in that it provides a gateway to a deeper understanding of the topic for readers. Many have said that substantive (as opposed to personal, diary-like) posts set blogs apart from other mediums in that the hyperlink's role is to provide access to verifiable facts published by credible sources. This allows the blogger to concentrate on communicating his or her opinion and possibly raising the credibility of the information present by linking to government reports or media articles supporting viewpoints communicated in the post.

The claims that hyperlinked material lets readers decide how they feel about an issue are true to a point. The blogger handpicks the hyperlink and source and has discarded ones with contrary evidence or views. Therefore, the hyperlink in these cases reinforces or further explains the message in the post.

Limitations and Future Research

This study is not without limitations. Since the sample was collected and analyzed, many more celebrities have begun blogging. Additionally, the blogging celebrity may be more politically active and outspoken than non-blogging celebrities. Even so, this data stand as an initial representation of celeblogs and their propensity for talking politics to their publics.

This area is ripe for future research. Not only should the impact of celebrity blogs be analyzed, but also the role that interaction plays on receptivity to political messages. Important questions regarding how readers view celebrities in regards to opinion leaders still need to be answered. Additionally, future research should expand beyond political messages on high-traffic celebrity blogs to investigate content on other political, and even nonpolitical, blogs written by noncelebrities. Finally, conversation in feedback mechanisms (comments, trackbacks) must be further investigated through a larger sample.

Conclusion

The blog is a personal, opinionated and interactive medium. Because of this, readers who do not know the blogger in person may develop a parasocial relationship and feel as though they know the blogger. As such, the reader may be more receptive to these political statements.

Survey data indicate that readers are not approaching celebrity blogs for political statements; however, they are not actively avoiding celebrity blogs with such statements either (Trammell, 2004). Political statements can be easily wrapped inside intensely personal statements or anecdotes of experiences. Therefore, this direct interpersonal (even though mass communicated) message has the opportunity to be more impactful than media coverage of the celebrity discussing his or her political beliefs.

Conventional wisdom and a reading of the literature on public opinion formation both indicate that celeblogs' political opinions have minimal impact on the opinions of fans. If the fan already agrees with the celebrity's political stance, those views might be reinforced. The question is, however, what of the fan who disagrees politically with a celebrity? Does that person's opinion undergo change in the direction of the celebrity's? Current scholarship, intuition and literature would say "no." That is why additional specific studies of blogs, bloggers, and blog users are needed.

Author's Note

The author would like to express appreciation to her doctoral dissertation committee for their assistance with this project: Drs. Lynda Lee Kaid, Spiro Kiousis, Rick Ferdig, and Meg Lamme.

References

Associated Press. (2003, March 14). Dixie Chicks remark irks country fans. Retrieved March 14, 2003 from http://story.news. yahoo.com/ news?tmpl=story2&u=/ ap/20030314/ap_on_en_mu/ people_dixie_chicks&e=1&ncid" http://story.news.yahoo.com/news?tmpl=story2&u=/ap/20030314/ ap_on_en_mu/people_dixie_chicks&e=1&ncid_=

Banwart, M.C. (2002). Videostyle and Webstyle in 2000: Comparing the gender differences of candidate presentation in political advertising on the Internet. Unpublished doctoral dissertation, University of Oklahoma.

Blood, R. (2002). The Weblog handbook: Practical advice on creating and maintaining your blog. Perseus Publishing: Cambridge, MA.

Boorstin, D.J. (1992). *The image: A guide to pseudo-events in America.* Vintage Books: New York.

Breznican, A. (2002, December 11). Hollywood stages counteroffensive against war. *Washington Post*, C10.

Bystrom, D.G., Banwart, M.C., Robertson, T., & Kaid, L.L. (2004). *Gender and political candidate communication: VideoStyle, WebStyle, and newsStyle.* Routledge Publishers: New York.

Herring, S.C., Scheidt, L.A., Bonus, S., & Wright, E. (2004). Bridging the gap: A genre analysis of Weblogs. Proceedings of the 37th Hawaii International Conference on System Sciences (HICSS-37). Los Alamitos: IEEE Press.

Rice, A. (2003). Use of blogs in the 2004 presidential election. Report retrieved Feb. 10, 2004, from http://www.campaignsonline.org/reports/blog.pdf http://www.campaignsonline.org/reports/blog.pdf_

Trammell, K.D. (2004). Celebrity blogs: Investigation in the persuasive nature of two-way communication regarding politics. Unpublished doctoral dissertation, University of Florida.

Trammell, K.D., & Gasser, U. (2004). Deconstructing Weblogs: An analytical framework for analyzing online journals. Paper presented at the International Communication Association, New Orleans, LA. May.

Trammell, K.D., Tarkowski, A., Hofmokl, J., & Sapp, A.M. (2006). Rzeczpospolita blogow [Republic of Blog]: Examining the motivations of Polish bloggers through content analysis. *Journal of Computer-Mediated Communication, 11*(3), article 2, http://jcmc.indiana.edu/vol11/issue3/trammell.html

DISCUSSION QUESTIONS

1. Why do people continue to follow the political advice of celebrities? What special insights do audiences think they possess that is important to the way they conduct their lives or form their opinions?

2. "Celeblogs" are the latest extension of celebrity opinion on important issues and public policies. How effective is this form of opinion sharing in developing support for social movements?

3. Celebrities, according to the study, were generally more critical about President George W. Bush and the 2003 Iraq War. To what extent has this "set the agenda" for discussion of these issues, and why would readers disagree with celebloggers they obviously expended effort to find on the Internet?

4. Interactivity is a hallmark of most blogging efforts, so how do blog readers contribute to the rehaping of opinions by the celebrities themselves?

5. Marketers understand the power of celebrity when opening shopping malls, selling shoes, or other merchandise. To what extent will marketers eventually use celebrities or links to celebrity pages to promote social or commercial causes? Give examples.

CHAPTER NINETEEN

BLOG DAY AFTERNOON: ARE BLOGS STEALING AUDIENCES AWAY FROM TRADITIONAL MEDIA SOURCES?

THOMAS J. JOHNSON AND BARBARA K. KAYE

The horrific images of five armed terrorists chopping off the head of American Nick Berg and then proudly displaying it like a hunting trophy was not featured on television news as editors deemed such images too graphically horrific for the American audience. But the networks' decision not to air the grisly video or images from the execution did not deter Americans from viewing them on the Internet or on Weblogs, which are diary-style Web sites offering news and opinions listed chronologically on the site as well as discussions by their hosts (bloggers) and audience.

The words "Nick," "Berg," "beheading" and "video" were among the top 10 words searched that week (May 11-17, 2004) on Lycos. Several leading Weblogs such as andrewsullivan.com provided links to the video or images from that video. Several political Weblogs also reported an "exponential jump" in the number of people visiting their blogs to discuss the beheading (Editorial: Whiplash and war, 2004). Recent studies suggest that almost a quarter of online users have seen graphic war images online and have visited Weblogs and other Internet sites to get news and images not available from the mainstream media (Fallows & Rainie, 2004).

Several studies have examined whether the Web is replacing or supplementing traditional media as a source of news and information. Less attention has been paid to whether components of the Internet such as Weblogs have been taking audience members away from traditional media. Bloggers and blog readers tend to harbor a deep distrust of traditional media. They view blogs as an improved form of journalism, one that is more opinionated, independent, personal, and in depth than traditional media (Palser, 2002; Cooper, 2006).

But while bloggers and their users may consider blogs an alternative to traditional media, few academics and journalists have studied whether blog users have actually reduced time spent with traditional media. Also, while studies have examined whether the Internet is replacing or complementing traditional media, much less attention has been paid to explaining why the Internet would serve as a supplement or replacement for traditional media sources.

This chapter focuses on the results of an online survey that was completed by 3,747 Weblog users. The survey examined whether blogs are supplanting or supplementing online sources for information on the 2003 Iraq War. More specifically, this study examines whether blogs users are reducing the amount of time spent with traditional media and their online counterparts. Furthermore, this study will try to explain why blogs may or may not be replacing other media sources by examining whether blog users say they receive war information they cannot find in traditional media as well as whether they see blogs as more believable, fair, accurate, and in-depth than the traditional media.

WEBLOGS AS AN ALTERNATIVE TO TRADITIONAL MEDIA

The emergence of the World Wide Web in the 1990s created fears among news organizations that the Net would rob them of their audiences. Researchers suggest that because people have only a finite amount of time, their use of traditional media would be expected to decline if they devote more time to a new technology that is viewed as more desirable than an old one (Dimmick, Kline & Stafford, 2000; Kang & Atkin, 1999; Lin, 2001a, 2001b). Max McCombs called this the "relative constancy hypothesis" (McCombs, 1972). Research on the relative constancy hypothesis has been mixed, partly because it appears that during the 20th century the amount of time people spend with mass media is actually growing, not static. Sociological theory also suggests that time spent with media will increase as societies become more structurally complex (Demers, 1994).

Research on the Internet has focused on the effects of that medium on television because it is structurally similar (Kaye & Medoff, 2001). However, studies from both academia (Kaye, 1998; Kaye & Johnson, 2003; Lin, 2001a) and the industry (Fallows & Rainie, 2004; Horrigan, Garrett, & Resnick, 2004) suggest that while television viewing has been hurt most by the Internet, most people say that have not cut back on television use. Studies have found that people interested in political news appear even less likely to cut back on traditional news use, using Web sites to supplement rather than replace traditional sources (Horrigan, Garrett & Resnick, 2004; Kaye & Johnson, 2003). Indeed, Horrigan and associates (2004) suggested that Internet users tend to be "news omnivores," feasting on news from various sources and from different points of view. Kaye and Johnson (2003) found that while the Internet tended to cut into news magazine use, newspaper use was unaffected and television viewing had actually increased. While online news sources as a whole might supplement rather than replace traditional media, evidence suggests that users might be turning away from traditional media and relying on blogs for news and information because they distrust traditional media.

Bloggers and blog readers grumble loudly about the quality of mainstream media, arguing that is dominated by an elitist, Eastern Establishment liberal bias (Seipp, 2002). The rising popularity of political blogs has mirrored a growing distrust and dislike of the traditional media (Hamdy & Mobarak, 2004). Indeed, studies suggest that bloggers consider themselves viable alternatives to corporate-controlled journalists and that they offer a different and superior product than that served by the traditional media (Blood, 2002; Cooper, 2006; Delwiche, 2004; Johnson & Kaye, 2004b). For instance, blogger Andrew Sullivan, in his "Blogger Manifesto," describes blogs as the Napster of journalism.

[J]ust as Napster by-passed record companies and brought music to people with barely any mediation, so Blogger by-passes established magazines, newspapers, editors and proprietors, and allowed direct peer-to-peer journalism to flourish.

Bloggers also set themselves apart from traditional media by skewering them for how they cover the news, castigating them for ignoring certain stories against journalists and taking considerably pleasure in pointing out errors journalists make (Cooper, 2006; Kurtz, 2002; Smolkin, 2004). Scholars suggest that one source of political distrust of traditional media is that Internet users feel that corporate-controlled media do not deliver the entire story about events such as the 2003 Iraqi war, while blogs connected to news sources around the world and ran stories that were either unavailable or ignored by the mainstream media. Blogs first gained notoriety in the days after September 11 (Jesdanun, 2001) and emerged as a key source of news for a cadre of

Internet users since the 2003 Iraq War (Hamilton, 2003; Simon, 2004). In fact, some observers suggest that blogs hit their stride after the bombs starting falling in Baghdad (Hastings, 2003).

Analysts suggest that blogs gained popularity during the Iraq War for several reasons:

- Several blogs were written by soldiers on the battlefield, providing more detail and insight than stories in traditional media (Bedell, 2002). Such blogs offered more than just war stories, but rather images of Iraq not seen anywhere else (Hebert, 2004; Simon, 2004).
- Blogs could present a more incisive and personal side of the war than traditional media. As Instapundit blogger Glenn Reynolds (2004) argues, "The arrival of war ... called for two things: an easy-to-parse overview for news junkie who wanted information from all sides, and a personal insight that bypassed the sanitizing Cuisinart of big-media news editing."

For instance, Salam Pax, a 29-year-old gay Iraqi architect, became the most celebrated reporter during the early days of the war as his blog "Where is Raed," brought readers personal glimpses into the bombing of Baghdad. For instance, on May 7, 2003, six days after President Bush declared, "mission accomplished," Pax lamented,

Let me tell you one thing first. War sucks big time. Don't let yourself ever be taken into having one waged in the name of your freedom. Somehow, when the bombs start dropping or you hear the sound of machinery at the end of your street, you don't think about your "imminent liberation"' any more (Dehnart, 2004).

While most information sources feature only one-way communication, most blogs allow readers to respond to their postings, promoting a healthy debate about the progress and the purpose of the war (Hastings, 2003; Papacharissi, 2004). Similarly, people visited blogs to gauge people's opinions about the war as well as to gain a sense of community by being able to share views with like-minded individuals (Carver, 2003; Katz, 2003; Seipp, 2002; Thompson, 2003).

Because many bloggers were on the front lines of the war they often present more varied and more up-to-date news than traditional news sources. Consequently, journalists are one of the main readers of blogs. They access blogs to find out about events and perspectives missing from traditional news reports (Ryan, 2003).

Blog supporters contend traditional media presented a negative perspective of the war, while Weblogs feature writers worldwide who hold a variety of perspectives, giving readers insights missing from the largely American traditional media (Hamilton, 2003; Hastings, 2003). War bloggers tended to be conservative and support the war efforts, undermining the efforts of traditional media to present a critical war image. As Reynolds (2004) notes,

> Weblogs have made a point of showing both sides—and of noting that other visitors to Iraq have reported that the story is far less negative than the drip, drip, drip coverage of bombings and anti-American demonstrations on network news broadcasts might suggest.

Because bloggers do not need to adhere to traditional journalistic standards and are not subjected to the advertising pressures of traditional media, they can interject their own views and run stories and show images, such as the beheadings of prisoners, that do not meet traditional standards of good taste (Fallows & Rainie, 2004; Grossman, Hamilton, Buechner & Whitaker, 2004; Sydell, 2003; Wall, 2003).

Some argue, however, that journalists and political observers are too quick to praise blogs as the rise of a powerful new kind of journalism. Only 11% of Internet users have ever visited a blog (Lenhart, Horrigan & Fallows, 2004). The average reader spends less than two minutes reading a blog, and blogs mainly preach to the converted (Petersen, 2004). Also, bloggers do very little reporting, but rather incessantly comment on information already gathered by mainstream media (Packer, 2004). Therefore, bloggers are more commentators and aggregators than reporters (Lamb, 2004). As long-time journalist Randal Rothenberg (2004) argues,

> Blogging is little more than hype dished out largely by the unemployable to the aimless. While there is a phenomenon that bears attention buried within them, blogs themselves are barely worth the attention politicians are paying to them.

For all the advantages and disadvantages of Weblogs, the question remains whether these online sites are taking time away from traditional media. The respondents to the online Weblog survey have indeed altered their media use habits since discovering Weblogs. Changes in the amount of time spent with media are not consistent across all media types. Broadcast television news has taken the hardest hit from Weblogs. More than four out of 10 respondents (45.7%) report watching less broadcast television news since they starting accessing Weblogs. Furthermore, broadcast television news sites are also looked at less frequently by 39% of Weblog users. About a quarter of all respondents also spend less time with traditionally delivered cable television news, newspapers, and news magazines. When comparing online sources to Weblogs, one-fourth (25.1%) of respondents favor using Weblogs to cable news sites, and about 20% have reduced their time with online newspapers, online radio, and online magazines.

Although Weblogs are taking time away from some traditional and online media, they are also being used as a supplement. In other words, in some cases a larger percentage of respondents have increased rather than have decreased the amount of time they spend with some media. For example, a greater percentage (42.4%) of Weblog users have increased the amount of time they spend reading online newspapers than have decreased their time spent with this source (19.1%). Such increases are also found with the amount of time spent with cable television news sites, online magazines, and traditionally delivered cable news. However, almost the same percentage of Weblog users (17.6%) claim they have reduced their time listening to talk radio as those who have increased their time listening (17.2%) since they discovered Weblogs.

Weblogs provide a convenient means of comparing traditional and online news stories. With some media, such as over-the-air and online broadcast television, users may find that Weblogs satisfy their appetites for news more so than do other sources. These Weblogs users presumably spend time on Weblogs that they once devoted to other sources. Yet, this is not always the case. In some instances, Weblog users have increased their time with other sources. This finding suggests that Weblogs may spark greater interest in news and current events, such as about the Iraqi war, and that this interest leads people to compare accounts among various media.

Weblogs also act as a catalyst for face-to-face discussion. Over half (52.2%) of Weblog users have increased their time talking with others about events, such as the war on Iraq, since they started using Weblogs. Presumably, links to in-depth information and the array of opinions expressed on Weblogs ignite interest, stimulate thought, solidify opinions, and arm readers with information, such that they feel compelled to discuss what they have learned with others.

WEBLOGS AS A SOURCE OF ALTERNATIVE INFORMATION

Weblog users consider blogs a viable alternative to the news churned out by traditional journalists. Indeed, Palser (2002) argues that blogs are the antithesis of traditional media: "unedited, unabashedly opinioned, sporadic and personal." As *American Journalism Review* writer Rachel Smolkin claimed, "Yes, in these hardened cynical times amid angst over media conglomerates and homogenization of the news, political junkies are using cyberspace to opine and whine, to preach and beseech" (Smolkin, 2004).

When Park (2004) studied the top four political bloggers — Glenn Reynolds' instapundit.com. Mickey Kaus' kausfiles on slate.com, Andrew Sullivan's andrewsullivan.com and Joshua Michal Marshall's talkingpointsmemo.com — he found that at least in the case of Reynolds and Sullivan, they perceived that their greatest strengths were that they were NOT traditional journalists. Traditional journalists, they argue, are trapped by the journalistic canons of objectivity. For instance, Kevin Drum, who blogs for *The Washington Monthly*, concedes that blogs don't meet the journalistic standards for sourcing and reporting, but that the whole point is that bloggers standards are lower:

> They're able to toss stuff out that a reporter on a daily newspaper couldn't. They express opinions loudly and with fervor. It's not clear for me how those two things can intersect.

Furthermore, mainstream reporters are restrained from either expressing their views or from covering sensitive stories because they work for media conglomerates that constantly fret about making a profit and not offending advertisers.

Bloggers set themselves apart from the traditional media because they are free to express their own views and their Web sites offer news and commentary that simply cannot be found in traditional media. Indeed, a study of the agendas of Weblogs and traditional media in 2003 found little correspondence between what was stressed on blogs and what appeared in traditional media (Dewiche, 2004). Park (2004) contends that while bloggers hold themselves at length from traditional journalists (even though they link heavily to traditional media stories), they align themselves with their readers and believe that they represent the views of their readers and run stories of interest to them. Indeed, studies suggest that just as most bloggers position themselves as libertarians or conservatives, blog readers also rate themselves as conservative supporters of the war and the Bush administration and are indeed attracted to blogs because they express their points of view (Johnson & Kaye, 2004b).

While bloggers and journalists argue over their differences, what really should be taken into account are Weblog users' perceptions of content. When asked about the similarity between the information provided by Weblogs and information provided by other online and traditional sources, respondents generally stated that Weblogs were very different from other media.

Regarding online sources, between 35.7% and 69.2% of respondents asserted that Weblog information was "not very similar/not similar at all" to broadcast television news sites, cable television news sites, online newspapers, online radio news, online magazines, electronic bulletin boards/mailing lists, and chat rooms. Online broadcast television news and online radio news sites are the two online sources considered the least similar to Weblogs. Almost 7 out of 10 respondents reported that online television news was nothing like Weblogs, with 61.4% responding in kind to the similarity between online radio news and Weblogs.

When considering traditionally delivered media, more than three-quarters of respondents marked that over-the-air television was "not similar at all/not very similar" to Weblogs. Cable television, radio news, newspapers, and news magazines were rated as dissimilar by 52.4%, 52.5%, 49.9%, and 46.7% of respondents, respectively.

The interactive nature of Weblogs could account for the perceptions of dissimilar content. Even though many bloggers copy and paste information gathered from other sources, the addition of commentary written by bloggers and other readers may be what sets Weblogs apart from other sources. On the other hand, Weblog commentary may make Weblogs seem similar to face-to-face discussion and to radio talk shows. A greater percentage of Weblog users (35.8%) said that Weblogs were "similar to/very similar to" face-to-face discussion than the percentage (26.7%) of those who said the opposite. Radio talk shows had almost the same percentage of respondents claiming these sources were as similar to Weblogs (30.2%) as those claiming they were dissimilar (34.9%).

Presumably, the ability to express an opinion, coupled with the interactive format of face-to-face discussion and radio talk shows, led to the perceptions of similarity between these sources and Weblogs. Face-to-face discussion centers on interpersonal expression and feedback, which is very similar to Weblog content — the major difference is that face-to-face discussion is usually verbal whereas Weblog discussion is written.

Talk radio hosts encourage listeners to call in, and rant and rave and express their opinions and beliefs, just as bloggers encourage their readers to engage in discussion, spout off their views and send in links to other sources. Again, the difference is that talk radio is verbal/auditory and Weblogs are written/visual sources. Interestingly, neither electronic bulletin boards/mailing lists nor chat rooms are deemed very similar to Weblogs. Even though both of these sources are venues where participants are free to express their opinions, a host does not typically moderate them, as is the case of Weblogs and talk radio.

These findings suggest that Weblogs are seen as most similar to face-to-face discussion and talk radio, which both revolve around expression of opinion, unfettered commentary, and interaction with a host. Therefore, perceptions of similarity are based on function, rather than on content.

WEBLOGS AND CREDIBILITY

While Weblog popularity is growing, political observers argue about how much stock to put into information found on them. Critics argue bloggers are not bound by the same ethical and professional standards of trained journalists such as objectivity. Most bloggers have strong views that they express openly on their sites (Ryan, 2003). Also,

> Weblogs do not undergo the scrutiny of editors who are responsible for flagging misinformation and for ensuring that coverage is balanced and fair (Amis, 2002).

Supporters contend that even though blogs do not go through an editorial review process as do the traditional media, users are constantly monitoring blogs for misinformation and that errors can be fixed immediately rather than waiting until the next day, as with newspapers (Carver, 2003; Seipp, 2002). Bloggers concede that they do not follow the canons of traditional journalism, but they see this as a virtue. As Lev Grossman and associates (2004) at *Time* magazine argue, "Bloggers are unconstrained by such journalistic conventions as good taste, accountability and objectivity—and that can be a good thing. Accusations of media bias are thick on the ground these days, and Americans are tired of it. Blogs don't pretend to be neutral; they're gleefully unabashedly, biased, and that makes them a lot more fun." As leading blogger Andrew Sullivan adds, "I don't have the pressure of an advertising executive telling me to lay off. It's incredibly liberating" (Grossman, et al., 2004).

While some have dismissed blogs as akin to small terriers nipping at the ankles of mainstream media, blogs have clearly achieved increased credibility among politicians and journalists. While evidence suggests that blogs may not have much of an influence on public opinion in general, they may have an impact on journalists and Washington insiders, who are heavy readers of blogs. Journalists are increasingly monitoring blogs to get a sense of the public debate about politics. Howard Fineman, *Newsweek's* chief political correspondent, says he reads blogs

> for the same reason I try not to sit on my tush inside the Beltway, and get outside the Beltway as much as possible. Cyberspace is a place you need to go (Smolkin, 2004).

Similarly, Karen Tumulty, *Time* magazine's national political correspondent, said blogs are a "good indicator of what's in the political bloodstream at any given moment" (Smolkin, 2004).

While bloggers rely heavily on traditional media to get their information, they can draw attention to issues ignored by the mainstream press and get those issues on the traditional press agenda (Drezner & Farrell, 2004; Grossman, et al., 2004). "Blogs act like a lens, focusing attention on an issue until it catches fire" (Grossman et al, 2004).

Blogs are credited with bringing to light then-Senate Majority Leader Trent Lott's perceived racist comments at the birthday party of Sen. Strom Thurman. After 60-Minutes aired a story contending that President Bush did not serve his time with the Alabama National Guard, four bloggers waged a campaign claiming that the documents that CBS relied on were not authentic. Although CBS did investigate the documents before the broadcast, there was still some doubt about their authenticity. CBS was later forced to apologize for running the story; an apology that probably would not have come about if it was not for the bloggers' influence (Boyd, 2004; Cooper, 2006; Karlgaard, 2004).

Finally, because blogs allow journalists to interject views and to personalize the news, many media organizations are starting their own blogs or co-opting existing ones (Berman, 2004; Heyboar & Rosen, 2003). For instance, Micky Kaus, a former writer for *The New Republic* and *Newsweek*, moved his blog Kausfiles to Slate.com and Reynolds blogs for MSNBC in addition to creating his own Instapundit site. Blogger J.D. Lasica believes that by creating their own blogs that traditional media are building trust with their readers. "Newsroom-sanctioned Weblogs promise to show journalists as human beings with opinions, emotions, and personal lives and yes, with warts and foibles" (Lasica, 2003).

Media consumers are screaming that traditional media are liberally biased. Yet blog readers consider Weblogs the most credible sources, even though bloggers themselves admit that they are biased, most often to the right, and that they are often pushing an agenda and trying to persuade readers to their point of view (Johnson & Kaye, 2004c). It seems that Weblog users embrace bias as long as it is conservative bias. Thus, users are not concerned about media bias, as such, but attack a medium if they perceive it too liberal.

It is not surprising that nearly three quarters of Weblogs users (73.6%), who eschew other media sources feel that Weblogs are the most credible source of news and information. If users thought that Weblogs were not credible they probably would not access them. Credibility is assessed by how accurate, believable, fair, and in-depth they find Weblogs as compared with other online and traditional sources.

When each of these elements of credibility are examined separately, Weblogs are seen as more accurate, believable, fair, and in-depth than all other online and traditionally delivered media. When comparing Weblogs to other sources in terms of accuracy, Weblogs are seen as the most accurate followed by traditionally delivered newspapers and news magazines. Apparently, because these printed sources are subject to fact-checking and journalistic standards they are viewed as highly accurate, as are their online counterparts. Yet, despite the lack of editorial review, Weblogs are still deemed more accurate than these printed sources and their online sites. It could be that even though much Weblog information is taken directly from these sources, Weblog users trust bloggers to verify information more than they do newspaper and news magazine editors.

Weblogs are also seen as the most believable medium. Printed newspapers and their online sites, and cable television news and their online sites are the next most believable media. Both online and traditionally delivered newspapers are deemed believable presumably because of strict editorial standards, but over-the-air and online cable television news sites are known for their biases, and some networks, such as Fox News, unabashedly display their right-leaning biases. Yet, these sources are deemed believable. These findings could indicate that Weblog users, who do tend to be conservative, white males with high incomes, also tend to gravitate toward cable news because it supports their worldview. In this case believability is equated to whether a source conforms to one's own views and prejudices. Weblogs, which mainly lean to the right and are read by conservatives (Johnson & Kaye, 2004c), may be seen as the most believable source because users agree with and trust the spin bloggers put on news accounts.

Despite their built-in biases, Weblogs are deemed the fairest source of news and information. However, Weblogs are deemed more believable, accurate, and in-depth than they are fair. This finding suggests that users may very well be aware of bloggers' biases and may recognize when only one-side of an issue is presented. Nevertheless, Weblogs are seen as the fairest sources, followed by printed newspapers, online cable television, cable television, news magazines, and broadcast radio news, which were all deemed as equally fair as the other.

Weblogs are viewed as being highly in-depth sources of news and information and are rated higher on this quality than they are on accuracy, believability, and fairness. Users appreciate insightful, in-depth commentary along with links to even more information. It is the interaction between the blogger and blog reader, the connection to more information, and the lack of limits to the length of story that sets Weblogs apart from any other source of information.

Regarding accuracy, believability, fairness, and depth of information, bulletin boards/electronic mailing lists and chat rooms are consistently ranked as the least credible sources. Weblog users recognize that with both of these sources, participants are free to express their views and impart information that may be factually incorrect. Unlike with Weblogs and traditional media sources, there is no one to correct misstatements. The lack of oversight and correction of misinformation may make these sources seem unbelievable as well as inaccurate to Weblog users. Additionally, it is acknowledged that participants are largely anonymous and, thus, may feel free to push a particular viewpoint that is unfairly presented. Further, bulletin boards and chat rooms participants usually dish out opinion and information in a few lines of text, wait for a response, and then add a few more lines, which leads to shallow commentary.

CONCLUSION

The increased attention and power attributed to blogs by journalists and political observers have caused some to gleefully predict that blogs have become the most powerful boost to journalism since the rise of the political pamphlet (Petersen, 2004) and that they challenge the power of mainstream media (Cooper, 2006; Pack, 2004). Others have gone further, predicting that the rise of blogs will signal the death of newspapers and television news (Karlgaard, 2004; Pohlig, 2003). No less an authority than *The New York Times* proclaimed in its election-day editorial headlined, "The revolution will be posted," (2004) that the Weblog constitutes the revolution that usually accompanies a presidential election.

Others note that while blogs offer an alternative to the traditional media, to paraphrase Mark Twain, reports of the imminent death of the traditional media are greatly exaggerated. First, the blogosphere represents a small island in the Internet world. Only 11% of Internet users have ever visited a blog (Lenhart, Horrigan & Fallows, 2004), and those who visit only stay a short time. One study found that the average reader spends less than two minutes on a blog (Petersen, 2004). Second, blogs do not seem poised to replace traditional media, but to work along side them, providing political junkies a more personal and opinionated take on the news than the mainstream media. As CyberJournalist.net blogger Jonathan Dube commented,

> Bloggers are not threatening traditional media, nor replacing it—bloggers are enhancing it, adding additional voices, another check and balance. Bloggers are part of the media now (Pack, 2004).

Indeed, our study suggests that blogs are supplementing rather than replacing information readers get from other sources. Blogging primarily hurts broadcast television, although a plurality still claim the amount of time they spend watching television news has remained the same. Similarly, the plurality or majority of both online and traditional cable television, newspaper, radio news, and news magazines users have indicated that blogs have not altered the time they spend with this sources. Indeed, blog readers are more likely to say that they have increased the time they spent with online and traditional cable television news, online newspapers, and online magazine sites. Blogs provide links in their articles to these online sources that blog readers can click to get a fuller view of the story.

Blogs have had a particularly profound influence on the degree to which people talk about politics. A majority said that face-to-face discussion has increased or greatly increased while only 3% said it declined. Blogs draw the politically interested online to discuss issues such as the Iraqi War. As evidence suggests that most bloggers are conservative and are attracted to blogs that express a conservative point of view on the war and other topics, presumably readers go to these sites to bolster their opinions and to learn new arguments that they can carry with them offline in discussions and debates with others.

Researchers suggest that people have only a finite amount of time to devote to media. When a new technology emerges that is viewed as superior in content, cost, and convenience than old technology people will reduce their time with the medium, particularly if it is perceived as functionally similar (Dimmick, Kline & Stafford, 2000; Kang & Atkin, 1999; Lin, 2001a, 2001b). For instance, CDs replaced records because of their superior quality and convenience and DVDs will soon render VHS tapes extinct for the same reason.

But our study suggests that blogs are not replacing traditional media because readers *do not* see them as functionally similar to traditional media. About 50% or more of those surveyed said blogs were "not similar at all" or "not very similar" to online and broadcast television news, cable news, newspapers, radio news, and magazines. Indeed bloggers take pride in the fact that blogs do not follow the canons of journalism such as objectivity and good taste, and that their sites are independent, unedited, opinionated, and personal.

On the other hand, blogs are considered functionally similar to radio talk shows. Earlier studies have compared blogs to digital versions of talk radio. Like bloggers, talk radio hosts openly attack both political opponents as well as what they perceive as liberal media coverage (Katz, 1992; Owens, 1997). Like talk shows, blogs allow the users to weigh in with their opinions on the issue. Finally, talk radio listeners may be more likely to trust the information they find on the shows because they believe talk show hosts openly express their biases while traditional journalists subtly interject their views into their stories (Davis, 1997).

Weblog users view blogs as a new and better form of journalism — one that is opinionated, analytical, independent, and personal. Almost three-quarters of those surveyed view Weblogs as moderately to very credible, and the more one relied on blogs the more credible users considered them (Johnson & Kaye, 2004a). Blog readers distinguished Weblogs from traditional media by claiming that Weblogs provide the depth lacking from mainstream media sources. They also judge blogs as accurate and believable. On the other hand, users do not necessary judge blogs as fair. But while fairness may be considered an important pillar of traditional journalism, blog users likely see bias as a virtue.

The majority of blog users rate themselves as conservative and almost two-thirds said they sought information from conservative or very conservative sites (Johnson & Kaye, 2004c). Therefore, blog readers do not judge blogs as credible based on whether they can get all sides of an issue. Blog users are seeking out information to support their already-held views, and they are likely to consider the conservative information they receive from blogs on issues like the Iraqi War as highly credible.

REFERENCES

Amis, D. (2002, Sept. 21). Web logs: Online navel gazing. [Online]. http://www.netfreedom.org.

Bedell, D. (2003, April 7). War blogs add personal edge to news. *The Dallas Morning News*. [Online] http://www.dallasnews.com

Berman, A.S. (2004, July/August). With election, every blog has its day, *Presstime*, p. 32.

Blood, R. (2002). Weblogs: A history and perspective. In *We've got blog: How Weblogs are changing our culture*, pp. 7-16. Cambridge, MA: Perseus Publishing.

Boyd, R. (2004, Sept. 13). How four blogs dealt a blow to CBS's credibility. *New York Sun*, p. 1

Carver, B. (2003). What would Dewey do? Librarians grapple with Internet. *Library Journal*, 128, 30-32.

Cooper, Stephen D. (2006). *Watching the Watchdog: Bloggers as the Fifth Estate*. Spokane, WA: Marquette Books.

Davis, R. (1997, July/September). Understanding broadcast political talk. *Political Communication*, 14, 323-332.

Delwiche, A.A. (2004). Agenda-setting, opinion leadership, and the world of weblogs. Presented at the annual meeting of the International Communication Association, May.

Demers, D. P. (1994). The relative constancy hypothesis, structural pluralism and national advertising expenditures. *Journal of Media Economics*, 7(4), 31-48.

Denhart, A. (2004, January 20). Tales of the Baghdad blogger. *Advocate*, p. 88.

Dimmick, J., Kline, S., & Stafford, l. (2000). The gratification niches of personal e-mail and the telephone. *Communication Research*, 27, 227-248.

Drenzer, D.W., & Farrell, H. (2004). Web of influence. *Foreign Policy*, 145, 32-40.

Editorial: Whiplash and war. (2004, May 14). SavannahNow. [Online] http://www.savannahnow.com/stories/051404/2158525.shtml

Fallows, D. & Rainie, L. (2004). The Internet as unique news source: Millions go online for news and images not covered in the mainstream press. [Online] http://www.pewinternet.org_, July 8, 2004.

Grossman, L., Hamilton, A., Buechner, M.M., & Whitaker, L. (2004,June 21). Meet Joe blog. Time, http:// www_.time.com/archive.

Hamdy, N. & Mobarak, R. (2004). Iraq war ushers in web-based era. In R.D. Berenger (ed), *Global media goes to war: Role of news and entertainment media during the 2003 Iraq War*, 245-254. Spokane, WA: Marquette Books.

Hamilton, A. (2993, April 7). Best of the war blogs. *Time*, 161, p. 91.

Hastings, M. (2003, April 7). Bloggers over Baghdad. *Newsweek*, 141, p. 48-49.

Hebert, J. (2004, August 2). Troop blogs offer voices, visions from Iraq. Copley News Service.

Heyboer, K, & Rosen, J. (2003 Dec./2004 Jan). Bloggin' in the newsroom. *American Journalism Review*, 245, 10-11.

Horrigan, J. Garrett, K., & Resnick, P. (2004 October 27). The Internet and democratic debate: Wired Americans hear more points of view about candidates and key issues than other citizens. They are not using the Internet to screen out ideas with which they disagree. http://www.pewinternet.org/reports, Oct. 27, 2004.

Jesdanun, A. (2001, October 14). In Online Logs, Web authors personalize attacks, retaliation, *The Florida Times-Union,* http://www.Jacksonville.com/tu-online/stories, October 14, 2001

Johnson, T.J., & Kaye, B.K. (2004a, August). The blogs of war: Reliance on Weblogs for information during the Iraqi War. Paper presented to the annual conference of the Association for Education in Journalism and Mass Communication, Toronto, Canada.

Johnson, T.J., & Kaye, B.K. (2004b). Wag the blog: How reliance on traditional media and the Internet influence credibility perceptions of Weblogs among blog users. *Journalism & Mass Communication Quarterly,* 81 (3) 622-642.

Johnson, T.J., & Kaye, B.K. (2004c). Weblogs as a source of information about the 2003 Iraq War. In R.D. Berenger (ed), *Global media goes to war: Role of news and entertainment media during the 2003 Iraq War.* Spokane, WA: Marquette Books, pp. 291-301.

Kang, M., & Atkin, D.J. (1999). Exploring the role of media uses and gratifications in multimedia cable adoption. *Telematics and Informatics,* 16, 59-74.

Karlgaard, R. (2004, Nov. 29). Net—one, TV—zero. *Forbes,* p. 41.

Katz, J. (2002). Here come the Weblogs. In *We've got blog: How Weblogs are changing our culture,* pp. 17-24. Cambridge, MA: Perseus Publishing.

Kaye, B.K. (1998). Uses and gratifications of the World Wide Web: From couch potato to Web potato. *New Jersey Journal of Communication,* 6, 21-40.

Kaye, B.K., &. Medoff, N.J. (2001). *The World Wide Web: A mass communication perspective.* Mountain View: Mayfield Publishing Company.

Kaye, B.K., & Johnson, T.J. (2003). From here to obscurity: The Internet and media substitution theory. *Journal of the American Society for Information Science and Technology,* 54 (3), 260-273.

Kurtz, H. (2002, July 21). How Weblogs keep the media honest. *Washington Post,* http://www.washingtonpost.com, July 21, 2002

Lamb, G.M. (2004, April 15). Blogs: Here to stay—with changes. *Christian Science Monitor,* p. 14.

Lasica, J.D. (2002a). Blogging as a form of journalism: Weblogs offer a vital, creative outlet for alternative voices. In *We've got blog: How Weblogs are changing our culture,* pp. 163-170. Cambridge, MA: Perseus Publishing.

Lasica, J.D. (2002b). Weblogs: A new source of news. In *We've got blog: How Weblogs are changing our culture,* pp. 171-182. Cambridge, MA: Perseus Publishing.

Lin, C.A. (2001a). Audience attributes, media supplementation, and likely online service adoption. *Mass Communication & Society,* 4, 19-38.

Lin, C.A. (2001b, August). Online use activity and user gratification-expectations. Paper presented at the Association for Education in Journalism and Mass Communication, Washington.

McCombs, M. (1972, February). Mass media in the marketplace. *Journalism Monographs,* Vol. 24.

Owen, D. (July/Sept. 1997). Talk radio and evaluations of President Clinton. *Political Communication,* 14, 333-353

Pack, T. (2004). Through the blogosphere. *Information Today,* 21, 41-42.

Packer, G. (May/June, 2004). The revolution will not be blogged. *Mother Jones,* p. 28-32.

Palser, B. (2002, July/August). Journalistic blogging. *American Journalism Review,* 24, p. 58.

Papacharissi, Z. (2004, May). The blogger revolution? Audiences as media producers. Presented at the annual meeting of the International Communication Association. May 2004.

Park, D. (2004, May). From many, a few: Intellectual authority and strategic positioning in the coverage of, and self-descriptions of, the "Big Four" Weblogs. Presented at the annual meeting of the International Communication Association.

Petersen, S. (2004, May 31). Another blog on the fire. *Eweek*, p. 34.

Pohlig, C. (2003). How a newspaper becomes H.I.P," *Nieman Reports*, 24-26.

"The revolution will be posted." (2004, Nov. 2). *The New York Times*, p. A27.

Reynolds, G. H. (2004). The blogs of War. *National Interest*, 75, 59-64.

Rothenberg, R. (2004, November 8). Reports on power of blogs have been greatly exaggerated. *Advertising Age*, p. 26.

Ryan, M. (2003, April 17). Blogs' rise stymies old media. *Chicago Tribune.* http://www.chicago.tribune.com.

Seipp, C. (2002, June). Online uprising. *American Journalism Review*, 24, 42-47.

Singer, J.B. (2003). Who are these guys? *Journalism*, 4, 139-163.

Simon, E. (2004, Sept. 27). U.S. soldiers' blogs detail life in Iraq: Unvarnished accounts comfort family, anger some commanders. [Online] http://www.msnbc.msn.com/id/6115600

Simon, S. (2003, March 29). Analysis: Web logs the newest way to convey war information. National Public Radio. http://npr.org.

Smolkin, R. (2004, June/July). The expanding blogosphere. *American Journalism Review*, 26, 38-43.

Sydell, L. (2003, March 29). Weblogs the newest way to convey war information. Weekend Edition. National Public Radio. http://www.npr.org

Wall, M.A. (2003, October) Blogs over Baghdad: Postmodern journalism and the Iraqi war. Paper presented to the Global Fusion Conference, Austin, Texas.

DISCUSSION QUESTIONS

1. Webloggers consider themselves "pure" journalists since their information efforts are most often unmediated by editors. To what extent is their self-assessment valid, and where is it off base?

2. One of the major problems bloggers face is getting their Weblogs recognized by major search engines, which limits potential audiences. As blogs grow in popularity, how can audiences be built and how are new blog readers "recruited"?

3. Some traditional news organizations encourage their reporters to write blogs, which are then carried on their Web sites, but other news organizations sometimes considers reporters-turned-bloggers as disloyal. How should these conflicts be remedied?

4. Why are some Weblogs more credible than others? Do traditional media "legitimize" blogs by quoting them in stories and opinion pieces? Or does this aspect have nothing to do with perceived credibility of Weblogs?

5. The authors do not see Weblogs supplanting traditional news agencies for

a variety of reasons, mostly that bloggers rely on traditional news for their links and news ideas about which they analyze and opine. What do you think? Are blogs the wave of the future?

Part V

Effects of Convergence Media

CHAPTER TWENTY

REMEMBERING THE "BIG PICTURE": A PHOTO-JOURNALISTIC ICON OF THE IRAQ WAR IN THE "IDS" AGE

DAVID D. PERLMUTTER

When thinking about the word "Fallujah," what is the first picture that pops into your mind?

Respondent #37: I think about Justin McCleese, a 20-year-old young man [and friend of mine] who was killed in while fighting in Fallujah [Iraq] in November of 2004.

Respondent #109: When I hear the word "Fallujah," the first picture that pops into my head is Muslims dressed in cloth from head to toe, covered. I also think about crazy men running around with bombs strapped to them, while innocent children get taught that Americans are evil and they should die to kill us.

Respondent #151: When I think of Fallujah, chaos comes to my mind. I see the bodies of three dead marines being pulled through the city streets, then being hung from a bridge to the delight of the Iraqi insurgent. The marines died trying to invoke peace and establish democracy for the people celebrating their death. Overall Fallujah is the perfect example of the grave mistake our wonderful president has committed us all to.

Respondent #204: I see soldiers in a jeep, on deserted looking land. Some look sad and lonely while others look hopeless and in despair. Things are physically calm but it seems as if crazy and chaotic thoughts are going on mentally in these poor soldiers ... .

Respondent #378: Some kind of food, like a Gyro. Possibly containing Garbonzo beans, pita bread, lettuce and some kind of thousand island looking sauce. Probably looking like a Mexican Fajita of some sort. Maybe it contains some kind of steak or chicken. All I know is that it sound very good. Mmmmm ... Fallujah.

Respondent #602: I've seen so many pictures from over there [Iraq]. I can't seem to focus on a single one. They are all bad, aren't they?

Introduction: Plato at the Speed of Light

"Journalism," stated *Washington Post* publisher Philip Graham, "is the first draft of history." Certainly, initial reports, wrong though they often are, create lasting impressions of the events defined by a news story. The actual words of initial spoken or printed narratives by on-the-scene or live-from-ground-zero reporters, however, are rarely recalled for longer than the instant. The few exceptions are legend: William Howard Russell's saber-sharp account of the Charge of the Light Brigade (Coughlan, 2004); Herbert Morrison's agitated but electric witnessing of the Hindenburg explosion; and Edward R. Murrow's composed anatomy of an air battle over London. Subsequent wordsmiths, from historians to textbook writers, supercede the initial reports from the field and create new narratives for contemporary audiences. Indeed, as many journalism-writing instructors have lectured, nobody reads yesterday's news — not even to expose themselves to great prose.

On the other hand, the mind's eye, when prompted by the merest suggestion of a famous occurrence, almost immediately focuses on one or several news pictures that became and remain our mnemonic telescope for symbolizing and summing up the event. For example, a person from the "greatest generation," if asked about the battle of Iwo Jima, would almost certainly visualize Joe Rosenthal's immortal still of the second flag-raising at Mount Suribachi. We may amend Graham, thus, to say that photojournalistic icons can be both the provisional sketch and the final illustration of history.

Other staples in the photo-iconic pantheon include: Robert Capa's *Dying Spanish Militiaman* (1936); Dorothea Lange's *Migrant Mother*

(1936); the photo by an unknown Nazi photographer of a small boy emerging from the rubble of the Warsaw ghetto (1943); Charles Moore's *Police Dogs Attacking Black Civil Rights Marchers in Birmingham, Alabama* (1963); Bob Jackson's *Jack Ruby Shooting Lee Harvey Oswald* (1963); Eddie Adams's *Saigon Street Execution* (1968); John Paul Filo's *Girl Screaming over a Dead Body at Kent State* (1970); Huynh Cong Ut's *Naked Little Girl and Other Children Fleeing Napalm Strike* (1972); and various photographers' *Man Confronting the Tanks at Tiananmen* (1989). Images of "The Fall of Saddam's Statue," "Abu Ghraib Prisoner Abuse," and "Cargo of Caskets" are more recent candidates for iconicity (e.g., Major & Perlmutter, 2005). Each serves the mind and society as an "instant replay" for our thinking about the past and present.

That we rely on "big pictures" to summarize and organize the way we think about knowledge is unsurprising. As it is for other primates, the visual system is our primary sense-gathering mode — the way we most prefer to receive, collect, and organize data (Canfield & Haith, 1991; Canfield & Kirkham, 2001; Gross, Heinze, Seiler & Stephan, 1999). Research has shown that holding "mental images" of objects greatly assists in their recall and affects the "view" we hold of them (Anderson, 1978; D'Agostino, O'Neill & Paivio, 1977; Elliot, 1973). Moreover, the vast weight of experimental research has found that visual images are recalled and recognized more quickly, more easily, and for a lengthier duration than are lexical words (Ackerman, 1985; Anglin & Levie, 1985; Joseph, Wain & Stone, 1984; Payne, 1986; Winograd, Smith & Simon, 1982). Furthermore, unlike any other creature on earth, humans create mediated images to express their understanding of the world and to impose order upon it. As the late paleontologist Stephen Jay Gould noted, "the pictures we draw betray our deepest convictions and display our current conceptual limitations" (1994, p. 85).

That certain images achieve stardom — or as is more often the case have celebrity thrust upon them — reveals much about the norms, codes, and ideologies at work within any society, polity, and system of news (Domke, Perlmutter & Spratt, 2002; Hariman & Lucaites, 2004; Perlmutter, 1998; Perlmutter & Wagner, 2004: Major & Perlmutter, 2005). Photo-icons typically are significant not only because of their fame, omnipresence, or mnemonic potential, but because it is commonly assumed that they have power over public opinion as well as policy-shaping toward the very events that they portray. Indeed, accompanying any famous news image, spoken of in today's news or in historical analysis, is usually some ascription by journalists, pundits, political and military leaders, and others that these images "changed the world."

The prospect of the visual image as policy-maker and demagogue has never been popular with traditional discourse elites. In Plato's *Republic,* for example, the philosophers argue that there should be few or no visual artists in an ideal state because painters and sculptors, by creating realistic visual images, fool the senses of ordinary people and lead them to make decisions based on emotion; such pursuits engender a "bad state of affairs in the mind of the individual, by encouraging the unreasoning part of it, which cannot distinguish greater and less but thinks the same things are now large and now small, and by creating images far removed from the truth" (Plato, 1987, X, 595c).

Many political and military leaders of the age of television and our current era of IDS (Internet-digital-satellite) convergence share such sentiments. Lyndon Johnson's National Security Adviser Ellsworth Bunker argued that "television is interested in the sensational, dramatic; this was the aspect of [the Vietnam] war they saw, saw things that happen in every war but had never been seen before. [That] turned opinion against it, made it impossible then for us to go through with our program" (Bunker, 1983). Later, during the Tiananmen crisis of 1989, Margaret Tutweiler, then press spokesperson for the State Department, insisted that her boss, James Baker, also watch the CNN coverage (Henry III, 1992, p. 25; Friedland, 1992, pp. 5-6). "You cannot *not* respond to these images on TV," she asserted, "you have got to say something that expresses the outrage people feel and about how unacceptable this behavior is" (Tyler, 1999, p. 10A). Bill Clinton's first secretary of state, Warren Christopher, similarly maintained, "television images cannot be the North Star of America's foreign policy" (Urschel, 1994). More recently, Secretary of Defense Donald Rumsfeld complained to Congress that "people are running around with digital cameras and taking these unbelievable photographs and then passing them off, against the law, to the media, to our surprise, when they have not even arrived in the Pentagon" (Rumsfeld, 2004).

A small but growing body of research seeks to examine closely the place such icons have in policy-making, public opinion, and in the historical memory of major events in our lives (Bailey & Lichty, 1974; Bossen, 1982; Domke, Perlmutter & Spratt, 2002; Hariman & Lucaites, 2004; Perlmutter & Major, 2004; Perlmutter & Major, 2005; Perlmutter & Golan, 2005; Perlmutter, 2005; Wright, 1993; Perlmutter, 1998; Perlmutter, 2006; Perlmutter, 2004; Goldberg, 1993; Monk, 1989; Bennett, Swenson & Wilkinson, 1992; Spruill, 1983; Whelan, 2002; Kleinman & Kleinman, 1996). The study of "big pictures" yields evidence that icons are thought of, argued about, shown, repeated, and magnified in importance far beyond the regular news stream of "coverage" of an event. At the same time, students of news icons appreciate that they are complicated, with their genesis, fame, effects, and even basic meaning both varied and often elusive. Worse, hoary myths often accompany them, much like legendary tales about heroes.

Some basic questions for those of us who study big pictures are:

- How are icons created within a news system and political culture?
- In determining the "effects" of news images, does the mass coverage matter as much as the icons?
- Do news icons have qualities or elements in common?
- Is there an identifiable process that governs their creation and exaltation?
- What are their effects on media, public opinion, policy-making, and ultimately on the events they portray?
- How has new media technology such as the Internet, blogs, cell phones, and digital editing affected icons themselves and our appreciation of them?

The plethora of issues raised by new media can be approached through a number of research methods, from experimentation to surveys to industrial sociology to critical cultural appraisals. I have conducted a series of studies of how my undergraduate students think of, recall, process, react to, draw meaning from, and develop policy-implicating opinions and actions from photojournalistic icons related to the Iraq War. Since the early part of the year 1999, I have been regularly surveying undergraduate students in introductory mass communication survey courses at our institution.

Questionnaires center on three areas of knowledge about photo-icons. First, to certain groups within the general study population, I show stills or video of celebrated big pictures and ask them to provide what information they can recall concerning the provenance and history of the images. Alternately, I ask groups of students to "tell me about the first picture that comes into your mind" when stimulated by minimal prompts such as "Hiroshima," "Iwo Jima," "Tiananmen," and "Oklahoma City bombing." A second set of questions deals with quasi-manipulations of the students' knowledge about particular pictures; most of these are not famous icons. Here I will change the captions, for example, and see whether or not that alteration affects the respondents' interest in, feeling of relevance toward, ascription of meaning for, or empathy and sympathy toward the subjects within a particular picture. Third, I try to gauge the "icon agenda": Which pictures students are paying most attention to at a particular time and, retroactively, which ones they remember most associated with recent news events. Specifically, I have tried to appraise how the "IDS" generation — a term I employ to mean both Internet-digital-satellite and also in the Freudian sense of one's "primitive" unconscious; that is, our fundamental inner drive for making sense and meaning about the world — processes news icons.

The research question was: What factors influence the lifespan of a "big picture"? If we live in an age of saturation from many sources of sensational images, all designed to elicit our attention, then the durability of the news icon, which in the pre-IDS era had a distinctive note of prominence, is challenged. If icons must compete with more images, do they diminish in status? What implications would such a phenomenon have for picture-makers and policy-shapers?

To suggest an answer to these queries, I examine the allegedly iconic images surrounding the killing of four American contractors in the city of Fallujah, Iraq on March 30, 2004. Every criteria of photo-iconic status was achieved by these images within 48 hours: They were celebrated, frequently repeated, widely commented on, appeared in many different kinds of media, occasioned controversy, and most of all were ascribed as having a "powerful" effect on the public and possibly on American war policy as well. Normally, those of us who study icons might have predicted that these images would become, as is commonly claimed, indelible. As discussed below, according to my surveys this is not the case. But speculation as to why the icons of Fallujah may have faded from the collective memory, at least in the group I studied, offers some insight into the process of iconization itself, especially in our IDS era.

BACKGROUND: POWER AND DISPOSITION IN PHOTO-ICONS

Preliminary research on news icons has yielded certain parameters for their study (Perlmutter, 1998; Perlmutter, 1999). To begin, famous news images tend to fall into two genera.

The first is called the *acute*, that is, the single still or moving picture or video image that shows an individual, not repeated, event that becomes idiosyncratically famous. Eddie Adams's notorious picture of a South Vietnamese police general summarily executing a "Viet Cong suspect" on the streets of Saigon during the Tet Offensive of 1968 is a case in point. There is one event in question, although it was captured in the film footage of other photographers as well as by Adams's still camera. In contrast are chronic icons, which typically are images showing scenes similar to each other in varied events and occurrences. For example, if I offer the prompt "African famine," a whole set of images of starving, fly-besotted, swollen-bellied, dark-skinned children may flood the news viewer's mind's eye. Certainly, some of these images — such as for example Kevin Carter's Pulitzer Prize-winning "Little Girl Refugee in the Sudan, 1992" — are more famous than others, but at the same time there is a host of pictures from individual African famines that are effectively both physically and symbolically interchangeable.

A corresponding insight about the nature of the news icon is the diffuse nature of its ascription of having "power." In a study of the alleged superlative influences of several "big pictures," thousands of descriptions of photo-icons fell into the vein of "they changed the world" or "they shocked the American public" or "they overturned policy." These descriptions were used habitually and often inaccurately. Research on news icons should attempt to parse out individual potential of differential powers for any particular picture. These powers include, in part, influence on public opinion (which may further be differentiated into influencing certain groups in a society but not others); influence on policy shaping or execution; mnemonic potency; symbolization; the stirring of political discourse; emotional incitement (which may or may not include the activation of empathy and sympathy for the subjects); and aesthetic reaction. In sum, a picture might contain a striking visual panoply or stir our emotions, but will have no particular measurable political impact — that is, not "change the world" or even our hearts.

A brief but notorious example will suffice to describe a larger research area. The Saigon execution picture still exists today frequently captioned as "the picture that lost the [Vietnam] war." Literally hundreds of commentators, from all over the political spectrum including super hawks and super doves, have made and continue to make this assertion, typically explained as that the American public was so "shocked" by the brutality of the slaying that, in its disgust, it turned against Lyndon Johnson's Vietnam War. Extraordinary claims, however, as any scientist will assert, will require extraordinary evidence. The problem for researchers is that the "power" of the Saigon picture is so commonly assumed that few have considered it necessary to provide any evidence for the assertion. Actual scrutiny, however, has found almost no evidence of any major or even minor impact on the psyche or sympathies of the American public by the famous scene from Saigon (Bailey & Lichty, 1972; Perlmutter, 1998). Public opinion polls, letters to periodical editors, epistles to Congress and the White House, and oral history projects all suggest either an absence of a "shocked" public or, in contrast, antipathy toward the victim of the shooting and indifference to his plight. In retrospect, from the point of view of political reality and psychological schema, this is in fact an unsurprising result. Surveys demonstrate that the American public's opposition to the war in Vietnam was largely based on the mortality rate of American soldiers and the interminability of the conflict (Mueller, 1971, 1973; Milstein, 1974; Kernell, 1978). Only the tiniest fraction of the U.S. public cheered or cared in the least for the fate of the enemy soldiers and guerillas, and civilians (or, indeed, our in-country indigenous allies).

In addition, those of us who study news icons typically challenge two of the very pillars of why they are worth studying: their universality and their mnemonicity. Other researchers and I have found that so-called famous pictures are not as famous as we would commonly suppose (Perlmutter, 1998; Messaris, 1994).

Generally, the accuracy of people's memories of icons and the details that they are able to provide about the events to which icons are linked is directly related to their familiarity with them. Familiarity, in turn, is affected by many factors. We know that audience recall of most news stories is low, although many variables may affect the strength, accuracy, and length of recall of any particular news item (D'Haenens, Jankowski & Heuvelman, 2004; Lang, Potter & Grabe, 2003; Gibbons, Vogl & Grimes, 2003; Grabe, Lang & Zhao, 2003). Sociologists, however, have discussed the phenomenon of "generational memory": People tend to have the sharpest memories of events that occurred during their years of maturation and early adulthood (Schuman, Belli & Bischoping, 1997; Wilkerson-Barker, 2003; Gongaware, 2003; Weispfenning, 2003; Haskins, 2003; Parry-Giles & Parry-Giles, 2000). This is a fact that most of us viscerally feel, whether or not we ponder it. Our cultural tastes, such as the kind of music we listen to, are determined at this critical life period. My research reveals that icons are regulated by generations as well as other conditions. People tend to remember the famous news pictures of their early adult years rather more than the pictures of previous generations. Culture, nationality, even gender and race can also be strong influences on which pictures are familiar to us. So, while there are certainly some "global icons" — say, the images of the 1969 Apollo moon landings — an 18-year-old white, southern Baptist college student may retain for his instant replay different images of different events than would a 70-year-old Muslim Iraqi grandmother.

In sum, we know much less than we should or can about the most famous and ubiquitous incarnations of journalism and history. The project worth engaging in by researchers from many disciplines as well as journalists is to try to investigate the anatomy of how icons are created, how certain meanings come to be attached to them, and what powers, influences, or effects they may have on events as well as ourselves.

IRAQ AS HYPERWAR: THE TEMPORAL DIMENSION OF THE ICON

New media — which, we should always recall, are not "new" to those exposed to them in early life — quantitatively affect icons in two ways. First, icons are speeded up — that is, they can arrive for our inspection faster than ever via the Internet or satellite. Second, there are many more venues now than ever for sending, processing, and receiving all news pictures including icons: millions of Web sites, many new news channels (some "24 hours"), cell phones, digital software, Personal Digital Assistants, and so on.

The *temporal* dimension of the news icon, thus, means not only how fast it gets to us from the field, but also its provenance in the general flow of pictures in our life (Perlmutter, 2006; Perlmutter, 2004). Updating Plato, we need to ask whether the nature of modern communications technology has changed the equation of the icon as an instrument of public affairs — in reporting, public opinion, and public policy-making. My method is to use the surveys of my students' knowledge of and opinions about news of the day or of the past. I seek to understand if the "instant replay" quality of the icon, its mnemonic aspect, is being affected by the IDS convergence.

The last 500 years has seen a series of inventions, including the popularization of moveable type, that allow for the delivery of accurate, repeatable visual images of events to be transmitted to home audiences. It is only in the last 150 years, however, that the modern picture world was both born and industrialized. Photography was the first step, of course, but a series of other breakthroughs later allowed the creation of what we call today photojournalism: black-and-white halftones (1880s), radio-wireless transmission (1895), hand-sized still cameras (1888), roll film (1889), the commercial single lens reflex camera (1925), and the rise of color photography (1950s). By the late 1930s pictures were routinely sent "over the wire".

The 1960s witnessed further acceleration in the delivery of news images. At the time of the Vietnam War it was still common to take news film from the battlefield and fly it to developing labs in the United States

— a 24-hour delay in reporting. Satellite transmission (1962), video (1970s), and fiber optics (mid-1970s) allowed the first "live broadcasts," although the technology "tail" was quite extensive, comprising a huge truck and a crew of technicians. The commercialization of the Internet, digital photography, and cell phones (1990s) finally created what was hinted at in the first Iraq War and now seems to have been fulfilled in the second: the ability to see news images "live from ground zero." It seems to be a situation in which, as one writer put it, we face the "death of distance" (Cairncross, 2001).

The impact of instant communication (and replay) on the news icon is, thus, one dimension for study (Perlmutter, 2006; Perlmutter, 2004; Wright, 1993). News icons are seldom delayed events; they emerge almost immediately after the occurrence that they depict. It is the rarest news picture that becomes famous only in a historical time frame. But the "speeded up" quality of temporary celebrity is just one measure of the means by which the news image has entered the pantheon of immortal images of news and public affairs. Often, yesterday's icon can become today's blurry disassociations.

Take an "icon" of a short time ago. On March 30, 2004, a group of Iraqis killed four American contractors who were driving through the city of Fallujah. A mob of civilians attacked the bodies and hung two of them from a bridge over the Euphrates River. Many onlookers and participants danced with joy and chanted anti-American slogans. The images — the burning car, a boy holding up a shoe with which he had beaten the bodies, the hanging men — were shown in video and in stills in most major newspapers and television networks in America and the world (Perlmutter & Major, 2004). Saturation coverage also brought controversy — and not just about the war. Various print and electronic media showed edited or cleaned up versions of the events. These are listed as follows:

A1- 'Contractors Hanging from Bridge'
A2- '3 Iraqis Cheering with Burning SUV'
A3- 'Burning SUV'
A4- 'Cheering Iraqis with Burning SUV'
A5- 'Iraqis Beating Burned SUV'
A6- 'Graveyard of America with Boy'
A7- 'Iraqis Dancing on Burned SUV'
A8- 'Joyous Iraqis with One Corpse on Bridge'
A9- 'Graveyard of Americans, Smoking SUV'
A10- Cropped photo of A4, 'Cheering Iraqi with Burning SUV'
A11- 'Beating Burned Corpses with Shoes'

A12- Cropped version of A3, 'Burning SUV'
A13- 'Man in White Shirt in Front of Burning SUV'
A14- 'Bridge Scene with Hand in Victory Salute'
A15- 'Iraqis on Roof of Burned SUV'
A16- '3 Iraqi Boys in Front of Burned SUV'
A17- Video capture of Americans engulfed in flames

The grisliness of the pictures occasioned much soul searching by news gatekeepers (quotes are from Perlmutter & Major, 2004). Ellen Soeteber, editor of the *St. Louis Post-Dispatch*, deemed the decision about which image in what form to print "one of the toughest calls I've ever had to make." Bill Keller, executive editor of the *New York Times*, ran "Contractors Hanging from Bridge." He commented, "On the one hand, you can't shy away from the news, and the news in this case is the indignities visited upon the victims and the jubilation of the crowd. At the same time you have to be mindful of the pain these pictures would cause to families and the potential revulsion of readers, and children, who are exposed to this over their breakfast table." Fort Lauderdale's *Sun Sentinel* printed no photographs of the incident because, as editor Earl Maucker put it, "I felt the story could be told without the horrific pictures to accompany it. When you have charred corpses that are hung from a bridge you can say that without putting it in front of a reader who really has no choice. There is no right or wrong answer."

Certainly such heavy coverage and discussion made the incident and the images famous. When, on April 5, 2004, 620 students were surveyed, most were able, when given the prompt "Fallujah," to cite at least *one* of the images of the contractors' deaths and the aftermath, from the jeering crowd to the desecrations of the bodies. Moreover, their accuracy of recall was high.

To proportionally measure such a phenomenon, qualitative responses were coded within a 1 to 5 scale. A "1" on the scale — *first-level recall* — is the highest level of accuracy and faithfulness of recall and is accorded when a respondent directly describes either the exact icon when an acute icon is in question or a reasonable facsimile of the portrayal of a generic icon. Furthermore, the respondent provides details of place, setting, time, main characters, event, and possibly significance. For example, as one student in the April 5 survey described his recollection of the events when prompted, "I am thinking of video I saw on the news that showed these people in the town of Fallujah, Iraq. They were jumping up and down and happy; they had just killed some civilian Americans. This happened just a few days ago. I remember being angry and saying, 'Hey, aren't we supposed to be saving these people?'"

Second-level recall, a "2" on the scale, is when, while some details of the picture or the corresponding information about its provenance may be indistinct. Overall, it is clear that the respondent has the basic icon in mind connected to the verbal prompt or, when shown the icon itself, has at least a moderate understanding of its place, time and event. For example, in the group to which I showed images of the dancing Iraqis with the burning car of the contractors in the background, one respondent stated, "This happened recently in Iraq. People were killed, and these [dancing] people were happy about it. I'm not sure who was killed."

Third-level recall is when the respondents have vague associations of image and narrative. When shown the picture, they know only the sketchiest details of its provenance. When given a verbal prompting, they provide a description of a picture that does not correspond strongly to the notorious news image. Of the respondents surveyed for the first time about Fallujah, for example, one reacted with the statement, "Something bad happened there. I have a picture in my head of some people on the street, dead. I think some Americans were killed there recently. I saw something on this."

Fourth-level recall is when there is minimal association between any kind of accurate description of time, space, or details of event and the corresponding image.

The final level of recall, the *fifth level*, is when there is obviously no correspondence whatsoever between word and image. People given a textual prompt do not recall any particular associated image, and people shown an image offer details which suggest no knowledge whatsoever about the event itself or familiarity with the icon. Typically, here a respondent will answer something like, "I don't know what that is; I don't remember anything about that picture," or will get the details completely wrong. Interestingly, and testament to the saturation coverage of the Fallujah killings, of the 620 respondents in the first survey, even those respondents with the barest level of recall were placed in category 4, because they were able to connect Fallujah with Iraq if shown the iconic image, or if offered a verbal prompt were able to recall (or perhaps guess) that Fallujah is in Iraq and that, as one put it, "something bad was happening there." The recall and accuracy rates for the April 5, May 1, June 10 and Oct. 23 surveys are listed in Table 22.1.

Such findings for April 5 are not surprising. The images were at the top of the news agenda for days and were displayed in every news source possible — on blogs as well as in mainstream media.

TABLE 20.1
"FALLUJAH" RECALL
(IN PERCENTAGE POINTS)

	April 5, 2004	May 1, 2004	June 10, 2004	Oct. 23, 2004	38430
Level of recall	N=620 %	N=603 %	N=89 %	N=480 %	N=365 %
Level 1 (highest)	70	53	30	12	3
Level 2	15	26	14	12	8
Level 3	10	13	20	30	32
Level 4	2	4	24	24	37
Level 5 (Lowest)	3	2	12	22	20

In addition, I sought to know where the students saw the image in the first place. For each respondent I asked whether they had seen images on television, the Internet, in print (as pictures), through text or verbal descriptions of the pictures, and/or through Web sources or some combination of the three. Here are the results:

Level 1 (Highest) — Combination of Television, Internet, Print
Level 2 — Combination of Television, Internet, Print
Level 3 — Television
Level 4 — Television
Level 5 (Lowest) — NA

On May 1, 2004, I surveyed (mostly) the same group of students. Accuracy had dropped. In Summer 2004, a small number of other students were surveyed. The Fallujah prompts received much lower rates of recall.

Then, on Oct. 23, 2004, a large body of students was surveyed. The recall and accuracy rates for this survey indicate a fading memory of the Fallujah incident. The most recent survey, March 20, 2005, two years after the Iraq War started, demonstrated the increasing erosion of memory of the Fallujah incident.

In sum, *highest-level recall was generated among respondents who reported seeing the original images from many sources.* Then, taking into account confounding factors such as the variation in respondents and the "memory" effect when the same group of respondents was used, there is a clear and sharp drop-off in recall of Fallujah "contractor killing" images. Basically, the prime word "Fallujah" became diffuse over time — prompting scenes of mayhem, combat, or bleakness in Iraq generally, but less tied to any specific picture or event. Consistently, however, in later surveys, American soldiers play a prominent role; respondents tended to include "American Marine" or some variation of such as part of the Fallujah panorama.

Conclusions: Why Did the Icons Fade Away?

To recapitulate, icon studies of the past have suggested that big pictures often avoid the fate of much news in our memory: They don't fade away. Icons encountered in early adult years as related to salient issues stay lodged in our memory and serve as summing up and symbols of the events for us. History itself — as recorded by historians, textbook writers, documentarians, scholars of visual culture, journalists, and political leaders — also contributes to the "indelibleness" of icons by repeating them and continuing to discuss them.

Such, however, was not the case here — at least by inference, since the same group of respondents was not surveyed again in the later surveys (after the first cohort). The icons of Fallujah have become something else, from the ridiculous to the general.

I argue that several forces are at work. First, as with all subjective, qualitative coding schemes, the coders and the primary researchers are called upon to make judgments of nuance in the responses. There is a well-known social desirability effect in political polling, for example, wherein participants strive not to appear ignorant on any given subject. So a certain number of responses in the 3 and 4 categories are most likely simply good guesses. After all, that America was involved in a war in Iraq in April 2004 was a generally known fact, even to college undergraduates. So a picture of Arabic-looking people in Arabic-looking dress with a Middle Eastern cityscape in the background would probably prompt the most oblivious news consumer to offer, "Something bad was happening in Iraq."

These kinds of responses, however, can themselves be of interest, and I have followed them up in questionnaires, because it is often the case that people may have little or no knowledge about a famous news icon, even though they may have encountered it somewhere — for example, in a high school textbook, or a more contemporary pop cultural reference such as in a program like "The Simpsons" or "The Daily Show." In surveys of historical icons, for instance, I find between 30 and 40 percent of students responding, when shown the flag-raising at Iwo Jima, that the events took place in Vietnam. This is less a statement concerning the general ignorance about allegedly famous pictures and more an insight into what events comprise the largest surface area in the historical imagination of young people. Even those who had not seen the images nor paid attention to them nor recalled them in any meaningful way still betrayed a vague impression of negativity about the insurgency war. In counter-example, American troops are still stationed in Bosnia, but in terms of news coverage they physically do not exist. It is not surprising that, when I show my students pictures from the American intervention in Bosnia, their recognition and recall is almost zero.

The "contractor killing" pictures themselves were heavily censored by media organizations. Some were digitally edited, cropped, or blurred. In terms of the topography of the icon, there was hardly a single mind's-eye slide that could be deeply imprinted on the synapses. Indeed, much of the controversy about the pictures was on their news value, the propriety of showing such grisly details to the American public and, if they were shown, how and with what contextual framing. Even if one icon emerged from the pack of pictures, it may have been physically as well as contextually distorted.

Moreover, the saturation of the icon's image probably did not assist in its long-term recall, because the events it showed were to be crowded out by so many other images of mayhem in general and Fallujah in particular. A survey of the mention of Fallujah in the context of other fighting — terrorist attacks and such — shows a whole series of nodes of prominence, with accompanying pictures, throughout 2004 and into 2005. Other candidates for photo-icons presented themselves as well in relation to Fallujah. For example, later, American Marines and other elements of the U.S. and British military conducted a city-wide campaign to "retake" the area, crushing pockets of resistance and rooting out insurgents. An image of an American Marine shooting an unarmed and wounded Iraqi civilian achieved sensational notoriety (Perlmutter, 2004). As noted above, however, by March 2005 the mention of Fallujah did not elicit this image from my respondents either.

In addition, when looking at thousands of responses to pictures or to text prompts concerning pictures, it is clear that another phenomenon is at work — what might be called "impression plug-in." Simply put, this means that when we are trying to fill in the details of sketchy images we tend — as gestalt psychologists noted long ago (Köhler, 1947) — to fill in details that we think *ought* to be present. Hence, in each survey a certain number of respondents "filled in" the images of the contractor killings as being related to "Marines." Such a fill-in makes sense since so many news stories from Iraq and especially from Fallujah are related to America's most prominent combat unit. As a recall mechanism of Fallujah, "civilian contactors" do not readily compute as victims or participants in the violence of the insurgency, whereas the headline "Marines killed in Iraq" has been a common one for the past two years.

Media saturation may also be inferred as influential. Obviously, human beings are trained to receive data at the speed and in the form in which their brain was most accustomed to doing so during the period of maturation. The modern 18-year-old is able to play a video game or watch a music video that would induce a headache in his grandparents. On the other hand, asking today's 18-year-olds to sit quietly for four hours and read St. Thomas Aquinas is an exercise in cruelty. But even if modern younger viewers are able to process hyperdata and saturated panoramas better than their elders, necessarily they will be more likely to have a faster replacement rate for images of importance. Correspondingly, news icons may now be appearing at a faster rate than in previous eras. This in itself may be a subject for greater scrutiny, not just by communication researchers but by historians, psychologists, sociologists and political scientists. If the replacement rate hypothesis is correct, one confirmation may be that the icons of yesterday, not just yester-generation, are more likely to be forgotten, or rather superceded, by newer imagery and icons.

Obviously, several complicating factors may be in operation. The icon of Tiananmen lingers — although not, as I have seen, in the minds of my students — not only because of its immense celebrity and repetition as the first sketch of history but also because no new icon of Tiananmen has replaced it. Since 1989, there have been no copious news stories emanating from the geographic location described by the word "Tiananmen." One may say the same thing of Oklahoma City, Iwo Jima, and Kent State.

I argue, then, that the Fallujah contractor killings did not stay famous, at least among this demographic of audience, because they were relatively unconnected to their major concerns, especially among students in a part of the country where proportionally more friends, family, and neighbors tend to be in the military. Although further research is necessary, I hope this study points out that we need to investigate how modern technology, with which it is so easy to convert war into an instant replay of itself, may, because of the exigencies of the IDS era — a 24-hour, 500-channel, 50 million-blog wall of imagery that any curious news seeker may confront

— result in what might be called an *"instant deplay."* That is, while an image may be famous for 15 minutes, the implication of that instant fame is that a new sensational image is yearned for by the maw of the image industry as well as the independents, and thus will naturally supercede those pictures that came before. Even more, as the "id" of IDS implies, in an era of podcasting, personalized media, niche communication, and targeted media market segmentation, we face a time where individuals can literally make (or select) their own media world and, by fiat, put their own icons in a pantheon of their own choosing. The inner will (id) becomes the outer reality.

The project of studying the icons of photojournalism as well as independent image production for the global visual marketplace, thus, is greatly complicated by new and convergent technology and perhaps a new *psychology* of viewing. Certain basic questions remain, however, for political scientists, communication researchers, psychologists, sociologists, and historians to answer: How are big pictures made and maintained, and how do they affect our world and us?

REFERENCES

Ackerman, B. P. (1985). The effects of specific and categorical orienting on children's incidental and intentional memory for pictures and words. *Journal of Experimental Child Psychology* 39: 300-325.

Anderson, J. R. (1978). Arguments concerning representations for mental imagery. *Psychological Review* 85: 249—277.

Anglin, G. J., & W. H. Levie. (1985). Role of visual richness in picture recognition memory. *Perceptual and Motor Skills* 61: 1303-1306.

Bailey, G. A., and L. Lichty. (1974). Rough justice on a Saigon street: A gatekeeper study of NBC's Tet execution film. *Journalism Quarterly* (Summer): 221-238.

Bennett, E. M., J. D. Swenson, & J. S. Wilkinson. (1992). Is the medium the message? An experimental test with morbid news. *Journalism Quarterly* 69: 921-928.

Bossen, H. (1982). A tall tale retold: The influence of photographs of William Henry Jackson upon the passage of the Yellowstone Act of 1872. *Studies in Visual Communication* 8(1): 8-109.

Cairncross, F. (2001). *The death of distance: How the communications revolution is changing our lives.* Boston: Harvard Business School Press.

Canfield, R. L., & M. M. Haith. (1991). Young infants' visual expectations for symmetric and asymmetric stimulus sequences. *Developmental Psychology* 27: 198—208.

Canfield, R. L., and N. Z. Kirkham. (2001). Infant cortical development and the prospective control of saccadic eye movements. *Infancyarchives.com*: 2(2).

Coopersmith, J. (2000). From lemons to lemonade: The development of AP Wirephoto. *American Journalism* 17(4): 55-72.

Coughlan, S. (2004, October 25). Why the charge of the Light Brigade still matters. *BBC News Online Magazine.* Retrieved from http://news.bbc.co.uk/go/pr/fr/-/1/hi/magazine/3944699.stm

D'Agostino, P. R., V. J. O'Neill, & A. Paivio. (1977). Memory of pictures and words as a function of level of processing: Depth or duel coding? *Memory and Cognition* 5(2): 252-256.

D'Haenens, L, N. Jankowski, & A. Heuvelman. (2004). News in online and print newspapers: Differences in reader consumption and recall. *New Media & Society* 6(3): 363-382.

Diaz, B. 1963. The conquest of New Spain. [J. M. Cohen, trans.]. Middlesex, England: Penguin Classics.

Domke, D., D. D. Perlmutter, & M. Spratt.(2002). The primes of our times: An examination of the "power" of visual images. *Journalism* 3(2): 131-159.

Elliot, L. (1973). Imagery vs. encoding in short- and long-term memory. *Journal of Experimental Psychology* 100(2): 270-276.

Friedland, L. A. (1992). *Covering the world: International television news service.* New York: Twentieth Century Fund.

Gibbons, J. A., R. J. Vogl, & T. Grimes. (2003). Memory misattributions for characters in a television news story. *Journal of Broadcasting and Electronic Media* 47(1): 99-112.

Goldberg, V. (1993). *The power of photography: How photographs changed our lives.* New York: Abbeville.

Gongaware, T.B. (2003). Collective memories and collective identities: Maintaining unity in native American educational social movements. *Journal of Contemporary Ethnography* 32(5): 483-520.

Gould, S. J. (October 1994). The evolution of life on earth. *Scientific American*, p 85.

Grabe, M.A., A. Lang,& X. Zhao. (2003). News content and form: Implications for memory and audience evaluations. *Communication Research* 30(4): 387-413.

Grant, M. (1950). *Roman anniversary issues.* Cambridge: Cambridge University Press, p. 8.

Gross, H. M., A. Heinze, T. Seiler, & V. Stephan. (1999). Generative character of perception: A neural architecture for sensorimotor anticipation. *Neural Networks* 12: 1101—1129.

Hariman, R., & J. L. Lucaites. (2004). Ritualizing modernity's gamble: The iconic photographs of the Hindenburg and Challenger explosions. *Visual Communication Quarterly* 11(1&2): 4-1.

Haskins, Ekaterina V. (2003). Put your stamp on history: The USPS commemorative program celebrates the century and postmodern collective memory. *Quarterly Journal of Speech* 89(1): 1-19.

Henry III, W. (1992, Jan 6). Man of the year: History as it happens. *Time*, p. 25.

Jones, E. E., & V. A. Harris. (1967). The attribution of attitudes. *Journal of Experimental Social Psychology* 3:1-24.

Joseph, C. A., R. F. Wain & D. R. Stone. (1984). Effects on free recall of grouping pictures, picture names, and complete picture descriptions. *Journal of General Psychology* 110: 69-73.

Kernell, S. (1978). Explaining presidential popularity. *American Political Science Review* 72: 506-22.

Kleinman, A., & J. Kleinman. (1996). The appeal of experience: The dismay of images: Cultural appropriations of suffering in our times. *Daedalus* 125(1): 1-23.

Köhler, W. (1947). *Gestalt psychology*. New York: Liverwright. p. 172.

Lang, A., D. Potter, & M.E. Grabe. (2003). Making news memorable: Applying theory to the production of local television news. *Journal of Broadcasting and Electronic Media* 47(1): 113-123.

Major, L.H. & D.D. Perlmutter. (2005). The fall of a pseudo-icon: The toppling of Saddam Hussein's statue as image management. *Visual Communication Quarterly, 12* (1 & 2): 38-45.

McNulty, T. J. (1996, July 14). World politics: Made in America. *Chicago Tribune*, p. 1C.

Messaris, P. (1994). *Visual "literacy": Image, mind, & reality*. Boulder: Westview Press, pp. 176-80.

Milstein, J. S. (1974). *Dynamics of the Vietnam War: A quantitative analysis and predictive computer simulation*. Columbus: Ohio State University Press.

Monk, L. (1989). *Photographs that changed the world: The camera as witness, the photograph as evidence*. New York: Doubleday.

Mueller J. E. (1973). *War, presidents, and public opinion*. New York: John Wiley and Sons, pp. 37, 167.

Mueller, J. E. (1971). Trends in popular support for the wars in Korea and Vietnam. *American Political Science Review* 65(June): 358-75.

Parry-Giles, S. J., & Trevor Parry-Giles. (2000). Collective memory, political nostalgia, and the rhetorical presidency. *Quarterly Journal of Speech* 86(4): 417.

Payne, D. G. (1986). Hypermnesia for pictures and words: Testing the recall level hypothesis. *Journal of Experimental Psychology: Learning, Memory and Cognition* 12: 16-29.

Perlmutter, D.D. (1992). The vision of war in high school social science textbooks. *Communication* 13: 143-160.

Perlmutter, D.D. (1994). Visual historical methods: Problems, prospects, applications. *Historical Methods* 27(4): 167-184.

Perlmutter, D.D. (1998). *Photojournalism and foreign policy: Framing icons of outrage in international crises*. Westport, CT: Greenwood.

Perlmutter, D.D. (1999). *Visions of war: Picturing warfare from the Stone Age to the Cyberage*. New York: St. Martin's.

Perlmutter, D.D. (2004). The Internet: Big pictures and interactors. In L. Gross, J.S. Katz, & J. Ruby (Eds.), *Image ethics in the digital age*, (p. 1-26). Minneapolis: University of Minnesota Press.

Perlmutter, D.D. (2004, November 19). Keep warfare in historical context. *Minneapolis Star Tribune*, p. A21.

Perlmutter, D.D. (2005). Photojournalism and foreign affairs. *Orbis* 49(1): 109-122.

Perlmutter, D.D. (2006). Hypericons: Famous news images in the Internet-Digital-Satellite Age. In P. Messaris (Ed.), *Digital media: Transformations in human communications*. New York: Peter Lang.

Perlmutter, D.D., & G. Golan. (2005). Counter-imaging: Myth-making and Americanization in Israeli Labor Party campaign ads, 2003. *Visual Communication*, 4(3): 304-332.

Perlmutter, D.D., & G.L. Wagner. (2004). The anatomy of a photojournalistic icon: Marginalization of dissent in the selection and framing of "A Death in Genoa." *Visual Communication*. 3(1): 91-108.

Perlmutter, D.D., & L.H. Major. (2004). Images of horror from Fallujah. *Nieman Reports* 58(2): 68-70.

Perlmutter, D.D., & L.H. Major. (2005). The Fall of a Pseudo-Icon: The Toppling of Saddam Hussein's Statue as Image Management. *Visual Communication Quarterly* 12:38-45.

Plato. (1987). *The Republic*. 2nd ed. D. Lee (trans.). New York: Penguin.

Rumsfeld Testimony before Senate Armed Services Committee, May 7, 2004.

Schuman, H., R. F. Belli, & K. Bischoping. (1997). The generational basis of historical knowledge. In J. W. Pennebaker, D. Paez, and P. Rimel Mahway (Eds.), *Collective memory of political events: Social psychological processes*. Mahway, NJ: Lawrence Erlbaum.

Spruill, L. H. (1983). Southern exposure: Photography and the civil rights movement, 1955-1968. Unpublished Ph.D. dissertation. State University of New York at Stony Brook.

Stauffer, J., R. Frost, & W. Rybolt. (1983). The attention factor in recalling network television news. *Journal of Communication* 33 (Winter): 29-37.

Transcript, Ellsworth Bunker Oral History Interview III, 10/12/83, by Michael L. Gillette, Internet Copy, LBJ Library. Lyndon Baines Johnson Library Oral History Collection. http://128.83.78.10/johnson/archives.hom/oralhistory.hom/bunker%2De/bunker3.pdf.

Turmoil at Tiananmen: A study of U.S. press coverage of the Beijing spring of 1989. Joan Shorenstein Barone Center on the Press, Politics and Public Policy, Harvard University, John F. Kennedy School of Government, June, 1992, p. 188.

Tyler, P. (1999). *A Great Wall: Six presidents and China, an investigative history*. New York: Public Affairs.

Urschel, J. (1994, Feb 10). Caution: Don't base policy on emotions. *USA Today*, p. 10A.

Webster, G. (1998). *The Roman imperial army (of the first and second centuries A.D.)* University of Oklahoma Press.

Weispfenning, J. (2003). Cultural functions of reruns: Time, memory, and television. *Journal of Communication* 53(1): 165-176.

Whelan, R. (2002). Robert Capa's falling soldier: A detective story. *Aperture* 166: 48-55.

Wilkerson-Barker, D. (2003). Photographic memories in Leila Sebbar's le Chinois vert d'Afrique. *Research in African Literatures* 34(2): 28-40.

Winograd, E., A. D. Smith, & E. W. Simon. (1982). Aging and the picture superiority effect in recall. *Journal of Gerontology* 37: 70-75.

Wright, D. B. (1993). Recall of the Hillsborough disaster over time: Systematic biases of flashbulb memories. *Applied Cognitive Psychology* 7(2): 129-138.

DISCUSSION QUESTIONS

1. It is said that some men and women are born great, some achieve greatness and some have greatness thrust upon them. How would you apply to same processes to a given news icon?

2. Think of some famous new events in your lifetime: What pictures do you associate with them? Why do you think they "define" the event?

3. Why did the "Fallujah" images, so famous in their time, fade away in memory?

4. Do you think news icons are "powerful," and, if so, in what ways can they affect public opinion or policy-making?
5. What, if any, lasting effects do news icons have on public opinion formation? Give examples.

CHAPTER TWENTY-ONE

CHANGING FACES: THE FIRST FIVE WEEKS OF THE IRAQ WAR

CAROL B. SCHWALBE

T hose of us who have never heard the scream of an incoming missile or cradled a dying comrade in our arms learn about actual war mainly through images and stories in newspapers and magazines, on TV, and, lately, on the Internet (Sontag, 2002, p. 87). Photos can provide evidence that can't be denied. Many people didn't believe eyewitness accounts of Nazi concentration camps until they saw photos of the skeleton-like survivors (Wheeler, 2002, p. 6). After the My Lai massacre in Vietnam, Secretary of Defense Melvin Laird wanted "to sweep it under the rug." Photos prevented a government cover-up (Becker, 2004, p. A1). More recently, pictures put the Abu Ghraib prison abuse directly in the public eye.

Photos can sway public opinion at home and abroad. The Abu Ghraib images tarnished America's stature as a superpower. In 1992 shots of starving children were credited with pushing the United States into Somalia. Less than a year later, a Pulitzer Prize-winning picture of a dead GI being dragged through Mogadishu was said to have hastened U.S. withdrawal from Somalia (Sharkey, 1993).

Americans have seen many faces of war since the U.S.-led coalition invaded Iraq on March 19, 2003. But there are many others they haven't seen — of war protesters and the Iraqi resistance, of women and coalition troops, of the injured and dead. This chapter looks at how mainstream U.S. news Web sites portrayed the first five weeks of the Iraq War. Whose faces did we see? Whose were seldom seen or even invisible? How have those images helped shape our perceptions of this war?

LIMITED SCOPE OF WAR IMAGES

In some ways, the images of war we do not see can be as important as those we do see. The mainstream U.S. media rarely publish gory photos of dead American troops or prisoners, botched military actions, or civilian casualties (Zelizer, 2004, p. 116). Overseas news photos of the Vietnam War were more likely than photos by U.S. news media to depict conflict, violence, and disaster (Tsang, 1984). Magazine photos of injured and dead U.S. soldiers accounted for a much smaller percentage of the total coverage than indicated by the later shift in U.S. public opinion against the Vietnam War (Patterson, 1984). Injured or dead troops rarely appeared on television, especially during the early years of the war (Hallin, 1986).

Vietnam was the last conflict where photojournalists could freely shoot events. Despite restricted access during the 1991 Gulf War, photographers recorded grisly scenes of charred vehicles, beheaded Iraqi soldiers, and bulldozers plowing dead bodies into a mass grave. These graphic images, however, were not published in the United States because editors considered them too shocking. As one scholar noted, Gulf War coverage was "void of images of real violence and suffering" (Robins, 1993, p. 325). Surprisingly few images published in *Time*, *Newsweek*, and *U.S. News & World Report* showed combat, let alone casualties, Iraqi troops, destruction, or protests (Griffin & Lee, 1995). Instead, more than half depicted U.S.-allied troops and hardware, U.S. political and military leaders, Iraqi political leaders, and Iraqi military hardware.

During the current war with Iraq, photojournalists embedded with the troops had greater access than they did during the Gulf War, but for the most part they saw only what the military wanted them to see (Elliott & Elliott, 2003). About half the photos in *Time*, *Newsweek*, and *U.S. News & World Report* from the weeks just before and during the Iraq invasion reinforced the prevailing theme of U.S. political and military might (Griffin, 2004). Rare were images that contributed "new, independent, or complex visual information," such as the Iraqi perspective, the human toll, or global economics (p. 399).

Observers have noted that the limited scope of war photography in the mainstream U.S. media may lead to a "sanitized" view. As photojournalist Peter Turnley (2002) wrote, gut-wrenching shots represent "a more accurate picture of what really does happen in war. I feel it is important and that citizens have the right to see these images."

VISUAL FRAMING

Framing refers to the way the mass media present news or, in some cases, "spin" a news event or issue through what they select, emphasize, elaborate, or exclude (Tankard, 1997). Entman (1993) provided a useful definition: "Framing essentially involves selection and salience. To frame is to select some aspects of a perceived reality and make them more salient" (p. 52). The news media, for example, could *select* to show the American perspective rather than the Iraqi, *emphasize* military victories instead of botched missions, *elaborate* frames of patriotism rather than protest, and *exclude* images of the injured and dead.

Framing helps journalists select and organize information. Many factors affect the production of media frames. Inside the newsroom, these include news values, journalistic practices and routines, personal preferences, competition from other stories, deadlines, declining interest in an ongoing event like war, and budgetary constraints. Outside the newsroom, these factors include access to events and sources, changing technology, cultural values, and sociopolitical forces.

Scholars debate whether framing is a deliberate or subconscious process (D'Angelo, 2002). Some maintain that news organizations select certain information and deliberately neglect other information in order to foster a viewpoint supportive of the status quo (Reese & Buckalew, 1995; Solomon, 1992; Watkins, 2001). Entman (2003) proposed a model that reflects the amount of influence different entities have on how the news media frame an event or issue. In this layered model, the president and his administration carry the most weight, followed by Congress and other elites, then the media, and finally the public. For breaking news, Entman (1991) wrote, "Official sources in the White House, State Department, Pentagon, and other administration outposts hold the commanding influence" (p. 25).

Photos are an important aspect of framing because they're so visible. Many people don't read a story, but everyone at least glances at the pictures. Most images are quickly understood, even without reading the caption. In addition, images can stir powerful emotions in ways that words often can't. A photo of a flag-draped coffin, for example, can be more poignant than a statistic about the number of war dead.

THE WAR ON THE WEB

The Iraq War marked the Internet's coming of age as a news medium. Iraq was the first U.S. ground war covered online. Although it ranked last as Americans' primary sources of war news when the U.S.-led coalition invaded Iraq (Palser, 2003), during the first week of hostilities 77% of Americans turned to the Web for war news (Rainie et al., 2003). At the time, three of every four Americans had Internet access (Hewitt, 2003).

Iraq was also the first U.S. war photographed by embedded journalists. High-quality digital cameras, satellite phones, and Internet access enabled instant dissemination of battlefield images. From warblogs and up-close images to the multimedia-rich Web sites of U.S. news giants like *The New York Times* and CNN, the Internet promised an unparalleled variety of coverage and alternative perspectives.

This chapter examines how mainstream U.S. news Web sites visually framed the first five weeks of the Iraq War. Which faces were emphasized? Why were certain groups seldom seen or even invisible? What are the implications of framing on our perceptions of this war?

To answer these questions, this chapter looks at the changing faces of war as portrayed in 492 war-related photos on 26 Web sites. They represent a broad spectrum of mainstream media outlets: 18 U.S. daily newspapers, three news magazines, three television networks, and two cable television news outlets:

Newspaper Web sites: The *Arizona Republic*'s azcentral.com, the *Atlanta Journal-Constitution*'s ajc.com, *The Chicago Tribune*'s chicagotribune.com, *The Dallas Morning News*' dallasnews.com, the *Houston Chronicle*'s chron.com, The *Los Angeles Times*' latimes.com, *The Miami Herald*'s miamiherald.com, the New York *Daily News*' nydailynews.com, *The New York Times*' nytimes.com, *Newsday*'s newsday.com, *The Oregonian* of Portland's oregonian.com, the *Rocky Mountain News* of Denver's rockymountainnews.com, *The Sacramento Bee*'s sacbee.com, the *St. Petersburg Times*' sptimes.com, *The Tampa Tribune*'s tbo.com, *USA Today*'s usatoday.com, the *Virginian-Pilot* of Norfolk's hamptonroads.com/pilotonline, and *The Washington Post*'s washingtonpost.com. News magazine Web sites: *Newsweek*'s newsweek.com, *Time*'s time.com, and *U.S. News & World Report*'s usnews.com. Television network Web sites: ABC News' abcnews.go.com, CBS News' cbsnews.com, and NBC News' msnbc.msn.com. Cable network Web sites: CNN's cnn.com and Fox News' foxnews.com.

These images provide a representative snapshot of how the U.S. news media structured their Internet coverage of the Iraq War when the conflict broke out, then at points one week, two weeks, three weeks, and four weeks later.

Two trained coders analyzed all the images. To test intercoder reliability, Scott's pi was calculated, yielding a coefficient of .90. The images were coded according to subject matter, size (dominant or not), and whether or not they depicted certain types of people, such as anti-war protesters, coalition troops, women, the Iraqi resistance, and the injured and dead. Since the "essence of framing is sizing," dominant images were put in a separate category (Entman, 1991, p. 9).

Week 1: March 19, 2003

The drumbeats of war had been pounding for weeks when President George W. Bush announced on March 19 that U.S.-led coalition forces had invaded Iraq. As troops massed on the Kuwaiti border, planes bombed military targets in Iraq. The foreign ministers of Germany, France, and Russia condemned the attack, saying the use of force had not been sanctioned by a UN resolution.

Previous studies of war images indicated that American weaponry, civilian leaders, and military leaders would figure prominently in the early visual coverage. Of the war images posted on 26 U.S. news Web sites, the theme of American military and political might comprised 79% of the dominant (largest) and 40% of all remaining images (see Table 21.1). The most dominant single image was Baghdad, which was pounded by U.S. air strikes the night of March 19.

Missing: Images of Protesters: For weeks, millions of people around the world had been protesting the impending invasion. On the first day of the war, tens of thousands of schoolchildren staged walkouts in the United Kingdom, and peace activists intensified their efforts in Vancouver. Even so, these events didn't appear on the 26 U.S. news Web sites, perhaps because they took place abroad and were pre-empted by invasion pictures. In fact, of the 492 war-related images studied over five weeks, only one dominant photo depicted protesters (University of Florida students, the *St. Petersburg Times'* sptimes.com, April 2), as did just one small picture (a female peace activist, *The Dallas Morning News'* dallasnews.com, March 19).

Even in an arena where women play a key role — that of protest — online images almost ignored anti-war sentiments at home and abroad. Why? Feminists contend that the powerful men who lead countries and head newsrooms "make sure that these views are berated and second-rated — thus ensuring that the dominant language of war and 'justice' conquers and that the patriarchal order which supports this rhetoric is sustained" (Magor, 2002, p. 143). Other reasons might include patriotism, support for our troops, or a preference for dramatic combat images.

TABLE 21.1
KEY VISUAL FRAMES*

	First Five Weeks of the Iraq War				
Dominant	3/19/03 n=19	3/26/03 n=24	4/2/03 n=22	4/9/03 n=23	4/16/03 n=19
Official war machine[1]	15 (79.0%)	9 (37.6%)	6 (27.3%)	0 (0.0%)	3 (15.9%)
Personal face of war[2]	3 (15.9%)	15 (62.7%)	16 (72.6%)	23 (100.0%)	16 (84.2%)
Other[3]	1 (5.3%)	0 (0.0%)	0 (0.0%)	0 (0.0%)	0 (0.0%)
All Other Images	3/19/03 n=55	3/26/03 n=96	4/2/03 n=82	4/9/03 n=92	4/16/03 n=60
Official war machine[1]	22 (40.0%)	27 (28.1%)	15 (18.3%)	16 (17.4%)	10 (16.7%)
Personal face of war[2]	17 (30.9%)	44 (45.8%)	48 (58.4%)	58 (63.1%)	38 (63.2%)
Other[3]	16 (29.1%)	25 (26.0%)	19 (23.2%)	18 (19.6%)	12 (20.0%)

* Because of rounding, some columns don't add up to 100%.
[1]Official war machine includes ordnance, civilian and military leaders, Baghdad air strikes, and destruction.
[2]Personal face of war includes troops, civilians, journalists, humanitarian relief, protesters, and home front.
[3]Other includes maps, flags, graphics, and miscellaneous images.

Week 2: March 26, 2003

A week after the invasion began, Iraq claimed that an American missile had killed many civilians in a busy Baghdad market. Although nighttime strikes failed to silence the national television station, U.S. paratroopers seized an airfield in northern Iraq.

News frames can change over time. By the second week, as embedded photojournalists moved with the invading troops toward Baghdad, the visuals focused less on the big, powerful, impersonal war machine (37.6%) than on the human face (62.7%), mainly U.S. troops and Iraqi civilians. This frame encompassed the troops who carried out the official policies as well as the people affected by the war.

Missing: Images of Coalition Troops: Some of America's closest allies didn't join the invading forces, so the Bush administration pointed instead to the support received from other nations. Of the 46 coalition partners, only the United Kingdom sent a substantial number of troops. Most of the armed forces came from the United States. The "Coalition of the Willing" included six unarmed nations — Costa Rica, Iceland, Marshall Islands, Micronesia, Palau, and Solomon Islands — but not major allies like France and Germany.

The relatively small size and the makeup of the Coalition of the Willing made it appear that the United States acted almost alone against the wishes of the international community. The lack of visual coverage on U.S. news Web sites reinforced that impression. Coalition troops appeared alone or with Iraqis in only three of the 107 dominant images (2.8%) and four of the 385 non-dominant images (1.0%). All three dominant photos showed troops from the United Kingdom: a British soldier fixing a tank near the city of Basra (Fox News' foxnews.com, March 26), a British soldier greeting Iraqi villagers (*The New York Times'* nytimes.com, March 26), and British soldiers checking Iraqis leaving Basra (*Time's* time.com, April 2).

Week 3: April 2, 2003

By the 14th day of the invasion, GIs had secured the southern city of Kerbala. To the north, troops drew to within 20 miles of Baghdad, inside the Red Line where it was feared Saddam's forces would deploy chemical weapons. Troops crushed a Republican Guard division and secured a key bridge over the Tigris River.

The dominant visual frame still showed the personal face of war (72.6%). This can be partly attributed to the big news of the day — the rescue of Private Jessica Lynch on April 1. Seven dominant images depicted Lynch as a hero standing in front of the American flag (the New York *Daily News'* nydailynews.com and *The Tampa Tribune's* tbo.com) or as a victim lying on a stretcher (*The Atlanta Journal-Constitution's* ajc.com, the *Houston Chronicle's* chron.com, *U.S. News & World Report's* usnews.com, the Norfolk *Virginian-Pilot's* hamptonroads.com/pilotonline, and *The Washington Post's* washingtonpost.com).

Missing: Images of Women: Many American women paid dearly at home and on the battlefield. Nonetheless, U.S. news Web sites focused on just a few of the injured, mainly Jessica Lynch, and killed, such as Lori Piestewa, the first female GI to die in Iraq. American women who stayed at home were affected as well, especially those whose family members were injured or killed. The war cast an even darker shadow on Iraqi women, who lost loved ones, homes, livelihoods — and sometimes even their own lives.

Nonetheless, the visual coverage on mainstream U.S. news Web sites all but ignored their contributions and sacrifices. Females make up almost 15% of the U.S. armed forces in Iraq and about half the populations of Iraq and the United States, yet they appeared in only 7% of the 492 war-related images studied. Males were featured in nearly half (45%), followed by people whose gender couldn't be identified because shadows, helmets, or military gear obscured their faces (23%).

Since size magnifies or shrinks an image's significance, it's important to look not only at percentages but also at dominance. Rarely were women the exclusive focus of the dominant photo on the home page. Only seven of the 107 dominant images depicted women exclusively. Five of those were of Jessica Lynch, the focus of media attention during the third week. The sixth image showed a female journalist (*The Arizona Republic*'s azcentral.com, April 16), while the seventh photo depicted an Iraqi woman in an overcrowded Baghdad hospital (*USA Today*'s usatoday.com, April 16).

Why was the face of the early weeks of the war mainly male? Although Iraqi women have long held professional positions and enjoyed freedoms uncommon in the Arab world, lawlessness and loss of jobs drove most of them inside, shielded from the invading troops and photographers' lenses (Morello, 2003, p. A1). In addition, journalistic routines may have played a role in keeping women on the sidelines. Since American women can't fight on the battlefront, photographers embedded with ground combat units can shoot pictures only of men. Action-filled images probably appealed more to photo editors than did images of female soldiers, who mostly supplied units, maintained vehicles, and filled other support roles. Thus, photographic access to men fighting on the frontlines tended to reinforce "the conventional paradigm of conflict where women have a particular place," such as peace protesters (Magor, 2002, p. 142).

Week 4: April 9, 2003

On the 21st day of the war, the visual focus online returned to Baghdad as U.S. forces secured the capital and Gen. Tommy Franks took control of the country. Saddam Hussein had vanished. Looters ransacked his seat of power, unhindered. Although intense fighting continued throughout the city, the toppling of Saddam's statue moved onto center stage.

The widely publicized toppling of the 40-foot-high bronze statue by a Marine tank recovery vehicle became an instant icon. The news media embraced the statue's fall as symbolic of Saddam's fall. Television newscasts led with the dramatic footage, and U.S. newspapers splashed pictures across their front pages. This victory frame was also the focal point of 60.9% of dominant online images. Different versions of the scene incorporated four visual themes of the war: the city of Baghdad, Saddam Hussein, cheering Iraqi civilians, and triumphant U.S. troops (Schwalbe et al., 2003).

This jubilant scene marked the visual re-emergence of Iraqi civilians, who had all but vanished from last week's home pages. Their reappearance bolstered the shifting of the visual frame from the U.S. war machine to intimate portraits of Americans and Iraqis. The statue's fall also provided a dramatic visual counterpoint to the scenes of Baghdad from the first night of the war. Devoid of people, those early images showed buildings under attack by unseen bombs and missiles. By contrast, the images from week four captured the war in human terms. The U.S. media showed crowds of jubilant Iraqis welcoming their American liberators. Wide-angle shots released later, however, revealed only a few hundred people gathered in Firdos Square. Some reports claimed the spectators were mostly American journalists and troops (Fisk, 2003; Litchfield, 2003).

Missing: Images of the Iraqi Resistance: Entman (1991) equated the "amount, prominence, and duration of coverage" with an event's importance. The large number of dominant images made the statue's toppling a supercharged event. Dramatizing the statue's fall implied that Iraqis overwhelmingly welcomed the Americans as liberators and that the war was over. "[B]attle stories imply a war is going on, statues falling ... imply the war is over" (Aday et al., 2005, p. 325).

By so quickly embracing the victory frame (and excluding others), U.S. news Web sites did not give viewers the complete picture, with its ominous portends of things to come. Missing were images of violent fighting in other parts of the city. Missing were images of Marines ducking for cover after gunmen fired at them as they got ready to pull down Saddam's statue. As Major & Perlmutter (2005) pointed out, "In hindsight, such a scene would have been the most appropriate image from that day to foreshadow what was to come" (p. 44). In the next week alone, 13 GIs lost their lives.

By the fifth week of the invasion, American officials were trumpeting the capture in Iraq of Palestinian Abu Abbas, who had masterminded the 1985 hijacking of an Italian cruise ship. They said this showed a link between Saddam and terrorism. Marines claimed to have discovered a terrorist training camp. President Bush urged the UN to lift the economic sanctions against Iraq, saying the country had been liberated.

Web images continued to spotlight the personal face of war (84.2%) rather than U.S. political and military might (15.9%). This is noteworthy because on April 16, Gen. Tommy Franks was photographed striding triumphantly through the ruins of one of Saddam's palaces. Even so, only one dominant online image marked this event. U.S. news Web sites focused instead on American POWs arriving in Germany and troops searching for Iraqi leaders.

As would be expected, nonwar-related dominant images were appearing more frequently, growing from none the first week to 23.1% the fifth week. In just two weeks President Bush would stand on the flight deck of the U.S.S. *Abraham Lincoln* and declare the end of major combat operations in Iraq. The war began to fade from home pages.

Missing: Images of the Injured and Dead: By the end of major combat operations, 139 U.S. troops and 33 British troops had died, and 542 U.S. troops had been injured (Department of Defense, 2005). Although no coalition troops died during this period, 15 journalists and one contractor lost their lives (Iraq Coalition Casualty Count, 2005). Thousands of Iraqi civilians were killed or injured. Fatality estimates range from 1,961 (CIVIC Worldwide, 2005) to 7,460 (Iraq Body Count, 2005), while injury estimates range from 4,881 (CIVIC Worldwide, 2005) to 17,425 (Iraq Body Count, 2005). Between 4,895 and 6,570 Iraqi soldiers died, and 5,103 were wounded (CBC News Online, 2005).

Most online news coverage of the injured or dead was devoted to Jessica Lynch during the third week of the war. Other than Lynch, only a scattering of dominant images told of the human costs — an American soldier carrying a wounded Iraqi soldier (*The Atlanta Journal-Constitution*'s ajc.com, March 26), grandparents holding a photo of a grandson killed in Iraq (the *St. Petersburg Times*' sptimes.com, March 26), a GI in a wheelchair (*USA Today*'s usatoday.com, April 2), a former POW on a stretcher (*Los Angeles Times*' latimes.com, April 16), an Iraqi woman in a Baghdad hospital

(*USA Today*'s usatoday.com, April 16), and a Marine's flag-draped coffin (the *St. Petersburg Times*' sptimes.com, April 16).

Other than Lynch, the injured and dead appeared in even fewer non-dominant images — an American soldier comforting an injured Iraqi boy (Fox News' foxnews.com, March 26), parents with a picture of their dead son (the *Tampa Tribune*'s tbo.com, March 26), and a soldier helping an injured comrade (*Newsweek*'s newsweek.com, April 2).

Although mainstream television and print outlets shy away from showing the injured and dead, their online counterparts sometimes run a greater number of violent images. The rationale is that Web sites can post warnings, and viewers have to seek out the pictures. Nonetheless, U.S. news Web sites didn't show many images of the injured and dead, American or Iraqi. Why?

Like other media gatekeepers, Internet editors and producers walk a fine line between informing viewers about the enormous toll of war and protecting sensitive viewers from violent images. Too much visual coverage carries the risk of sensationalism and offending people, while too little oversimplifies complex issues and fails to inform the public about the magnitude of horrors.

Wartime controls can prevent photographers from covering battle scenes or releasing certain images to the public (Elliott & Lester, 2001). The Pentagon's ban on shots of flag-draped coffins returning from Iraq limits the public's awareness of the body count. Some observers worry that censorship, pool coverage, and other types of government control can weaken the watchdog function of the press and lead to an overly upbeat or skewed view of war. Longtime journalist Pete Hamill (2004) perceived political motivation behind the "sanitized" images of the Iraq War: "We are seeing a war without blood. ... This accomplishes one great goal for the people who are running the war. The war almost never becomes real" (p. 30). Sontag (2003) wrote that portraying the vicious side of war would be deemed unpatriotic: "If governments had their way, war photographers ... would drum up support for soldiers' sacrifice" (p. 48).

As both a product of and a reflection of their society, the media "reflect, express and sometimes actively serve the 'national interest,' as determined by other, more powerful actors and institutions" (McQuail, 1994, p. 121). Although the media often resist or challenge the official line, during crises they tend to promote the government's interests and consensus values (Hallin, 1994; Solomon, 1992).

CONCLUSION

Images of war on U.S. news Web sites have been filtered through at least two layers — first the photographer's lens, then the editor's or producer's eyes. Those who shoot photos and those who select which ones to publish have an obligation to show as complete a picture as possible, not just the most graphic or compelling images. "Photojournalism must be about the big picture, not just the great shot" (Major & Perlmutter, 2005, p. 43). Peter Turnley (2002) wrote, "I feel that it is part of my role as a photojournalist to offer the viewer the opportunity to draw from as much information as possible, and develop his or her own judgment."

To bypass the traditional media filters, WarShooter.com was launched in late 2005. Here, photographers covering conflict and disaster can post all their work, "not just the great shot." WarShooter.com links to photos, first-person accounts, and news that photojournalists "feel is important and being overlooked."

Although U.S. news Web sites didn't show the complete picture, they did provide an intimate glimpse of some of the faces of war during the early weeks. Nonetheless, many faces were missing or hardly visible. Why? Does this even matter?

In terms of why certain groups of people were ignored, the reasons vary. For one, "The U.S. media appear generally to encourage more empathy with American than with foreign victims of disaster or violence, responding to and reinforcing Americans' notorious ethnocentrism" (Entman, 1991, p. 17). Accessibility reinforces this tendency. It's easier and safer for photojournalists to shoot U.S. troops than Iraqis, including civilians, who might be armed. Yet even the accessibility of our own troops is limited because of government controls. Reasons for not portraying the injured and dead include patriotism, support for our troops, not upsetting family and friends, and the Pentagon ban against showing flag-draped coffins returning home from Iraq.

For the most part, the visual framing by U.S. news Web sites focused attention on the narrow, government-friendly perspective rather than on the broader sociopolitical picture. Ignoring the antiwar protesters reinforced that patriotic view. Failing to show many coalition troops or women ignored their contributions. Neglecting the injured and dead rendered the early weeks of the war as a relatively bloodless march to Baghdad. Not showing the Iraqi resistance gave the impression that everyone welcomed the American troops as liberators. This victory frame led to reduced coverage of the conflict and less prominence in the public eye. Not surprisingly, American adults who thought the war was over rallied from 32% on April 10 to 52% a week later (Pew Research Center, 2003). President Bush's popularity rose from 69% on April 3 to 73% on April 14, which was his highest approval rating since July 2002 (CBS News, 2003).

Framing is "an expression of power" that shapes our perceptions and understanding of news events such as war (Watkins, 2001, p. 84). Although framing doesn't determine what people think, the way stories are packaged can add meaning by telling viewers *what to think about* the news and also *how to think about it* (Pfau et al., 2004). Certain aspects of war appear more significant, while others become negligible or invisible.

Framing can also affect public opinion and, in turn, policy decisions. As Dwight David Eisenhower said during World War II, "Public opinion wins wars." When Congress responded to declining public support for the Iraq War in late November 2005, some GIs blamed the media for the movement to cut and run. They voiced the popular complaint that journalists over-report violence and death but under-represent good news and progress. Insurgents realize they can affect U.S. policy by continued violence, which is reported by the media. A peaceful day at a school or rebuilt hospital in Baghdad, however, isn't front-page news.

During the early weeks of the war, Americans who didn't see images of war protesters and war victims were probably more likely to support the government policy in Iraq. Those who viewed the war as a military success would likely be more supportive. The heroic rescue of Jessica Lynch, it could be argued, was used to win support for the war (Kumar, 2004). By not showing alternative perspectives or opposing views, the media helped boost morale and build consensus on a potentially divisive issue.

By studying visual frames on news Web sites, scholars can learn how what we see (and don't see) molds and modifies public opinion. Further research could embrace other media to see how they framed the Iraq War for their readers and viewers. It would also be beneficial to examine the routines emerging at news Web sites to determine why some images are chosen and others are not. Another key area of inquiry is the interplay between journalistic autonomy and government influence with regard to visual news frames. They're important not only for their portrayal of a particular event or issue but also for their implications about the broader social order and public policy. More research will enhance our understanding of how online news frames serve as expressions of power for what we do see as well as what we do not see.

References

Aday, S., Cluverius, J., & Livingston, S. (2005). As goes the statue, so goes the war: The emergence of the victory frame in television coverage of the Iraq War. *Journal of Broadcasting & Electronic Media, 49* (3), 314-331.

Becker, E. (2004, May 27). Kissinger tapes describe crises, war and stark photos of abuse. *New York Times,* p. A1.

CBC News Online. (2005, November 25). Casualties in the Iraq war. Available online: http://www.cbc.ca/news/background/iraq/casualties.html. Accessed November 26, 2005.

CBS News. (2003, April 14). Polls: Americans more optimistic now. Available online: http://www.cbsnews.com/stories/2003/04/14/opinion/polls/main549300.shtml. Accessed November 28, 2005.

CIVIC Worldwide. (2003). Iraqi civilian war casualties. Available online: http://civilians.info/iraq/. Accessed November 20, 2005.

D'Angelo, P. (2002, December). News framing as a multiparadigmatic research program: A response to Entman. *Journal of Communication, 52* (4), 870-888.

Department of Defense. (2005). U.S. military casualties—Operation Iraqi Freedom. Available online: http://www.dior.whs.mil/mmid/casualty/castop.htm. Accessed November 20, 2005.

Elliott, D., & Elliott, P.M. (2003, September). Manipulation: The word we love to hate (Part 2). *News Photographer, 58* (9), 12-13.

Elliott, D., & Lester, P.M. (2001, November). 9-11 and the ethics of patriotism: When is it okay to break the law? *News Photographer, 56* (11), 10-12.

Entman, R.M. (1991, Autumn). Framing: Toward clarification of a fractured paradigm. *Journal of Communication, 41* (4), 6-27.

Entman, R.M. (1993, Autumn). Framing U.S. coverage of international news: Contrasts in narratives of the KAL and Iran Air incidents. *Journal of Communication, 43* (4), 51-58.

Entman, R.M. (2003, October-December). Cascading activation: Contesting the White House's frame after 9/11. *Political Communication, 20* (4), 415-432.

Fisk, R. (2003, April 10). Baghdad: The day after. *The Independent,* p. 1.

Griffin, M. (2004). Picturing America's 'war on terrorism' in Afghanistan and Iraq: Photographic motifs as news frames. *Journalism, 5* (4), 381-402.

Griffin, M., & Lee, J. (1995, Winter). Picturing the Gulf War: Constructing an image of the war in *Time, Newsweek,* and *U.S. News & World Report. Journalism & Mass Communication Quarterly, 72* (4), 813-825.

Hallin, D.C. (1986). *The "uncensored war": The media and Vietnam.* Berkeley: University of California Press.

Hallin, D.C. (1994). *We keep America on top of the world: Television journalism and the public sphere.* London: Routledge.

Hamill, P. (2004, September). The war without blood. *The Journalist: A Supplement to Quill Magazine,* 24-34.

Hewitt, G. (2003, March 25). The war on the Web. Available online: http://www.globalsecurity.org/org/news/2003/030325-warweb01.htm. Posted March 25, 2003. Accessed July 14, 2005.

Iraq Body Count. (2005). The Iraq Body Count database. Available online: http://www.iraqbodycount.org/. Accessed November 20, 2005.

Iraq Coalition Casualty Count. (2005). Available online: http://icasualties.org/oif/. Accessed November 20, 2005.

Kumar, D. (2004, November). War propaganda and the (ab)uses of women: Media constructions of the Jessica Lynch story. *Feminist Media Studies, 4* (3), 297-313.

Litchfield, J. (2003, April 10). Single pictures that capture history's turning points. *The Independent*, p. 10.

Magor, M. (2002, March). News terrorism: Misogyny exposed and the easy journalism of conflict. *Feminist Media Studies, 2* (1), 141-144.

Major, L.H., & Perlmutter, D.D. (2005, Winter/Spring). The fall of a pseudo-icon. *Visual Communication Quarterly, 12* (1 & 2), 38-45.

McQuail, D. (1994). *Mass communication theory: An introduction.* London: Sage.

Morello, C. (2003, May 17). Iraqi women out of the picture: Prominence in public life disappears in postwar fear. *The Washington Post,* p. A1.

Palser, B. (2003, May). Online advances. *American Journalism Review, 25* (4), 40-45.

Patterson III, O. (1984, Spring). Television's living room war in print: Vietnam in the news magazines. *Journalism Quarterly, 61* (1), 35-39, 136.

Pew Research Center for the People and the Press. (2003, April 18). Modest Bush approval rating boost at war's end: Economy now top national issue. Available online: http://people-press.org/reports/display.php3?ReportID=182. Accessed November 27, 2005.

Pfau, M., Haigh, M., Gettle, M., Donnelly, M., Scott, G., Warr, D., & Wittenberg, E. (2004, Spring). Embedding journalists in military combat units: Impact on newspaper story frames and tones. *Journalism & Mass Communication Quarterly, 81* (1), 74-88.

Rainie, L., Fox, S., & Fallows, D. (2003). The Internet and the Iraq war: How online Americans have used the Internet to learn war news, understand events, and promote their views. Pew Internet & American Life Project. Available online: http://www.pewinternet.org/reports/toc.asp?Report=87. Posted April 1, 2003. Accessed November 17, 2004.

Reese, S.D., & Buckalew, B. (1995, March). The militarism of local television: The routine framing of the Persian Gulf War. *Critical Studies in Mass Communication, 12* (1), 40-61.

Robins, K. (1993, April). The war, the screen, the crazy dog and poor mankind. *Media, Culture and Society, 15* (2), 321-327.

Schwalbe, C.B., Keith, S., & Silcock, B.W. (2003, November 21). Flames, faces, and flags: Framing images of the Iraq War in an era of convergent media. Presented at the National Communication Association convention, Miami Beach.

Sharkey, J. (1993, December). When pictures drive foreign policy. *American Journalism Review, 15* (10), 14-19.

Solomon, W.S. (1992, March). News frames and media packages: Covering El Salvador. *Critical Studies in Mass Communication, 9* (1), 56-74.

Sontag, S. (2002, December 9). Looking at war: Photography's view of devastation and death. *The New Yorker, 78* (38), 82-98.

Sontag, S. (2003). *Regarding the pain of others.* New York: Farrar, Straus and Giroux.

Tankard, J.W. (1997). PR goes to war: The effects of public relations campaigns on media framing of the Kuwaiti and Bosnian crises. Presented at the Association for Education in Journalism and Mass Communication convention, Chicago.

Tsang, K. (1984, Summer). News photos in *Time* and *Newsweek. Journalism Quarterly, 61* (2), 578-84, 723.

Turnley, P. (2002, December). The unseen Gulf War. *The Digital Journalist*. Available online: http://www.digitaljournalist.org/issue0212/pt_intro.html. Accessed November 29, 2005.

Watkins, S.C. (2001, March). Framing protest: News media frames of the Million Man March. *Critical Studies in Media Communication, 18* (1), 83-101.

Wheeler, T.H. (2002). *Phototruth or photofiction? Ethics and media imagery in the digital age.* Mahwah, NJ: Lawrence Erlbaum.

Zelizer, B. (2004). When war is reduced to a photograph. In S. Allen & B. Zelizer (Eds.) *Reporting War: Journalism in Wartime*, pp. 115-135. London: Routledge.

DISCUSSION QUESTIONS

1. How does the adage "seeing is believing" support the author's claim that images on the Internet of prisoner abuse at Abu Ghraib "tarnished the image of America as a superpower"? Were these images perceived as examples of local abuse of individual power or as a symbol of America's abuse of its superpower status? How did this affect public opinion in the United States?

2. The author discusses various "missing images" during the war. To what extent did omission of certain images contribute to how the war was perceived by audiences?

3. In the case of international conflict, how do attempts by news media to concentrate on their home countries and exclude others in the conflict contribute to inaccurate frames of the effects of war? Explain.

4. How does framing theory apply in the case of photographs? Are there multiple layers of framing going on when photographers and editors publish those images? If so, examine in greater detail.

5. News consumers "select" the stories they want to view, read, or listen to. How do Web site editors know what news will interest their audiences since news, by its nature, might occur spontaneously?

Chapter Twenty-Two

Net Narcissism: Leading TV News Web Site's Self-Reflexive Coverage of Operation Iraqi Freedom

Andrew Paul Williams

Not only was Operation Iraqi Freedom an unprecedented war in terms of journalistic access to military action in general, it was also the first official U.S. Web war. The Web was still in its infantile stages when the 1991 Gulf War occurred, but it has since developed into a significant news source. During the 2003 war, not only were reports being broadcast electronically through the medium of television as they occurred, they were also being reported in real time and in multimedia on the Web.

Overall, the use of the Web as a news information-seeking tool has seen a dramatic increase during the last decade. This was specifically noteworthy in the 2000 presidential election, when unlike the 1996 American general election cycle, politicians turned to the Web to communicate directly with voters, and citizens turned to the Web to seek the most up-to-date and accurate election results (Berenger, 2002).

This increasing use of the Web for information seeking proved to be evident during the 2003 U.S. war with Iraq. According to a survey conducted by the Pew Internet and American Life Project (2003), the online news audience increased significantly from the time before the war began. The study found that 77% of U.S. Internet users reported seeking information on the Web about the war and 56% of American Web users accessed a Web site for the express purpose of getting news or other information about the war in Iraq. The study also reported that 20% of American Internet users relied on the Web in order to form opinions about the war.

Since the proliferation of the Internet as a major source of news, numerous studies have examined how effectively news Web sites function. Such studies have examined how national breaking news is covered (Dimitrova et al., 2003). There are numerous studies on the effectiveness and use of online newspapers, magazines, and television news Web sites. Such studies examine the work of online reporters (Deuze, 1998), the use of the Web for information gathering (Garrison, 2001), and the pragmatics of news Web sites organizational operations and journalistic practice (Singer 2001, 2003).

In an initial study of international coverage of the first few hours following the U.S. attack on Iraq, Dimitrova et al. (2003) found that most news Web sites had immediately updated their homepages and were offering breaking news of the onset of this new war.

MEDIA FRAMING

Framing theory suggests that the media place a frame of reference around its audience's thought process. Tuchman (1978) considers the organization of everyday reality to be the most important function of media frames.

A media frame is the "central organizing idea for news content that supplies context and suggests what the issue is using selection, emphasis, exclusion, and elaboration" (Tankard, 2001; Tankard et al., 1991). According to Gitlin (1980), "media frames" organize the world both for journalists who report it and, in some important degree, for consumers who rely on their reports. Gamson and Modigliani (1997) suggest that journalists' framing of the news is due to professional norms and the influence of special interest groups. Similarly, Edelman (1997, 1993) views the act of framing as being clearly impacted by authorities and groups.

Simply put, Entman (1993) states that "to frame is to select some aspects of a perceived reality and make them more salient in a communicating text." Holloway (2001) points out are two key components of Entman's definition of framing: selection and salience. In a prior study that applied framing to media war discourse, Kelman's (1995) research about the 1991 Gulf War, offered 10 dominant frames that the U.S. administration used to shape public discourse:

- no negotiations;
- fear of reward for aggression;
- blinkmanship;
- unbalanced cost-benefit analysis;

- human costs for the enemy;
- self-glorification;
- stigmatization of dissent;
- rallying around the flag;
- overcoming the Vietnam Syndrome; and
- a New World Order.

MEDIA NARCISSISM

Media narcissism, self-reflexive reporting, and metacommunication are three terms that are being used to describe how the media have shifted their focus more and more to their apparently favorite subject: themselves. While the terms are different and moving towards a theory of metacommunication is relatively new, the concept of media self-coverage and the concerns of the impact of such reporting are decades old.

Broadly, "metacommunication is defined as the news media's response to a new, third force in news making: professional political PR. Metacommunication is defined as the news media's self referential reflections on the nature of the interplay between political public relations and political journalism" (Esser & D'Angelo, 2001a). Specifically, self-reflexive reporting refers to coverage that describes the role the media are playing in political campaigns. (D'Angelo, 1999, 2002; D'Angelo & Esser, 2003; Esser, 2000, 2001a, 2001b; Esser & D'Angelo, 2002, 2003; Esser, Reinemann & Fan 1999, 2000, 2001; Esser & Spanier, 2003).

Stebenne (1993) argues that this trend in media self coverage is "a logical outgrowth of the new emphasis on the political process and the growing sense of the media's central place within it" (p. 87-88), and indeed research indicates that the metacoverage frame has become increasingly prevalent in political campaign reporting. Studies of the 1992 and 1996 presidential campaigns found use of this self-reflexive frame accounted for 20% of the coverage in the 1992 election cycle and increased to 25% in the 1996 coverage (Kerbel, 1998; Kerbel, Apee & Ross, 2000).

It is argued that instead of sitting on the sidelines and reporting the facts, "The news media no longer simply report; they interpret. Journalists are quick to insert their own construction of events and issues between candidates and voters" (Lichter, Noyes & Kaid, 2000, p. 363-364). It is also of concern that, "the media become part of the dialectic process of the production of consent, shaping the consensus while reflecting it" (Jensen, 1992, p. 2).

A study that explicated and applied the research of

metacommunication to a crisis situation; specifically, the first four hours of televised news coverage following the terrorist attacks of September 11, 2001. Connolly-Ahern, et al. (2002) found that both categories of metacommunication were prevalent in that reporting. The researchers found that self-reflexive reporting accounted for 43% of the stories. This is one of the rare cases in which the concept of metacommunication was applied to non political campaign coverage, and even though it only focuses on initial coverage, the study indicates that metacommunication in news content is not limited to election coverage but is also prevalent during a crisis situation.

METHOD

This study used content from U.S. Web coverage from March 20, 2003 — the first official day of news coverage about the U.S. military strikes on Iraq — through May 1, 2003, when President Bush made a declaration of victory. For purposes of this study, the story was the unit of analysis, and all war-related stories collected during this time period were used. The total sample for this study was 983 Web stories.

The Web sites' data were systematically downloaded daily. The Web news coverage sample consisted stories from four sites: abcnews.com (171 stories), cbsnews.com (249 stories), cnn.com (151 stories), and foxnews.com (412 stories), which newsknife.com rated in their list of the top Iraq War news sites, and in their rating of the overall top U.S. news sites of 2003 (newsknife.com, 2003).

A constraint that affected the sample size and prevented using the entire universe of television network Web site coverage for these networks was the problem faced by NBC's Web site format. The initial goal of this study was to include the Web sites from NBC and MSNBC in the sample. The barrier to doing so was that they do not have separate Web sites, but instead during the time of this data collection, NBC had a Web site that merged its multiple media products including NBC, MSNBC, CNBC, and *Newsweek*. This hybrid Web site often did not distinguish which original media channel its content was attributed to, and made it impossible to do a balanced and accurate comparison with the other Web coverage being analyzed for this study.

For purposes of this study, the news story was the unit of analysis. A story consisted of the use of a headline and subsequent text. Story length was determined by a word count, and the coders coded for the manifest textual content of each Web story. Only the Web stories for each given day were coded — not the archived coverage that was linked to from a given story, but instead just the current story with a byline and date for each day in the time-period analyzed.

The list of frames coded as present or absent in each story were:

- *Military Conflict* — frames that emphasize the military battle itself on macro or micro levels;
- *American Patriotism* — frames that emphasize citizens rallying around the flag and a resurgence of American patriotism in various manifestations;
- *Protest* — frames that show individuals or groups, in the United States or abroad protesting or the discussion of protest of the war;
- *Human Interest* — frames that emphasize the human element of the war, including soldiers, their families, and any citizens;
- *Responsibility* — frames that assign responsibility for the military conflict to a given individual, government, or regime;
- *Economic Consequences* — frames that focus on the either short or long-term economic consequences that the war will have domestically, in the Middle East, or internationally;
- *Diagnostic* — frames that emphasize an assessment of how and why this military conflict developed;
- *Prognostic* — frames that emphasize what outcome of the military conflict will be, including the removal of Saddam/regime change, regional stability, loss of U.S. soldiers, etc.;
- *Rebuilding of Iraq* — frames that specifically deal with the rebuilding of Iraqi and the future of the country and its people after the war is finished; and
- *Metacommunication* — a frame that emphasizes the media's self-reflexivity.

More specifically, the self-reflexive metacommunication frame was characterized as any coverage that referred directly or indirectly to the media's role in bringing news about the U.S. military effort against Iraq to the public. Incidents of self-reflexive reporting include: information about the impact the coverage of the military campaign was having on the public; references to the work of the television news network or Web sites' own reporters (such as embedded journalists); referrals to the electronic media's other news products for more information; members of the media used as news sources; and mentions of the work of other news media outlets. If the self-reflexive metacommunication frame was coded as being present, the coders identified which of the following types of coverage best characterized this frame:

- Role of Technology in Attaining Coverage;
- Anchors or Media Personalities Discussing their Opinions;
- Reporters Discussing Personal Experience of Covering the War;
- Reporters Interviewing/Reporting about other Journalists from their News Organization, Network, or Publication;
- Reporters Interviewing/Reporting about other Journalists from another News; Organization, Network, or Publications;
- The News Media Emphasizing their Role as a Participant in the Event;
- Cross Promotion and Cross Referencing of Media; or
- Insider Views of the War or War Strategizing.

RESULTS

Frame Prevalence

In any given story, a number of frames could be present. The total frames present in the Web coverage totaled 2,333.

Overall, the self-reflexive metacommunication frame ranked as the second-most prominent frame in the Web coverage of Operation Iraqi freedom. Of the four Web sites analyzed for this study percentile rankings of the self-reflexive frame were as follows: foxnews.com had the most at 38%; followed by cbsnews.com at 30%; cnn.com at 23%; and with abacnews.com having the least at 19%.

The most prevalent frames, from highest to lowest presence, were: military conflict (33% of total frames); metacommunication (27%); human interest diagnostic (13%); rebuilding of Iraq (5%); diagnostic (5%); economic consequences (4%); protest (4%); prognostic (4%); American patriotism (3%); and responsibility (2%).

Self-Reflexive Metacommunication Frames

Additionally, this study examined what types of self-reflexive frames were relied on in the Web coverage of the war. The most prevalent self-reflexive metacommunication frames, from highest to lowest presence, were: cross promotion and cross referencing of media (36%); reporters reporting about journalists from their organization or network (25%); reporters reporting about journalist from other organizations or networks (17%); reporters discussing personal experience of covering the war (8%); news media emphasizing their role as participant in event (7%); insider views of the war or war strategizing (4%); media reporters or personalities discussing their opinions (2%); and the role of technology in attaining coverage (1%).

In terms of prevalent frames in the media coverage of the war, the military conflict frame was the most prevalent frame overall, and the self-reflexive metacommunication frame was the second-most prevalent frame.

The sheer volume of metacommunication frame presence is a finding that is striking for several reasons. While military conflict was the most prevalent frame, it was a frame that included a broad number of scenarios that dealt with actual conflict and events in the war in general. The other eight frames ranged from very specific, such as American patriotism, human interest, diagnostic, and prognostic to broad, such as economic consequences, protest, responsibility, and rebuilding of Iraq.

The high level of self-reflexive coverage prevalence is a key finding of this study. It indicates that, other than broad military conflict information, the media are, indeed, providing coverage that is self-reflexive and emphasizing the media's role in the news-gathering process much more than they are the specific events, issues, and people involved in the military conflict.

The use of embedded reporters during Operation Iraqi Freedom is one possible reason that could have led to such coverage. From the Jessica Lynch rescue, to the toppling of the Statue of Saddam Hussein, to the day-to-day activities of the U.S. military personnel, to President Bush's parachute landing and official declaration of the end of the war, embedded reporters were right there telling this unfolding story. This unprecedented access given to the media created a situation in which reporters were not only more like participants, the also became daily storytellers who would tend to focus on incidents and events rather than broader issues.

The results of this research indicate that the self-reflexive type of metacommunication frame, in which media frequently insert themselves into the coverage and evaluate their role in the news process, was the second-most dominant media frame. The finding that Web story authors frequently offered opinions and emphasized their roles in the news means that they spent less time conveying substantive news. Examples of reporters interviewing embedded reporters in the field were frequently occurring types of self-reflexive coverage and a mainstay of the electronic war coverage analyzed in this study. This is not surprising, since certain major media outlets had access to more data and the actual troops, and the media sources offered perspectives that were not available through other independent sources that were not on the front line.

The finding that cross-promotion and cross-referencing of the media was high in the Web coverage could be attributed to the structural nature of this media channel. Since the Web offers a practically infinite news hole and more coverage possibilities.

Future work the existing data collected during Operation Iraqi Freedom include examining which sources were most frequently associated with given frames to see what patterns emerge, and to examine if and how these patterns are related to the media channels, the time periods, and the episodic and/or thematic frame characterizations, as well as other categories and subcategories of metacommunication frames.

The opportunities to address media narcissism and self-reflexive reporting are seemingly myriad, not only in terms of differing contexts but also in differing media outlets and areas of the world. Also, after considerably more work has been done with content analysis, experimental studies to measure the effects of metacommunication on respondents will provide further chances to advance understanding of this media practice.

The findings of this study are, overall, troublesome and especially so in regard to journalistic objectivity. As the public does indeed rely on the media for factual information on a regular basis, the need for facts from the media during a time of crisis, such as war or terrorist attacks is paramount. The issues and events are much more important to the public than being educated about the news gathering process.

REFERENCES

Berenger, R.D. (2002). Frame theory and political behavior by candidates, national media and voters in the 2000 primary election. Unpublished doctoral dissertation. Pocatello: Idaho State University.

Connolly-Ahern, C., Williams, A.P., Flowers, K., Floyd, S., Khang, H., & Mills, L. (2002). Look who's talking: The role of media narcissism in the news coverage of the September 11, 2001 terrorist attacks. Paper presented to the annual convention of the International Communication Association, Seoul, Korea.

D'Angelo, P. (1999). Framing the press: A new approach to assessing the cynical nature of press self-coverage and its implications for information processing in the political campaign context. Paper presented to the Mass Communication Division at the 49th Annual conference of the International Communication Association, San Francisco, CA.

D'Angelo, P. (2002). Framing the press: A new model for observing press frames in presidential campaign news. Unpublished doctoral dissertation. Philadelphia: Temple University,.

Deuze, M. (1998). The Web communicators: Issues in research into online journalism and journalists. *First Monday 3* (12). Retrived April 13, 2005 from http://www.firstmonday.dk/issues/issue3_12/deuze/index.html.

Dimitrova, D.V., Connolly-Ahern, C., Williams, A.P., Reid A., & Kaid, L.L. (2003). Hyperlinking as gatekeeping: Online newspaper coverage of the execution of an American terrorist. *Journalism Studies, 4(3)*, pp. 401-414.

Dimitrova, D.V., Kaid, L.L., Williams, A.P., & Trammell, K.D. (2003, August). *War on the Web: The first hours of Operation Iraqi Freedom.* Paper presented at the Entertainment Studies Special Interest Division, Association for Education in Journalism and Mass Communication, Kansas City, Missouri.

Entman, R. (1991). Framing U.S.coverage of international news: Contrasts in narratives of the KAL and Iran air accidents. *Journal of Communication, 41(4)*, 6-27.

Entman, R. (1993). Framing: Toward a clarification of a fractured paradigm. *Journal of Communication.* 43 (4), 51-58.

Esser, F. (2000). Tabloidization of news. A comparative analysis of Anglo-American and German press journalism. *European Journal of Communication, 14(3),* 291-324.

Esser, F. (2001a). *A news stage in political reporting: Metacommunication in election coverage.* Paper presented to the Political Communications Division, International Communication Association, Washington, DC.

Esser, F. (2001b). *Reflexive reporting on political journalism and political PR in the 2000 presidential campaign: Toward a theory of metacommunication.* Paper presented to the Political Communications Division, International Communication Association, Washington, DC.

Esser, F., & D'Angelo, P. (2002). Framing the press and the publicity process: A content analysis of meta-coverage in campaign 2000 network news. *American Behavioural Scientist, 46(5), 617-641.*

Esser, F., & D'Angelo, P. (2003*). Framing the press and publicity process in German, British and U.S. general election campaigns: A comparative study of metacoverage.* Paper Presented to the Political Communications Division, International Communication Association, San Diego, CA.

Esser, F., Reinemann, C., & Fan, D. (1999). Spin Doctoring im deutschen Wahlkampf. *Medin Tenor, 86,* 40-43.

Esser, F., Reinemann. C., & Fan, D. (2000). Spin doctoring in British and German election campaigns: How the press is becoming confronted with a new quality of political PR. *European Journal of Communication, 15(2),* 209-39.

Esser, F., Reinemann, C., & Fan, D. (2001). Spin doctors in the United States, Great Britain, and Germany: Metacommunication about media manipulation. *The Harvard International Journal of Press/Politics, 6(1),* 16-45.

Esser, F., & Spanier, B. (2003). *Media politics and media self-coverage in the British press.* Paper presented to the Political Communications Division, International Communication Association, San Diego, CA.

Gamson, W.A., & Modigliani, A. (1997). The changing culture of affirmative action. *Research in Political Sociology, 95,* 1-37.

Garrison, B. (20010. Computer-assisted reporting near complete adoption. *Newspaper Research Journal, 22(1),* 65-80.

Gitlin, T. (1980). *The whole world is watching: Mass media in the making and unmaking of the new left.* Berkeley: University of California Press.

Holloway, R. (2001). One nation, after all: Convention frames and political culture. In R. E. Denton (Ed.), *The 2000 presidential campaign: A communication perspective* (pp. 117-134). Westport, CT: Praeger.

Jensen, R. (1992). Fighting objectivity: The illusion of journalistic neutrality in coverage of the Persian Gulf War. *Journal of Communication, 16,* (1), 20-32.

Kelman, H.C. (1995). Decision making and public discourse in the Gulf War: An assessment of underlying psychological and moral assumptions. *Journal of Peace Psychology, 1(2),* 117-130.

Kerbel, M.R. (1995). *Remote & Controlled: Media politics in a cynical age.* Boulder, CO: Westview Press.

Kerbel, M.R. (1998). *Edited for television: CNN, ABC, and American presidential elections.* Boulder, CO: Westview Press.

Kerbel, M.R., Apee, S., & Ross, M.H. (2000). PBS ain't so different: Public broadcasting, election frames, and democratic empowerment. *Harvard International Journal of Press/Politics, 5(4),* 8-32

Lichter, R.S., Noyes, R.E., & Kaid, L.L. (2000). No News or Negative News: How the Networks nixed the '96 Campaign, In L.L. Kaid & D. Bystrom (Eds.), *The Electronic Election* (pp. 3-13). Mahwah, NJ: Lawrence Erlbaum Associates, Inc.

Pew Internet & American Life Project. (2003). The Internet and the Iraq war: How online Americans have used the Internet to learn war news, understand events, and promote their views. http://www.pewinternet.org/reports/toc.asp?Report=87.

Singer, J. (2001). The metro wide web: Changes in newspaper's gatekeeeping role online. *Journalism & Mass Communication Quarterly, 78(1),* 65-73.

Singer, J. (2003). Campaign contributions: Online newspaper coverage of election 2000. *Journalism & Mass Communication Quarterly, 80(1),* 39-57.

Tankard, J.W. Jr. (2001). The empirical approach to the study of media framing. In S.D. Reese, O.H. Gandy, Jr., & A.E. Grant (Eds.), *Framing public life: Perspectives on the media and our understandings of the social world.* Mahwah, NJ: Lawrence Erlbaum Associates, Inc., pp. 95-106.

Tankard, J., Hendrickson, L., Silberman, J,. Bliss, K., & Ghanem, S. (1991). *Media frames: Approaches to conceptualization and measurement.* Paper presented at the annual convention of the Association for Education in Journalism and Mass Communication, Boston.

Tuchman, G. (1978). *Making news.* New York: Free Press.

DISCUSSION QUESTIONS

1. This chapter discusses the trend of media inserting themselves in their stories, instead of just sitting on the sidelines and reporting the facts. Do you perceive this to be a problematic issue in terms of Web coverage as compared with televised news broadcasts or print news stories?

2. This chapter reports findings that the "self-reflexive metacommunication frame" ranked as the second-most-prominent frame in the Web's coverage of Operation Iraqi Freedom. Is this an example of a media bias towards

the media, or is it possibly positive, since embedded journalist were able to upload stories via the Web about a military conflict from a closer proximity than ever before?

3. The most prevalent self-reflexive metacommunication frames are "cross promotion" and "cross-referencing" of media. Since the Web allows much user control, does this cross promotion and cross-referencing of media really appear to be a troubling finding?

4. Should Web news sites focus on offering more coverage and linking to other stories and sources instead of emphasizing the role of the journalist or the news organization? Or should the responsibility of the Web user be to seek out additional information?

5. Do you agree with the assessment that Web stories which offer authors' opinions and emphasize their roles in the news means that substantive news was limited?

CHAPTER TWENTY-THREE

ONLINE IRAQ WAR NEWS: WHY IT HAD AS MUCH APPEAL AS SPINACH AND LIVER TO YOUNGER AUDIENCES

DAVID WEINSTOCK AND TIM BOUDREAU

"Eat your spinach. It's good for you," your mother probably told you when you were a child. But no matter how much you tried to think about all the good vitamin A it contained, you couldn't get past the way it tasted and slid around your mouth.

"Eat your liver. It's good for you," your dad probably told you. But, you thought, meat shouldn't be crumbly, should it? And is there some reason why it should taste like dirt? If you put salt or pepper on it, why does liver taste like salty or peppery dirt? Yes, nothing delivers iron quite like liver does, but it is still ... well, liver.

For about two-thirds of people in this country under the age of 35, the news is like spinach and liver. There it sits — every day, sometimes two or three times a day — on their favorite media, sometimes as a side dish, sometimes as the main course, in media they really like for all sorts of other reasons that have nothing to do with the news.

Supposedly, the news is good for us. We could be better citizens. We could be more aware of what is happening around us. Some of us could even make more money if all we did was take some of it in, digest it and convert it to something useful.

But most of us don't. In fact, as time goes on, fewer and fewer of us do. And like spinach and liver, it seems as if when we don't consume the news that we are none the worse for it.

Take the 2003 Iraq War, for example. For a little more than a year and a half, the people of several countries have launched missiles and air strikes at each other, bombed each other, shot guns at each other, and generally waged war with each other. Americans have been wounded or have died there — people you may know.

You could read about it if you were interested or if you cared. But if you are young and American, you probably don't follow the news.

Who Likes and Dislikes News

In his recent book, *Tuned Out: Why Americans Under 40 Don't Follow the News*, media scholar David T. Z. Mindich carefully analyzed a number of studies to determine who reads the news and who doesn't (Mindich, 2005). Based on his analysis of Pew Research Center, DDB Needham and Roper data, he derived an interesting picture of the American news audience around the year 2000.

About 32% of Americans between the ages of 18 and 24 agreed with the statement: "I need to get the news every day." Beginning at age 35, however, and on up through age 65, the percentage of people who agreed with this statement ranged from 46% to 68%. Mindich also reviewed data from two studies that looked at the ages of people who read newspapers "every day" from 1972 to 2002 (Peiser, 200). He found that slightly fewer than half of people between 18 and 27 read newspapers every day in 1972 and that by 2002 this number had slipped to about 20%. There was also a slide for older Americans. About 75% of Americans aged 33 to 72, read a newspaper every day in 1972 and that dropped to about 50% in 2002.

These data, which show that newspaper reading has clearly declined over time and that younger people are far less interested than older people in the news, also is reflected in more recent studies. According to an April 2004 Pew Research Center survey, 23% of Americans 18 to 29 read a newspaper yesterday, compared to about 50% of those 30 to 65+ (Pew, 2004). The numbers were slightly higher for TV news, with 44% of younger Americans saying they watched the news yesterday vs. about 66% of Americans 30 to 65+. In terms of attention to war news, Pew Research also found that 17% of its subjects use the Internet to find war news (Rainie, Fox & Fallows, 2003).

While not focusing specifically on war news, Mindich, in his evaluation of Roper data (RoperASW, 2002) found only 11% of U.S. respondents 18 to 24 used the Internet to find information about "current events." Interestingly, he noted that young adults from Canada, France, Great Britain, Italy, Japan, Mexico and Sweden were more likely to use the Internet to find news about current events (Mindich, p. 33). The Pew data underscores the data reported in Mindich's book. They also report

24% of their subjects said "they went online for news on the previous day" (Pew, 2004).

WHAT WE FOUND

In spring 2003, the authors of this chapter conducted a survey of young people and focused specifically on their interest in war news (Weinstock & Boudreau, 2004). We found that young people professed a high interest in Iraq War news (92%). However, they seemed to be unexcited about the way in which the news was presented. Only 19% accessed war news online. Was the medium boring? Or was it the way in which the news was presented that made it so indigestible by younger audiences.

In fall 2004, we went back into the field again and conducted another online survey of 429 students at a Midwest public university, this time focusing more on their use of online news. Almost nine in 10 (88.8%) were 22 or younger, with 17% age 18 or younger. Females made up 72% of the sample. The largest numbers of respondents (30%) were majoring in education, followed by those studying fine arts and business administration. Just over 90% of the students were white; 4% were African-American and 1% Hispanic. Nearly four in 10 (38.5%) said they had a family member or relative in the armed forces.

Students gave seemingly contradictory responses to questions designed to measure their interest in news about the war in Iraq. While nearly three in four (72.5%) expressed interest in war news, only 7.2% said they actively seek out such news. Almost 90% said they acquire news about the war only when they happen upon it. And while 30% of the students said they had sought out a new source for news since the war had begun, that new source was most often TV news.

Questions about media preferences elicited some predictable responses. Three in four students said either TV news (49.1%) or the Web (25.5%) was the most convenient media for information about the war. Newspapers fared better on measures of credibility. Almost a third (32.5%) cited newspapers as the most credible source, slightly behind the 34% who chose TV news. Only 10% listed the Web as most credible. A news triad formed on measures of "informativeness." TV news was selected by 34% of students as the most informative medium, followed by newspapers (28%) and the Web (19.5%).

Fewer than half of the respondents (44%) regularly sought war news on the Web. Within that group, most (74%) turned to online network TV news sites for war news. The much-ballyhooed blogs attracted only 3.2%

of those who sought war news online.

When students seek war news online, they delve into the story. About eight in 10 (80.7%) said they click to access the full story from online sites, and 91% of those said they read more than half of the story. Similar numbers look at the photos (95.7%) or read the captions (91.5%). Those numbers begin to fall off dramatically with video links. Fewer than half (48.3%) of the students said they click on the video links, and fewer than a third (31%) said they click audio links.

The great majority of students (93%) said they had cable modem, DSL or on-campus Ethernet access, so speed of access seems not to explain any reluctance to seek out news online.

STILL BORED

We thought young people would be more interested in consuming news through the Internet, since it is the medium of their choice. In fact, 72% of people 18-29 access the Internet (Pew Internet, 2004).

However, disinterest in war news was strong among younger audiences on the Web, too. Only 19% of the 18- to 24-year-old U.S. news audience used the Internet to find war news (Weinstock & Boudreau, 2004). This was true, not only in our study, but also in one done by the Pew Internet and American Life Project in 2003. That project surveyed some 10,000 Internet users about their media preferences at the outbreak of the Iraq War and found that when Internet users of all ages sought news about the Iraq War their medium of choice was TV. The Internet and online news ranked last among their choices.

Why?

What our numbers have told us in two Iraq War news media preference studies — one at the beginning of the war and a second a year and a half later — is that no matter how it is dressed it up, no matter how it is delivered, Iraq War news, is pretty much just liver and spinach for younger audiences.

When it was new news, it was just fresh liver and fresh spinach. The numbers at the beginning of the Iraq War told us that while younger audiences seemed very interested in the concept of being interested in war news, they didn't morph into actual news consumers. Though the vast majority of young people were still interested in war news, a far smaller amount of young people actually sought it out and consumed it.

Overall, our subjects' interest in Iraq War news dropped by nearly 20% from 2003 to 2004. News-seeking behavior dropped even more dramatically. At the outbreak of the war, 77% of our sample actively sought war news; a year and a half later, only 7.2% actively sought out war news. What is even more staggering about this number is that nearly 40% of our sample said they had "a family member or someone else close to them" currently serving in the U.S. or the U.K.'s armed forces.

Certainly, some of this can be explained by the loss of the war's novelty news value. Further evidence of this declining interest in Iraq War news is that almost 90% of our sample in our second study said they did not actively seek Iraq War news but instead "happened to encounter it."

This is not an unusual finding.

Pew research showed that in the fall of 2004 nearly 64 million adults logged onto the Internet each day. Based on data they collected in May and June 2004, only 27% of these people logged on to "get news." In another study it published at the same time, Pew identified a class of Internet users called "inadvertent news consumers" and reported nearly three-fourths "of Internet users come across the news this way." They noted 82% of people under the age of 30 found news in this fashion on the Web (Pew, 2004).

All this lends credence to one of the conclusions that we came to in our first study: that young people are not very interested in the news media. The trend in accessing the Internet for people in general, including younger segments, has increased steadily since 1994. In all the 2004 studies we've mentioned so far, fewer than a third of research subjects reported actually getting news online but nearly everyone reported "encountering it."

This "passive" behavior toward online news is interesting. The numbers, in both our studies and the Pew research, shows audiences of all ages to be far more interested in seeking news from TV, newspapers and radio and far less interested in seeking news from magazines and the Web. If the audience wants it but is not getting it online, something appears to be missing from the online news offering.

These findings force us to look at the media that more people use to actively seek out Iraq War news. In our surveys, TV and newspapers were the only two media to outscore the Internet in several key measures. Interestingly, our survey subjects reported that TV news was the single greatest "new source of Iraq War news information" they had acquired recently (newspapers were second on this list and the Web was third). They also identified TV as the most informative of all media (34%), the most credible (34%) and most convenient (49%). Newspapers scored a close second in credibility (32.5%) and a slightly more distant second in being informative (28%).

By contrast, the Web came in second on convenience (25.5%) and third on being informative (19%). Perhaps most surprising is the Web finished a distant last on credibility (10%). This finding helps explain why fewer people actually seek out Web news.

There are a number of possible explanations for these findings. Convenience is a relatively easy one to interpret. There is very little difference between turning on a television and a computer, choosing a channel to watch or finding a Web page to view, and viewing the information.

In terms of the Web being less informative, a measure of that may be blamed on the writing style currently being advocated among Web news operations. The current wisdom among online content producers is to require news consumers to scroll screens as little as possible because research has shown them that less scrolling facilitates greater attention being placed on content. The idea is to write tightly and succinctly; brevity is valued far more than deeper analysis is online. The brevity of writing may play a role in the Web's lack of credibility.

Then, too, there is less distinction between opinion and fact online. In the traditional news media, the professionals there take painstaking care to differentiate between what is news and what is not news. The lines between fact and opinion tend to be blurred on the Web. Making this kind of distinction among various Web sites can be especially difficult for novices.

There is also another factor here that may change over time. Today, Web news sites can be updated the moment a news event takes place. In fact, it is not uncommon for online news operations to update their sites numerous times during the day. Again, younger audiences, less expert at spotting or even looking for time/date stamps on news sites, might perceive the constant change in content or even the apparent discrepancies between news reports in traditional media and Web media as inaccuracy. As this audience segment grows older and becomes more sophisticated as news consumers, its views may change about online news credibility.

Still another factor in the overall credibility question may be related to the younger audience's Web-savvy. Although they are relatively naïve about Web news and how Web news sites operate, they are suspicious of the credibility of information found on the Web. They may fail to distinguish, as older audiences might, between the value of information found on the Web, overall, and news published on the Web.

Finally, perhaps younger audiences perceive the Web as more of an entertainment medium, and other media, such as TV and newspapers, as the media-of-choice for news.

So who are the people who actually do seek out the news online? Our study showed these people's behavior more closely mimicked that of students than just regular people. Primary among these findings is that those who seek out news are data-miners. Slightly more than 8 of 10 of our subjects who said they were interested in Iraq War news clicked through to the full story to read it. Nearly all these readers claimed they read more than half of what they found on the full story level. While there, similar numbers of subjects examined photos and read their captions.

When it came to multimedia offerings, our subjects' desire to mine data fell off by nearly half. Slightly fewer than half accessed video links and fewer than one-third accessed audio links, despite the fact that 93% used cable modems to access the Web. The good news is that multimedia access rates are about 10% higher than they were in our first study.

Still it would have been reasonable to expect higher access because, at the time of our first study, only a third of our subjects reported using high-speed Internet access. A year later, with high-speed access at 93%, audio and video link usage was surprisingly low.

One possible explanation for this is that our subjects are university students and half (50.1%) said they accessed war news on campus. Since access would have occurred in public space, such as libraries, classrooms and computer labs, it would have been inconsiderate to play this content in these places. Furthermore, only 2.8% reported listening to computer audio with headphones and only 16% reported using computers equipped with speakers. In our first study, we dubbed this lack of multimedia access as a de-convergence phenomenon. Now, however, it seems possible this phenomenon may be an artifact of this particular audience segment and not one that might be generalized to a nonuniversity segment. Should multimedia access increase and access location shift off campus, then it is very likely the de-convergence we identified earlier is, indeed, nothing more than artifact.

CHANGING TIMES, CHANGING TASTES

Clearly, the Web has not come of age as a news medium in the eyes of younger audiences. When they seek news, both in our studies and others, TV remains the medium of choice for news, followed somewhat distantly by newspapers. Online news is a distant third.

Contrast these findings to media preference studies in the 1970s and 1980s in which news audiences generally preferred newspapers to TV for news acquisition. There is a fundamental shift in media preference toward electronic media, away from print media and not toward online media. On its face, it is surprising when print media's ability to deliver a more analytical and in-depth presentation of events or the Web's seemingly limitless ability to deliver related material via links to other stories and other sites is considered. In short, credibility and "informativeness" seem to be far less important to younger audiences than convenience.

Additionally, we think one of the more plausible explanations we've offered is this notion that the younger audience purposes the media — TV and newspapers for news and the Web for entertainment and recreation. Thus, they devalue whatever news they find on the Web since it runs counter to what they are seeking from the Web.

Lastly, it is important to note that at no time in our studies or in the Pew research did interest in daily news even approach the 50-percentile mark. Our subjects should have been very interested in the Iraq War. More than a third of them have people who matter to them serving in the armed forces — people who are either fighting in the war or may very likely be fighting in the war in the near future — and yet fewer than 10% actively seek out war news.

For younger audiences, media and the consumption of its content is still more about what they want and far less about what they need. Just as there was no way our parents could convince us to eat our liver or spinach, no matter how good for us it was, there is no way younger audiences will read the news until it is proven to them that it *is*, in fact, good for them.

REFERENCES

Mindich, D. T. (2005). *Tuned out: Why Americans under 40 don't follow the news.* New York: Oxford University Press.

Peiser, W. (2000). Cohort replacement and downward trend in newspaper readership. *Newspaper Research Journal, 21*(2), 15-16.

Pew Center for the People and the Press. (2004, June). News audiences increasingly politicized: Online news audiences larger, more diverse (chap.) Retrieved November 7, 2004, from http://people-press.org/

Pew Internet and American Life Project. (2004, December). Post election 2004 and November 2004 tracking surveys (chap.) Retrieved December, 2004, from http://www.pewinternet.org/.

Putnam, R. D. (2002). *Bowling alone: The collapse and revival of American community.* New York: Simon & Schuster.

Rainie, L., Fox, S., & Fallows, D. (2003, April). *The Internet and the Iraq War: How online Americans have used the Internet to learn war news.* Retrieved May 1, 2003, from http://www.pewinternet.org/

RoperASW. (2002). National Geographic-RoperASW 2002 global geographic literacy survey (chap.) Retrieved November, 2002, from http://news.nationalgeographic.com/

Weinstock, D., & Boudreau, T. (2004). Were young people bored with Iraq war news or bored with the media? In R.D. Berenger (Ed.), *Global media go to war: Role of news and entertainment media in the 2003 Iraq war.* Spokane: Marquette Books, pp. 305-312.

DISCUSSION QUESTIONS

1. Young people do not seem particularly interested in what traditionally has been defined as news, even on the Internet. Is this problem attributed to characteristics of youth or to characteristics of what has been defined by an older generation as news?
2. To make information more attractive to youth, should there be greater convergence of entertainment, stories about personalities, music and games in what has been traditional news-oriented programming?
3. In general, what could news organizations do to make such events as wars and international relations more attractive to younger audiences?
4. Interestingly this study found that television (and presumably converged visual media on the Internet) was more credible than the printed word in newspapers, even though media Web sites use information from print sources? What does this tell us about the Marshall McLuhanesque notion that the medium is more important than the message?
5. Eventually, how would the interactivity potential of the Internet affect the news use "passivity" of youth this study found?

Name Index

A

A.C. Nielsen, 206
Aeschlus, 19
al-Din, Salah, 218
al-Iraqi, Abu-Maysara, 216
al-Sistani, Ali, 220
al-Walid, Khalid Ibn, 218
Al-Zarqawi, Abu Musab, 213, 215
Alcorn, Gay, 207
Ali, Tariq, 206
Amin, Hussein Y., 34
Anderson, Richard, 117
Anderson, Gillian, 307
Arden, Jann, 307
Arnison, Mathew, 161
Austen, Jane, 289
Ayoub, Tareq, 120, 131
Aznar, Jose Maria, 133

B

Badran, Mona, 35
Baker, James, 339
Bartlett, Fredric, 117
Bayh, Birch, 188
Beardow, Peter, 45
Berenger, Ralph D., 7, 12, 20, 23
Berg, Nick, 316
Bilbasey, Nadia, 50
bin Laden, Osama 109, 111, 217, 223, 226, 230
Bin-Ziyad, Tariq, 218
Blades, Joan, 187, 189
Blair, Tony, 57, 68, 96, 132, 133, 285, 309
Bloom, David, 46
Bossert, Pattie, 193
Boyd, Andrew, 190
Boyd, Wes, 187

Flea, 307
Franks, Tommy, 142, 364, 366
Friedrich, Art, 177, 178, 182

G

Gaiman, Neil, 307
Gates, Bill, 5, 272
Gibson, William, 307
Gillette, Penn, 307
Gilligan, Andrew, 93
Gould, Stephen Jay, 338
Greenwald, Robert, 193, 195
Grossman, Lev, 324

H

Hall, Stuart, 121
Hamdy, Naila, 24, 35
Hamill, Pete, 367
Hashem, Sultan, 139
Hazen, Don, 192
Herron, Ken, 46
Highfield, Ashley, 93
Hitler, Adolf, 56
Howard, John, 201
Hussein, Saddam, 24, 56, 78, 81, 137-139, 141, 143, 145, 146, 201, 214, 223, 235, 242, 247, 252, 297-299, 308, 309, 364, 365, 379

I

Imrie, Ariel, 194

J

Jones, Andy, 177, 178, 182, 184

K

Kaid, Lynda Lee, 314
Kazziha, Khalid, 51
Keller, Bill, 346
Kelley, David, 31, 93, 102
Kincer, Aaron, 187

P

R

S

SUBJECT INDEX

1967 War with Israel, 121
1991 Iraq War, 23, 72
2003 Iraq War, 2, 3, 7, 8, 12, 15, 17, 19, 20, 23, 25-30, 32, 33, 37, 70, 72, 76, 85, 90, 92,
    93, 95, 100, 101, 103, 113, 115, 123, 124, 152, 161, 184, 213, 214, 231, 234, 235,
    250-254, 256, 258, 260, 267, 269, 291, 294, 302, 303, 305, 315, 317, 319, 330, 331,
    384, 392
2003 Arab Human Development Report, 272, 275
7E Communications, 45
9/11 (see September 11, 2001)

A

Abbasid period, 223
abcnews.com, 376
Abyssinian Baptist Church in Harlem, 160
accurate, 40, 73, 131, 241, 253, 317, 326, 327, 329, 344, 347, 358, 373, 376
action, 46, 57, 59, 64-66, 81, 82, 96, 97, 99, 129, 139, 155, 156, 169, 192-195, 202-204,
    207, 238, 243-245, 247, 248, 272, 299, 304, 364, 373, 381
Adbusters, 158
Advanced Research Projects Agency (ARPA), 234
Advanced Journalist Technology Project, 49
advertiser, 73, 75
advertising, 11, 12, 16, 17, 75, 248, 250, 314, 320, 324, 330, 332
advocacy video, 153, 157
Afghanistan, 24, 39, 40, 43-45, 50, 55, 104, 105, 110, 167, 178, 201, 215, 216, 223, 370
Africa, 17, 27, 47, 50, 51, 64, 162, 167, 174, 230, 275
agenda setting, 18, 27, 69, 188, 197, 330
aggregators, 320
agit prop, 235
air battle over London, 337
aircraft carriers, 135
Al-Jazeera, 7, 12, 24, 72, 103, 104, 106-125, 127, 131, 140, 149, 222, 224, 225, 228,
    262, 263, 268
Al-Qaeda Organization for Holy War, 215
Al-Qaeda, 55, 110, 133, 200, 203, 213-215, 217, 226, 229, 230
al-Rashid forum, 217, 225, 230
al-Saqifa, 217, 230
Alabama National Guard, 325
Alta Vista, 105

alternative media, 7, 13, 14, 18, 20, 28, 30, 32, 33, 103, 105, 107, 113-116, 152-163, 168, 173, 185, 188, 189
Alternative Media Asia, 161
American Civil War, 39
American occupation of Iraq, 215
American University in Cairo, 11, 12, 15, 18, 21, 258, 265
American Journalism Review, 89, 322, 330-332, 371
Amman, 99
Anglo-American, 8, 66, 69, 126-128, 146, 147, 381
Ansar al-Sunna Army, 217, 223, 225, 227, 230
Ansar al-Sunna, 215, 217, 223, 225, 227, 230
Ansar al-Islam, 215, 216, 230
anti-Americanism, 72
anti-Bush, 160, 235, 244, 247
anti-nuclear power movement, 190
anti-war rallies, 180, 183
anti-war protest frame, 97
anti-war movement, 210
Apple's Final Cut Pro, 42
Arab culture, 35, 275
Arab Dialogue Forum, 217, 230
Arab Diaspora, 273
Arab identity, 15, 32, 122
Arab League, 143, 145
Arab perspective, 31, 103, 106, 147
Arab Street, 145
Arab World, 12, 25, 96, 121, 126-128, 130, 133, 143, 147-149, 254, 272-274, 278-280, 364
Arabic Language, 275
Armageddon of the 21st Century, 128
Asian, 17, 112, 201
Associated Press Television News (APTN), 11, 44, 53
Associated Press, 11, 44, 51, 53, 314
asynchronous communication, 236
audiences, 9, 23, 25, 26, 29-31, 33, 34, 39, 40, 49, 65, 69, 75, 78, 80, 90, 93, 95, 100, 101, 103, 106, 113, 116, 123, 125, 127, 130, 131, 138, 149, 152, 158, 161, 174, 207, 213, 236, 251, 253, 256, 301, 315-317, 332, 337, 344, 372, 384, 386-392
Australia, 12, 16, 96, 144, 161, 168, 202, 206, 209, 210, 275
Australian Jewish Democratic Society, 204
Azores Summit, 133, 138

B

B-52 bombers, 135
Ba'ath Party, 140, 214, 219, 220, 224, 227
Ba'athist, 217, 220, 221, 224, 227, 231
Badr Corps, 221
Baghdad al-Rashid, 217, 225, 230

Baghdad, 9, 33, 34, 44, 62-64, 70, 81, 99, 118-123, 128, 131, 132, 138, 141-143, 145-147, 183, 210, 217, 220, 223-225, 229, 230, 294, 296, 298-300, 304, 308, 310, 319, 330, 332, 361-366, 368-370
Basra, 137, 139, 141-143, 219, 363
Battle of Baghdad, 128
BBC World, 263
BBC, 7, 24, 31, 40, 43, 44, 46-48, 51, 92-102, 106, 127, 262, 263, 268, 353
bearers of the cross, 221
beheading, 221, 229, 316
believability, 326, 327
Benton Foundation, 157
Bhuj earthquake, 43
Big Media Effect, 114
Big Oil, 166
Black House, 222
black-and-white halftones, 344
Blogger Manifesto, 318
bloggers, 2, 20, 27, 108, 109, 294, 295, 297, 300, 301, 304, 305, 314-320, 322-326, 328-330, 332, 333
blogging, 9, 32, 33, 99, 292, 301, 303, 304, 313, 315, 320, 328, 331
Boeing, 172, 183
bombings in London, 127
books, 2-4, 12, 14, 16, 28, 34, 101, 113, 114, 169, 184, 197, 250, 251, 261, 267-269, 276, 302, 315, 330, 331, 392
Bosnia, 350
branding, 270
Britain, 65, 110, 201, 381, 385
broadcast television news, 320, 321, 323, 329
broadcasting, 12, 15, 43, 50, 52, 53, 76, 90, 92, 116, 119, 225, 250, 251, 267, 302, 353, 354, 370, 382
Budapest, 50
Bull Run, 39
Bush Administration, 55, 133-137, 160, 167, 192, 197, 201, 202, 235, 242, 244, 245, 247-249, 276, 323, 363
Bush doctrine, 201, 211

C

Cable News Network (CNN), 7, 24, 31, 40, 43-45, 50, 72, 102, 106, 109, 110, 113, 115-120, 122-124, 161, 251, 262, 263, 268, 288, 290, 296, 339, 360, 376, 378, 382
Cairo, 11, 12, 15, 18, 21, 117, 134, 144, 258, 265
Caliph, 222
Campaign Embed, 40
Canada, 93, 104, 134, 190, 201, 250, 275, 331, 385
card stacking, 252
Cargo of Caskets, 338
casualties of war, 94, 97
cbsnews.com, 360, 370, 376, 378
celeblogs, 305-307, 309, 313, 315

censorship, 52, 74, 81, 230, 367
Center for Islamic Studies and Research, 214, 230
Central Command Center, 135
Challenger shuttle, 44
Charge of the Light Brigade, 337, 353
chemical weapons, 363
child pornography, 165
Chile, 43
China, 64, 79, 89, 143, 144, 355
Chinese, 43, 61, 153
Chinese Revolution, 153
CIA, 298
citizens' media, 153, 154
Civilian Oversight Board, 178
Clueless, 9, 282, 288, 289
cluster bombs, 136
CNN International, 50, 263
Coalition of the Willing, 95, 99, 201, 246, 363
Cold War, 39, 55, 234
collective memory, 121, 341, 353-355
color photography, 344
Colorado, 76
Columbia Broadcast System (CBS), 48, 52, 325, 360, 369, 370
community radio, 160, 163
Community Arts and Media Project (CAMP), 132, 142, 145, 171, 182-184, 221, 228,
    230, 366
computer-mediated communication, 18, 148, 192, 254, 267, 280, 315
Congo, 51
conspiracy theory, 122, 123
context, 17, 20, 29, 63, 68, 69, 74, 97, 106, 129, 130, 136, 144, 146, 152, 156, 158, 166,
    167, 173, 174, 191, 209, 217, 235, 272, 279, 300, 350, 354, 374, 380
contextualizing, 112
convergence, 7, 12, 16, 20, 39, 40, 53, 54, 126, 148, 176, 270, 334, 339, 344, 390, 392
convergent media, 7, 9, 30, 33, 37, 371
core opinion frames, 116
counter-cultural medium, 188
counter-flow, 112
credibility, 27, 28, 33, 109, 117, 120, 123, 124, 131, 148, 294, 313, 324-326, 330-332,
    386, 388, 389, 391
Crimea War, 30, 39
cross-promotion, 380
cross-referencing, 380
Crow, 217
Cruise missiles, 135, 136
Cuba, 120
cyber-insurgency, 8, 32, 213, 214, 228
Cyberjournalist.net, 128, 148, 328
cyberspace, 5, 20, 21, 23-25, 27-29, 163, 173, 185, 189, 200, 203, 204, 208, 210, 211,
    213, 254, 267, 270, 273, 280, 300, 322, 325

D

Daily Show, 350
Daily Mirror, 132
Dallas, 124, 132, 330, 360, 361
Danish political cartoon controversy, 25
David-Goliath (analogy), 143, 146, 147
DDB Needham, 385
death of newspapers, 327
Deep Dish TV, 160, 162
delegitimization, 65, 68
Democratic convention, 160
diffusion, 126, 155, 234, 236
digital video cameras, 39
Do-It-Yourself (DIY) punk ethic, 161
domestic policy, 57
Dubai, 44, 224
Dying Spanish Militiaman, 338

E

e-mail bombing, 237
e-mail, 8, 19, 21, 23, 24, 26, 32, 46, 52, 100, 164, 187, 190, 194, 195, 206, 208,
    234-237, 239, 240, 242, 243, 245-251, 254, 256, 258-261, 263-265, 271, 277, 330
e-revolution, 203
e-zines, 157
Earth Worker, 205
Editor & Publisher, 30, 76
Egypt, 12, 15, 110, 121, 130, 134, 143, 145, 148, 254, 258, 266, 274
Egyptian media, 118, 123
electronic mail, 258-260
electronic media technologies, 153
embedded journalists, 360, 377
embedded reporters, 19, 40, 53, 294, 379
Emirates Media Incorporated online, 127
Emma, 282, 289
emoticons, 270
England, 34, 48, 89, 113, 157, 353
English, 7, 12, 15, 24, 31, 42, 44, 103-114, 131, 148, 158, 165, 166, 226, 274, 275, 283
Enron, 166
Ethernet, 387
Euphrates, 141, 297, 345
Europe, 15, 126, 153, 162, 163, 169, 174, 201, 210, 211
European Union, 96, 144

F

face-to-face discussion, 321, 323, 324, 328
Fahrenheit 9/11, 195, 311

information technologies, 176, 182, 185, 273
information warfare, 8, 234, 235, 237, 239, 242, 248-252
Information Age, 185, 203, 210
Inside Edition, 52
Instapundit, 319, 322, 325
International Newspaper Marketing Association, 41
International Atomic Energy Agency (IAEA), 64
Internet Digital Satellite (IDS), 9, 336, 339, 341, 344, 351, 352
Internetworked Social Movements, 175
invasion of Iraq, 7, 42-44, 115, 126, 127, 133, 145, 192, 235, 244, 246, 247
inverted pyramid, 53
Iran, 24, 69, 251, 370, 381
Iraq, 2, 3, 7-9, 11, 12, 15, 17, 19, 20, 23-33, 37, 39, 40, 42-44, 46, 47, 52, 53, 55-57, 59, 61-66, 68, 70, 72, 76-88, 90, 92-95, 97-101, 103-105, 112-115, 119-124, 126-128, 132-140, 142-147, 149, 152, 157, 161, 166, 167, 173, 175, 177-180, 182-186, 190, 192, 193, 196, 197, 200-204, 206, 208-211, 213-217, 219-226, 228-231, 234, 235, 239, 240, 242, 244-248, 250-254, 256, 258, 260, 263, 266-269, 272, 274, 276, 281-291, 294-296, 298, 302-307, 310, 315, 317, 319-321, 330-332, 336, 340, 341, 344-349, 351, 357-362, 364, 366-371, 373, 374, 376-379, 382, 384, 386-388, 390-392
Iraq Patrol, 217, 220, 231
Iraqi TV, 138
Iraqi Muslim Scholars Council, 225
Iraqi forces, 141, 146, 213
Islam, 17, 25, 147, 215, 216, 219, 220, 230, 231
Islamic Caliphate, 223
Islamic Council of Victoria, 204
Islamic Advantages Network, 217, 231
Islamic Army in Iraq, 216, 224, 229
Islamic law, 225
Islamic Renewal Organization, 216, 231
Islamic Dialogue Open Forum, 217, 231
Islamonline, 127
Israel, 24, 121, 134, 179, 244, 281
Israeli flag, 219
Italy, 143, 163, 175, 366, 385

J

Japan, 57, 229, 385
Jefferson Barracks, 177
Jordan, 11, 12, 96, 134, 143, 145, 158, 169, 216
journalism, 11-18, 20, 28, 34, 39-43, 47, 50, 53, 54, 63, 69, 73, 89, 90, 93, 101, 102, 126-130, 148, 149, 184, 185, 250, 280, 294, 301, 302, 316, 318, 320, 322, 324, 327, 329-332, 337, 344, 352, 353, 370-372, 375, 381, 382

K

Kabul, 43

Q

R

S

U

V

W

war casualties, 209, 370
war in Vietnam, 343
war on terror, 127
war profiteering, 183
war protesters, 173, 174, 212, 357, 361, 369
war correspondents, 30, 90
War for oil, 180
warblogs, 268, 294, 295, 300, 303, 360
Warsaw Ghetto, 338
warshooter.com, 368
Washington, 3, 4, 13, 15, 17, 18, 39, 53, 56, 62-64, 68, 70, 79, 89, 114, 133, 144, 145, 147, 157, 159, 167, 177, 201, 222, 251, 267, 268, 296, 300, 315, 322, 325, 331, 337, 360, 363, 371, 381
Washington, D.C., 13, 133, 144, 145, 157, 296
Washington Post, The, 56, 62-64, 70, 79, 315, 331, 337, 371
weapons of mass destruction (WMD), 24, 67, 78, 81, 87, 93, 102, 133, 135, 137, 183, 203, 208, 244, 245
Web sites, 7, 15, 23, 26-28, 30, 33, 72, 73, 76, 80, 89, 102-115, 127, 130, 156, 157, 161, 175, 185, 189, 190, 194, 196, 213-217, 219, 220, 222, 225, 226, 230, 231, 236, 237, 244, 246, 250, 263, 264, 266, 268, 270, 274-277, 296, 306, 316, 318, 322, 332, 344, 357, 360, 361, 363-369, 374, 376, 378, 389, 392
Weblogs, 23, 24, 27, 28, 32, 33, 264, 302-304, 315-317, 320-327, 329-332
West Africa, 47, 51, 167
Western Mass IMC, 162
Where is Raed?, 298
White House, 144, 166, 222, 343, 359
Wizard of Oz, 160
Women for Peace: No Weapons No War, 205
World Trade Center, 43, 179, 200
World Wide Web, 5, 16, 19, 89, 126, 148, 253, 255, 257-259, 261, 270, 275, 279, 280, 317, 331
World War II, 39, 43, 52, 92, 369
World Trade Organization, 174
World Agricultural Forum, 176
worms, 237, 246

Y

Yahoo, 7, 27, 31, 72, 79, 80, 83, 85-90, 191, 243, 262, 265, 274, 314
Yemen, 134, 143, 216
Young Labour Left, 205

Z

Zebra Network, 161
zine, 159, 160, 183